FREEDOM RIDERS

FREEDOM
RIDERS

1961 and the Struggle for Racial Justice

Abridged Edition

RAYMOND ARSENAULT

OXFORD
UNIVERSITY PRESS

OXFORD
UNIVERSITY PRESS

Oxford University Press, Inc., publishes works that further
Oxford University's objective of excellence
in research, scholarship, and education.

Oxford   New York
Auckland   Cape Town   Dar es Salaam   Hong Kong   Karachi
Kuala Lumpur   Madrid   Melbourne   Mexico City   Nairobi
New Delhi   Shanghai   Taipei   Toronto

With offices in
Argentina   Austria   Brazil   Chile   Czech Republic   France   Greece
Guatemala   Hungary   Italy   Japan   Poland   Portugal   Singapore
South Korea   Switzerland   Thailand   Turkey   Ukraine   Vietnam

Copyright © 2006, 2011 by Raymond Arsenault

Published by Oxford University Press, Inc.
198 Madison Avenue, New York, NY 10016

www.oup.com

Oxford is a registered trademark of Oxford University Press

Library of Congress Cataloging-in-Publication Data
Arsenault, Raymond.
Freedom riders : 1961 and the struggle for racial justice /
Raymond Arsenault. — Abridged ed.
p. cm. — (Pivotal moments in American history)
Includes bibliographical references and index.
ISBN 978-0-19-975431-1 (pbk.)
1. African American civil rights workers—History—20th century.
2. Civil rights workers—United States—History—20th century.
3. African Americans—Segregation—Southern States—History—20th century.
4. Segregation in transportation—Southern States—History—20th century.
5. African Americans—Civil rights—Southern States—History—20th century.
6. Civil rights movements—Southern States—History—20th century.
7. Southern States—Race relations—History—20th century. I. Title.
E185.61.A69   2011
323.092—dc22   2010037533

9 8 7 6 5 4 3 2 1

Printed in the United States of America
on acid-free paper

*For
John Hope Franklin—
the Freedom Writer
1915–2009*

Parts of this manuscript previously appeared in a different form and are republished with permission: " 'You Don't Have to Ride Jim Crow': CORE and the 1947 Journey of Reconciliation," in *Before* Brown: *Civil Rights and White Backlash in the Modern South.* ed. Glen Feldman, 21–67 (Tuscaloosa: University of Alabama Press, 2004); "You Don't Have to Ride Jim Crow," *Stetson Law Review* 34 (Winter 2005): 343–411; "One Brick at a Time: The Montgomery Bus Boycott, Nonviolent Direct Action, and the Development of a National Civil Rights Movement," in *Sunbelt Revolution: The Historical Progression of the Civil Rights Struggle in the Gulf South, 1866–2000*, ed. Samuel C. Hyde Jr., 153–89 (Gainesville: University Press of Florida, 2003); and "Taking the Road to Freedom," *Forum* 28 (Spring 2004): 30–35.

Contents

List of Maps   viii
Preface   ix
Author's Note   xiii

Introduction   3

1. You Don't Have to Ride Jim Crow   13

2. Beside the Weary Road   43

3. Hallelujah! I'm A-Travelin'   61

4. Alabama Bound   93

5. Get on Board, Little Children   125

6. If You Miss Me from the Back of the Bus   148

7. Freedom's Coming and It Won't Be Long   183

8. Ain't Gonna Let No Jail House Turn Me 'Round   214

9. Woke Up This Morning with My Mind Stayed on Freedom   246

10. Oh, Freedom   263

Epilogue: Glory Bound   287

Note on Sources   303

List of Maps

1. Journey of Reconciliation, April 1947   34
2. CORE Freedom Ride, May 4–May 17, 1961   75
3. Anniston, Alabama, May 14, 1961   95
4. Birmingham, Alabama, May 14–20, 1961   104
5. Montgomery, Alabama, May 20–24, 1961   150
6. Mississippi, 1961   186
7. Jackson, Mississippi, 1961   191
8. Freedom Rides, April–December 1961   221

Preface

Fifty years ago, during the spring and summer of 1961, the Freedom Riders set out to change the world. Amazingly, they did so by simply boarding a bus, not as blacks or whites restricted by an outmoded system of racial discrimination, but as free and full citizens of a democratic nation. The Freedom Riders knew that federal law and the Constitution of the United States protected their right to travel together, even in the Deep South where local law and custom mandated racial separation. But they also knew that they might be injured or even killed for trying to exercise that right. When riots ensued, the potential violence became all too real, and a nation recoiled in horror. Unfazed, the Freedom Riders kept coming, more than four hundred in all, filling the freedom buses and marching into the jails of the Jim Crow South. In the process, this interracial, nonviolent army forced John F. Kennedy's administration to confront the immediacy of a civil rights struggle that had captured the world's attention. By the end of the year, a sweeping desegregation order was in effect, and the federal government was moving toward active involvement in the struggle for racial justice.

The Freedom Riders' victory was the first of many civil rights triumphs achieved during the 1960s. Indeed, as the decade progressed the improbable story of the Freedom Rides became part of an unfolding saga of democratic promise and renewal. Almost inevitably, however, as the spotlight shifted from the burning bus in Anniston to the attack dogs and fire hoses of Birmingham, and later to Freedom Summer in Mississippi, Bloody Sunday in Selma, and the mean streets of Chicago and Watts, the Freedom Rides were reduced to a mere prelude, both in the public mind and in the world of civil rights scholarship.

This was the unfortunate situation that I discovered in 1998, as I began to research and write the first scholarly book on the Freedom Rides. Amazingly, nearly four decades had passed since the end of the Freedom Rides, yet historians had failed to produce a single book or article on the subject. Though puzzled by this curious oversight, I embraced the opportunity to amend the historical record, especially after signing a contract to publish my book in Oxford University Press's new Pivotal Moments in American History series. At this early stage in my research, I couldn't be sure that the Freedom Rides represented an historical milestone of that magnitude. Indeed, no one other than me, my editors, and the Freedom Riders themselves seemed to regard the Freedom Rides as anything approaching a pivotal moment in American history. Fortunately, the 1998 publication of Congressman John Lewis's eloquent memoir, *Walking with the Wind,* which includes a riveting narrative of his participation in the Freedom Rides, steeled my courage and spurred me onward.

As I dug deeper into the Freedom Rider story, poring over archival records and interviewing scores of Riders, any doubts about the pivotal nature of the Rides disappeared. The resolute courage and commitment of the Freedom Riders had brought nonviolent direct action and grassroots insurgency to the center stage of American public life, prompting an unprecedented governmental response to unconstitutional infringements of freedom and civic equality. Initiating an era of tumultuous social change, the decision to challenge Jim Crow frontally but nonviolently provided a new model of activist citizenship, radically altering the nation's prospects for democratic reform. Considering all that followed, from the student and women's movements to the broader "rights revolution," the Freedom Rides more than met the standard of pivotal importance.

Even so, the American public, including the scholarly community, has been slow to recognize the significance of the Freedom Rides as an historical turning point. As recently as 2001, when the Freedom Riders held two fortieth-anniversary celebrations—one in Jackson, Mississippi, where many Riders had been arrested in 1961, and a second "rolling reunion" featuring a partial recreation of the first Freedom Ride from Atlanta to Anniston and Birmingham—there was minimal press coverage and little scholarly attention, other than my feverish attempt to interview as many Freedom Riders as I could.

But that was then, before the recent rediscovery of the Freedom Riders' extraordinary sacrifices and contributions. How different the landscape of history and memory looks now as we approach the fiftieth anniversary of the Rides. No fewer than four books on the Freedom Rides have appeared during the last seven years. In 2008, the National Endowment for the Humanities awarded a million-dollar grant to WGBH Public Television to produce an *American Experience* documentary on the Freedom Rides. Based on *Freedom Riders* and directed by the award-winning filmmaker Stanley Nelson, the two-hour film played to enthusiastic audiences at several 2010 film festivals, including the prestigious Sundance documentary competition, and it is scheduled for a national public television broadcast in May 2011.

In coordination with the broadcast, a busload of forty college students, accompanied by former Freedom Riders and civil rights scholars, will spend ten days traveling from Washington to New Orleans, replicating the original CORE Freedom Ride of 1961. In January 2011, an exhibit on the Freedom Rides curated by the Gilder-Lehrman Institute of American History will begin a national tour of public libraries, and the annual meeting of the American Historical Association will host a special session presenting a fifty-year retrospective on the Rides. In February, the Smithsonian Institution's National Museum of American History will sponsor a simulcast symposium and "national town meeting" for high school students, focusing on the Freedom Rides. In May 2011, three major Freedom Rider reunions are scheduled to commemorate the fiftieth anniversary, and local groups in Montgomery, Anniston, and Jackson are currently preparing historical exhibits and markers to acknowledge the significance and legacy of the Freedom Rides. Finally, in Montgomery, a collaborative effort by Alabama State University and the Alabama Historical Commission to create a Freedom Rider museum is well under away.

Civil rights scholars are actively involved in all of these activities, but the Freedom Riders themselves have been no less essential to the resurgence of interest in the events of 1961. Rep. John Lewis, in particular, never misses an opportunity to rally his fellow Freedom Riders, urging them to tell their stories to a new generation of Americans. Lewis is a powerful legislative leader closely tied to a black president born coincidently during the Freedom Rides. But, fundamentally, he remains a preacher of the "beloved community" gospel, a living testament to the long legacy of the Rides.

Whatever role my book may have played in fostering the revival of historical interest in the Freedom Rides is of little consequence compared with the historic and continuing contributions of the Freedom Riders themselves. But I cannot help feeling a certain pride in my association with the Freedom Riders, as well as a sense of satisfaction from the overwhelmingly positive responses to a book that has dominated more than a decade of my life. My only regret, after attempting to write a comprehensive and authoritative work, is that the original 2006 edition was too long, and perhaps too intimidating, for some potential readers. For undergraduates straining to complete weekly reading assignments and for casual readers seeking the basic story of the Freedom Rides minus the occasional digressions and scholarly apparatus of an academic study, a shorter book was clearly in order.

As soon as *Freedom Riders* appeared in 2006, friends and colleagues urged me to consider an abridged edition accessible to a broader spectrum of readers; and now, just in time for the fiftieth anniversary of the Freedom Rides, I am pleased to oblige them. The 2011 edition is much shorter than the original text, but it tells the same powerful story, an improbable tale of struggle and sacrifice, of seemingly ordinary Americans committing extraordinary acts of courage, of young kids daring their elders to live up to the nation's professed ideals of freedom and justice. Conceived in blood and tears a half century ago, it is a story for today and tomorrow, a potential source of wonder and empowerment, and perhaps even wisdom. As we travel forward with all of our diversity and individual interests, the ideal of the beloved community—so central to the hopes and dreams of the Freedom Riders—still beckons.

Author's Note

The 2011 edition of *Freedom Riders* represents a scaled-down version of the volume published in 2006. While the author and publisher have made every effort to preserve the character of the original book, the text has been abridged, and certain elements such as notes and appendices have been eliminated. Readers interested in source materials and documentation are invited to consult the extensive endnotes and bibliography in the original volume. With the exception of the original Chapters 8 and 9—which appear as Chapter 8 in the 2011 edition—the chapter titles remain the same, and the sequence of presentation is unaltered. Thus, matching the abridged text with the original documentation should be a fairly straightforward matter. The complete notes and bibliography are also accessible online at http://www.oup.com/us/brochure/Freedom_Riders/.

An updated version of "Appendix: Roster of Freedom Riders," a chronological list of Freedom Rides that includes brief biographical sketches of 436 Freedom Riders, is also available online at the same site.

Eight of the ten maps included in the original volume have been retained in the 2011 edition.

Readers interested in the collaborative and collegial effort that produced *Freedom Riders* are welcome to consult the lengthy acknowledgments section in the original edition. But as an important addendum to the original acknowledgments, I would like to thank those who were instrumental in breathing life into the 2011 edition. First, I am extremely grateful to the staff of Oxford University Press, especially Senior Production Editor Joellyn Ausanka, who oversaw the final stages of the abridgment, and Tim Bent, my talented and patient editor. Without his steady hand (and his willingness to hold *my* hand through the dark passages of editorial surgery), the new edition would not have seen the light of day. Second, I would like to thank Marty Beiser for undertaking the difficult task of abridging a tightly woven narrative. His professionalism and editorial skill were essential to the success of the project, and I am proud to have worked with him. Third, I owe a great debt to my wonderful agent, Wendy Strothman, who was with me every step of the way—guiding, advising, and sometimes consoling.

Finally, I would like to thank the editors and producers of *American Experience* and Firelight Media for joining forces to create a remarkable documentary film based on *Freedom Riders*. Their skill in compressing and accurately representing a larger work of history served as a model for this abridgment. Special thanks to Susan Bellows, Jim Dunford, Lewis Erskine, Vanessa Esersky, Laurens Grant, Sharon Grimberg, Stacy Holman, Lewanne Jones, Stanley Nelson, Tom Phillips, Lauren Prestileo, Marc Samels, Robert Shepard, Paul Taylor, and Algernon Tunsil. Thanks also to Gary Nicolai, a gifted and dedicated teacher who offered sage advice during the abridgment process, and to four talented young students: Peyton Jones, my irrepressible research assistant; Daun Fletcher, program assistant in the Florida Studies Program at the University of South Florida, St. Petersburg; Theresa Collington, my technical wizard; and Zoë Samels of Williams College. As an undergraduate at the University of Chicago, where I was a visiting professor and her teacher in 2007, Zoë urged her father, *American Experience* executive producer Marc Samels, to read *Freedom Riders*. The rest, as they say, is history.

FREEDOM RIDERS

Introduction

The plan was ... simplicity itself. In any sane, even half-civilized society it would have been completely innocuous, hardly worth a second thought or meriting any comment at all. CORE would be sending an integrated team—black and white together—from the nation's capital to New Orleans on public transportation. That's all. Except, of course, that they would sit randomly on the buses in integrated pairs, and in the stations they would use waiting room facilities casually, ignoring the white/colored signs. What could be more harmless ... in any even marginally healthy society?
—Stokely Carmichael

May 21, 1961. It was Sunday night on the New Frontier, and freedom was on the line in Montgomery, Alabama. Earlier in the evening, more than a thousand black Americans, including the Reverend Martin Luther King Jr. and several other nationally prominent civil rights leaders, had gathered at the First Baptist Church (Colored) to show their support for a visiting band of activists known as Freedom Riders. Located just a few blocks from the state capitol where President Jefferson Davis had sworn allegiance to the Confederate cause in 1861, First Baptist had been the setting for a number of dramatic events over the years. But the historic church had never witnessed anything quite like the situation that was unfolding both inside and outside its walls. For several hours the Freedom Riders and the congregation sang hymns and freedom songs and listened to testimonials about courage and commitment. But as the spirit of hope and justice rose inside the crowded sanctuary, a wholly different mood of defiance and outrage developed outside.

By nightfall the church was surrounded and besieged by a swelling mob of white protesters determined to defend a time-honored system of racial segregation. Screaming racial epithets and hurling rocks and Molotov cocktails, the protesters threatened to overwhelm a beleaguered group of federal marshals who feared that some members of the mob were intent on burning the church to the ground. When it became obvious that the marshals were overmatched, the governor of Alabama deployed a battalion of National Guardsmen to disperse the crowd, and tragedy was averted. But it would be early morning before the surrounding streets were secure enough for the Freedom Riders and their supporters to leave the church. Loaded into a convoy of military trucks and looking much like wartime refugees, the troublesome visitors and their embattled hosts were escorted back to a black community that must have wondered what other indignities and challenges lay ahead. The battle of May 21 was over, but the centuries-old struggle for racial justice would continue.

How the Freedom Riders came to be at First Baptist, why they inspired so much hope and fear, and what happened to them—and the hundreds of other Americans who joined their ranks—are the questions that drive this book. As the epigram from Stokely Carmichael suggests, these are important and perplexing questions that should engage anyone concerned with freedom, justice, and the realization of America's democratic ideals. With characters and plot lines rivaling those of the most imaginative fiction, the saga of the Freedom Rides is an improbable, almost unbelievable story. And from start to finish it is a tale of heroic sacrifice and unexpected triumph. In 1961, during the first year of John F. Kennedy's presidency, more than four hundred Americans participated in a dangerous experiment designed to awaken the conscience of a complacent nation. Inspired by visions of social revolution and moral regeneration, these self-proclaimed Freedom Riders challenged the mores of a racially segregated society by performing a disarmingly simple act. Traveling together in small interracial groups, they sat where they pleased on buses and trains and demanded unrestricted access to terminal restaurants and waiting rooms, even in areas of the Deep South where such behavior was forbidden by law and custom.

Patterned after a 1947 Congress of Racial Equality (CORE) project known as the Journey of Reconciliation, the Freedom Rides began in early May with a single group of thirteen Riders recruited and trained by CORE's national staff. But by early summer the Rides had evolved into a broad-based movement involving hundreds of activists representing a number of allied local, regional, and national civil rights organizations. Attracting a diverse assortment of volunteers—black and white, young and old, male and female, religious and secular, Northern and Southern—the Freedom Rider movement transcended the traditional legalistic approach to civil rights, taking the struggle out of the courtroom and into the streets and jails of the Jim Crow South. Empowered by two

U.S. Supreme Court decisions mandating the desegregation of interstate travel facilities, the Freedom Riders brazenly flouted state and local segregation statutes, all but daring Southern officials to arrest them.

Deliberately provoking a crisis of authority, the Riders challenged federal officials to enforce the law and uphold the constitutional right to travel without being subjected to degrading and humiliating racial restrictions. Most amazingly, they did so knowing that their actions would almost certainly provoke a savage and violent response from militant white supremacists. Invoking the philosophy of nonviolent direct action, they willingly put their bodies on the line for the cause of racial justice. Openly defying the social conventions of a security-conscious society, they appeared to court martyrdom with a reckless disregard for personal safety or civic order. None of the obstacles placed in their path—not widespread censure, not political and financial pressure, not arrest and imprisonment, not even the threat of death—seemed to weaken their commitment to nonviolent struggle. On the contrary, the hardships and suffering imposed upon them appeared to stiffen their resolve, confounding their white supremacist antagonists and testing the patience of even those who sympathized with their cause. Time and again, the Riders seemed on the verge of defeat, but in every instance they found a way to sustain and expand their challenge to Jim Crow segregation. After marauding Alabama Klansmen used bombs and mob violence to disrupt and disband the original CORE Freedom Ride, student activists from Nashville stepped forward to organize a Ride of their own, eventually forcing federal officials to intervene on their behalf. Later, when Mississippi officials placed hundreds of Freedom Riders in prison and imposed bond payments that threatened the financial solvency of CORE, the net effect was to strengthen rather than to weaken the nonviolent movement. And on a number of other occasions attempts to intimidate the Freedom Riders and their supporters backfired, reinvigorating and prolonging a crisis that would not go away.

It is little wonder, then, that the Freedom Rides sent shock waves through American society, evoking fears of widespread social disorder, racial polarization, and a messy constitutional crisis. In the mid-1950s, the Montgomery Bus Boycott and its Gandhian leader, Martin Luther King Jr., had familiarized Americans with the tactics and philosophy of nonviolent resistance. And in 1960 the sit-in movement conducted by black college students in Greensboro, North Carolina, and scores of other Southern cities had introduced direct action on a mass scale. But nothing in the recent past had fully prepared the American public for the Freedom Riders' interracial "invasion" of the segregated South. With the Freedom Rides, the civil rights struggle reached a level of intensity that even the sit-ins, potentially the most disruptive episode of the pre-1961 era, had managed to avoid. Loosely organized by local student activists and only tangentially connected to federal court mandates, the sit-in movement had skirted the potentially explosive issues of states' rights and outside agitation by Northern-based civil rights organizations.

The closest thing to a national civil rights crisis prior to the Freedom Rides was the school desegregation fight following the *Brown v. Board of Education* implementation decision of 1955. But the refusal of Dwight Eisenhower's administration to press for anything more than token integration had seemingly defused the crisis by the end of the decade. Even in Little Rock, Arkansas, where Eisenhower had dispatched troops to enforce a court order in 1957, the spirit of intense confrontation had largely subsided by the time of the Freedom Rides. By then John Kennedy's New Frontier was in full swing. But there was no indication that the new administration was willing to sacrifice civic peace or political capital in the interests of school desegregation or any other civil rights issue, despite periodic pledges to abide by the Supreme Court's "with all deliberate speed" implementation order. Indeed, with public opinion polls showing little interest in civil rights among white Americans, there was no compelling reason, other than a personal commitment to abstract principles of freedom and justice, for any national political leader to challenge the racial orthodoxies and mores of Jim Crow culture.

During and after the fall campaign, Kennedy proclaimed that his New Frontier policies would transcend the stolid conservatism of the Eisenhower era; and in a stirring inaugural address he declared that the United States would "pay any price, bear any burden, meet any hardship, support any friend, oppose any foe to assure the survival and success of liberty." But in the winter and early spring of 1961, the New Frontier manifested itself primarily in an assertive presence abroad, not in enhanced social justice at home. As civil rights leaders waited for the first sign of a bold initiative on the domestic front, superheated rhetoric about "missile gaps" and Soviet expansionism heightened Cold War tensions, fostering a crisis mentality that led to the ill-fated Bay of Pigs invasion in April. Marginalizing all other issues, including civil rights, the military and diplomatic fiasco in Cuba only served to sharpen the administration's focus on international affairs.

The president himself set the tone, and by early May there was no longer any doubt, as the journalist Richard Reeves later observed, that the Cold Warrior in the White House regarded civil rights matters as an unwelcome "diversion from the priority business of promoting and winning freedom around the world." Father Theodore Hesburgh, the chairman of the U.S. Civil Rights Commission, was one of the first to learn this sobering truth. During an early briefing held two weeks after the inauguration, Kennedy made it clear that he considered white supremacist transgressions such as the Alabama National Guard's illegal exclusion of black soldiers to be a trivial matter in the grand scheme of world affairs. "Look, Father," he explained, "I may have to send the Alabama National

Guard to Berlin tomorrow and I don't want to have to do it in the middle of a revolution at home." Ironically, neither he nor Hesburgh had the faintest suspicion that in three months' time these same Alabama Guardsmen would be called not to Berlin but rather to a besieged black church in Montgomery where Freedom Riders required protection from a white supremacist mob. In early February, neither man had any reason to believe that a group of American citizens would deliberately place themselves in jeopardy by traveling to Alabama, counting "upon the racists of the South to create a crisis, so that the federal government would be compelled to enforce federal law," as CORE's national director, Jim Farmer, put it.

To many Americans, including the president, the rationale behind the Freedom Rides bordered on madness. But Farmer and other proponents of direct action reasoned that they could turn the president's passion for Cold War politics to their advantage by exposing and dramatizing the hypocrisy of promoting freedom abroad while maintaining Jim Crow in places like Alabama and Mississippi. With the onset of decolonization, the "colored" nations of Africa and Asia had emerged as important players in the escalating struggle between the United States and the Soviet Union. And it was no secret that America's long and continuing association with racial discrimination posed a potential threat to the State Department's continuing efforts to secure the loyalty and respect of the so-called Third World. If movement leaders could find some means of highlighting the diplomatic costs of Jim Crow, the administration would be forced to address civil rights issues as a function of national security.

Putting this strategy into practice, however, was extremely risky in a nation still reeling from a decade of hyper-patriotic McCarthyism. To embarrass the nation on the world stage, for whatever reason, was to invite charges of disloyalty and collusion with Communist enemies. Even though a growing number of Americans acknowledged the connection between civil rights and the legitimacy of America's claims to democratic virtue and moral authority, very few, even among self-professed liberals, were willing to place the nation's international stature at risk for the purpose of accelerating the pace of social change. Such considerations extended to the civil rights movement itself, where internecine Red-baiting and periodic purges had been common since the late 1940s. In varying degrees, every civil rights organization from the NAACP to CORE had to guard against charges of subversion and "fellow-traveling," and even the most cautious advocates of racial justice were sometimes subject to Cold War suspicions.

Civil rights activists of all persuasions faced an uphill struggle in the Cold War context of 1961. For the Freedom Riders, however, the challenge of mounting an effective protest movement was compounded by the fundamental conservatism of a nation wedded to consensus politics. As earlier generations of radical activists had discovered, enlisting support for direct action, economic boycotts, and other disruptive tactics was a difficult task in a society infused with the mythology of superior national virtue and equal access to legal redress. While a majority of Americans endorsed the goal of desegregating interstate transportation, a much smaller proportion supported the use of direct action, nonviolent or otherwise. According to a Gallup poll conducted in late May and early June 1961, 66 percent of Americans agreed with the Supreme Court's recent ruling "that racial segregation on trains, buses, and in public waiting rooms must end," but only 24 percent approved "of what the 'freedom riders' are doing." When asked if sit-ins, Freedom Rides, and "other demonstrations by Negroes" would "hurt or help the Negro's chances of being integrated in the South," only 27 percent of the respondents thought they would help.

In many communities, public opposition to the Rides was reinforced by negative press coverage. Editorial condemnation of CORE's intrusive direct action campaign was almost universal in the white South. But negative characterizations of the Freedom Rides as foolhardy and unnecessarily confrontational were also common in the national press. Although most of the nation's leading editors and commentators embraced the ideal of desegregation, very few acknowledged that Freedom Rides and other disruptive tactics were a necessary catalyst for timely social change. Indeed, many journalists, like many of their readers and listeners, seemed to accept the moral equivalency of pro- and anti-civil rights demonstrators, blaming one side as much as the other for the social disorder surrounding the Rides. In later years it would become fashionable to hail the Freedom Riders as courageous visionaries, but such sentiments were rare in 1961.

The Freedom Riders' negative public image was the product of many factors, but two of their most obvious problems were bad timing and a deeply rooted suspicion of radical agitation by "outsiders." Set against the backdrop of the Civil War Centennial celebration, which began in April 1961, the Freedom Rides evoked vivid memories of meddling Abolitionists and invading armies. This was especially true in the white South, where a resurgent "siege mentality" was in full force during the post-*Brown* era. But "outside agitators" were also unpopular in the North, where Cold War anxieties mingled with the ambiguous legacy of Reconstruction. When trying to comprehend the motivations behind the Freedom Rides, Americans of all regions and of all political leanings drew upon the one historical example that had influenced national life for nearly a century: the allegedly misguided attempt to bring about a Radical Reconstruction of the Confederate South. While some Americans appreciated the moral and political imperatives of Reconstruction, the dominant image of the tumultuous decade following the Civil War was that of a "tragic era" sullied by corruption and opportunism.

Among black Americans and white liberals the *Brown* decision had given rise to the idea of a long overdue Second Reconstruction, but even in the civil rights community there was some reluctance to embrace a neo-Abolitionist approach to social change. Some civil rights advocates, including Thurgood Marshall and Roy Wilkins of the NAACP, feared that Freedom Riders and other proponents of direct action would actually slow the process of change by needlessly provoking a white backlash and squandering the movement's financial and legal resources. To Wilkins, who admired the Riders' courage but questioned their sanity, the CORE project represented "a desperately brave, reckless strategy," a judgment seconded by Leslie Dunbar, the executive director of the Southern Regional Council. "When I heard about all those Northerners heading south, I was sure they were going to catch hell and maybe even get themselves killed," Dunbar recalled many years later.

Dunbar had good reason to be concerned. In a nation where the mystique of states' rights and local control enjoyed considerable popularity, crossing state lines for the purpose of challenging parochial mores was a highly provocative act. The notion that Freedom Riders were outside agitators and provocateurs cast serious doubt on their legitimacy, eliminating most of the moral capital that normally accompanied nonviolent struggle. Freedom Rides, by their very nature, involved physical mobility and a measure of outside involvement, if only in the form of traveling from one place to another. But the discovery—or in some cases, the assumption—that most of the Freedom Riders were Northerners deepened the sense of public anxiety surrounding the Rides. Judging by the national press and contemporary public commentary, the archetypal Freedom Rider was an idealistic but naive white activist from the North, probably a college student but possibly an older religious or labor leader. In actuality, however, the Freedom Riders were much more diverse than most Americans realized. While many Freedom Riders resembled the description above, many others did not. Black activists born and raised in the South accounted for five of the original thirteen Freedom Riders and approximately one-third of the four hundred-plus Riders who later joined the movement. The Freedom Rider movement was as interregional as it was interracial, but for some reason the indigenous contribution to the Rides did not seem to register in the public consciousness, then or later. Part of the explanation undoubtedly resides in the conventional wisdom that Southern blacks were too beaten down to become involved in their own liberation. Even after the Montgomery bus boycott and the 1960 sit-ins suggested otherwise, this misconception plagued popular and even scholarly explanations of the civil rights struggle, including accounts of the Freedom Rides.

Redressing this misconception is reason enough to write a revisionist history of the Freedom Rides. But there are a number of other issues, both interpretative and factual, that merit attention. Chief among them is the tendency to treat the

Freedom Rides as little more than a dramatic prelude to the climactic events of the mid- and late-1960s. In the rush to tell the stories of Birmingham, Freedom Summer, the Civil Rights Acts of 1964 and 1965, the Black Power movement, and the urban riots, assassinations, and political and cultural crises that have come to define a decade of breathless change, the Freedom Rides have often gotten lost. Occupying the mid-point between the 1954 *Brown* decision and the 1968 assassination of Martin Luther King, the events of 1961 would seem to be a likely choice as the pivot of a pivotal era in civil rights history. But that is not the way the Rides are generally depicted in civil rights historiography. While virtually every historical survey of the civil rights movement includes a brief section on the Freedom Rides, they have not attracted the attention that they deserve. The first scholarly monograph on the subject was published in 2003, and amazingly the present volume represents the first attempt by a professional historian to write a book-length account of the Freedom Rides.

The reasons for this scholarly neglect are not altogether clear, but in recent years part of the problem has been the deceptive familiarity of the Freedom Rider story. Beginning with Taylor Branch's *Parting the Waters: America in the King Years 1954–63*, published in 1988, several prominent journalists, including Diane McWhorter and David Halberstam, have written long chapters that cover significant portions of the Freedom Rider experience. Representing popular history at its best, both Branch's book and McWhorter's *Carry Me Home: Birmingham, Alabama: The Climactic Battle of the Civil Rights Revolution*, published in 2000, attracted wide readership and won the coveted Pulitzer Prize for their authors. Halberstam's 1998 best-seller, *The Children*, has also been influential, bringing the Nashville movement of the early 1960s back to life for thousands of Americans, including many historians. Written in vivid prose, these three books convey much of the drama and some of the meaning of the Freedom Rides.

And yet as good as they are, these books do not do full justice to an historical episode that warrants careful and sustained attention from professional scholars. The Freedom Rides deserve a comprehensive and targeted treatment unhampered by the distraction of a broader agenda. Every major episode of the civil rights struggle merits a full study of its own. But none is more deserving than the insistent and innovative movement that seized the attention of the nation in 1961, bringing nonviolent direct action to the forefront of the fight for racial justice. Foreshadowed by Montgomery and the sit-ins, the Freedom Rides initiated a turbulent decade of insurgent citizen politics that transformed the nature of American democracy. Animated by a wide range of grievances, from war and poverty to disfranchisement and social intolerance, a new generation of Americans marched, protested, and sometimes committed acts of civil disobedience in the pursuit of liberty and justice. And many of them did so with the knowledge that the Freedom Riders had come before them.

As the first historical study of this remarkable group of activists, *Freedom Riders* attempts to reconstruct the text and context of a pivotal moment in American history. At the mythic level, the saga of the Freedom Riders is a fairly simple tale of collective engagement and empowerment, of the pursuit and realization of democratic ideals, and of good triumphing over evil. But a carefully reconstructed history reveals a much more interesting story. Lying just below the surface, encased in memory and long overlooked documents, is the real story of the Freedom Rides, a complicated mesh of commitment and indecision, cooperation and conflict, triumph and disappointment. In an attempt to recapture the meaning and significance of the Freedom Rides without sacrificing the drama of personal experience and historical contingency, I have written a book that is chronological and narrative in form. From the outset my goal has been to produce a "braided narrative" that addresses major analytical questions related to cause and consequence. But I have done so in a way that allows the art of storytelling to dominate the structure of the work.

Whenever possible, I have let the historical actors speak for themselves, and much of the book relies on interviews with former Freedom Riders, journalists, and government officials. Focusing on individual stories, I have tried to be faithful to the complexity of human experience, to treat the Freedom Riders and their contemporaries as flesh-and-blood human beings capable of inconsistency, confusion, and varying modes of behavior and belief. The Freedom Riders, no less than the other civil rights activists who transformed American life in the decades following World War II, were dynamic figures. Indeed, the ability to adapt and to learn from their experiences, both good and bad, was an essential element of their success. Early on, they learned that pushing a reluctant nation into action required nimble minds and subtle judgments, not to mention a measure of luck.

While they sometimes characterized the civil rights movement as an irrepressible force, the Freedom Rides knew all too well that they faced powerful and resilient enemies backed by regional and national institutions and traditions. Fortunately, the men and women who participated in the Freedom Rides had access to institutions and traditions of their own. When they boarded the "freedom buses" in 1961, they knew that others had gone before them, figuratively in the case of crusading Abolitionists and the black and white soldiers who marched into the South during the Civil War and Reconstruction, and literally in the case of the CORE veterans who participated in the 1947 Journey of Reconciliation. In the early twentieth century, local black activists in several Southern cities had staged successful boycotts of segregated streetcars; in the 1930s and 1940s, labor and peace activists had employed sit-ins and other forms of direct action, and more recently the Gandhian liberation of India and the unexpected mass movements in Montgomery, Tallahassee, Greensboro, Nashville, and other centers of insurgency had demonstrated that the power of nonviolence was more than a philosophical chimera. At the same time, the legal successes of the NAACP and the gathering strength of the civil rights movement in the years since the Second World War, not to mention the emerging decolonization of the Third World, infused Freedom Riders with the belief that the arc of history was finally tilting in the right direction. Racial progress, if not inevitable, was at least possible, and the Riders were determined to do all they could to accelerate the pace of change.

Convincing their fellow Americans, black or white, that nonviolent struggle was a reliable and acceptable means of combating racial discrimination would not be easy. Indeed, even getting the nation's leaders to acknowledge that such discrimination required immediate and sustained attention was a major challenge. Notwithstanding the empowering and instructive legacy left by earlier generations of freedom fighters, the Freedom Riders knew that the road to racial equality remained long and hard, and that advancing down that road would test their composure and fortitude.

The Riders' dangerous passage through the bus terminals and jails of the Jim Crow South represented only one part of an extended journey for justice that stretched back to the dawn of American history and beyond. But once that passage was completed, there was renewed hope that the nation would eventually find its way to a true and inclusive democracy. For the brave activists who led the way, and for those of us who can only marvel at their courage and determination, this link to a brighter future was a great victory. Yet, as we shall see, it came with the sobering reminder that "power concedes nothing without a demand," as the abolitionist and former slave Frederick Douglass wrote in 1857.

The story of the Freedom Rides is largely the story of a single year, and most of this book deals with a rush of events that took place during the spring and summer of 1961. But, like most of the transformative experiences of the 1960s, the Freedom Rides had important antecedents in the mid-century convulsions of depression and war. Though frequently associated with a decade of student revolts that began with Greensboro and ended with a full-scale generational assault on authority, the Rides were rooted in earlier rebellions, both youthful and otherwise. Choosing a starting point for the Freedom Rider saga is difficult, and no single individual or event can lay claim to its origins. But perhaps the best place to begin is 1944, the year of D-Day and global promise, when a young woman from Baltimore named Irene Morgan committed a seminal act of courage.

1

You Don't Have to Ride Jim Crow

You don't have to ride Jim Crow,
You don't have to ride Jim Crow,
Get on the bus, set any place,
'Cause Irene Morgan won her case,
You don't have to ride Jim Crow.
—1947 freedom song

When Irene Morgan boarded a Greyhound bus in Hayes Store, Virginia, on July 16, 1944, she had no inkling of what was about to happen—no idea that her trip to Baltimore would alter the course of American history. Having recently had a miscarriage, the twenty-seven-year-old defense worker and mother of two had more mundane things on her mind. It was a sweltering morning in the Virginia Tidewater, and she was anxious to get home to her husband, a stevedore who worked on the docks of Baltimore's bustling inner harbor. Now she was going back to Baltimore for a doctor's appointment and perhaps a clean bill of health that would allow her to resume work at the Martin bomber plant where she helped build B-26 Marauders. The restful stay in Gloucester, Virginia—where her mother's family had lived and worked since the early nineteenth century, and where she had visited many times since childhood—had restored some of her physical strength. But it had also confirmed the stark realities of a rural folk culture shouldering the burdens of three centuries of plantation life. Despite Gloucester's proximity to Hampton Roads and Norfolk, the war had brought surprisingly few changes to the area, most of which remained mired in suffocating poverty and a rigid caste system.

As Irene Morgan knew all too well, Baltimore had its own problems related to race and class. Still, she could not help feeling fortunate to live in a community where it was relatively common for people of "color" to own homes and businesses, to vote on election day, to attend high school or college, and to aspire to middle-class respectability. Bright and self-assured, with a strong sense of right and wrong, she was determined to make her way in the world, despite the very real obstacles of prejudice and discrimination.

The Greyhound from Norfolk was jammed that morning, especially in the back, where several black passengers had no choice but to stand in the aisle. As the bus pulled away from the storefront, Morgan was still searching for an empty seat. When none materialized, she accepted the invitation of a young black woman who graciously offered her a lap to sit on. Later she moved to a seat relinquished by a departing passenger. Although only three rows from the back, she found herself sitting directly in front of a white couple—an arrangement that violated Southern custom and a 1930 Virginia statute prohibiting racially mixed seating on public conveyances. Since she was not actually sitting next to a white person, Morgan did not think the driver would ask her to move. And perhaps he would not have done so if two additional white passengers had not boarded the bus a few seconds after she sat down. Suddenly the driver turned toward Morgan and her seatmate, a young black woman holding an infant, and barked: "You'll have to get up and give your seats to these people." The young woman with the baby complied immediately, scurrying into the aisle near the back of the bus. But Irene Morgan, perhaps forgetting where she was, suggested a compromise: She would be happy to exchange seats with a white passenger sitting behind her, she calmly explained, but she was unwilling to stand for any length of time. Growing impatient, the driver repeated his order, this time with a barely controlled rage. Once again Morgan refused to give up her seat. As an uneasy murmur filled the bus, the driver shook his head in disgust and rushed down the steps to fetch the local sheriff.

Irene Morgan's impulsive act—like Rosa Parks's more celebrated refusal to give up a seat on a Montgomery bus eleven years later—placed her in a difficult and dangerous position. In such situations, there were no mitigating circumstances, no conventions of humanity or even paternalism that might shield her from the full force of the law. To the driver and to the sheriff of Middlesex County, the fact that she was a woman and in ill health mattered little. Irene Morgan had challenged both the sanctity of segregation and the driver's authority, disturbing the delicate balance of Southern racial etiquette.

The sheriff and his deputy showed no mercy as they dragged her out of the bus. Both men claimed that they resorted to force only after Morgan tore up the arrest warrant and threw it out the window. According to the deputy's sworn testimony, the unruly young woman also kicked him three times in the leg. Morgan herself later insisted that propriety and male pride prevented him from telling what really happened. "He touched me," she recalled in a recent interview. "That's when I kicked him in a very bad place. He hobbled off, and another one came on. He was trying to put his hands on me to get me off. I was going to bite him, but he was dirty, so I clawed him instead. I ripped his shirt. We were both pulling at each other. He said he'd use his nightstick. I said, 'We'll whip each other.' " In the end, it took both officers to subdue her, and when she complained that they were hurting her arms, the deputy shouted: "Wait till I get you to jail, I'll beat your head with a stick." Charged with resisting arrest and violating Virginia's Jim Crow transit law, she spent the next seven hours slumped in the corner of a county jail cell. Late in the afternoon, after her mother posted a $500 bond, she was released by county authorities confident that they had made their point: No uppity Negro from Baltimore could flout the law in the Virginia Tidewater and get away with it.

As Morgan and her mother left the jail, Middlesex County officials had good reason to believe that they had seen the last of the feisty young woman from Baltimore. In their experience, any Negro with a lick of sense would do whatever was necessary to avoid a court appearance. If she knew what was good for her, she would hurry back to Maryland and stay there, even if it meant forfeiting a $500 bond. They had seen this calculus of survival operate on countless occasions, and they didn't expect anything different from Morgan. What they did not anticipate was her determination to achieve simple justice. "I was just minding my own business," she recalled many years later. "I'd paid my money. I was sitting where I was supposed to sit. And I wasn't going to take it." As she waited for her day in court, discussions with friends and relatives, some of whom belonged to the Baltimore branch of the NAACP, brought the significance of her challenge to Jim Crow into focus. Her personal saga was part of a larger story—an ever-widening struggle for human dignity that promised to recast the nature of American democracy. Driven, as one family member put it, by "the pent-up bitterness of years of seeing the colored people pushed around," she embraced the responsibility of bearing witness and confronting her oppressors in a court of law.

On October 18 Morgan stood before Middlesex County Circuit Judge J. Douglas Mitchell and pleaded her case. Although she represented herself as best she could, arguing that Virginia's segregation laws did not apply to interstate passengers, the outcome was never in doubt. Pleading guilty on the resisting arrest charge, she agreed to pay the $100 fine assessed by Judge Mitchell. The conviction on the segregation violation charge was, however, an altogether different matter. To Mitchell's dismay, Morgan refused to pay the $10 fine and court costs, announcing her intention to appeal the second conviction to the Virginia Supreme Court. She vowed to take her case all the way to Washington if necessary.

Morgan's appeal raised more than a few eyebrows in the capital city of Richmond, where it was no secret that the NAACP had been searching for suitable test cases that would challenge the constitutionality of the state's Jim Crow transit law. Segregated transit was a special concern in Virginia, which served as a gateway for southbound bus and railway passengers. Crossing into the Old Dominion from the District of Columbia, which had no Jim Crow restrictions, or from Maryland, which, unlike Virginia, limited its segregationist mandate to local and intrastate passengers, could be a jarring and bewildering experience for travelers unfamiliar with the complexities of border-state life. This was an old problem, dating back at least a half-century, but the number of violations and interracial incidents involving interstate passengers had multiplied in recent years, especially since the outbreak of World War II. With the growing number of black soldiers and sailors and with the rising militancy of the Double V campaign, which sought twin victories over enemies abroad and racial discrimination at home, Virginia had become a legal and cultural battleground for black Americans willing to challenge the dictates of Jim Crow.

In 1942 the state legal committee of the Virginia NAACP, led by three Howard University–trained attorneys—Spottswood Robinson, Oliver Hill, and Martin A. Martin—began the search for a case that would bring the interstate issue before the U.S. Supreme Court. Working closely with the brilliant legal theorist Thurgood Marshall and the NAACP's national legal staff, the committee considered and rejected a number of potential clients before discovering Irene Morgan in the fall of 1944. Almost immediately they sensed that this was the case and the defendant they needed. Not only was the basis of her conviction clear, but she also had the makings of an exemplary client.

With Thurgood Marshall's blessing, the Virginia NAACP filed a carefully crafted appellate brief emphasizing the interstate commerce clause and *Hall v. DeCuir*, an 1877 decision that, ironically, had invalidated a state law prohibiting racial segregation among interstate steamboat passengers. But, as expected, the seven justices of the Virginia Supreme Court unanimously affirmed Morgan's conviction. In a rambling sixteen-page opinion issued on June 6, 1945, the court upheld the constitutionality of the 1930 Jim Crow transit law. Speaking for the court, Justice Herbert Gregory did not deny that *Hall v. DeCuir* established a legal precedent for invoking the commerce clause as a barrier to state statutes that interfered with interstate commerce, but he summarily dismissed the NAACP's claim that the 1930 law involved such interference. "Our conclusion," he declared at the end of the opinion, "is that the statute challenged is a reasonable police regulation and applies to both intrastate and interstate passengers. It is not obnoxious to the commerce clause of the Constitution."

Gregory's forthright words were just what the NAACP wanted to hear. With a little help from the Virginia Supreme Court, *Morgan v. Commonwealth of Virginia* had become a near-perfect test case. When the Virginia court denied the

NAACP's petition for a rehearing in September, Spot Robinson could hardly wait to file an appeal to the U.S. Supreme Court. In January 1946 the court agreed to hear the case, and two months later Robinson joined Marshall and Hastie for the oral argument in Washington. Although this was the first time that the NAACP had argued a segregated transit case in front of the court, the organization's talented team of attorneys made short work of Virginia attorney general Abram Staples's predictable arguments on behalf of the status quo. Focusing on the Virginia statute's broad reach, they argued that forcibly segregating interstate passengers violated the commerce clause, infringed upon congressional authority, and threatened the nation's tradition of free movement across state lines. Insisting that this misuse of state segregation laws placed an unnecessary and unconstitutional burden on individuals as well as interstate bus companies, the NAACP gave the court a compelling rationale for overruling the Virginia court's judicial and racial conservatism. "Today, we are just emerging from a war in which all of the people of the United States were joined in a death struggle against the apostles of racism," the NAACP brief reminded the justices. Surely it was time for the court to declare that federal law no longer sanctioned "disruptive local practices bred of racial notions alien to our national ideals, and to the solemn undertakings of the community of civilized nations as well."

Since this was essentially the same court that had struck down the Texas "white primary" electoral system in the *Smith v. Allwright* decision of April 1944, NAACP leaders were cautiously optimistic. But in the unsettled atmosphere of postwar America, no one could be certain how the court would rule or how white Americans would respond to an NAACP victory over Jim Crow transit. The year 1946 had already brought a number of surprises, both bitter and sweet, ranging from the brutal repression of black veterans in Columbia, Tennessee, to the signing of Jackie Robinson by the Brooklyn Dodgers. Although change was in the air, it was not entirely clear which way the nation was headed on matters of race.

When the Supreme Court announced its decision on June 3, 1946, Marshall was both relieved and elated. With only one dissenting vote, the justices sustained Morgan's appeal. In a carefully worded opinion delivered by Associate Justice Stanley Reed, the court accepted the NAACP's argument that segregating interstate passengers violated the spirit of the interstate commerce clause. "As there is no Federal act dealing with the separation of races," Reed explained, "we must decide the validity of this Virginia statute on the challenge that it interferes with commerce, as a matter of balance between exercise of the local police power and the need for National uniformity in the regulations for interstate travel. It seems clear to us that seating arrangements for the different races in interstate motor travel requires a single uniform rule to promote and protect national travel."

The ruling affirmed the NAACP's claim that the Virginia statute requiring segregation of interstate bus passengers was unconstitutional. But the opinion, cast in narrow terms, said nothing about intrastate passengers, its applicability to other means of conveyance such as railroads, or how and when desegregation of interstate buses might be implemented, and it offered no clear sign that the court was moving closer to an outright rejection of the notorious *Plessy v. Ferguson* doctrine of 1896 that gave sanction to separate but equal facilities for the two races. On June 4 the *Morgan* decision was front-page news throughout the nation, and by the end of the day the NAACP's national office was flooded with congratulatory telegrams. Many hailed the *Morgan* decision as a legal milestone comparable to *Smith v. Allwright*, but NAACP officials knew that praise from friends and allies, however welcome, was less important than the responses of editors, reporters, public officials, and bus company executives.

Immediately following the *Morgan* decision, the NAACP's victorious legal strategy drew praise from a wide variety of civil rights activists, including Morgan herself. Having left Baltimore for New York City, where she found work as a practical nurse, Morgan expressed confidence that the court's decision would "abolish jim crow for northerners going south." "Jim-crow tension has been removed by the edict," she proclaimed, "and the insult and degradation to colored people is gone."

Unfortunately, the situation looked much different two months later. Segregated transit, with all its insults and degradation, remained firmly in place; Morgan herself was all but forgotten; and the leadership of the NAACP was ready to move on to new challenges. Despite their disappointment, Marshall and his colleagues were not about to let the *Morgan* case disrupt their long-term plan to dismantle the legal structure of Jim Crow. After more than a decade of careful legal maneuvering, they remained committed to a patient struggle based on the belief that American constitutional law provided the only viable means of achieving civil rights and racial equality.

Within the NAACP, some local activists—especially in the Youth Councils—felt constrained by this narrow, legalistic approach, but their restlessness had little impact on the organization's national leaders, who maintained tight control over all NAACP activities. Alternative strategies such as economic boycotts, protest marches, and picketing were anathema in the national office, which saw itself as the guardian of the organization's respectability. In the midst of the Cold War, NAACP leaders did not want to do anything to invite charges of radicalism or subversion. Even though the NAACP prided itself on being a militant organization, public association with direct action tactics or with groups that might be termed "red" or even "pink" was to be avoided at all costs. In the Cold War context such caution was understandable, but in a number of instances, including the *Morgan* case, it placed severe limits on the NAACP's capacity to represent the interests of black Americans. Other than counseling patience, the nation's largest civil rights organization had no real answer to the white South's refusal to take *Morgan* seriously.

In the fall of 1946 the NAACP's disengagement from the fading, unresolved controversy over the *Morgan* decision created an opening for the radical wing of the civil rights movement. Though no one realized it at the time, this opening represented an important turning point in the history of the modern American freedom struggle. When the NAACP fell by the wayside, a small but determined group of radical activists seized the opportunity to take the desegregation struggle out of the courts and into the streets. Inspired by an international tradition of nonviolent direct action, this response to segregationist intransigence transcended the cautious legal pragmatism of the NAACP. In the short run, as we shall see, their efforts to breathe life into the *Morgan* decision failed, but in the long run, their use of direct action in the late 1940s planted the seeds of a larger idea that bore remarkable fruit a decade and a half later. Although called a "Journey of Reconciliation," this nonviolent foray into the world of Jim Crow represented the first formal "freedom ride."

To most Americans, then and now, the pioneer freedom riders were obscure figures, men and women who lived and labored outside the spotlight of celebrity and notoriety. During the immediate postwar era, the radical wing of the civil rights struggle was small, predominantly white, and fragmented among several organizations. Concentrated in New York, Chicago, and other large Northern cities, the radicals included followers of Mohandas Gandhi, Christian socialists, labor and peace activists, Quaker pacifists, Communists, and a varied assortment of left-wing intellectuals. Though ideologically diverse, they shared a commitment to militant agitation aimed at bringing about fundamental and even revolutionary change. Like India's Gandhi, they dreamed of a world liberated from the scourges of racial prejudice, class oppression, and colonialism.

In 1946 the most active members of this radical vanguard were affiliated with two interrelated organizations, the Congress of Racial Equality (CORE) and its parent organization, the Fellowship of Reconciliation (FOR). It was within these groups that the idea of the Freedom Ride was born. Founded in Chicago in 1942, CORE drew inspiration from the wartime stirrings of decolonization in Africa and Asia and from the recent success of nonviolent mass resistance in Gandhi's India. It also drew upon a somewhat older tradition of nonviolent protest nurtured by FOR, an organization formed in 1914 at an international gathering of Christian pacifists in London.

Among the FOR/CORE stalwarts were three men destined to play pivotal roles in the Freedom Rider saga: Bayard Rustin, James Peck, and James Farmer. A founding member of CORE and the co-secretary of FOR's Racial-Industrial Department, Rustin—along with co-secretary George Houser—organized and led the Journey of Reconciliation of 1947 and later served as an advisor to Dr. Martin Luther King Jr. He played no direct role in the Freedom Rides of 1961, spending most of the early 1960s in Africa and Europe. Yet, perhaps more than anyone else, Rustin was the intellectual godfather of the Freedom Rider movement. Peck, a radical journalist who acted as CORE's chief publicist, was the only person to participate in both the Journey of Reconciliation and the 1961 Freedom Rides. Severely beaten by Klansmen in Alabama in May 1961, he later wrote a revealing memoir of his experiences as a Freedom Rider. Farmer, like Rustin, was one of the founders of CORE. Although personal circumstances prevented him from participating in the Journey of Reconciliation, he was the guiding spirit behind CORE's 1961 Freedom Rides. As national director of CORE from 1961 to 1966, he presided over the organization's resurgence, crafting and sustaining the legacy of the Freedom Rides. Together, these three activists provided a critical link between the nonviolent civil rights initiatives of the 1940s and the full-blown movement of the 1960s. While none of these men achieved national fame in the manner of King or Rosa Parks, each in his own way exerted a powerful influence on the development of nonviolence in the United States. Their personal stories reveal a great deal about the origins and context of the Freedom Rides and about the hidden history of the civil rights struggle—especially the complex connections between North and South, blacks and whites, liberalism and radicalism, and religious and secular motivation.

Rustin, the oldest of the three, was born in 1912, in West Chester, Pennsylvania. The child of Florence Rustin, an unwed black teenager, and Archie Hopkins, an itinerant black laborer who barely acknowledged his son's existence, he was adopted by Florence's parents, Julia and Janifer Rustin, and raised by an extended family of grandparents, aunts, and uncles who collectively eked out a living by cooking and catering for the local Quaker gentry. Julia Rustin was a member of the local Quaker meeting before joining her husband's African Methodist Episcopal (AME) church following their marriage in 1891. And she remained a Quaker "at heart," naming her grandson for Bayard Taylor, a celebrated mid-nineteenth-century Quaker leader. A woman of substance and deep moral conviction, Julia was the most important influence in Bayard's upbringing and the primary source of the pacifist doctrines that would anchor his lifelong commitment to nonviolence. Indulged as the favorite child of the Rustin clan, he gained a reputation as a brilliant student and gifted singer and musician, first as one of a handful of black students at West Chester High School, where he also excelled as a track and football star, and later at all-black Wilberforce University in Ohio, where he studied history and literature and toured as the lead soloist of the Wilberforce Quartet. Despite these accomplishments, he eventually ran afoul of the Wilberforce administration by challenging the school's compulsory ROTC program and by engaging in homosexual activity (he reportedly fell in love with the son of the university president). Expelled in December 1933, he returned to Pennsylvania and enrolled at Cheyney State Teachers College the following fall.

At Cheyney, where he remained for three years, Rustin gained a reputation as a multi-talented student leader, distinguishing himself as a singer, a keen student of philosophy, and a committed peace activist. When Cheyney's president, Leslie Pinckney Hill, a devout black Quaker, invited the American Friends Service Committee to hold an international peace institute on the campus in the spring of 1937, Rustin was a willing and eager participant. Inspired by the dedicated pacifists who attended the institute and already primed for social action by his family and religious background, he soon accepted a position as a "peace volunteer" with the American Friends Service Committee's Emergency Peace Campaign. During a training session, he received further inspiration from Muriel Lester, a noted British pacifist and Gandhi protégé. After listening to Lester's eloquent plea for pacifism and nonviolent struggle, he threw himself into the peace campaign with an uncommon zeal that would later become his trademark. Along with three other volunteers—including Carl Rachlin, who would later serve as a CORE and Freedom Rider attorney—he spent the summer of 1937 in the upstate New York town of Auburn, where he honed his skills as a lecturer and organizer.

At the end of the summer, he returned to West Chester and Cheyney, but not for long. In the early fall, propelled by a growing disenchantment with southeastern Pennsylvania's political and cultural scene, and by a second scandalous (and interracial) homosexual incident, he moved northward to the alluring uncertainties of metropolitan Harlem, the unofficial capital of black America. Cast adrift from the relatively secure world of college life and facing the vagaries of the Great Depression, Rustin embarked on a remarkable odyssey of survival and discovery that took him through a labyrinth of radical politics and bohemian culture. Along the way, he became a professional singer, a dedicated Communist, and an uncloseted homosexual. During the late thirties, he sang backup for Josh White and Huddie "Leadbelly" Ledbetter, worked as a recruiter for the Young Communist League, preached revolution and brotherhood on countless street corners, and even squeezed in a few classes at City College, all the while gaining a reputation as one of Harlem's most colorful characters.

In early 1941, the Young Communist League asked Rustin to organize a campaign against segregation in the American armed forces, but later in the year, following the unexpected German attack on the Soviet Union, League leaders ordered him to cancel the campaign in the interests of Allied military solidarity. With this apparent shift away from racial and social justice agitation, Rustin became deeply disillusioned with the Communist Party. "You can all go to hell," he told his New York comrades, "I see that the Communist movement is only interested in what happens in Russia. You don't give a damn about Negroes." In June 1941, he left the Communist fold for good and transferred his allegiance to A. Philip Randolph, the legendary black socialist and labor leader who was busy planning a mass march on Washington to protest the Roosevelt administration's refusal to guarantee equal employment opportunities for black and white defense workers. Randolph appointed Rustin the youth organizer for the march, but the two men soon had a serious falling out. After Roosevelt responded to Randolph's threatened march with an executive order creating a Fair Employment Practices Committee (FEPC), Randolph agreed to call off the march. But many of his young supporters, including Rustin, thought the protest march should continue as planned. Later in the war Rustin and Randolph resumed their friendship and collaboration, but the temporary break prompted the young activist to look elsewhere for a political and spiritual home. Consequently, in the fall of 1941, he accepted a staff position with A. J. Muste's Fellowship of Reconciliation.

As FOR youth secretary, Rustin returned to the pacifist track that he had followed as an American Friends Service Committee volunteer, immersing himself in the writings and teachings of Gandhi and pledging his loyalty to nonviolence, not just as a strategy for change, but as a way of life. Muste encouraged and nurtured Rustin's determination to apply Gandhian precepts to the black struggle for racial equality, and in the spring of 1942 the two men joined forces with other FOR activists to found the Committee (later "Congress") of Racial Equality. "Certainly the Negro possesses qualities essential for nonviolent direct action." Rustin wrote prophetically in October 1942. "He has long since learned to endure suffering. He can admit his own share of guilt and has to be pushed hard to become bitter . . . He is creative and has learned to adjust himself to conditions easily. But above all he possesses a rich religious heritage and today finds the church the center of his life."

As a CORE stalwart, Rustin participated in a number of nonviolent protests, including an impromptu refusal to move to the back of a bus during a trip from Louisville, Kentucky, to Nashville, Tennessee, in the early summer of 1942. This particular episode earned him a roadside beating at the hands of the Nashville police, who later hauled him off to jail. A month after the incident Rustin offered the readers of the FOR journal, *Fellowship*, a somewhat whimsical description of his arrest:

> I was put into the back seat of the police car, between two policemen. Two others sat in front. During the thirteen-mile ride to town they called me every conceivable name and said anything they could think of to incite me to violence . . . When we reached Nashville, a number of policemen were lined up on both sides of the hallway down which I had to pass on my way to the captain's office. They tossed me from one to

another like a volleyball. By the time I reached the office, the lining of my best coat was torn, and I was considerably rumpled. I straightened myself as best I could and went in. They had my bag, and went through it and my papers, finding much of interest, especially in the *Christian Century* and *Fellowship*. Finally the captain said, "Come here, nigger." I walked directly to him, "What can I do for you?" I asked. "Nigger," he said menacingly, "you're supposed to be scared when you come in here!" "I am fortified by the truth, justice, and Christ," I said. "There's no need for me to fear." He was flabbergasted and, for a time, completely at a loss for words. Finally he said to another officer, "I believe the nigger's crazy!"

In the end, the timely intervention of a sympathetic white bystander who had witnessed the roadside beating and the restraint of a cool-headed assistant district attorney (Ben West, a future Nashville mayor who would draw widespread praise for his moderate response to the student sit-ins of 1960 and 1961) kept Rustin out of jail, reinforcing his suspicion that even the white South could be redeemed through nonviolent struggle.

Soon after his narrow escape from Nashville justice, Rustin became a friend and devoted follower of Krishnalal Shridharani, a leading Gandhian scholar and the author of *War Without Violence*. This discipleship deepened his commitment to nonviolent resistance and noncooperation with evil, and in 1943 he rejected the traditional Quaker compromise of alternative service in an army hospital. Convicted of draft evasion, he spent the next twenty-eight months in federal prison. For nearly two years, he was imprisoned at the federal penitentiary in Ashland, Ohio, where he waged spirited if futile campaigns against everything from the censorship of reading materials to racial segregation. In August 1945, a final effort to desegregate the prison dining hall led to solitary confinement, but soon thereafter he and several other pacifist malcontents were transferred to a federal facility in Lewisburg, Pennsylvania.

Following his release from Lewisburg in June 1946, Rustin returned to New York to accept an appointment as co-secretary (with George Houser) of FOR's Race and Industrial Department, a position that he promptly turned into a roving mission for Gandhian nonviolence. Though physically weak and emaciated, he took to the road, preaching the gospel of nonviolent direct action to anyone who would listen. As his biographer Jervis Anderson has noted, during the critical postwar year of 1946 Rustin "functioned as a one-man civil disobedience movement in his travels across the United States. He occupied 'white only' railroad compartments; sat in at 'white only' hotels; and refused to budge unless he was forcibly ejected." All of this reinforced his dual reputation as a fearless activist and a Gandhian sage. He was both irrepressible and imaginative; and no one who knew him well was surprised when he, along with Houser, came up with the provocative idea of an interracial bus ride through the South. After the Journey of Reconciliation proposal was hatched, Rustin acted as a relentless advocate, eventually winning over, or at least wearing down, those who thought the plan was too dangerous. Without his involvement, the Journey—and per-haps even the Freedom Rides of 1961—would never have taken place.

Jim Peck followed a somewhat different path to the Journey of Reconcilia-tion. Three years younger than Rustin, he grew up in one of Manhattan's most prosperous households. The son of Samuel Peck, a wealthy clothing wholesaler (who died when his son was eleven years old), he spent the early years of the Great Depression at Choate, an elite prep school in Wallingford, Connecticut. Despite his family's conversion from Judaism to Christianity, Peck was a social outsider at Choate, which used a strict quota system to limit the number of reli-gious and ethnic minorities on campus. The primary factor separating him from his fellow students was not religion or ethnicity, however. Politically precocious, he cultivated a reputation as an independent thinker who espoused idealistic political doctrines and who preferred the company of bookish intellectuals.

In the fall of 1933, he enrolled at Harvard, where he honed his skills as a writer while assuming the role of a campus radical. At Harvard, he missed few opportunities to challenge the social and political conventions of the Ivy League elite and shocked his classmates by showing up at the freshman dance with a black date. As he recalled, this particular act of defiance was directed not only at "the soberly dressed Boston matrons on the sidelines" who "stared at us, whis-pered, and then stared again," but also at his own mother who "referred to Negroes as 'coons' " and "frequently remarked that she would never hire one as a servant because 'they are dirty and they steal.' " By the end of his freshman year, he was a pariah, and his alienation from his family and the American establish-ment was complete. Dropping out of school, he immigrated to Paris, where he lived as an avant-garde expatriate for two years. His years in Europe, where he witnessed the ascendance of authoritarian and totalitarian regimes, deepened his commitment to activism and social justice. In the late thirties a severe case of wanderlust and a desire to identify with the working class led to a series of jobs as a merchant seaman, an experience that eventually propelled him into the tur-bulent world of radical unionism. His years at sea also reinforced his commit-ment to civil rights. "Living and working aboard ships with interracial crews," he later wrote, "strengthened my beliefs in equality."

Returning to the United States in 1938, Peck helped to organize the National Maritime Union, which made good use of his skills as a writer and publicist. During these years, he also became a friend and follower of Roger Baldwin, the strong-willed founder of the American Civil Liberties Union (ACLU). Baldwin encouraged him to become involved in a number of social justice organizations, including the War Resisters League, and helped him find work with a trade union news syndicate. By the end of the decade, Peck was an avowed pacifist who spent much of his time publicizing the activities of the War Resisters League. Like Rustin, he refused to submit to the draft and was imprisoned for his defiance in 1942. He spent almost three years in the federal prison in Danbury, Connecticut, where he helped to organize a work strike that led to the desegregation of the prison mess hall. After his release in 1945, he rededicated himself to pacifism and militant trade unionism, offering his services to a number of progressive organizations. For a time he devoted most of his energies to the War Resisters League and to editing the Workers Defense League *News Bulletin*. But in late 1946 he became increasingly absorbed with the race issue, especially after discovering and joining CORE. Recent events had convinced him that the struggle for racial equality was an essential precondition for the transformation of American society, and the direct action philosophy of CORE provided him with a means of acting upon his convictions. With the zeal of a new recruit, he embraced the idea of the Journey of Reconciliation, which would be his first venture as a CORE volunteer.

Jim Farmer shared Peck's passion for direct action and nonviolent protest. But in most other respects, from style and temperament to racial and regional background, the two men represented a study in contrasts. Born in Marshall, Texas, in 1920, Farmer was a black Southerner who had first-hand experience with the institutions of the Jim Crow South. Raised in a middle-class family, he was fortunate enough to avoid the degrading economic insecurities of the rural poor. But as the aspiring son of educated parents, he was forced to endure the painful psychological and social indignities of a racial caste system that warped and restricted his prospects. His mother, Pearl Houston Farmer, was a graduate of Florida's Bethune Cookman Institute and a former teacher; his father, James Leonard Farmer Sr., was a learned Methodist minister who had earned a PhD in theology at Boston University. One of the few blacks in early-twentieth-century Texas to hold a doctoral degree, Farmer's father spoke seven languages and held academic positions at a number of black colleges, including Rust College in Holly Springs, Mississippi, and Samuel Houston College in Austin, Texas. A towering figure in black academic circles, he was nonetheless cautious and deferential in his dealings with whites. This inconsistency troubled his young son, who idealized his father's moral and intellectual stature but who eventually recoiled from what he came to see as a cringing hypocrisy that perpetuated racial injustice.

A brilliant student, young Jim Farmer entered school at the age of four and graduated from Wiley College at eighteen. At Wiley, he came under the influence of Melvin Tolson, an English professor and debating coach who nurtured his young protégé's oratorical skills. Farmer possessed a deep, mellifluous voice that was perfectly suited to a dramatic style of oratory; and by the time Tolson got through with him, his studied intonations carried the barest hint of an east Texas twang. This remarkable speaking voice became Farmer's trademark and the cornerstone of a grand manner that struck some observers as pretentious and condescending. Even as a teenager, he was a large and imposing figure with an ego to match. Ambitious and articulate, he felt constrained by the small-town, segregated culture of Marshall. His first taste of the outside world came in 1937 when he represented Wiley at a National Conference of Methodist Youth at Miami University in Oxford, Ohio. Although there were only a handful of black delegates in attendance, Farmer emerged as one of the stars of the conference, persuading his fellow Methodists to approve a resolution urging Congress to pass anti-lynching legislation. "Everyone here wants to stop lynching," he informed the assembled delegates, "The only question is how long do we have to wait? How long, oh, Lord, how long? The purpose of this motion is not to damn the South and the many decent people who live there . . . The purpose of this motion is to *stop lynching now*." The audience responded with a standing ovation and approval by acclamation, providing him with the "first taste of the heady wine of public acclaim." The conference later elected him to its governance committee, a remarkable achievement for a seventeen-year-old black boy from east Texas.

The exhilarating triumph in Ohio reinforced Farmer's determination to become involved in the widening struggle for racial justice, and a few weeks later he accepted an invitation to attend a joint meeting of the National Negro Congress and the Southern Negro Youth Conference. Held in Richmond, Virginia, the meeting attracted some of the nation's most prominent black leaders, including A. Philip Randolph, Howard University President Mordecai Johnson, and Howard political scientist Ralph Bunche. Traveling the thousand miles to Richmond by car, Farmer and two companions, one of whom was a white delegate from the University of Texas, encountered the inevitable frustrations of finding food, shelter, and restroom facilities along the Jim Crow highways of the Deep South. By the time the young travelers arrived at the conference, they had seen and experienced enough to fuel a growing sense of outrage. But the conference itself was even more eye-opening. Here Farmer received his first exposure to the passionate militance of left-wing politics. He also got more than a glimpse of the sectarian intrigue and political infighting between Communists and socialists that threatened to tear the National Negro Congress apart. Founded in 1936 as a national clearinghouse for civil rights and labor organizations concerned about fair employment issues, the National Negro Congress had elected Randolph as its first chairman. But during the organization's first two years, the black socialist leader had grown increasingly suspicious of Communist activists who were reportedly exploiting the National Negro Congress for selfish political purposes. Randolph's anger boiled over at the Richmond conference, where his explosive resignation speech both shocked and thrilled Farmer.

To his conservative father's dismay, Farmer was never quite the same after the Richmond conference. The dream of becoming a theologian and following in his father's footsteps was still alive, and in the fall of 1938 he dutifully entered the Howard University School of Theology, where his father had recently accepted a position as a professor of Greek and New Testament studies. But during his years at Howard the young divinity student continued to gravitate toward radical politics. Inspired by Howard Thurman, a charismatic professor of social ethics and dean of the chapel whom he later described as a "mystic, poet, philosopher, preacher," Farmer became intrigued with Gandhianism, pacifism, and radical versions of the social gospel. Under Thurman's direction, he wrote his thesis on "A Critical Analysis of the Interrelationships Between Religion and Racism." Thurman also helped him secure a position as a part-time secretary in the Washington office of the Fellowship of Reconciliation, and by the time he graduated in 1941 he was completely captivated by FOR's philosophy of nonviolent interracial activism. Refusing ordination as a Methodist minister–a decision clinched by the news that his choice of pastorates was limited to all-black congregations—he accepted a full-time position as FOR's race relations secretary. Assigned to FOR's regional office in Chicago, he arrived in the Windy City in August 1941, ready, as he put it, to lead "an assault on the demons of violence and bigotry."

For the next two years, he spearheaded a series of direct action campaigns in Chicago and also traveled throughout the Midwest spreading the FOR gospel of pacifism and nonviolent resistance to social injustice. Though barely old enough to vote, he exuded an aura of confidence and command that belied his youth. Some found him arrogant and a bit overbearing, but no one doubted his intelligence or his passionate belief in the struggle for racial justice. At the University of Chicago, he organized an interracial study group on Gandhianism and encouraged students and others to engage in sit-ins and picketing campaigns at segregated coffeehouses, restaurants, roller rinks, and theaters. Working closely with both Rustin and George Houser, FOR's white field secretary, he also created Fellowship House, "an interracial men's cooperative" designed to challenge a restrictive covenant that segregated the neighborhood surrounding the university. In the spring of 1942, these efforts led to the formation of the Chicago Committee of Racial Equality, which Farmer conceived as part of a national direct action network known as the "Brotherhood Mobilization." By 1943, the organization had evolved into the Committees of Racial Equality, and a year later the name was changed to Congress of Racial Equality. At first, A. J. Muste resisted Farmer's insistence that CORE should be allowed to have an identity largely independent of FOR, but the FOR chairman eventually relented. Adopted at the organization's first annual meeting, the CORE charter stated that "the purpose of the organization shall be to federate local interracial groups working to abolish the color line through direct non-violent action." With Muste's blessing, Farmer became CORE's first national chairman, though not for long.

Muste's acceptance of CORE's partial autonomy came at a price, one that eventually proved too costly for Farmer to bear. In June 1943, he received a "promotion" that required relocation to New York. "I knew at once what it all meant," he later wrote, "New York, where they could watch me closely, and full time so I would have less time to freewheel for CORE. I was being given bigger wings, but they would be clipped wings." Muste was not unsympathetic to the aims and activities of CORE, but his primary loyalty was to pacifism and FOR. And he expected the same from Farmer, whose primary job, in his view, was to organize and recruit new members for FOR. As long as FOR was paying Farmer's salary, the interests of the parent organization, not CORE, had to come first. Moreover, Farmer was a notoriously inattentive administrator who preferred public speaking to the background work of building and maintaining an organization. Well aware of Muste's concerns, Farmer made a valiant effort to satisfy his obligations to FOR and to pay more attention to administrative matters. But by the spring of 1945 it was clear to both men that the dual arrangement was not working. In May, following an awkward meeting in Muste's office, Farmer resigned from his FOR staff position—and from his cherished unpaid position as CORE's national chairman.

Following Farmer's departure, CORE reorganized its leadership structure, creating an executive directorship filled by Houser. But the troubled relationship between FOR and CORE continued to plague both organizations in the postwar years. While the split between Muste and Farmer was largely personal and organizational in nature, the nonviolent movement also harbored persistent philosophical and ideological divisions, including disagreements over the connection between pacifism and social justice and the competing claims of morality and pragmatism as the primary rationale for nonviolent direct action.

Farmer himself would later participate in these ongoing debates, especially during and after the Freedom Rides of 1961. But in the immediate postwar era he found himself somewhat removed from the world of FOR and CORE. In late 1945, he accepted a position with the Upholsterers International Union of North America (UIU), which sent him to Virginia and later to High Point, North Carolina, to organize furniture workers. Throughout his stay in the Piedmont he maintained contact with Houser, who kept him abreast of CORE affairs, including the Journey of Reconciliation. And as soon as Farmer heard about the idea of the Journey, which he considered "exciting and intriguing," he was sorely tempted to abandon the frustrations of union organizing and join the ride. But, with a new wife to support, he could not afford to leave a steady-paying job. Turning down a chance to take part in the Journey of Reconciliation was a difficult decision that isolated him from the cause that still excited his deepest passions; and when the UIU transferred him to Cincinnati, he felt even farther removed from the action. Later, after learning that Rustin and several other old friends had been arrested in North Carolina, he "felt pangs of guilt for not having been there." This failure to take part in the Journey would bother him for many years, and only in 1961—when he returned to CORE as national director and the leader of the Freedom Rides—would he begin to feel that he had atoned for his absence from CORE's first great adventure below the Mason-Dixon line.

The plan for an interracial bus ride through the segregated South grew out of a series of discussions between Bayard Rustin and George Houser held during the summer of 1946. Like Rustin, Houser was a Northerner with little firsthand experience in the South. For them the timing of the *Morgan* decision and the ensuing controversy over compliance and enforcement could not have been better. During its first four years, CORE had operated as "a loose federation of local groups which were united mostly by their aim of tackling discrimination by a particular method: nonviolent direct action." In addition to enhancing CORE's national stature and autonomy, a project like the Journey of Reconciliation also promised to provide "an entering wedge for CORE into the South." As Houser explained, "We had no local groups in the South, and it wasn't easy to organize them at this point, especially with the two words 'racial equality' in our name. Those were fighting words in the South. But with a definite project around which to rally, we felt there was a possibility of opening up an area seemingly out of reach." Rustin and Houser were confident that the issue of Jim Crow transit— which, in Houser's words, "touched virtually every black person, was demeaning in its effect, and a source of frequent conflict"—represented a perfect target for CORE's first national project. Even if the project failed to desegregate interstate buses, "challenging discrimination in transportation, by striking a raw nerve, would get public attention."

During the summer of 1946, as expectations of compliance with the *Morgan* ruling faded, the idea of a CORE-sponsored freedom ride became a frequent topic of conversation among CORE stalwarts in New York. Some predicted that the proposed ride would reveal a liberalizing trend in the postwar South, but others were less hopeful. The original plan involved a region-wide journey from Washington, D.C., to New Orleans, Louisiana, but after several of CORE's Southern contacts warned that an interracial journey through the Deep South would provoke "wholesale violence," Rustin and Houser reluctantly agreed to restrict the ride to what was perceived as the more moderate Upper South. "The Deep South may be touched later," they explained, "depending on what comes out of this first experience." After much debate, they also agreed that all of the riders would be men, acknowledging "that mixing the races and sexes would possibly exacerbate an already volatile situation." Less controversially, Rustin and Houser also came up with an official name for the project: the Journey of Reconciliation. This redemptive phrase lent an air of moral authority to the project.

For reasons of safety and to ensure that the compliance tests would be valid, CORE leaders did not seek any advance publicity for the Journey. Within the confines of the movement, though, they quietly spread the word that CORE was about to invade the South. The proposed ride received enthusiastic endorsements from a number of black leaders—most notably Howard Thurman, A. Philip Randolph, and Mary McLeod Bethune—and from several organizations, including the Fellowship of Southern Churchmen, an interracial group of liberal Southern clergyman. The one organization that expressly refused to endorse the ride was, predictably, the NAACP. When CORE leaders first broached the subject with national NAACP officials in early October, Thurgood Marshall and his colleagues were preoccupied with a recent District of Columbia Court of Appeals decision that extended the applicability of *Morgan* to interstate railways. In *Matthews v. Southern Railway*, the court ruled that there was "no valid distinction between segregation in buses and railway cars." For a time, this ruling gave NAACP attorneys renewed hope that the *Morgan* decision would actually have an effect on interstate travel. In the aftermath of the ruling, however, only one railway—the Richmond, Fredericksburg, and Potomac Railroad—actually desegregated its interstate trains. The vast majority of Southern railways continued to segregate all passengers, interstate or not. Several railroad officials insisted that the ruling only applied to the District of Columbia, but to protect their companies from possible federal interference they also adopted the same "company rules" strategy used by some interstate bus lines. The basis for segregation, they now claimed, was not state law but company policy. Racial separation in railroad coaches was thus a private matter allegedly beyond the bounds of public policy or constitutional intrusion.

In mid-November Marshall and the NAACP legal brain trust held a two-day strategy meeting in New York to address the challenge of privatized segregation. No firm solution emerged from the meeting, but the attorneys did reach a consensus that CORE's proposal for an interracial ride through the South was a very bad idea. The last thing the NAACP needed at this point, or so its leaders believed, was a provocative diversion led by a bunch of impractical agitators. Marshall publicly denounced the plans.

Rustin responded in a public letter:

I am sure that Marshall is either ill-informed on the principles and techniques of non-violence or ignorant of the processes of social change.

Unjust social laws and patterns do not change because supreme courts deliver just opinions. One need merely observe the continued practices of jim crow in interstate travel six months after the Supreme Court's decision to see the necessity of resistance. Social progress comes from struggle; all freedom demands a price.

At times freedom will demand that its followers go into situations where even death is to be faced . . . Direct action means picketing, striking and boycotting as well as disobedience against unjust conditions, and all of these methods have already been used with some success by Negroes and sympathetic whites . . .

I cannot believe that Thurgood Marshall thinks that such a program would lead to wholesale slaughter . . . But if anyone at this date in history believes that the "white problem," which is one of privilege, can be settled without some violence, he is mistaken and fails to realize the ends to which man can be driven to hold on to what they consider privileges.

This is why Negroes and whites who participate in direct action must pledge themselves to non-violence in word and deed. For in this way alone can the inevitable violence be reduced to a minimum. The simple truth is this: unless we find non-violent methods which can be used by the rank-and-file who more and more tend to resist, they will more and more resort to violence. And court-room argumentation will not suffice for the activization which the Negro masses are today demanding.

Rustin's provocative and prophetic manifesto did not soften Marshall's opposition to direct action, but it did help to convince Marshall and NAACP executive secretary Walter White that CORE was determined to follow through with the Journey of Reconciliation, with or without their cooperation. CORE leaders had already announced that the two-week Journey would begin on April 9, and there was no turning back for activists like Rustin and Houser who believed that the time for resolute action had arrived. For them, all the signs—including Harry Truman's unexpected decision, in December 1946, to create a President's Commission on Civil Rights—suggested that the movement for racial justice had reached a crossroads. It was time to turn ideas into action, to demonstrate the power of nonviolence as Gandhi and others were already doing in India.

Even so, the Journey remained a dangerous prospect, and finding sixteen qualified and dependable volunteers who had the time and money to spend two weeks on the road was not easy. The organizers' determination to enlist riders who had already demonstrated a commitment to nonviolent direct action narrowed the field. When it proved impossible to find a full complement of volunteers who could commit themselves to the entire Journey, Rustin and Houser reluctantly allowed the riders to come and go as personal circumstances dictated. In the end, fewer than half of the riders completed the entire trip.

The sixteen volunteers who traveled to Washington in early April to undergo two days of training and orientation represented a broad range of nonviolent activists. There were eight whites and eight blacks and an interesting mix of secular and religious backgrounds. In addition to Houser, the white volunteers included Jim Peck; Homer Jack, a Unitarian minister and founding member of CORE, who headed the Chicago Council Against Racial and Religious Discrimination; Worth Randle, a biologist and CORE stalwart from Cincinnati; Igal Roodenko, a peace activist from upstate New York; Joseph Felmet, a conscientious objector from Asheville, North Carolina, representing the Southern Workers Defense League; and two FOR-affiliated Methodist ministers from North Carolina, Ernest Bromley and Louis Adams. The black volunteers included Rustin; Dennis Banks, a jazz musician from Chicago; Conrad Lynn, a civil rights attorney from New York City; Eugene Stanley, an agronomy instructor at North Carolina A&T College in Greensboro; William Worthy, a radical journalist affiliated with the New York Council for a Permanent FEPC; and three CORE activists from Ohio—law student Andrew Johnson, pacifist lecturer Wallace Nelson, and social worker Nathan Wright.

Faced with so many unknowns and the challenge of taking an untried corps of volunteers into the heart of darkness, Rustin and Houser fashioned an intensive orientation program. Meeting at FOR's Washington Fellowship House, nine of the riders participated in a series of seminars that "taught not only the principles but the practices of nonviolence in specific situations that would arise aboard the buses." Using techniques pioneered by FOR peace activists and CORE chapters, the seminars addressed expected problems by staging dramatic role-playing sessions. Two days of this regimen left the riders exhausted but better prepared for the challenges to come.

Leaving little to chance, Rustin and Houser also provided each rider with a detailed list of instructions. Later reprinted in a pamphlet entitled *You Don't Have to Ride Jim Crow*, the instructions made it clear that the task at hand was not, strictly speaking, civil disobedience but rather establishing "the fact that the word of the U.S. Supreme Court is law." Throughout the training sessions for the trip, Rustin and Houser kept reiterating that Jim Crow could not be vanquished by courage alone; careful organization, tight discipline, and strict adherence to nonviolence were also essential.

When the riders gathered at the Greyhound and Trailways stations in downtown Washington on the morning of April 9 for the beginning of the Journey, the predominant mood was anxious but upbeat. As the riders boarded the buses they were accompanied by Ollie Stewart of the *Baltimore Afro-American* and Lem Graves of the *Pittsburgh Courier*, two black journalists who had agreed to cover the first week of the Journey. Joking with the reporters, Rustin, as always, set a jovial tone that helped to relieve the worst tensions of the moment. But there was also a general air of confidence that belied the dangers ahead. Sitting on the bus prior to departure, Peck thought to himself that "it would not be too long until Greyhound and Trailways would 'give up segregation practices' in the South." Years later, following the struggles surrounding the Freedom Rides of 1961, he would look back on this early and unwarranted optimism with a rueful eye. But during the first stage of the Journey, his hopeful expectations seemed justified.

The ride from Washington to Richmond was uneventful for both groups of riders. For a few minutes, Rustin even sat in the seat directly behind the Greyhound driver. Most gratifying was the decision by several regular passengers to sit outside the section designated for their race. Everyone, including the drivers, seemed to take desegregated transit in stride, confirming a CORE report that claimed the Jim Crow line had broken down in northern Virginia in recent months. "Today any trouble is unlikely until you get south of Richmond," the report concluded.

The prospects for white compliance and black militance were less promising on the second leg of the Journey, but even in southern Virginia, where most judges and law enforcement officials had yet to acknowledge the *Morgan* decision, the riders encountered little resistance. During the short stint from Richmond to Petersburg, there were no incidents other than a warning from a black passenger who remarked that black protesters like Nelson and Lynn might get away with sitting in the front of the bus in Virginia, but farther south things would get tougher. "Some bus drivers are crazy," he insisted, "and the farther south you go, the crazier they get." As if to prove the point, a segregationist Greyhound driver had a run-in with Rustin the following morning. Ten miles south of Petersburg, the driver ordered the black activist, who was seated next to Peck, to the back of the bus. After Rustin politely but firmly refused to move, the driver vowed to take care of the situation once the bus reached North Carolina. At Oxford the driver called the local police, but after several minutes of interrogation the officer in charge declined to make an arrest.

A more serious incident occurred on the Trailways bus. Before the bus left the Petersburg station, the driver informed Lynn that he could not remain in the front section reserved for whites. The unflappable New Yorker's refusal to move led to his arrest on a charge of disorderly conduct, but only after the local magistrate talked with the bus company's attorney in Richmond. During a two-hour delay, several of the CORE riders conducted a spirited but largely futile campaign to drum up support among the regular passengers. A white Navy man in

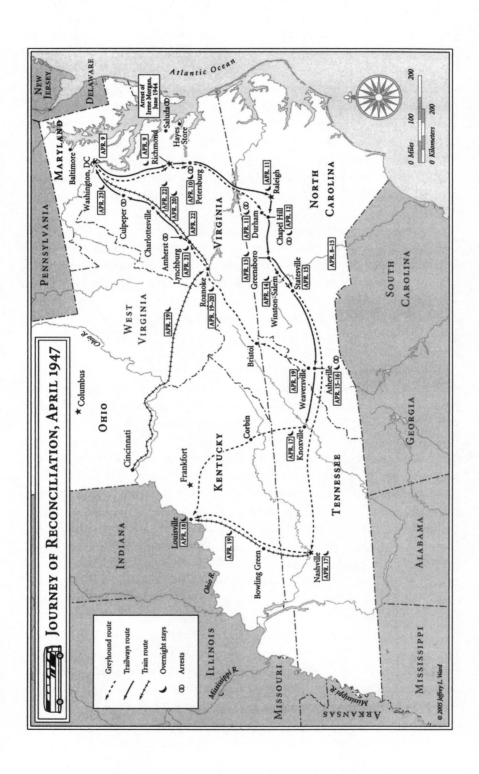

Journey of Reconciliation, April 1947

Greyhound route
Trailways route
Train route
Overnight stays
Arrests

Arrest of Irene Morgan, June 1944

Atlantic Ocean

NEW JERSEY
DELAWARE
MARYLAND
PENNSYLVANIA
WEST VIRGINIA
VIRGINIA
NORTH CAROLINA
SOUTH CAROLINA
OHIO
KENTUCKY
TENNESSEE
GEORGIA
INDIANA
ILLINOIS
MISSOURI
ARKANSAS
ALABAMA
MISSISSIPPI

Baltimore
Washington, DC — APR. 9 / APR. 23
Richmond — APR. 9
Hayes Store
Saluda
Columbus
Cincinnati
Culpeper — APR. 22
Charlottesville — APR. 20
Amherst — APR. 22
Lynchburg — APR. 21
Petersburg — APR. 10
Raleigh — APR. 11
Durham — APR. 11
Chapel Hill — APR. 12
Greensboro — APR. 13
Winston-Salem — APR. 14
Statesville — APR. 15
Roanoke — APR. 19-20
APR. 19
APR. 8-15
Bristol
Weaversville — APR. 19
Asheville — APR. 15-16
Frankfort
Corbin
Knoxville — APR. 17
Louisville — APR. 18
Bowling Green — APR. 19
Nashville — APR. 17

Ohio R.
Mississippi R.
Missouri R.

0 Miles 100 200
0 Kilometers 200

© 2005 Jeffrey L. Ward

uniform grumbled that Lynn's behavior merited a response from the Ku Klux Klan, and an incredulous black porter (who reminded Houser of a fawning "Uncle Tom" character in Richard Wright's *Black Boy*) challenged Lynn's sanity. "What's the matter with him? He's crazy. Where does he think he is?" the porter demanded, adding "We know how to deal with him. We ought to drag him off." As a menacing crowd gathered around the bus, Lynn feared that he might be beaten up or even killed, especially after the porter screamed: "Let's take the nigger off! We don't want him down here!" In the end, he managed to escape the vigilantism of both races. Released on a $25 bail bond, he soon rejoined his comrades in Raleigh.

New challenges awaited the riders in Durham, where three members of the Trailways group—Rustin, Peck, and Johnson—were arrested on the morning of April 12. While Rustin and Johnson were being hauled off for ignoring the station superintendent's order to move to the black section of the bus, Peck informed the police: "If you arrest them, you'll have to arrest me, too, for I'm going to sit in the rear." The arresting officers promptly obliged him. When Joe Felmet and local NAACP attorney C. Jerry Gates showed up at the jail a half hour later to secure their release, the charges were dropped, but a conversation with the Trailways superintendent revealed that there was more trouble ahead. "We know all about this," the superintendent declared. "Greyhound is letting them ride. But we are not." Even more disturbing was the effort by a number of local black leaders to pressure Gates and the Durham NAACP to shun the riders as unwelcome outside agitators. A rally in support of the Journey drew an unexpectedly large crowd, and the local branch of the NAACP refused to abandon the riders. Still, the rift within Durham's black community reminded the riders that white segregationists were not the only obstruction to the movement for racial equality.

The next stop was Chapel Hill, the home of the University of North Carolina. Here, for the first time, the CORE riders would depend on the hospitality of white Southerners. Their host was the Reverend Charles M. Jones, the courageous pastor of a Presbyterian congregation that included the university's president, Frank Porter Graham—a member of President Truman's Committee on Civil Rights—and several other outspoken liberals. Earlier in the year, the black singer Dorothy Maynor had performed before a racially integrated audience on campus, and Jones's church had hosted an interracial union meeting sponsored by the Congress of Industrial Organizations (CIO). These and other breaches of segregationist orthodoxy signaled a rising tolerance in the university community, but they also stoked the fires of reaction among local defenders of Jim Crow. By the time the CORE riders arrived, the town's most militant segregationists were primed and ready for a confrontation that would serve warning that Chapel Hill, despite the influence of the university and its liberal president, was still white man's country.

The riders' first few hours in Chapel Hill seemed to confirm the town's reputation as an outpost of racial moderation. Jones and several church elders welcomed them at the station, and a Saturday night meeting with students and faculty at the university went off without a hitch. On Sunday morning most of the riders, including several blacks, attended services at Jones's church and later met with a delegation representing the Fellowship of Southern Churchmen. At this point there was no hint of trouble. As the riders boarded a Trailways bus for the next leg of the journey, they could only hope that things would continue to go as smoothly in Greensboro. Five of the riders—Johnson, Felmet, Peck, Rustin, and Roodenko—boarded the first bus just after lunch. But they never made it out of the station. As soon as Felmet and Johnson sat down in adjoining seats near the front of the bus, the driver, Ned Leonard, ordered Johnson to the "colored" section in the rear. The two riders explained "that they were inter-state passengers . . . 'covered' by the Irene Morgan decision." Unmoved, Leonard walked to the nearby police station to arrange for their arrest. While he was gone, Rustin and Roodenko engaged several of the passengers in conversation, creating an "open forum" that revealed that many of the passengers supported Felmet's and Johnson's protest. By this time Felmet and Johnson had been carted off to the police station, and Peck had followed them to the station to arrange bail. But Leonard soon discovered that he had two more protesters to deal with. Encouraged by the sympathetic reaction among the regular passengers, Rustin and Roodenko moved to the seat vacated by the arrested riders, which prompted a second round of arrests.

While the four men waited for Houser and Jones to arrive with the bail money, Peck shuttled back and forth from the police station to the bus, checking on his colleagues' bags and trying to keep tabs on the situation at the bus station. By this point the bus had been delayed almost two hours, and it was obvious to everyone at the scene that a group of "outside agitators" had provoked an incident. A few minutes later Peck found himself surrounded by five angry cab drivers as he crossed the street. Snarling, "Coming down here to stir up the niggers," one of the drivers punched Peck in the side of the head. When Peck refused to retaliate and simply asked, "What's the matter?" the man gave him "a perplexed look and started to walk away awkwardly." Moments later, two men—an unidentified local white minister and Eugene Stanley, the black rider who taught at North Carolina A&T—urged the driver to leave Peck alone but were told to mind their own business. Thinking that both men were part of the CORE group, the cab drivers rushed toward them menacingly, but after learning that both were North Carolinians, they let them go. Returning to the police station, Peck warned Jones and Houser, who had finally arrived with the bail money, that trouble was brewing.

After surveying the situation, Jones concluded that the riders would have to travel to Greensboro by car. Once bond had been posted for the arrested riders, the group piled into Jones's car and headed to the parsonage for a brief stop before leaving town. Unfortunately, two cabs filled with irate whites sped after them. As Peck recalled the harrowing scene: "We succeeded in getting to Reverend Jones's home before them. When we got inside and looked out the window, we saw two of the drivers getting out with big sticks. Others started to pick up rocks by the roadside. Then, two of the drivers, apparently scared, motioned to the others to stop. They drove away. But a few minutes later Reverend Jones, who since the CIO meeting in his church had been marked as a 'nigger lover,' received an anonymous phone call. 'Get the niggers out of town by midnight or we'll burn down your house,' threatened a quivering voice." Determined to get the riders out of Chapel Hill before nightfall, Jones rounded up three university students willing to drive the group to Greensboro and also called the police, who reluctantly agreed to provide an escort to the county line.

As soon as the riders left, Jones took his wife and two children to a friend's house for protection, a precaution that seemed warranted by subsequent events. When Jones returned home Sunday evening accompanied by a friend, Hilton Seals, he found a crowd of angry white protesters in his front yard. The two men tried to ignore the crowd's taunts, but as they walked to the door Seals was struck with a rock. On Monday morning Jones received a second anonymous call threatening him with death. Later in the day several cabdrivers milling around the bus station attacked Martin Walker, a disabled white war veteran and university student, after he was seen "talking to a Negro woman." A second university student, Ray Sylvester, "was knocked unconscious by a cabdriver for 'being too liberal.' " During the next few days, Jones received additional death threats by mail, and several anonymous calls threatened his church, prompting an emergency meeting of the congregation. When they learned of the threats, several university students volunteered to guard Jones's home and church, but this proved unnecessary, thanks in part to President Frank Graham's forceful consultation with the local police. By the end of the week the wave of intimidation had subsided, even though the controversy surrounding the bus station incident continued to simmer.

In the wake of the Chapel Hill incident, the CORE riders were somewhat apprehensive about the remaining ten days of the Journey. But whatever doubts they may have had about the wisdom of continuing the trip disappeared during a rousing mass meeting in Greensboro on Sunday evening. At the Shiloh Baptist Church—the same church that would welcome the Freedom Riders fourteen years later—the congregation's emotional embrace reminded them of why they had come south seeking justice. "The church was crowded to capacity and an atmosphere of excitement prevailed," Peck recalled in 1962. "Word had spread about what had happened to us and why we were late . . . After the usual invocation, hymn-singing, scripture-reading, and prayer, Rustin, who is a particularly talented speaker, told our story. He interrupted it only to get one or another of us to rise and tell about a specific incident or experience. Then he continued. When he finished, the people in the crowded church came forward to shake hands and congratulate us. A number of women had tears in their eyes. A few shook my hand more than once."

The mass meeting in Greensboro was the emotional high point of the Journey, and for most of the riders the last ten days on the road represented little more than a long anticlimax. There were, however, a few tense moments—and a few surprises—as the riders wound their way through the mountains of western North Carolina, Tennessee, Kentucky, and Virginia. No two bus drivers—and no two groups of passengers—were quite the same. On the way from Greensboro to Winston-Salem, a white passenger from South Carolina expressed his disgust that no one had removed Lynn from a front seat. "In my state," he declared, "he would either move or be killed." The following day, during a Greyhound run from Winston-Salem to Statesville, Nelson occupied a front seat without incident, but after the riders transferred to a Trailways bus in Statesville, the driver ordered him to the rear. Nelson explained that he was an interstate passenger protected by the *Morgan* decision, and the driver relented, but this did not satisfy several white passengers, including a soldier who demanded to know why Nelson had not been moved or arrested. "If you want to do something about this," the driver responded, "don't blame this man [Nelson]; kill those bastards up in Washington." Following several stops north of Asheville, the white section of the bus became so crowded that two white women had to stand in the aisle. When they asked why Nelson had not been forced to give up his seat, the driver cited the *Morgan* decision.

Asheville, the next stop, was the hometown of Joe Felmet, the young Southern Workers Defense League activist who had been arrested in Chapel Hill, and several of the riders spent the night at his parents' house. This did not please at least one neighbor, who shouted, "How're your nigger friends this morning?" as Felmet and the other riders left for the station. After the riders boarded a Trailways bus headed for Knoxville, Tennessee, a white woman complained to the driver that Dennis Banks, a black musician from Chicago who had just joined the Journey, was sitting in the whites-only section. When Banks, who was sitting next to Peck, politely refused to comply with the driver's order to move, the police were summoned. Twenty minutes of haggling over the law ensued before Banks was finally arrested. The police also arrested Peck, but only after he moved to the Jim Crow section, insisting that he be treated the same as his black traveling companion.

Brought before Judge Sam Cathey, a blind and notoriously hard-edged Asheville politician, the two defendants created a sensation by hiring Curtiss Todd to represent them in court. Neither Cathey nor the local prosecutor had ever heard of *Morgan*, and they had to borrow Todd's copy of the decision during the trial. An NAACP-affiliated attorney from Winston-Salem, Todd was the first black lawyer ever to practice in an Asheville courtroom. Despite this breach of local racial etiquette, Judge Cathey—who reminded the defendants that "we pride ourselves on our race relations here"—made sure that other shibboleths of Jim Crow justice remained in force. "In the courtroom where we were tried," Peck later declared, "I saw the most fantastic extreme of segregation in my experience—Jim Crow Bibles. Along the edges of one Bible had been printed in large letters the words 'white.' Along the page edges of the other Bible was the word 'colored.' When a white person swore in he simply raised his right hand while the clerk held the Bible. When a Negro swore in, he had to raise his right hand while holding the colored Bible in his left hand. The white clerk could not touch the colored Bible." The Jim Crow ethos did not prevent the white and black defendants from receiving the same sentence: thirty days on the road gang, the maximum under North Carolina law. But both riders were relieved when Todd arrived with the required $800 bail bond a few hours later.

While Peck and Banks were detained in Asheville, the rest of the riders went on to Knoxville, where they welcomed three new riders: Homer Jack, Nathan Wright, and Bill Worthy. A seasoned veteran of Chicago direct action campaigns, Jack could hardly wait to join the Journey, but he found the "taut morale" of his CORE colleagues a bit unnerving. "The whites were beginning to know the terror that many Negroes have to live with all the days of their lives," he noted. "All members of the party were dead-tired, not only from the constant tenseness, but also from participating in many meetings and conferences at every stop."

Jack himself soon experienced the emotional highs and lows of direct action in the South. After a full day of interracial meetings in Knoxville, he and Wright tested compliance on the night Greyhound run to Nashville. With Houser serving as the designated observer, they sat in adjoining seats four rows behind the driver. "Slowly heads began to turn around and within five minutes the driver asked Wright to go to the back of the bus," Jack recalled. "Wright answered, 'I prefer to sit here.' I said I and Wright were friends, that we were riding together, that we could legally do so because of the *Morgan* decision. The bus driver then pleaded, 'Wouldn't you like to move?' We said we would like to stay where we were. The driver left the bus, apparently to talk to bus officials and police. After much ogling by passengers and bus employees . . . the driver finally reappeared and started the bus, without any more words to us." *So far so good*, Jack thought to himself, but as the bus left the outskirts of Knoxville he started to worry "that the hard part of the Journey was still ahead." Unaccustomed to the isolation of the rural South, he began to conjure up images of impending doom. "Ours was the first night test of the entire Journey," he later noted. "The southern night, to Northerners at least, is full of vigilante justice and the lynch rope from pine trees if not palms. We wondered whether . . . the bus company—or one of its more militant employees—would telephone ahead for a road block and vigilantes to greet us in one of the Tennessee mountain towns. Neither of us slept a moment that night. We just watched the road." When nothing of this sort actually happened, Jack felt more than a little foolish, concluding that the South, or at least Tennessee, was less benighted than he had been led to believe. "The reaction of the passengers on the trip was not one of evident anger," he observed, "and certainly not of violence. It was first surprise, then astonishment, and even tittering. On that bus, anyway, there was only apathy, certainly no eager leadership in preserving the ways of the Old South."

A second team of riders traveled from Knoxville to Louisville by Greyhound, and they too escaped arrest. Worthy and Roodenko shared a seat in the front of the bus, and no one commented on the arrangement until they reached the small town of Corbin, a hundred miles north of Knoxville. When the young black journalist refused to move to the back, the driver called the police and "hinted that there would be violence from the crowd if Worthy did not move." However, the driver and the local police relented after one of the white passengers, a woman from Tennessee, defended Worthy's legal right to sit wherever he pleased. Once again there was hard evidence that at least some white Southerners were willing to accept desegregated transit.

Several of the riders, including Jack and Wright, left the Journey in Louisville on April 19, but approximately half of the riders participated in the final four days of testing, as three small groups of riders converged on Washington. Although most of these concluding bus and train trips were uneventful, there were two arrests in western Virginia, Nelson in Amherst and Banks in Culpeper. In both cases, the drivers and law enforcement officers involved displayed confusion about the law and some reluctance to follow through with actual arrests, suggesting that Virginia officials were still trying to sort out the implications of *Morgan*. And, despite the arrests, the behavior of several bystanders indicated that race relations in Virginia were changing. In Culpeper, one courageous black woman who sold bus tickets at a local concession stand boarded the bus and offered to help Banks in any way she could, and two local whites spoke out on Banks's behalf. "If I had been you I would have fought them before letting them take me off the bus," one of them told Banks, as the young musician calmly went off to jail.

For the riders, the return to Washington on April 23 brought a sense of relief— and a measure of pride in their perseverance. To their disappointment, however, there was no public event to mark the conclusion of a remarkable collective experience. "At the end of our Journey," Peck recalled in 1962, "there were no reporters flocking around us to ask whether it had been worth it or whether we would do it again—as they did after the Freedom Ride fourteen years later. If there had been, most of us would have answered yes." The Journey's official balance sheet, as reported by CORE, listed twenty-six tests of compliance, twelve arrests, and only one act of violent resistance, but the project's accomplishments drew little attention from the mainstream press in the spring of 1947. Even among white reporters interested in racial matters, the Journey could not compete with the unfolding drama of Jackie Robinson's first few weeks in a Brooklyn Dodgers uniform.

In the weeks and months following the Journey, several riders published reports on their recent experiences in the South. Rustin and Houser—in CORE's official report, *We Challenged Jim Crow*—offered both a day-by-day narrative and general commentary on what the Journey had revealed. "The one word which most universally describes the attitude of police, of passengers, and of the Negro and white bus riders is 'confusion,' " they concluded. "Persons taking part in the psychological struggle in the buses and trains either did not know of the *Morgan* decision or, if they did, possessed no clear understanding of it." Yet there were clear indications that the confusion could be alleviated. "Much was gained when someone in our group took the lead in discussion with bus drivers or train conductors and when police appeared," they reported, adding: "As the trip progressed it became evident that the police and the bus drivers were learning about the Irene Morgan decision as word of the 'test cases' was passed from city to city and from driver to driver." To Rustin and Houser, the Journey demonstrated "the need for incidents as 'teaching techniques.' " "It is our belief that without direct action on the part of groups and individuals, the Jim Crow pattern in the South cannot be broken," they insisted. "We are equally certain that such action must be nonviolent." Homer Jack, writing in the Unitarian magazine, *Common Ground*, offered a similar assessment. "What, finally, did the Journey of Reconciliation accomplish?" he asked rhetorically, answering: "It showed progressive Americans that the *Morgan* decision must be implemented by constant 'testing'—in the spirit of goodwill—and by subsequent law enforcement. The Journey helped implement the decision at least by spreading knowledge of it to bus drivers and some law-enforcement officers (both policemen and judges) in the upper South. The Journey also showed whites and Negroes living in that area that the *Morgan* decision could be enforced without disastrous results, if the proper psychological and legal techniques were used. The Journey gave these techniques—and accompanying inspiration—to thousands of whites and Negroes in the South."

As they wrote these and other reflections, Rustin, Houser, and Jack were well aware of the unfinished business in the courts. Six separate incidents during the Journey had produced twelve arrests, the legal and financial consequences of which were still looming in late April 1947. Fortunately, local officials had already dropped the charges against the three men arrested in Durham, and in May the district attorney in Asheville did the same when Curtiss Todd appealed the convictions of Peck and Banks. The three Virginia arrests were under review by the state supreme court, which would eventually rule in favor of the riders. Thus CORE's major concern was the fate of the four men arrested in Chapel Hill, all of whom, after appeals to the North Carolina Supreme Court, were sentenced to thirty-day jail sentences.

Rustin and Houser welcomed this ruling as the basis for an appeal to the U. S. Supreme Court—an appeal that would clarify and extend the nearly three-year-old *Morgan* decision—but it soon became all too apparent that NAACP leaders had no interest in filing any further appeals. Financially strapped and preoccupied with school desegregation cases and other legal challenges to Jim Crow, the NAACP national office informed CORE and FOR leaders that it could neither fund nor participate in an appeal of the North Carolina Supreme Court's decision. The committee decided that the best means of demonstrating CORE's commitment to nonviolence was to accept the sentences. Although Andrew Johnson, who was then finishing his senior year at the University of Cincinnati, declined to return to North Carolina, confessing that he was "both mentally and physically unprepared to serve thirty days on the road gang," the other three defendants embraced the committee's decision. Rustin predicted that his impending imprisonment would help to expose the hypocrisy of America's democratic pretensions. "Our conviction, unfortunately, is one more demonstration to the colored majority of the world of the failure of American democracy," he declared upon arriving in New York. "America cannot maintain its leadership in the struggle for world democracy as long as the conditions exist which caused our arrest and conviction. We don't fool anybody. People abroad know and are losing faith."

On March 21, 1949, Rustin, Felmet, and Roodenko surrendered to authorities at the Orange County Courthouse in Hillsboro, North Carolina. Assigned to the state prison camp at Roxboro, they braced themselves for thirty days of harsh punishment and humiliation. Fortunately, the actual sentence turned out to be only twenty-two days, thanks to an early release for good behavior. All three men survived the ordeal, but as the decade drew to a close it was all too obvious that the Journey of Reconciliation's primary objective remained unfulfilled. While the first freedom ride had demonstrated the viability of nonviolent direct action in the Upper South, it had not precipitated wholesale desegregation or even protest on a mass scale. With few exceptions, company rules and social inertia still kept the races apart on interstate buses and trains, and no one, other than a few die-hard optimists, expected the situation to change anytime soon. As it had done so many times in the past, the shape-shifting monster known as Jim Crow had adapted to changing legal and political realities without sacrificing the cold heart of racial discrimination. Irene Morgan and the CORE activists who followed her lead would have to wait a bit longer for the day of jubilee.

2

Beside the Weary Road

And ye, beneath life's crushing load, Whose forms are bending low,
Who toil along the climbing way With painful steps and slow,
Look now! For glad and golden hours Come swiftly on the wing:
O rest beside the weary road, And hear the angels sing.
—from the hymn "It Came Upon the Midnight Clear"

Despite the stubborn persistence of segregated travel in the late 1940s, most CORE activists regarded the Journey of Reconciliation as a qualified success. Some even talked of organizing a series of interracial rides and other direct action challenges to Jim Crow in the Deep South. Speaking at an April 1948 Council Against Intolerance in America dinner in New York, Bayard Rustin hailed the Journey as the first of many interracial bus rides and "a training ground for similar peaceful projects against discrimination in employment and the armed services." At the time, neither he nor anyone else in CORE suspected that more than a decade would pass before even one more "freedom ride" materialized.

During the early 1950s CORE and the broader nonviolent movement entered a period of steady decline. As Jim Peck later recalled, "These were CORE's lean years—the years when social consciences throughout the United States were numbed by the infection of McCarthyism." In the 1960s civil rights advocates of all persuasions would become adept at turning the Cold War to their advantage by pointing out the international vulnerability of a nation that failed to practice what it preached on matters of race and democracy. But this was not the case in the 1950s, before the decolonization of Africa and Asia heightened State Department sensitivity to public opinion in the "colored" nations of the Third World.

Following Houser's departure from CORE in early 1954, the burden of leadership fell upon the shoulders of Peck, the editor of the organization's newsletter, *CORE-lator*, and Billie Ames, a talented and energetic St. Louis woman who served as CORE's national group coordinator. In the summer of 1954, Ames tried to revive CORE's flagging spirit by proposing a "Ride for Freedom," a second Journey of Reconciliation that would recapture the momentum of the organization's glory days. Ames planned to challenge segregated railway coaches and terminals as far south as Birmingham, but the project collapsed when the NAACP, which had provided legal support for the original 1947 freedom ride, refused to cooperate. Arguing that an impending Interstate Commerce Commission ruling made the "Ride for Freedom" unnecessary, NAACP leaders advised CORE to devote its attention "to some other purpose." This disappointment, combined with continuing factionalism and dissension, brought CORE to the verge of dissolution. In desperation, CORE's 1955 national convention voted to hire a national field organizer with experience in the South. Even though the potential for nonviolent direct action in the region was unproven, many regarded the South as CORE's last best hope.

In early December 1955, during the same fateful week that witnessed the arrest of Rosa Parks—a forty-three-year-old black seamstress and NAACP leader who refused to give up her seat on a Montgomery, Alabama, bus—LeRoy Carter became CORE's first national field organizer. A former NAACP field secretary with twenty years of experience in the civil rights struggle, Carter seemed well suited to the task of spreading the CORE philosophy to the South. Soft-spoken and deliberate, yet full of determination, he could have been an important asset to the cause of nonviolent resistance in the Deep South, especially during the early weeks of the bus boycott triggered by Parks's arrest. Led by Dr. Martin Luther King Jr.—the charismatic twenty-six-year-old minister of Montgomery's Dexter Avenue Baptist Church and newly elected president of the Montgomery Improvement Association (MIA)—the boycotters faced an uphill struggle against local white supremacists and were in desperate need of help. Unfortunately for King and the MIA, the national leadership of CORE was slow to react to the unexpected events in Alabama and did not dispatch Carter to Montgomery until late March 1956.

In early April, Carter spent several days conferring with King and other MIA leaders, but it soon became evident that he had arrived too late to exert any measurable influence on the Montgomery movement. While the boycotters welcomed CORE's support, they were understandably wary of an organization that presumed to teach them the "rules" of nonviolent protest. Even King, who knew something about CORE's longstanding commitment to direct action, had mixed feelings about what appeared to be a belated and opportunistic attempt to capitalize on the boycotters' struggle. To his surprise, when the spring 1956 issue of *CORE-lator* ran a picture of MIA officials standing on the steps of the Holt Street Baptist Church, it identified them as the "LEADERS OF THE CORE-TYPE

PROTEST IN MONTGOMERY." In the accompanying story, editor Jim Peck proclaimed, "The CORE technique of non-violence has been spotlighted to the entire world through the effective protest action which the Montgomery Improvement Association has been conducting since December 5." And in an adjoining column, Peck proudly quoted a *New York Post* article that reminded the world that CORE had employed Gandhian techniques "long before Montgomery joined the passive resistance movement."

For Peck, as for most CORE veterans, the "miracle of Montgomery" was a bittersweet development. Having suffered through the lean years of the early 1950s, when nonviolent resistance was routinely dismissed as an irrelevant pipe dream, they could not help viewing the boycott with a mixture of pride and jealousy. "I had labored a decade and a half in the vineyards of nonviolence," Jim Farmer explained in his 1985 memoir. "Now, out of nowhere, someone comes and harvests the grapes and drinks the wine." He, along with most of his colleagues, eventually overcame such feelings, acknowledging that Montgomery gave nonviolence a new legitimacy and probably saved CORE from extinction. As he put it, "No longer did we have to explain nonviolence to people. Thanks to Martin Luther King, it was a household word." But such graciousness was the product of years of reflection and common struggle. In the uncertain atmosphere of the mid-1950s, charity did not come so easily, even among men and women who had dedicated their lives to social justice.

The Montgomery Bus Boycott was an important connecting link between the nonviolent movement of the 1940s and the freedom struggle of the 1960s. And it was also part of a great historical divide. Along with the *Brown v. Board of Education* decision, the rise of massive resistance in the white South, and other related developments of the 1950s, the boycott and the subsequent emergence of the Southern Christian Leadership Conference (SCLC) radically altered the context of racial and regional conflict. Even more important, the 1950s was an era of broad and deep social change. In the international arena, the passing of the Stalinist regime, the escalating tensions of the Cold War, the nuclear arms race, the economic recovery of Europe, and the decolonization of the Third World brought a new tone to world affairs.

The pace of change was equally dramatic on the domestic front, as significant shifts in political, legal, and popular culture transformed the nature of American life. The excesses of McCarthyism, the "rights revolution" initiated by the Warren Court, the proliferation of television, the growing influence of consumerism and corporate power, the emergence of a distinct youth culture that found expression in the racially subversive medium of rock 'n' roll, the desegregation of professional sports and the entertainment industry, and the massive postwar migration of blacks to the North and whites to the suburbs all contributed to this transformation. In many cases, the full impact of these changes did not become manifest until the mid-1960s, but the relative calm of the Eisenhower years should not obscure the shifting realities that the fifties represented—realities that helped to lay the groundwork for the social upheavals of the following decade.

As difficult as they are to unravel, the themes of continuity and discontinuity are an important part of the Freedom Rider story. The celebrated Freedom Rides of 1961 represented a reprise of the lesser-known Journey of Reconciliation of 1947; and the tactics, guiding philosophy, organizational roots, and goals of these two experiments in nonviolent resistance were strikingly similar. And yet, the impact—and the ultimate meaning—of the two historical episodes could hardly have been more different. While the Journey of Reconciliation brought about little change and was soon forgotten by all but a handful of nonviolent activists, the Freedom Rides triggered a major political crisis that forced the federal government to fulfill an unkept promise to desegregate public transit, revitalizing the nonviolent movement and bringing direct action to the forefront of a widening struggle.

This contrast in consequences can be traced to a number of factors—including chance and a web of contingency. But the relative success of the Freedom Rides was largely a function of historical context. America—and the world—was a different place in 1961, especially with respect to expectations of racial and social change. For those who dreamed of a nonviolent transformation of American race relations, there were new strands of experience and hope that subverted the moral authority of white culture—strands from which the fabric of the modern civil rights movement was woven.

The Montgomery bus boycott prepared the way for the creation of the modern civil rights movement, but it did not eliminate the difficulties of bridging long-standing ideological, regional organizational, and personal divisions. Years of negotiation, compromise, sacrifice, and struggle lay ahead. The bus boycott reintroduced the idea of nonviolent direct action, and the lessons learned on the streets of Montgomery clearly encouraged blacks to quicken their steps on the road to freedom. But the road itself remained long and hard. In the absence of a fully developed, cohesive national movement, the task of turning a small step into a meaningful "stride toward freedom," to borrow Martin Luther King's apt phrase, would prove far more difficult than he or anyone else realized during the heady days of the bus boycott.

The boycott itself ended triumphantly in December 1956, following the Supreme Court's unanimous ruling in *Gayle v. Browder*. Applying the same logic used in *Brown*, the court struck down Montgomery's bus segregation ordinance and by implication all similar local and state laws. But the decision did not address the legality of segregating interstate passengers, nor did it challenge mandated segregation in bus or train terminals. Indeed, its immediate impact was limited to local buses in Montgomery and a handful of other Southern cities. Predictably, political leaders in most Southern communities insisted that *Gayle* only applied to Montgomery, forcing local civil rights advocates to file a series of legal challenges. Armed with the legal precedent set in *Gayle*, NAACP attorneys were "virtually assured . . . ultimate victory in any legal contest over segregated carriers," as one legal historian put it. But the actual process of local transit desegregation was often painfully slow and limited in its effect. By 1960, local buses had been desegregated in 47 Southern cities, but more than half of the region's local bus lines remained legally segregated. In the Deep South states of Alabama, Mississippi, Georgia, and Louisiana, Jim Crow transit prevailed in all but three communities. And, despite *Gayle*, there was no sign that local and state officials in these states recognized the inevitability of bus desegregation. On the contrary, their resistance to change gained new life in November 1959, when Federal District Judge J. Hobart Grooms upheld the legality of the Birmingham city commission's strategy of sustaining segregation with a law authorizing bus companies to establish "private" segregation rules designed to maintain public order on buses. Asserting that private discrimination was sanctioned by the Fourteenth Amendment, Grooms's ruling virtually ensured that the legal struggle over segregated buses would continue into the next decade.

The battle in the courts ultimately proved to be only one part of a wider struggle against the indignities of Jim Crow transit. But this wider struggle took much longer to develop than anyone anticipated in the immediate aftermath of the victory in Montgomery. In early 1957, King and others predicted that the Montgomery experience would serve as a catalyst for a region-wide movement of nonviolent direct action. But to the dismay and puzzlement of those who had come to believe that Southern blacks were on the verge of self-liberation, the spirit of Montgomery did not spread readily to other cities. Indeed, in Montgomery itself the local movement atrophied as factional and internal strife weakened the MIA's hold over the black community. While nearly every Southern city boasted a local civil rights movement of some kind by the late 1950s, there was little momentum and no expectation of successful mass protest. Even in Birmingham, where the Reverend Fred Shuttlesworth and the Alabama Christian Movement for Human Rights (ACMHR) were engaged in a valiant and long-standing struggle against local white supremacists, mass support for nonviolent direct action seemed to be slipping away. Despite the recent victory in Montgomery, the black South at large, it seemed, harbored little interest in direct action and even less interest in the abstract philosophy of nonviolence.

Part of the explanation resides in the politics of massive resistance. In the aftermath of Montgomery, civil rights activists faced an increasingly militant white South. The signs of white supremacist mobilization were everywhere: in the resurgence of the Ku Klux Klan; in the spread of the White Citizens' Councils; in the angry rhetoric of demagogic politicians; and especially in the taut faces of white Southerners who seemed ready to challenge even the most minor breaches of racial etiquette. As the voices of moderation fell silent, a rising chorus of angry whites ready to defend the "Southern way of life" gave the appearance of regional and racial solidarity. Not all white Southerners were comfortable with the harsh turn in race relations, and some even harbored sympathy for the civil rights movement. But as the decade drew to a close the liberal dream that the white South would somehow find the moral strength to overcome its racial fears faded from view. This temporary loss of faith forced civil rights activists to reevaluate their plans and strategies for desegregation. In the long run, white intransigence left black Southerners with little choice but to take to the streets. But in the intimidating atmosphere of the late 1950s even the most committed proponents of direct action must have wondered about its viability in the Deep South.

Ironically, the paucity of direct action in these years also stemmed from an unfounded but expectant faith in the Eisenhower administration's commitment to civil rights. For a brief period in 1957 and 1958, federal enforcement of *Brown* and other aspects of civic equality appeared imminent. In August 1957, Congress approved the first federal civil rights act in eighty-two years, creating a U. S. Commission on Civil Rights and confirming the Fifteenth Amendment's guarantee of black voting rights. A threatened filibuster by white Southern senators and opposition from conservative Republicans weakened the enforcement provisions of the bill, reducing its meaning to symbolic proportions. But disappointment with the final version did not prevent civil rights leaders from hailing the 1957 act as a step in the right direction. This cautious optimism received further encouragement during the tumultuous school desegregation crisis in Little Rock, Arkansas. On September 24, two weeks after signing the 1957 Civil Rights Act, President Eisenhower answered the defiant challenge of Governor Orval Faubus and an angry white mob by federalizing the Arkansas National Guard and dispatching soldiers of the 101st Airborne Division to Little Rock's Central High School. The soldiers remained in Little Rock for nearly a year, protecting the rights of the nine black children attending Central High while asserting the preeminence of federal law. The belief that this show of federal force heralded a new attitude in the White House eventually turned into disillusionment, as the pace of school desegregation ground to a halt during the final two years of the Eisenhower era. But for a time the clash in Little Rock provided support for those who advocated a legalistic approach to social change. Even among advocates of nonviolent resistance, Little Rock confirmed the suspicion that the streets of the Jim Crow South were mean and dangerous, especially for unarmed civil rights activists.

This confusing combination of fear and hope produced an understandable wariness that inhibited risk-taking and innovation. As movement leaders watched and waited, organizational and ideological inertia set in, perpetuating the dominance of the NAACP and delaying the dreams of those who hoped to infuse the civil rights struggle with the spirit of Montgomery. For better or for worse, the NAACP, which celebrated its fiftieth anniversary in 1959, continued to steer the movement toward a legalistic resolution of social injustice. Despite its willingness to represent the MIA in court, the national leadership of the NAACP had mixed emotions about the emergence of Martin Luther King and his philosophy of nonviolence. Among the rank-and-file members of the NAACP local branches and youth councils, King enjoyed considerable popularity. But this was not the case at the national NAACP office in New York, where Roy Wilkins and others resented King's fame and regarded him as an unwelcome rival for funds and influence.

During the bus boycott, the national office had allowed local NAACP branches to raise funds for the MIA. But this sharing of resources ended in early 1957, when King became the leader of a rival national organization, the Southern Christian Leadership Conference (SCLC). Wilkins, Thurgood Marshall, and other NAACP leaders felt that they had already paid an exorbitant price (including the virtual dissolution of the Alabama NAACP, which was driven underground by the state legislature) for what Wilkins's assistant John Morsell called "the hullabaloo of the boycott." Suspicious of anything that complicated their carefully designed program of litigation and legislation, they were determined to avoid the emotional diversions of mass protest and the risk of being tarnished with charges of radicalism and civil disobedience. As Wilkins later explained, "My own view was that the particular form of direct action used in Montgomery was effective only for certain kinds of local problems and could not be applied safely on a national scale. Although there was a great deal of excited talk about adapting the tactics of Gandhi to the South, the fact remained that the America of the Eisenhower era and the Silent Generation was not the India of Gandhi and the Salt March . . . The danger I feared was that the Montgomery model would lead to a string of unsuccessful boycotts . . . at a time when defeats could only encourage white supremacists to fight all the harder."

In the short run, NAACP leaders had little to worry about, as King and others struggled with the problem of getting a new organization off the ground. Planning and logistical details consumed most of SCLC's energy during the late 1950s. In 1957 King visited the new nation of Ghana, helped organize a "Prayer Pilgrimage" to Washington to commemorate the third anniversary of *Brown*, and headlined a four-day institute on Non-Violence and Social Change held in Tallahassee, Florida, where SCLC vice-president C. K. Steele was trying to fend off white backlash following a local bus boycott that had driven the municipal bus company into bankruptcy. In 1958 SCLC established an Atlanta office run by Ella Baker, a Nashville affiliate (Nashville Christian Leadership Council, or NCLC) spearheaded by the Reverend Kelly Miller Smith, and a modest voting rights project known as the "Crusade for Citizenship"; and in 1959 King visited India, hired Rustin as a part-time public relations director, and moved from Montgomery to Atlanta. But none of this did much to rekindle the fires of nonviolent resistance. By the end of the decade, the notion that King possessed the capacity or the will to lead a liberation movement in the Deep South had all but disappeared, and even he had begun to wonder if the spirit of Montgomery would ever return.

The organizational obstacles to nonviolent direct action were formidable. But, as King and his colleagues at SCLC knew all too well, the greatest challenge to nonviolence was cultural. No amount of lofty rhetoric could disguise the hard truth that proponents of nonviolent struggle were operating in an inhospitable cultural environment. Reliance on force, gun ownership, and armed self-defense were deeply rooted American traditions, especially in the South where the interwoven legacies of slavery, frontier vigilantism, and a rigid code of personal honor held sway. The classic form of southern violence was most evident among whites, but the regional ethos of life below "the Smith and Wesson line" extended to black southerners as well. Weapons and armed conflict were an accepted fact of life, and even among the most religious members of southern black society the philosophy of nonviolence cut across the grain of cultural experience and expectation. According to white regional mythology, the uneasy racial peace that had existed since the collapse of Radical Reconstruction rested almost exclusively on the twin foundations of white resolve and black accommodation. But in reality historic patterns of racial negotiation involved a complicated mix of accommodation and resistance. If knowing one's "place" was an important survival skill in the Jim Crow South, in certain circumstances so was the willingness to engage in what Robert Williams called "armed self-reliance."

As the militant leader of the Monroe County, North Carolina, branch of the NAACP, Williams created a storm of controversy in October 1957 when he and other local blacks engaged in a shoot-out with marauding Klansmen. Openly brandishing a shotgun, and carrying a .45-caliber pistol on his hip, the thirty-two-year-old Army and Marine corps veteran urged all black southerners to do whatever was necessary to defend themselves and their families from white violence and oppression. Defying local whites as well as national NAACP leaders, he refused to disarm or to eschew violence as a means of taming "that social jungle called Dixie." In May 1959, expressing outrage over the acquittal of a white man who had beaten and raped a local black woman, he told reporters: "We must be willing to kill if necessary . . . We cannot rely on the law. We get no justice under the present system. If we feel injustice is done, we must right then and there on the spot be prepared to inflict punishment on these people." Horrified by Williams's angry outburst, Wilkins suspended him as president of the Monroe branch, and Thurgood Marshall even urged the FBI to investigate his role as a "communist" provocateur. But Williams refused to back down.

In July 1959, he began to disseminate his views in a weekly newspaper called *The Crusader*, attracting the attention of everyone from an admiring Malcolm X of the Nation of Islam to Martin Luther King, who felt compelled to speak out against him. In September, the pacifist magazine *Liberation* featured a debate between King and Williams, in which Williams expressed "great respect" for pacifists but insisted that nonviolence was something "that most of my people" cannot embrace. "Negroes must be willing to defend themselves, their women, their children and their homes," he declared, "Nowhere in the annals of history does the record show a people delivered from bondage by patience alone." King countered with an eloquent distillation of nonviolent philosophy, but acknowledged that even Gandhi recognized the moral validity of self-defense. The exchange, later reprinted in the *Southern Patriot*, left editor Anne Braden and many other nonviolent activists with the uneasy feeling that Williams spoke for a broad cross-section of the black South. As Braden conceded, Williams's views on armed self-reliance were not only common, they were likely to spread "unless change comes rapidly." The dim prospects for such change in the absence of direct action on a mass scale underscored the dilemma that all civil rights activists faced in the late 1950s. As the decade drew to a close, no one seemed to have a firm grasp on how to turn social philosophy into mass action, or how to awaken the black South without risking mass violence.

During the fallow years of the late 1950s, local NAACP youth councils, and in one case the SCLC, conducted sit-ins protesting discrimination in stores and restaurants in several Southern or border-state communities. However, none of these early efforts garnered much organizational or popular support. Initiated by local leaders at the grassroots level, these short-lived precursors of the famous 1960 Greensboro, North Carolina, sit-in received little attention in the press and only grudging recognition from the regional and national leaders of the NAACP and SCLC. Consequently, they produced meager results, leaving their participants isolated, frustrated, and vulnerable. During these years, the only national organization that evidenced a clear determination to translate the philosophy of nonviolence into action on behalf of civil rights was CORE. And, unfortunately for the nonviolent movement, CORE's resolve was tempered by the limitations of a small organization hampered by inadequate funding and limited experience in the South. Despite lofty goals, CORE activity in the late 1950s was restricted to a handful of communities where local chapters, generally consisting of a few brave individuals, mustered only occasional challenges to the institutional power of Jim Crow. Most of this activity took place in the border states of Missouri, West Virginia, and Kentucky, where several CORE chapters organized brief but sometimes successful picketing and sit-in campaigns directed at discrimination in employment and public accommodations. Farther south, in the ex-Confederate states, early efforts at direct action were much rarer and seldom successful, though not entirely unknown.

In Nashville, a group led by Anna Holden, a white activist originally from Florida, established an interracial committee that pressured the local school board to comply with *Brown*; and in Richmond CORE volunteers organized a 1959 New Year's Day rally that brought two thousand people to the Virginia capital to protest against the state's "massive resistance" plan. In Miami, a newly organized CORE chapter staged a series of sit-ins at segregated downtown lunch counters in the spring and summer of 1959, hosted a two-week-long Interracial Action Institute in September that brought the national staff to the city and forced the closing of a segregated lunch counter at Jackson-Byron's department store, and later joined forces with the local NAACP branch in an effort to desegregate a whites-only beach. In Tallahassee, a chapter organized by students at Florida A&M University in October 1959 anticipated the Freedom Rides by conducting observation exercises that documented segregated seating on city and interstate buses, as well as segregation patterns at downtown department stores, restaurants, and other public accommodations. In South Carolina, CORE's Southern field secretary, Jim McCain, led a statewide black voter registration project and presided over several local protests, including one that desegregated an ice cream stand in Marion in 1959. Taken together, these activities constituted a vanguard, giving the Southern nonviolent movement a handhold on the towering cliff of desegregation. But few if any CORE activists held out much hope that such activities would actually take the movement to the proverbial mountaintop, much less to the promised land on the other side.

At CORE headquarters in New York—a tiny office on Park Row "not much bigger than a closet"—Executive Secretary Jimmy Robinson presided over a small but dedicated staff that included *CORE-lator* editor Jim Peck, field secretaries Jim McCain and Gordon Carey, and community relations director Marvin Rich. During the late 1950s, Robinson and the staff worked closely with the National Council in an effort to raise CORE's profile. But the absence of a mass following continued to limit the organization's influence. While CORE claimed more than twelve thousand "associated members" by early 1960, only a small fraction of this following was actively involved in direct action campaigns. Despite recent gains in membership, the number of available volunteers remained well below the threshold needed to effect broad social change, especially in the South. To have any hope of transforming the region most in need of change, CORE would have to provoke a general crisis of conscience among white Southerners. And for that they would need an army of nonviolent insurgents, a mass of men and women willing to put themselves at considerable risk, including the very real possibility of going to jail for their beliefs. Where this hypothetical nonviolent army might come from was unclear, and none of the most likely sources, from organized labor to the black churches of SCLC, looked very promising as the new decade began. Rebellious and impatient students would soon fill the void, but when the student sit-in movement burst upon the scene in the late winter of 1960, it took almost everyone by surprise.

Ignited by the unexpected daring of four black freshmen at North Carolina A&T College in Greensboro—Ezell Blair Jr., Joseph McNeil, Franklin McCain, and David Richmond—the shift to mass protest was sudden and dramatic. Unlike the scattered and short-term sit-ins of the 1950s, the Woolworth's lunch counter sit-in that began on February 1, 1960, drew the rapt attention of national civil rights leaders, especially after the scale of the protest widened beyond anyone's expectations. As the number of participants multiplied, from twenty-nine on the second day to more than three hundred on the fifth, the Greensboro students realized that they needed help. Hoping to keep the situation under control, they turned to Dr. George Simkins, the president of the Greensboro NAACP, and to Floyd McKissick and the Reverend Douglas Moore, two black activists who had been experimenting with direct action in nearby Durham since 1957. After McKissick agreed to serve as legal counsel for the original four participants, he and Moore began to contact local activists in several other cities, including Nashville, where Moore's old friend and SCLC colleague Jim Lawson had been conducting nonviolent workshops in preparation for a sit-in campaign even more ambitious than Greensboro's. The student activists who had been attending his NCLC-sponsored workshops were eager to follow Greensboro's lead, he assured Moore. Other SCLC leaders, including King and the Reverend C. K. Steele in Tallahassee, shared Lawson's enthusiasm for the unexpected developments in North Carolina. But this was not the case among national NAACP leaders. When Simkins informed the national office that the Greensboro branch had endorsed the student sit-ins at its February 2 meeting, he was rebuked for violating organizational policy. Unmoved by the revelation that the originators of the Greensboro sit-ins were all NAACP Youth Council veterans, the national staff left Simkins with no choice but to look elsewhere for support.

Simkins's plaintive call to Jimmy Robinson on February 4—an action that, as Jim Farmer later commented, "did not endear him" to his NAACP superiors— sent shock waves through the CORE office. Sensing that this was the break they had been waiting for, CORE leaders immediately turned all of their attention to sustaining and publicizing the Greensboro sit-in. By February 5, both of CORE's field secretaries were on their way to the Carolinas, Carey to Greensboro and McCain to Rock Hill, South Carolina; and back in New York Peck and Rich were initiating negotiations with Woolworth and Kress executives and planning a nationwide campaign of sympathy demonstrations. Within a week, the first sympathy demonstration was held in Harlem, and before long CORE chapters were picketing dime stores across the country. All of this elicited considerable press attention, especially after the sit-ins spread to other North Carolina cities and beyond. By February 14, the ever-widening sit-in movement stretched across five states and fourteen cities, involving hundreds of young black demonstrators. Over the next three months it spread to more than a hundred Southern towns and cities, as thousands of students experienced the bittersweet combination of civil disobedience and criminal prosecution. By July, nearly three-fourths of these local movements had achieved at least token desegregation, dispelling the myth that the Jim Crow South was invulnerable to direct action. The fact that virtually none of this desegregation took place in the cities and towns of the Deep South was disturbing, but the partial victories in the upper or "rim" South represented an empowering development to a regional movement that had been virtually moribund six months earlier.

CORE's early involvement in the sit-ins brought the organization unprecedented notoriety, particularly among white segregationists who rushed to protect the South from "outside agitators." Following his arrest at a Durham sit-in on February 9, an almost giddy Carey informed his New York colleagues that "CORE has been on the front page of every newspaper in North Carolina for two days. CORE has been on radio and TV every hour . . . I can't move without the press covering my movement." Later, as Carey and McCain shuttled from sit-in to sit-in, it appeared to some that CORE had assumed control of the student movement. In actuality, however, CORE activists made little headway in their campaign to provide the movement with ideological and organizational discipline. Most student demonstrators exhibited only a passing interest in the subtleties of Gandhian philosophy, and many were suspicious of any effort to check the spontaneous and largely untutored nature of the sit-ins.

This spirit of independence became manifest when nearly two hundred student activists—including 126 black students representing fifty-six colleges and high schools across the South—met at Shaw University in Raleigh in mid-April. The Raleigh conference was the brainchild of fifty-six-year-old Ella Baker, who after years of false starts and dashed hopes had grown disenchanted with the cautious policies of SCLC and the NAACP. Representatives of all the major civil rights organizations were present, but Baker made sure that the students themselves ran the show. Though still an employee of SCLC, she urged the student activists to plot their own course and to avoid the controlling influence of any existing organization. Just before the opening of the Raleigh meeting, King issued a lengthy press conference statement outlining a proposed strategy for the student movement. But the speaker who aroused the most interest among the delegates was Jim Lawson, recently expelled from Vanderbilt University's School of Divinity for his leadership role in the Nashville sit-ins.

Born in western Pennsylvania in 1931 and raised in Massillon, Ohio, Lawson was an articulate and sophisticated student of Gandhian philosophy who had already served a year in prison as a conscientious objector during the Korean War and three years as a Methodist missionary in India. After meeting King at Oberlin College in 1956, Lawson took the Montgomery minister's advice to postpone his divinity studies and head south to spread the word about nonviolence. Subsequent conversations with A. J. Muste and Glenn Smiley, whom he had known for years, led to his appointment as FOR's Southern field secretary. At Smiley's suggestion, he soon moved to Nashville, Tennessee, where he helped organize the Nashville Christian Leadership Council (NCLC) and where his nonviolent workshops eventually attracted a dedicated following of young disciples, including John Lewis, Diane Nash, Bernard Lafayette, and others who would later gain prominence as Freedom Riders. Grounded in a mixture of social gospel Methodism and insurgent Gandhianism, Lawson's intellectual and moral leadership gave the local Nashville movement strength of purpose that no other student group could match. With the blessing of Nashville Christian Leadership Council president Kelly Miller Smith, Lawson's increasingly restless disciples had recently formed a Student Central Committee to mediate the relationship between local student activists and the older and generally more cautious ministers of the NCLC. Together, the students and the NCLC constituted a powerful if sometimes uneasy tandem that made the Nashville Nonviolent Movement the most effective local direct-action organization since the early Montgomery Improvement Association. Speaking at Fisk University in the immediate aftermath of the Raleigh conference, an admiring King called the Nashville movement "the best organized and most disciplined in the Southland," a judgment later confirmed by the Nashville Nonviolent Movement's critical role in the Freedom Rides.

In Raleigh, Lawson and the Nashville delegation dazzled King and many of the student activists with concrete visions of social justice and the "beloved community." To some, Lawson's sermon-like keynote speech seemed long on religion and a bit short on practical politics. But even the most secular delegates applauded when he warned established movement leaders that the sit-ins represented a "judgment upon middle-class conventional, half-way efforts to deal with radical social evil." In an obvious slap at the NAACP, he insisted that the civil rights struggle could no longer tolerate a narrow reliance on "fund-raising and court action." Instead, it had to cultivate "our greatest resource, a people no longer the victims of racial evil who can act in a disciplined manner to implement the constitution." Baker later echoed these words in a stirring speech that called for a broad assertion of civil rights, rights that involved "more than a hamburger," as she put it. All of this inspired the young delegates to take themselves seriously, and on the second day of the conference they voted to form an independent organization known as the Student Nonviolent Coordinating Committee (SNCC). Marion Barry, a twenty-two-year-old Fisk University chemistry graduate student and future mayor of Washington, D.C., won election as SNCC's first chairman, solidifying the Nashville group's influence.

In May, SNCC reaffirmed its independence at an organizational meeting held in Atlanta. But at this point the student organization constituted little more than a "clearinghouse for the exchange of information about localized protests." With no permanent staff and no financial backing to speak of, SNCC leaders had little choice but to draw upon the resources of older organizations such as SCLC, which allowed them to establish a small office at SCLC headquarters. The national leadership of the NAACP, despite serious misgivings about the sit-in movement, provided SNCC activists with free legal representation, and even hired the Reverend Benjamin Elton Cox, an outspoken, courageous black minister and future Freedom Rider from High Point, North Carolina, to serve as a roving ambassador of nonviolence. Paralleling the efforts of CORE field secretaries Carey and McCain, Cox traveled across the South during the spring and summer of 1960, spreading the gospel of nonviolence to as many students as possible. Most student activists were receptive to the nonviolent message, if only for pragmatic reasons; and despite numerous provocations by angry white supremacists, the sit-ins proceeded without unleashing the violent race war that some observers had predicted. At the same time, however, the students were unwilling to sacrifice the intellectual and organizational independence of the movement, even when confronted with elders who invoked religious, moral, or paternal authority. All of this led historian and activist Howard Zinn to marvel that "for the first time in our history, a major social movement, shaking the nation to its bone, is being led by youngsters."

CORE's failure to absorb the student movement was a disappointment. But the organization took pride in the fact that a number of the movement's most committed activists gravitated toward CORE's demanding brand of nonviolence. In Tallahassee, Florida A&M coed Pat Stephens and seven other young CORE volunteers became the first sit-in demonstrators of their era to acknowledge the importance of "unmerited suffering." By refusing to accept bail and remaining behind bars for sixty days in the spring of 1960, they introduced a new tactic known as the "jail-in." In an eloquent statement composed in her cell, Stephens reminded her fellow activists of Martin Luther King's admonition that "we've got to fill the jails in order to win our equal rights." At the time, it was standard practice for arrested demonstrators to seek an early release from jail. Most demonstrators, as well as most movement leaders, agreed with Thurgood Marshall, who insisted that only a fool would refuse to be bailed out from a Southern jail. "Once you've been arrested," he told a crowd at Fisk on April 6, "you've made your point. If someone offers to get you out, man, get out."

Convincing arrested demonstrators to ignore such advice soon became a cornerstone of CORE policy, and one of the activists most responsible for this new emphasis was Tom Gaither, another rising star among CORE recruits. When he first met McCain in March 1960, Gaither was a biology major and student leader at all-black Claflin College in Orangeburg, South Carolina. Following a mass protest in Orangeburg, he was one of more than 350 students "arrested and herded into an open-air stockade." This was the largest number of demonstrators arrested in any Southern city up to that point, and McCain couldn't help being impressed with the courage of the Orangeburg students. Gaither's leadership in the face of tear gas and fire hoses prompted CORE to offer him a staff position, and by September he found himself in the midst of a major sit-in campaign in Rock Hill. Working closely with McCain and student leaders at Friendship Junior College, he helped to turn Rock Hill into one of the movement's most militant battlegrounds. In February 1961, Rock Hill became the site of the movement's first widely publicized "jail-in." A month later, following his release from a county road-gang, Gaither agreed to serve as an advance scout for a new CORE project known as the Freedom Ride—a fitting assignment for someone who had been one of the first to promote the idea of such a ride earlier in the year.

The youthful dynamism of Stephens, Gaither, and other recruits helped to revitalize CORE, which was brimming with optimism by the summer of 1960. At the national CORE convention in July, Carey—recently promoted to the position of field director—claimed that the organization was on the verge of becoming "a major race relations group." In August, CORE's expanding staff gathered in Miami for a second "interracial action institute," during which they experimented with the tactic of "jail-no-bail." Following a sit-in at a Miami lunch counter, seven participants, including Gaither, Stephens, Executive Director Jimmy Robinson, and future Freedom Rider Bernard Lafayette, spent ten days in jail. Such actions enhanced CORE's reputation for militance and boosted expectations of increased activity. By September, CORE's field staff had grown to five "field secretaries": McCain; Gaither; Joe Perkins, a black graduate student at the University of Michigan; Richard Haley, a black Tallahassee activist and former music professor at Florida A&M; and Genevieve Hughes, a twenty-eight-year-old white financial analyst who had spearheaded the New York City chapter's dime-store boycott.

In October 1960, the CORE field staff fanned out across the South looking for new centers of struggle. What they found—especially in New Orleans where a committed band of activists was engaged in an all-out assault on Jim Crow, and in South Carolina where more and more students were responding to McCain and Gaither's organizing efforts—demonstrated that the spirit of nonviolent resistance was still on the rise. But, at the time, none of CORE's advances into the Southern hinterland drew much attention. In the movement at large, all eyes were on Atlanta. Part of the excitement was the reorganization of SNCC, which, during a fateful meeting at Atlanta University, moved toward a more secular ori-entation that placed "a greater emphasis on political issues." The influence of Lawson and the Nashville movement on SNCC was declining, and Orangeburg sit-in veteran Chuck McDew, a black Ohioan who had converted to Judaism, soon replaced Marion Barry as SNCC chairman. The biggest news, however, was the arrest and imprisonment of Martin Luther King following a sit-in at Rich's department store on October 19.

The first of eighty demonstrators to be arraigned, King refused Judge James Webb's offer to release him on a $500 bond. "I cannot accept bond," the SCLC leader proclaimed. "I will stay in jail one year, or ten years." This was the kind of courageous leadership that the militants of SNCC and CORE had been advo-cating, but they got more than they had bargained for when Georgia authorities dropped the charges against all of the defendants but King. The apparent sin-gling out of the nation's most celebrated civil rights leader raised doubts about his safety, a concern that turned into near panic after he was moved from the relative security of his Atlanta jail cell, first to the DeKalb County Jail and later to the maximum security prison at Reidsville. Fearing that King's life was in danger, SCLC and other movement leaders urged the U.S. Justice Department to inter-vene, but got no response—a development that set the stage for one of the most fateful decisions in modern American political history.

Harris Wofford, a liberal campaign aide to Democratic presidential candidate John Kennedy, had known King since 1957 and had even raised funds for the SCLC leader's trip to India, where Wofford had spent several years studying Gandhian philosophy. Frustrated by Kennedy's reluctance to take a forthright stand on civil rights, he sensed that King's endangerment provided his candidate with a golden opportunity to make up for past mistakes. After receiving a phone call from an obviously desperate Coretta King, Wofford made the political and ethical case for an expression of sympathy. "If the Senator would only call Mrs. King and wish her well," he told his boss, Sargent Shriver, "it would reverberate all through the Negro community in the United States. All he's got to do is say he's thinking about her and he hopes everything will be all right. All he's got to do is show a little heart." While campaigning with Kennedy in Chicago, Shriver relayed Wofford's suggestion, which, to the surprise of the entire campaign staff, led to an impulsive late-night phone call. Startled and touched by Kennedy's expression of concern, Mrs. King later made it clear to the press that she appre-ciated the senator's gesture, which stood out in stark contrast with Vice Presi-dent Richard Nixon's refusal to comment on her husband's situation.

Nixon's inaction widened the opening for the Kennedy campaign, allowing the Democratic candidate's younger brother Bobby to exploit the situation. Though initially opposed to any public association with King, he soon matched his brother's impulsiveness by calling Georgia Judge Oscar Mitchell to demand

King's release from prison. Following some additional prodding from Atlanta's progressive mayor, William Hartsfield, Mitchell complied, and after eight harrowing days behind bars King was out on bail. Following a joyful reunion with his family, King expressed his gratitude to the Kennedy brothers—and his intention to vote Democratic, something he had not done in previous presidential elections. Coming during the final week of the campaign, this delighted Kennedy's staff. But the best was yet to come. On the Sunday before the election, more than two million copies of a pro-Kennedy pamphlet entitled *The Case of Martin Luther King: "No Comment" Nixon versus a Candidate with a Heart* appeared in black churches across the nation, thanks in part to the efforts of Gardner Taylor, a leading figure in the National Baptist Convention who also served on the National Action Council of CORE. Later known as the "blue bomb," the brightly colored comic-book–style pamphlet produced a groundswell of support for Kennedy, who received approximately 70 percent of the black vote, 30 percent more than Adlai Stevenson had garnered in 1956. Some observers even went so far as to suggest that Kennedy, who defeated Nixon by a mere 114, 673 votes in the closest presidential election to date, owed his victory to a late surge in black support.

Kennedy's election brought renewed hope of federal civil rights enforcement. Even though he said relatively little about race or civil rights during the fall campaign, and the calls to Coretta King and Judge Mitchell were not much to go on, most civil rights advocates reasoned that the young president-elect could hardly be worse than Dwight Eisenhower. Personally conservative on matters of race and preoccupied with the Cold War and foreign affairs, Eisenhower had allowed the executive branch's commitment to civil rights to lag far behind that of the federal courts. While Kennedy, too, was an inveterate Cold Warrior with a weak civil rights record, the soaring rhetoric of the New Frontier suggested that the new president planned to pursue an ambitious agenda of domestic reform that included civil rights advances. Despite his reluctance to make specific promises, he often talked about the moral imperatives of a true democracy, and on one occasion he even alluded to the need for a presidency that would "help bring equal access to public facilities from churches to lunch counters and . . . support the right of every American to stand up for his rights, even if on occasion he must sit down for them." This implicit endorsement of the sit-ins did not go unnoticed in the civil rights community, though by inauguration day there were increasing suspicions that the new president's commitment to social change was more rhetorical than real. Civil rights leaders were disappointed when he passed over Wofford and appointed Burke Marshall, a corporate lawyer with no track record on civil rights, as the Assistant Attorney General for Civil Rights; and they were stunned when he failed to mention civil rights in his inaugural address—or to include Martin Luther King in the list of black leaders invited to the inauguration. These mixed signals left King and others in a state of confusion, though most activists remained hopeful that the arc of American politics was at least tilting toward racial justice.

As Washington and the nation weathered the transition to the Kennedy administration, CORE experienced its own administrative overhaul. A staff revolt against Executive Secretary Jimmy Robinson, who left on an extended European vacation in October, prompted a general bureaucratic reorganization and a search for someone to fill the newly created position of national director. "Jimmy Robinson was skilled at fund-raising, a tiger on details, and as fiercely dedicated as anyone alive," Jim Farmer recalled many years later, "But he was unprepossessing and could not lead Gideon's army, nor sound the call for battle. Furthermore he was white. If CORE was to be at the center of the struggle, its leader and spokesperson had to be black."

The search for a national director quickly focused on King, who briefly entertained an offer tendered by search committee chair Val Coleman. At first, King agreed to consider the offer if CORE would consent to a formal merger with SCLC. But the obvious impracticality of combining a secular, Northern-based organization with a group of devout, Southern black ministers soon convinced him to withdraw his name from consideration. The committee's second choice was Farmer, who had been languishing as a minor official at the national NAACP office since 1959. Frustrated by the cautious policies and bureaucratic inertia of Roy Wilkins and other NAACP leaders, Farmer leaped at the chance to rejoin and lead the organization that he had helped to found nineteen years earlier. When Wilkins heard about the offer, he urged Farmer to take it and even acknowledged a bit of envy. "You're going to be riding a mustang pony," he confessed to his departing assistant, "while I'm riding a dinosaur."

3

Hallelujah! I'm A-Travelin'

Stand up and rejoice! A great day is here!
We're fighting Jim Crow and the victory's near!
Hallelujah! I'm a-travelin,' Hallelujah, ain't it fine.
Hallelujah! I'm a-travelin' down freedom's main line!
—1961 freedom song

True to Wilkins's prediction, Farmer's directorship of CORE began with a gallop. His first day on the job, February 1, 1961, was the first anniversary of the landmark Greensboro sit-in, and all across the South demonstrators were engaging in commemorative acts of courage. As Farmer sat at his desk that first morning waiting for reports from the Southern front, he made his way through a stack of accumulated correspondence. Among the letters that caught his attention were several inquiries about *Boynton v. Virginia*, a recent Supreme Court decision involving Bruce Boynton, a Howard University law student from Selma, Alabama, arrested in 1958 for attempting to desegregate the whites-only Trailways terminal restaurant in Richmond. In December 1960 the court overturned Boynton's conviction by ruling that state laws mandating segregated waiting rooms, lunch counters, and restroom facilities for interstate passengers were unconstitutional. With this ruling, the court extended the 1946 *Morgan* decision, which had outlawed legally enforced segregation on interstate buses and trains. But, according to the letter writers, neither of these decisions was being enforced. Why, they asked, were black Americans still being harassed or arrested when they tried to exercise their constitutional right to sit in the front of the bus or to drink a cup of coffee at a bus terminal restaurant?

At a late-morning meeting, Farmer relayed this troubling question to his staff. To his surprise, two staff members had already come up with a tentative plan to address the problem of nonenforcement. As Gordon Carey explained, during an unexpectedly long bus trip from South Carolina to New York in mid-January he and Tom Gaither had discussed the feasibility of a second Journey of Reconciliation. Adapting the phrase "Ride for Freedom" originated by Billie Ames in the mid-1950s, they had come up with a catchy name for the project: "Freedom Ride." And thanks to a blizzard that forced them to spend a night on the floor of a Howard Johnson's restaurant along the New Jersey Turnpike, they had even gone so far as to map out a proposed route from Washington to New Orleans. Patterned after Gandhi's famous march to the sea—throughout the bus trip Carey had been reading Louis Fischer's biography of Gandhi—the second Journey, like the first, would last two weeks. But, taking advantage of the Southern movement's gathering momentum, it would also extend the effort to test compliance with the Constitution into the heart of the Deep South. Despite the obvious logistical problems in mounting such an effort, everyone in the room—including Farmer—immediately sensed that Carey and Gaither were on the right track. By the end of the meeting there was a consensus that the staff should seek formal approval of the project at the next meeting of CORE's National Action Committee, scheduled for February 11–12 in Lexington, Kentucky. There was also general agreement that, unlike the more staid "Journey of Reconciliation," the name "Freedom Ride" was in keeping with "the scrappy nonviolent movement that had emerged" since the Greensboro sit-ins. As a symbol of the new CORE, the project, in Farmer's estimation, required a name that expressed the organization's determination to put "the movement on wheels . . . to cut across state lines and establish the position that we were entitled to act any place in the country, no matter where we hung our hat and called home, because it was our country."

Later in the day, as the news of sit-ins and mass arrests reached the CORE office, Farmer became even more convinced that the time was right for a bold initiative in the Jim Crow South. In Nashville, James Bevel, Diane Nash, and dozens of other local black activists celebrated the Greensboro anniversary by picketing downtown movie theaters, and in Rock Hill, South Carolina, Gaither and nine others ended up in jail after staging a sit-in at a segregated McCrory's lunch counter. When nine of the ten Rock Hill defendants chose thirty days on a road gang rather than a $100 fine, the "jail—no bail" policy that CORE had been advocating for nearly a year took on new life.

The courage of the Rock Hill Nine was a major topic of conversation when leaders of the Student Nonviolent Coordinating Committee met in Atlanta on February 3. Jim Lawson had always encouraged his Nashville followers to refuse bail—both as a matter of principle and as an effective tactic—but to date no one in SNCC had chosen to remain behind bars. A heated discussion of the Rock Hill situation and other topics engaged the SNCC leaders well into the night but seemed to be going nowhere until a phone call from Gaither focused their atten-tion. Speaking from a York County jail phone, Gaither promised them that the Rock Hill Nine were committed to serving out their thirty days of hard labor, but he pleaded for reinforcements that would magnify the impact of the Rock Hill jail-in.

Following the call, four students—Diane Nash of Fisk, Charles Jones of John-son C. Smith University in Charlotte, Ruby Doris Smith of Atlanta's Spelman College, and Charles Sherrod of Virginia Union Seminary—vowed to join the Rock Hill Nine. The next day the four volunteers were on their way to South Carolina and jail. A SNCC press release urging other nonviolent activists to join the second wave of Rock Hill inmates found no takers, but the jail-in movement soon spread to Atlanta and Lynchburg, Virginia, raising the total number of stu-dents choosing jail over bail to nearly one hundred. On February 12, Abraham Lincoln's birthday, more than a thousand marchers, some local and some from as far away as Florida, demonstrated their support with a "pilgrimage to Rock Hill," suggesting that Gaither and CORE had started something big.

After his release on March 2, Gaither traveled to New York, where he was greeted as a hero by his CORE colleagues. By this time the office was abuzz with tentative plans for a Freedom Ride scheduled for early May. The Freedom Ride, now sanctioned by CORE's National Action Committee, followed the basic out-line of Rustin and Houser's original 1947 Washington-to-New Orleans plan, which had been adapted by Carey and Gaither in January. In Farmer's words, CORE planned to "recruit from twelve to fourteen persons, call them to Wash-ington, D.C., for a week of intensive training and preparation, and then embark on the Ride. Half would go by Greyhound and half by Trailways." The Riders would leave Washington on May 4, travel through Virginia, North and South Carolina, Georgia, Alabama, and Mississippi, and arrive—it was hoped—in New Orleans on May 17, the seventh anniversary of the *Brown* decision.

Realizing that the trip posed a series of potential dangers and logistical challenges, Farmer asked Gaither to act as the Riders' advance scout, just as Rustin and Houser had done in 1947. Setting out in early April, Gaither scouted the entire route from Washington to New Orleans. At each stop, he surveyed the layout of terminal facilities, met with black leaders to arrange housing and speaking engagements for the Riders, and assessed the tenor of local race relations. As he made his way across the region, news of the impend-ing Freedom Ride drew a mixed response among Southern blacks. Some weren't sure how they felt about CORE or the Ride, and others wanted nothing to do with the troublemakers from the North, but in virtually every black com-munity along the route Gaither found some support for the Riders. In the end, he was able to secure local sponsors in a dozen communities from Virginia to Louisiana.

His assessment of the white South was less sanguine. In the Upper South states of Virginia and North Carolina, the prospects for compliance with *Morgan* and *Boynton* looked promising, but from South Carolina on down Gaither didn't like what he saw. He already had firsthand experience with the harshness of segregationist resistance in Rock Hill and other South Carolina communities, but the belligerence and defiance that he encountered in Alabama and Mississippi shocked him. If the Freedom Riders challenged the ultra-segregationists of the Deep South without benefit of police protection, he concluded, they would be lucky to escape with their lives. In his report, he identified the white supremacist strongholds where the Riders would be most likely to encounter violence, including Birmingham and Anniston, which he termed "a very explosive trouble spot without a doubt."

While Gaither was checking out the route, other CORE staffers were busy recruiting and selecting the dozen or so Riders with the requisite skills and courage to survive. More than anything else, CORE wanted recruits who had already demonstrated a strong commitment to nonviolence and who knew what was being asked of them. Recruitment material made no attempt to hide the potential dangers of the Ride or to minimize the difficulty of fulfilling the responsibilities of nonviolent resistance. Only the most committed and the stoutest of heart were encouraged to apply. Freedom Riders could expect to be harassed and arrested, as fifteen members of the St. Louis and Columbia, Missouri, CORE chapters discovered in mid-April when they participated in what the *CORE-lator* later dubbed a "Little Freedom Ride." Setting out by bus from East St. Louis, the interracial band only made it as far as the southeastern Missouri town of Sikeston, 150 miles down the road, before being arrested at a whites-only terminal restaurant for "disturbing the peace." With their cases still pending in late April, the "little" Freedom Riders provided potential recruits with a sobering preview of what the "big" Freedom Ride might entail. As Carey warned in a letter sent to CORE leaders on May 1, "If bus protests end in arrest in Missouri, what can be expected when the Freedom Ride gets to Georgia and points South?"

The first Freedom Riders selected were Farmer himself and Peck. As a veteran of the Journey of Reconciliation, Peck was an obvious choice. But Farmer's decision to put himself in harm's way raised more than a few eyebrows. Known more as an office and idea man than as a hands-on activist, CORE's forty-one-year-old leader had never exhibited much interest in risking arrest and imprisonment. Those who knew him well, however, understood his motivation. The Freedom Ride was Farmer's personal ticket to glory, his best chance to join King, Randolph, and Marshall in the front rank of civil rights heroes. Having missed the 1947 ride, he wasn't about to miss this one.

In selecting the remaining Riders, Farmer and his staff tried to come up with a reasonably balanced mixture of black and white, young and old, religious and secular, Northern and Southern. The only deliberate imbalance was a lack of women. Although, unlike the Journey of Reconciliation, the Freedom Ride would not be limited to men, Farmer and Carey were reluctant to expose women, especially black women, to potentially violent confrontations with white supremacists. Their decision to limit the number of female Freedom Riders to two was undoubtedly rooted in patriarchal conservatism, but they also feared that a balanced contingent of men and women might be interpreted as a provocative pattern of sexual pairing. The situation was dangerous enough, they reasoned, without taunting the segregationists with visions of interracial sex.

CORE asked each applicant to include a recommendation from a teacher, pastor, or coworker, and to write an essay outlining his or her commitment to nonviolence and the struggle for civil rights. Volunteers under the age of twenty-one also had to submit proof of parental permission. By late April, the CORE office had received several dozen applications, all filled with testimonials of courage and conviction and eagerness to serve the cause. From this pool, Farmer and Carey chose fourteen riders. Three of those chosen were unable to make it to Washington in time for the Ride: the Reverend J. Metz Rollins, a veteran of the 1956 Tallahassee bus boycott who had become the Nashville-based field director of the United Presbyterian Church; and Julia Aaron and Jerome Smith, two members of New Orleans CORE who were languishing in a Louisiana jail. But those who did show up provided CORE with an experienced and committed band of activists.

The eleven Freedom Riders who joined Farmer and Peck in Washington on May 1 represented a wide range of backgrounds and movement experiences. Two of the eleven, Genevieve Hughes and Joe Perkins, were CORE staff members. A tall, attractive twenty-eight-year-old white woman, Hughes was a relative newcomer to the movement who had spent most of her life in the prosperous Washington suburb of Chevy Chase. Following her graduation from Cornell, she had moved to New York City to work as a financial analyst at Dunn and Bradstreet. During the late 1950s, she became active in the local chapter of CORE, eventually helping to rejuvenate the chapter by coordinating a boycott of dime stores affiliated with chains resisting the sit-in movement in the South. Exhilarated by the boycott and increasingly alienated from the conservative complacency of Wall Street, she gravitated toward a commitment to full-time activism, accepting a CORE field secretary position in the fall of 1960. At twenty-seven, Perkins was a year younger than Hughes, and he too had been on the CORE staff for less than a year. Born and raised in Owensboro, Kentucky, he attended Kentucky State University and Howard before transferring to the University of Michigan, where he and several other black graduate students became passionately involved in the Ann Arbor Direct Action Committee in the spring of 1960.

Rounding out the Michigan contingent were the Bergmans, Walter and Frances, two white activists who brought a unique set of experiences to the Freedom Ride. At sixty-one, Walter Bergman was the oldest of the Freedom Riders, and Frances, a former elementary school teacher and assistant principal, was the second oldest at fifty-seven. A retired school administrator who had taught at the University of Michigan and Wayne State University, he had been a leading figure in the teachers' union movement of the 1930s and 1940s, serving as the first president of the Michigan Federation of Teachers. Both Bergmans were committed socialists and admirers of Norman Thomas, as well as leaders of the Michigan affiliate of the ACLU. Since 1958 they had become increasingly active in CORE picketing campaigns against segregated hotels, chain stores, and swimming pools in Detroit. By the time they volunteered for the Freedom Ride, they were veteran civil rights activists, though virtually all of their movement experience was in the North.

The Bergmans were not the only Freedom Riders to have limited experience in the South. Four others—Albert Bigelow, Jimmy McDonald, Ed Blankenheim, and John Moody—were unmistakably Northern in background. A fifty-five-year-old former navy captain and World War II veteran, Bigelow had earned an architecture degree at Harvard and served as the state housing commissioner of Massachusetts before moving to Connecticut in the 1950s. Repulsed by the dropping of atomic bombs on Hiroshima and Nagasaki, he became a devout Quaker and pacifist who opened his home to Hiroshima survivors undergoing plastic surgery in American hospitals. A founding member of the Committee for Non-Violent Action (CNVA), he gained an international reputation as a militant anti-nuclear activist in 1958 when he captained the *Golden Rule*, a protest ship sponsored by CNVA and the National Committee for a Sane Nuclear Policy (SANE). Sailing the thirty-foot ketch into a drop zone in the Pacific to protest America's scheduled testing of nuclear weapons near the island of Eniwetok, he warned President Eisenhower that even though "our voices have been lost in the massive effort of those responsible for preparing this country for war . . . We mean to speak now with the weight of our whole lives." A square-shouldered, imposing man with a commanding presence, he did not fit the stereotypic image of a peace crusader. But no one who knew him well doubted the depth of his commitment to pacifism and nonviolent direct action.

Jimmy McDonald was a twenty-nine-year-old black folk singer from New York City known for his vast repertoire of labor and freedom songs. As a precocious seventeen-year-old, he had campaigned for Progressive Party presidential candidate Henry Wallace in 1948, inspired in part by a Wallace rally featuring the radical black activist and singer Paul Robeson. Asked to perform at a CORE fund-raiser in Brooklyn in 1956, McDonald later participated in a number of New York CORE direct-action campaigns, and for a brief period in 1960 he worked at CORE headquarters as a part-time clerk. "A very playful, bohemian,

Greenwich Village kind of guy," as John Lewis later described him, he added comic relief and a touch of whimsy to the band of Freedom Riders.

Two years younger than McDonald, Ed Blankenheim was a carpenter's apprentice and part-time chemistry student at the University of Arizona in Tucson. Feisty and full of resolve, he had talked his way into the Marine Corps in 1950 at the age of sixteen. Eleven years later, as a Korean War veteran and father of two, he traveled more than two thousand miles to join the Freedom Ride. Blankenheim had seen enough of the South as a young Marine recruit at Parris Island, South Carolina, to be wary of directly challenging the region's racial shibboleths, and he knew full well that he "was being invited on a trip into the Deep South as part of a mixed-race bomb." But, after a little prodding from Farmer, he could not resist joining the Ride. "I was no less concerned about the danger of my commitment," he later explained, "but all that I had seen in the South . . . stared me down. I had come too far, and I couldn't turn back."

John Moody was a thirty-year-old student at Howard University and an active member of the SNCC-affiliated Nonviolent Action Group (NAG), which had staged a series of successful sit-ins in Washington, Maryland, and northern Virginia. Born and raised in Philadelphia, where he was a leader of the local NAACP Youth Council, Moody threw himself into student and movement politics soon after transferring to Howard from Lincoln University. Self-conscious about his Northern background, he was both fascinated and frightened by images of black life in the Jim Crow South. As a young boy in Philadelphia, he listened with rapt attention to a transplanted North Carolina-born cousin who often reminisced about violent encounters with white Southern racists. Such stories, combined with his experiences at Howard, helped to draw him into the movement, but he remained very apprehensive about actually visiting the Deep South. As he confessed to his roommate in late April, even though he had volunteered to join the Freedom Ride, he didn't really want to go. This ambivalence soon plunged Moody into a physical and mental crisis that forced him to drop out on the last day of orientation. Less than a month later, after regaining his health and composure, he would take part in a Freedom Ride from Montgomery to Jackson, serving six weeks in a Mississippi jail cell for his trouble. But in early May he was in no condition to head south with the original Riders.

Realizing this, Farmer and Carey accepted Moody's young roommate, Hank Thomas, as a last-minute replacement. Although Thomas did not have the chance to go through the orientation, the strapping nineteen-year-old sophomore was well prepared for the challenges of the Ride. Like Moody, Thomas had been active in the NAG protests. But he also had the benefit of years of first-hand experience in the Jim Crow South and had even attended the founding conference of SNCC in April 1960. A native Georgian with rural roots, he grew up in an impoverished and troubled family headed by an abusive stepfather. One of ten children, he picked cotton and worked on the roads of southern Georgia before moving to St. Augustine, Florida, in his early teens. As a Deep South migrant and scholarship student, he never felt completely comfortable at Howard, an institution dominated by the sons and daughters of the black bourgeoisie. For him, the Freedom Ride provided a welcome escape from the stuffy complacency and condescension of privileged students who displayed little concern for the plight of their vulnerable Southern cousins. "When folks ask me what incident led me to ride," he explained many years later, "I can't say it was one. When you grow up and face this humiliation every day, there is no one thing. You always felt that way."

The rest of the Riders, like Thomas, were young black Southerners raised in the midst of rigidly segregated institutions. The youngest was eighteen-year-old Charles Person, a freshman at Atlanta's Morehouse College. Born and raised in Atlanta, where his father worked as an orderly at the Emory University Hospital, Person was a gifted math and physics student who dreamed of a career as a scientist. After being denied admission to the all-white Georgia Institute of Technology, he enrolled at Morehouse in the fall of 1960. A member of the local NAACP Youth Council during his senior year in high school, he and several other Morehouse freshmen, including future Freedom Rider Frank Holloway, became active in a student protest organization known as the Atlanta Committee on Appeals for Human Rights. In early 1961, one sit-in earned him a sixteen-day jail sentence, an experience that deepened his commitment to the struggle and drew the attention of CORE recruiters looking for a Freedom Rider who could represent the Atlanta sit-in movement. Since he was still a minor, he had to talk his mother (his father refused) into signing a CORE permission form, but his persistence ultimately prevailed. As he left his tearful parents in Atlanta to embark on the long bus ride to Washington, he reluctantly took a seat in the back of the bus—perhaps, he hoped, for the last time.

The oldest of the "Southern" Freedom Riders (aside from Farmer) was the Reverend Benjamin Elton Cox. Though only twenty-nine, he had packed a lot of living—and talking—into his three decades of existence. A native of Whiteville, Tennessee, Cox was a loquacious and eloquent preacher who earned the nickname "Beltin' Elton" during the course of the Freedom Ride. The seventh of sixteen children, he moved to Kankakee, Illinois, at the age of five. A high-school drop out, he shined shoes for eighteen months before completing the work for his diploma at the age of twenty. He later attended Livingstone College, an A.M.E. Zion institution in Salisbury, North Carolina, before studying for a divinity degree at Howard, and even spent a year as a visiting student at a seminary in Cambridge, Massachusetts. Following his ordination in 1958, he became the pastor of the Pilgrim Congregational Church in High Point, North Carolina, a small city fifteen miles southwest of Greensboro. In High Point he quickly gained a reputation as a militant civil rights advocate by spearheading local school de-segregation efforts, serving as an advisor for the local NAACP Youth Council, and acting as an observer for the American Friends Service Committee. Following the early Greensboro sit-ins in February 1960, he encouraged local students to stage their own sit-ins, but only if they were willing to keep them nonviolent. Forceful in his public commitment to nonviolence, he soon drew the attention of national NAACP leaders, including Farmer, who hired him to stump the South. Later, after Farmer became executive director of CORE, Cox received a call from his former boss, who wanted at least one ordained minister to join the Freedom Ride. Cox agreed without hesitation and, honoring the spirit of Farmer's request, showed up in Washington wearing a formal clerical collar, just in case anyone doubted that the Ride lacked divine guidance.

The roster of Freedom Riders originally included two ordained ministers, Cox and the Reverend J. Metz Rollins of Nashville. Rollins was also one of two Riders recruited from Nashville, but in late April he had to bow out, leaving Cox as the lone preacher and John Lewis as the sole representative of the Nashville movement. Destined to be the most celebrated Freedom Rider of them all, Lewis first learned about the Freedom Ride when Rollins showed him a CORE advertisement in *The Student Voice*. At twenty-one, the future Georgia congressman was one of the youngest Freedom Riders, but with five arrests he was already a jail-tested veteran of the nonviolent movement. Born on a hardscrabble tenant farm in Pike County, Alabama, a few miles outside the town of Troy, Lewis was a dedicated student who dreamed of being the first person in his family to go college. Despite a natural shyness, he wanted to be a preacher, especially after listening to a stirring radio sermon by Martin Luther King Jr. in 1955. Two years later, he enrolled at American Baptist Theological Seminary (ABT), a small, unaccredited college in Nashville, Tennessee. At ABT, he became a student and protégé of the Reverend Kelly Miller Smith, the founder of the Nashville Christian Leadership Council (NCLC), and by the fall of 1958 he had been drawn into the orbit of Jim Lawson and the emerging Nashville movement. Along with several ABT class-mates, including his close friends Bernard Lafayette and Jim Bevel, Lewis eagerly absorbed the lessons of Lawson's weekly workshops on nonviolence. And in November his commitment to nonviolent struggle deepened during a memo-rable weekend at the Highlander Folk School in Monteagle, Tennessee, where Septima Clark, Myles Horton, and others movement veterans shared their experiences and ideas. "I left Highlander on fire," he recalled.

Over the next year, Lawson's workshops strengthened his young disciple's religious and moral faith with visions of the "redemptive suffering," "soul force," and the "beloved community" concepts that would inform and animate Lewis's long and influential career as a civil rights leader. Instrumental in the founding of the Nashville Student Central Committee in October 1959, Lewis found an opportunity to put his evolving philosophy into action the following winter when downtown Nashville became a center of sit-in activity. Arrested along with scores of other student demonstrators during a February 1960 sit-in, he underwent what he later characterized as a conversion-like experience, "crossing over . . . into total, unquestioning commitment." More arrests followed, pushing thoughts of the ministry and school and family ties farther and farther into the background of his life. By the spring of 1961, when he volunteered for the Freedom Ride, the movement had become his surrogate "family." "At this time," he wrote revealingly on his application, "human dignity is the most important thing in my life. This is [the] most important decision in my life, to decide to give up all if necessary for the Freedom Ride, that Justice and Freedom might come to the Deep South." The depth of his commitment was already a source of inspiration for other Nashville activists, and those who knew him well realized that the CORE initiative would not be his first freedom ride.

In late December 1959, while traveling home for the Christmas break, Lewis and Bernard Lafayette impulsively decided to exercise their rights as interstate passengers by sitting in the front section of a bus from Nashville to Birmingham. Lafayette sat right behind the driver, and Lewis sat a few rows back on the opposite side. When the driver ordered them to the rear, they refused to budge. The driver then left the bus to call the Nashville police, but later returned in a rage after the police refused to intervene. At one point, he pushed his seat backwards crushing Lafayette's suitcase, but the two "freedom riders" stubbornly remained in the front as the bus headed southward. At several stops, the driver left the bus to use the phone, convincing Lewis and Lafayette that he was alerting the Klan. No Klansmen actually appeared, but when the two friends parted company later that night in Troy, they nervously joked that they might not see each other again. For Lafayette, who still had four hundred miles to travel before reaching his home in Tampa, the situation seemed especially dangerous. But in the end both students arrived home safely, suffering no more than the broken suitcase and the driver's scowls in the process. The whole experience filled them with a strange mixture of exhilaration and outrage, and after their return to Nashville a discussion of their narrow escape led to the idea of a second and more ambitious ride.

For more than a year they let the idea simmer, but in March 1961 they sent a letter to the Reverend Fred Shuttlesworth, Birmingham's leading civil right activist, proposing a test of both the *Morgan* and *Boynton* decisions. As Lewis recalled many years later, "Our idea was to have a core group of us ride the bus down to Birmingham and test the waiting areas, rest rooms, and eating facilities in the Greyhound station there—perhaps the most rigidly segregated bus terminal in the South—applying the same tactics we'd used with our sit-ins and stand-ins in Nashville." Though appreciative of their bravery, Shuttlesworth urged the

Nashville insurgents to find some other way to serve the cause. Birmingham, he warned, was a racial powder keg that would explode if local white supremacists were unduly provoked, especially by outsiders. This was not what Lewis and Lafayette wanted to hear, but their disappointment turned to vindication a few days later when they discovered CORE's plan for a Freedom Ride. Lafayette, like Lewis, was determined to join the Ride, but he was not yet twenty-one and needed his parents' permission. Already exercised over her son's role in the Nashville sit-ins, Lafayette's mother refused to sign the permission form, reminding him that she had sent him "to Nashville to study, not to aggravate white folks." Lafayette's father, an itinerant carpenter who had spent most of his life in the tough Ybor City section of Tampa, was even more emphatic, thundering: "Boy, you're asking me to sign your death warrant." Three weeks later young Lafayette would ignore his parents' wishes and join an NCLC-sponsored Freedom Ride that would land him in Mississippi's Parchman Prison. But at this point the best he could do was to accompany Lewis and Bevel on a wild car ride to Murphreesboro, where Lewis—who had missed his connection in Nashville—caught the morning bus to Washington.

Lewis arrived in Washington on the morning of April 30, just in time to join the other Freedom Riders for four days of intensive preparation and training in nonviolence. All thirteen Riders stayed at Fellowship House, a well-known Quaker meeting house and dormitory on L Street that had served generations of pacifists and social activists. "Inside was room after room filled with books and posters and pieces of art," Lewis later recalled, "all centered around the themes of peace and community." To many of the Riders, such a scene was familiar, but the young Alabaman "had never been in a building like this," nor "among people like this." In this enclave of interracial brotherhood, the beloved community that Lawson had conjured up suddenly seemed less abstract and more achievable, at least until Farmer's rather heavy-handed welcoming speech complicated this ethereal vision.

In greeting his fellow Riders, Farmer made it clear that he was in charge and that the Freedom Ride was first and foremost a CORE project. Anyone unwilling to abide by CORE's strict adherence to nonviolence should withdraw from the project, he informed them in his best stentorian voice. This was followed by short courses on constitutional law, sociology, and social activism—all a prelude to what CORE leaders considered to be the most important part of the Riders' training: "intense role-playing sessions" designed to give them a sense of what they were about to face. Coordinated by Carey, the sessions were carefully constructed "sociodramas—with some of the group playing the part of Freedom Riders sitting at simulated lunch counters or sitting on the front-seats of a make-believe bus. Others acted out the roles of functionaries, adversaries, or observers. Several played the role of white hoodlums coming to beat up the Freedom Riders on the buses or at lunch counters at the terminals." The sessions, which at times became "all too realistic," according to Farmer, went on for three grueling days, as the participants swapped and re-swapped places.

At a group dinner on May 3, the eve of the departure, Farmer made a soul-searching speech. Obviously pleased with what had transpired since the Riders had arrived in Washington, he wanted them to know that he had faith in their ability to meet any challenge, but he went on to insist that he was the only "one obligated to go on this trip," that "there was still time for any person to decide not to go." If one or more of them chose not to go, "there would be no recrimination, no blame, and CORE would pay transportation back home." After a moment of silence, Farmer told them that they did not have to make an immediate decision; they could tell him "later that night or just not show up at the bus terminal in the morning, whichever was easiest."

During the long, hard night before the departure, as he replayed the evening's events in his mind, Farmer began to worry that he had unwittingly sown the seeds of failure with his offer to let the volunteers back out. Why hadn't he left well enough alone? Had he come this far only to see his dream dissolve in a torrent of needless panic fostered by his own well-meaning but careless words? What would happen to CORE and the movement if word got out, as it surely would, that the Freedom Riders had lost their nerve?

Only when Farmer arrived at the breakfast table and saw the determination in the eyes of his fellow Riders did he realize that his fears were unfounded. "They were prepared for anything, even death," he later insisted. No one had withdrawn. The time had come to challenge the hypocrisy and complacency of a nation that refused to enforce its own laws and somehow failed to acknowledge the utter indecency of racial discrimination.

The scene at the downtown Trailways and Greyhound stations that morning gave little indication that something momentous was about to unfold. There were no identifying banners, no protest signs—nothing to signify the start of a revolution other than a few well-wishers representing CORE, NAG, and SCLC. Despite a spate of CORE press releases, the beginning of the Freedom Ride drew only token coverage. No television cameras or radio microphones were on hand to record the event, and the only members of the national press corps covering the departure were an Associated Press correspondent and two reporters from the *Washington Post* and the *Washington Evening Star*.

The only other journalists present were three brave individuals who had agreed to accompany the Riders to New Orleans: Charlotte Devree, a fifty-year-old white freelance writer and CORE activist from New York who hoped to publish a firsthand account of the Freedom Ride (and who frequently would be misidentified as a Freedom Rider); Simeon Booker, a forty-three-year-old black feature writer originally from Baltimore representing Johnson Publications' *Jet* and *Ebony* magazines; and Ted Gaffney, a thirty-three-year-old Washington-based photographer and Johnson stringer. A fourth journalist, Moses Newson, the thirty-four-year-old city editor of the *Baltimore Afro-American*, would later join the Ride in Greensboro, North Carolina.

Two weeks earlier the CORE office had sent letters describing the impending Freedom Ride to newly inaugurated President John F. Kennedy, FBI director J. Edgar Hoover, Attorney General Robert Kennedy, the chairman of the ICC, and the presidents of Trailways and Greyhound. But no one had responded, and as the Riders prepared to board the buses there was no sign of official surveillance or concern. At Farmer's request, Simeon Booker, who was known to have several close contacts in the Washington bureaucracy, called the FBI to remind the agency that the Freedom Ride was about to begin, and on the eve of the Ride Booker had a brief meeting at the Justice Department with Attorney General Kennedy and his assistant John Seigenthaler. Booker warned Kennedy that the Riders might need protection from segregationist thugs, but the young attorney general did not seem to appreciate the gravity of the situation. After telling the black journalist to "call" him if trouble arose, Kennedy quipped: "I wish I could go with you." All of this left Booker wondering if Kennedy had been paying full attention to their conversation, a suspicion confirmed when the attorney general later claimed that he had been blindsided by the Freedom Ride.

Once all of the Freedom Riders had arrived at the bus stations, Farmer held a brief press conference, during which he tried to explain both the philosophy of nonviolence and CORE's "jail—no bail" policy. "If there is an arrest, we will accept that arrest," he told the handful of reporters, "and if there is violence we will accept that violence without responding in kind." Accepting bail was contrary to the spirit of noncooperation with evil, he added: "We will not pay fines because we feel that by paying money to a segregated state we would help it perpetuate segregation."

After checking their bags, the Riders received last-minute instructions about seating arrangements. A proper test of the *Morgan* decision required a careful seating plan, and Farmer left nothing to chance. Each group made sure that one black Freedom Rider sat in a seat normally reserved for whites, that at least one interracial pair of Riders sat in adjoining seats, and that the remaining Riders scattered throughout the bus. One Rider on each bus served as a designated observer and as such remained aloof from the other Riders; by obeying the conventions of segregated travel, he or she ensured that at least one Rider would avoid arrest and be in a position to contact CORE officials or arrange legal council for those arrested. Most of the Riders, however, were free to mingle with the other passengers and to discuss the purpose of the Freedom Ride with anyone who would listen. Exercising the constitutional right to sit anywhere on the bus had educational as well as legal implications, and the Riders were encouraged to think of themselves as teachers and role models. Farmer imposed a strict dress code—coats and ties for the men and dresses and high heels for the women—and all of the Riders were asked to represent the cause of social justice openly and honestly without resorting to needlessly provocative or confrontational behavior.

All of these precautions took on new meaning as the buses actually headed south on Route 1. At first the regular passengers, both black and white, paid little attention to the Freedom Riders. No one, including the drivers, voiced any objection to the Riders' unusual seating pattern. This was encouraging and somewhat unexpected, but the first true test of tolerance did not come until the Greyhound stopped at Fredericksburg, fifty miles south of Washington. A small river town with a rich Confederate heritage and the site of one of the Union Army's most crushing defeats, Fredericksburg had a long tradition of strict adherence to racial segregation and white supremacy. Gaither's scouting report had warned the Riders that the facilities at Fredericksburg's bus terminals featured the all too familiar WHITE ONLY and COLORED ONLY signs. When they arrived at the Greyhound terminal, the Jim Crow signs were prominently displayed above the restroom doors. Nevertheless, someone in a position of authority had decided that there would be no trouble in Fredericksburg on May 4. Peck used the colored restroom, and Person, the designated black tester for the day, used the white restroom and later ordered a drink at the previously whites-only lunch counter, all without incident. To the Riders' surprise, the service was cordial, and not a harsh word was spoken by anyone. This apparent lack of rancor in the state that had spawned the "massive resistance" movement only a few years earlier was almost eerie, and as the Riders reboarded the bus, they couldn't help wondering what other surprises lay ahead.

The next stop was Richmond, where the Riders were scheduled to spend the night at Virginia Union College, a black Baptist institution located a few blocks north of the city's downtown business district. Understandably wary of a city that had served as the capital of the Confederacy for four years, they did not expect a warm welcome, especially after Farmer informed them that local NAACP leaders had urged their followers to avoid any association with the Freedom Ride. Even so, the fear that local whites would try to prevent them from desegregating the city's bus terminals proved unfounded. As Lewis later recalled, the Riders encountered "No signs. No trouble. Nothing but a few cold stares." There were, however, a few disheartening moments, at least for Peck. As he wandered through the Greyhound terminal—the same terminal that he had visited fourteen years earlier—he realized that the absence of Jim Crow signs had not led to any apparent changes in behavior. Unaware of or unmoved by the *Boynton* decision, "Negroes were sticking to the formerly separate and grossly unequal colored waiting rooms and restaurants." The same was true at the nearby Trailways station,

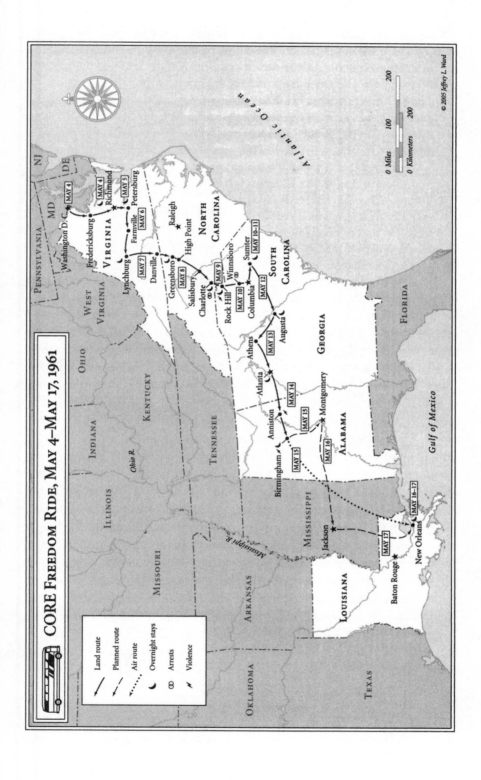

CORE FREEDOM RIDE, MAY 4–MAY 17, 1961

Land route
Planned route
Air route
Overnight stays
Arrests
Violence

MAY 4 Washington D.C.
MAY 4 Fredericksburg
Richmond MAY 5
Petersburg MAY 6
Farmville
Lynchburg MAY 7
Danville
Greensboro MAY 8
High Point
Salisbury MAY 9
Charlotte
Rock Hill MAY 10
Winnsboro
Columbia MAY 10–11
Sumter
Augusta MAY 12
Athens MAY 13
Atlanta
Anniston MAY 14
Montgomery MAY 15
Birmingham MAY 15
MAY 16
Jackson MAY 17
New Orleans MAY 16–17
Baton Rouge

Raleigh

PENNSYLVANIA
MD
DE
NJ
WEST VIRGINIA
VIRGINIA
OHIO
KENTUCKY
INDIANA
ILLINOIS
MISSOURI
TENNESSEE
NORTH CAROLINA
SOUTH CAROLINA
GEORGIA
ALABAMA
ARKANSAS
MISSISSIPPI
LOUISIANA
OKLAHOMA
TEXAS
FLORIDA

Ohio R.
Mississippi R.

Atlantic Ocean
Gulf of Mexico

0 Miles 100 200
0 Kilometers 200

© 2005 Jeffrey L. Ward

where traditional patterns of separation and deference still prevailed. Such scenes were profoundly discouraging to a man who had devoted his entire adult life to the struggle for racial equality.

Peck knew that, as a white man and a Northerner, he had no right to pass judgment on the frailties of black Southerners. Later that evening, however, as he sat through a sparsely attended meeting at the Virginia Union chapel, he felt a twinge of sadness, not only for the blacks still ensnared in the indignities of Jim Crow but also for the Freedom Riders who were taking such grave risks for a potentially empty victory. After interviewing several apathetic Virginia Union students, the New York writer Charlotte Devree shared some of Peck's concerns. But a late-night conversation with Charles Sherrod, a campus hero who had just gained his release from the Rock Hill jail, restored some of her faith in the black student movement. Speaking with a "cold fury" that stunned Devree, Sherrod insisted: "Some of us have to be willing to die."

Sherrod's words were enough to give anyone pause, especially a New Yorker facing her first visit to the Deep South. But when it came time to board the bus for the second day of the Freedom Ride, Devree overcame her fears and headed south with the rest of the group, realizing full well that the Freedom Riders were prepared to make the ultimate sacrifice for the cause of freedom. Fortunately, no such sacrifice was expected any time soon. Still in the Upper South, the Riders did not foresee much resistance in towns like Petersburg, where they disembarked for an overnight stay on May 5. Only twenty miles south of Richmond, Petersburg was a rough-and-tumble railroad town that had witnessed more than its share of carnage during the Civil War. As Gaither's scouting report had promised, despite recent tensions the town had seen relatively few manifestations of ultra-segregationist extremism. On the contrary, it had become a major center of movement activity and one of the few communities in the South where sit-ins had already led to desegregated bus terminals. As expected, the testing at the Petersburg terminals went off without incident, and the Riders received an enthusiastic welcome from a crowd that included some of the fifty-five sit-in veterans arrested at the Trailways terminal the previous summer.

Petersburg was encouraging, but Farmville, the first scheduled rest stop on Saturday morning, was the kind of place where almost anything could happen. The seat of Prince Edward County, the small farming and college town was the birthplace of Virginia's "Massive Resistance" campaign. In 1959, local officials had closed the county's public schools rather than submit to desegregation, establishing Farmville as a symbol of white supremacist defiance. The white children of Prince Edward County attended an array of private segregationist academies, but most local black children had no affordable options, a situation that didn't seem to bother county school officials or other local whites. The Freedom Riders expected trouble in Farmville, but to their surprise the signs designating segregated terminal facilities were hidden under a fresh coat of paint. Although the Riders could still make out the letters that had traditionally directed "white" and "colored" where to go, they met no resistance when they violated the color line in the restrooms and at the lunch counter. Farmville's white establishment clearly wanted nothing to do with the Freedom Riders and was willing to overlook a momentary lapse in racial etiquette to ensure the Riders' quick departure.

The next stop was Lynchburg, which despite its foreboding name, had a reputation for moderate race relations. Upon their arrival, the Freedom Riders were pleased to discover that the city's bus terminals were free of Jim Crow signs, but at the Trailways lunch counter they encountered a towering partition "making persons on one side virtually invisible to those on the other." Whether the absence of signs represented social progress or merely white supremacist cunning was a subject of debate and some puzzlement as the Riders mingled with their hosts later that evening. Dispersed among eight black churches, the Riders encountered a wide range of attitudes among local black leaders. If the quickening spirit of the movement was palpable in Lynchburg, so too were the lingering effects of decades of white intimidation and black accommodation. The raw emotionalism and political contradictions of the black South were familiar to the Southern-born Freedom Riders, especially to Lewis and Cox, but among the more secular Northern volunteers the Ride was turning out to be quite an educational experience. All this, and the Freedom Ride had yet to penetrate the Deep South.

The Freedom Riders' experience in Danville, a mill town sixty-five miles south of Lynchburg, represented a milestone of sorts. Here for the first time the Riders encountered open hostility and resistance. At the combined Greyhound-Trailways station, a black waiter refused to serve Ed Blankenheim when he insisted on sitting at the "colored counter." After several minutes of waiting and after the waiter explained that his white boss had promised to fire him if he served a Freedom Rider on the wrong side of the color line, Blankenheim gave up and reboarded the bus. An hour or so later, three white Riders from the second bus—Jim Peck, Genevieve Hughes, and Walter Bergman—renewed the challenge. Following a curt refusal and a brief standoff, Peck convinced the station manager to relent. While the seeming irrationality of insisting on eating at an inferior facility undoubtedly puzzled the manager and his staff, the Freedom Riders knew they had won a small but significant victory.

By mid-Sunday afternoon, both buses had crossed the North Carolina border, leaving proud but perplexed Virginia to its own devices. The day's final destination was Greensboro, the birthplace of the 1960 sit-in movement. Greensboro's leaders had traditionally taken pride in the city's enlightened paternalism, but more than a year of militant civil rights agitation had angered the white community. By the time the Freedom Riders arrived, the city's "civil" approach to racial accommodation had long since given way to the politics of racial polarization and white backlash.

While a few local white leaders continued to push for moderate gradualism, the dominant mood was anything but conciliatory. This confusion was obvious at the Greensboro Trailways station, where the Riders encountered huge signs pointing to a "colored" lunch counter that had been closed down earlier in the week.

Following an afternoon meeting with student leaders at all-black Bennett College, the Riders attended a mass meeting at Shiloh Baptist Church, the same church that had welcomed CORE riders in 1947, after the beatings at Chapel Hill. Shiloh's pastor, the Reverend Otis Hairston, was a fearless activist who had spearheaded a local NAACP membership drive in 1959 and turned his church into an unofficial command center during the early stages of the sit-in movement. He was proud that two of the four students who participated in the original February 1, 1960, sit-in were Shiloh members, and he was equally pleased to host the Freedom Riders. After a rousing invocation, he turned the meeting over to Dr. George Simkins Jr., the NAACP leader who had urged CORE to become involved in the Greensboro sit-ins. Perhaps more than any other NAACP official, Simkins had been an active supporter of the Freedom Ride, beginning with his insistence to Gaither that the Riders spend at least one night in Greensboro. He could hardly contain himself as he introduced the Riders to an overflow crowd of well-wishers.

Later, when Farmer addressed the congregation, expressing both his fear that the desegregation fight had lost some of its "steam" and his determination to make segregation "so costly the South can't afford it," the sanctuary reverberated with amens and other words of encouragement. "Life is not so dear and sweet," Farmer added, "that we must passively accept Jim Crow and segregation . . . If our parents had gone to jail we wouldn't have to go through the ordeal now. Our nation cannot afford segregation. Overseas it gives Uncle Sam a black eye. Future generations will thank us for what we have done." On and on he went, crying out for a resurgence of the spirit that had nurtured and sustained the city's famous sit-ins. By the end of the evening, both Farmer and the audience were emotionally spent. But as the Freedom Riders and their hosts filed out of the sanctuary, the dual message of empowerment and responsibility was clear. Before they could hope to redeem the white South, Farmer and the Freedom Riders felt they had to embolden the black South, to stir things up to a point where a critical mass of activists demanded fundamental change. Although they realized that mobilizing and sustaining such a critical mass would not be easy, the warm welcome that the Riders received in Greensboro suggested that at least one local movement was poised to take an unequivocal stand for freedom.

The upper North Carolina Piedmont was as far south as CORE's 1947 Journey of Reconciliation had dared to go, so when the Freedom Riders headed down Highway 29 on Monday morning, May 8, they were entering uncharted territory. In Salisbury, fifty-two miles southwest of Greensboro, the Riders encountered

Jim Crow signs at both bus terminals but were able to desegregate the restrooms and lunch counters without incident. Even more encouraging was the unexpected bravado of two black women, both regular passengers on the bus, who followed the Riders' example of demanding service at the white counter. They, too, received prompt and reasonably courteous service.

From Salisbury, the buses continued southward, on to Charlotte. The largest city in the Carolina Piedmont, Charlotte was a banking and textile center with a flair for New South commercialism. The "Queen City," as North Carolinians often called it, was 28 percent black and almost 100 percent segregated in 1961. As in Greensboro, city leaders cultivated an image of moderation and urbane paternalism, but they did so with the expectation that all local citizens, black and white, knew their place. The immutability of racial segregation, even in the most mundane aspects of life, was a given, and anyone who crossed the color line in Charlotte or Mecklenburg County was asking for trouble. Charles Person discovered just how true this was when he tried to get a shoeshine in Charlotte's Union Station. As Jim Peck later explained, the young Atlanta student "didn't even think of it as a test. He simply looked at his shoes and thought he needed a shine." But after being rebuffed, he decided to remain in the whites-only shoeshine chair until someone either changed the policy or arrested him. Within minutes, a policeman arrived and threatened to handcuff him and haul him off the jail if he didn't move. At this point, Person decided to avoid arrest and scurried back to tell the other Riders what had happened.

After an impromptu strategy session, the Riders designated Joe Perkins as the group's official shoeshine segregation tester. The whole scene carried a touch of the absurd—the Riders later referred to the incident as the South's first "shoe-in"—but Perkins agreed to sit in the shoeshine chair until somebody came and arrested him. A few minutes later, the young CORE field secretary became the first Freedom Rider to be arrested. The formal charge was trespassing, and bail was set at $50. Ed Blankenheim, the designated observer in Charlotte, was on hand with the required bail money, but Perkins bravely chose to spend two nights in jail instead. On Monday evening, while the rest of the Riders met with Charles Jones and other Johnson C. Smith University student activists—including twenty-year-old Gus Griffin of Tampa, Florida, who volunteered to replace Perkins on the Tuesday-morning Freedom Ride to Rock Hill, South Carolina—Perkins was at the city jail. And he remained there until his trial on Wednesday morning. With Blankenheim looking on, Perkins went before Judge Howard B. Arbuckle expecting the worst. But to his surprise, and to the amazement of his NAACP attorney, Thomas Wyche, Arbuckle promptly rendered an acquittal based on the *Boynton* decision. Elated, Perkins and Blankenheim headed for Union Station. But as they left the courthouse the same police officer who had arrested Perkins on Monday confronted them. Advising the interracial duo "to get the hell out of town," the officer declared that he wasn't about "to let no New York nigger come down here and make trouble for us and our good nigras." Though tempted to argue the point, Perkins and Blankenheim decided to let the comment pass and proceeded on to the terminal, where they caught an early afternoon bus to Rock Hill. Arriving in the South Carolina mill town too late to rejoin the other Riders, who had already headed southward, they traveled on to Sumter, where they finally caught up with their colleagues on Wednesday evening. Separated from the other Riders for two days, the two stragglers soon discovered that a great deal had happened during their absence.

Rock Hill, South Carolina, which had been seething with racial tension since the celebrated jail-in three months earlier, turned out to be the first serious trouble spot for the Freedom Ride. Gaither, who had spent considerable time there, both in and out of jail, warned the Riders that the town was literally crawling with Klansmen and other hard-line white supremacists. But the relative ease of the journey through Virginia and North Carolina left many of the Riders unprepared for the rude welcome they encountered during their first stop in the state. A cotton mill town with a chip on its shoulder, Rock Hill harbored a large contingent of what Senator Ben Tillman once called "the damned factory trash," displaced farmers who had been pushed off the land by declining cotton prices and a brutal crop-lien system. Over the years their economic and cultural grievances spawned a hardy tradition of racial scapegoating. As Lewis, who had traveled to Rock Hill earlier in the year to visit his jailed SNCC colleagues, put it, "I could tell we were in trouble as soon as I stepped off the bus."

As Lewis approached the "White" waiting room, some young toughs confronted him. When he proceeded, the men punched him to the floor and then kicked him. At that point Al Bigelow stepped in, placing his body between Lewis's and the men , standing square with his arms at his sides, Lewis later recalled. After the men attacked Bigelow, who did not defend himself, Genevieve Hughes intervened, and she too was knocked to the floor. Whether out of chivalry or just plain common sense, a white police officer who had witnessed the entire assault finally intervened and grabbed one of the assailants. "All right, boys," he stated with some authority. "Y'all've done about enough now. Get on home."

After a few parting epithets, the boys retreated to the street, leaving the Freedom Riders and the policeman to wait for several other officers who had been called to the scene. To Lewis's surprise, one of the officers appeared to be sympathetic to the injured Riders and asked them if they wanted to file charges against their attackers. But they declined the offer. Though still shaken and bleeding, Lewis, Bigelow, and Hughes then staggered into the terminal restaurant to join the rest of the Riders. Lewis, who had suffered bruised ribs and severe cuts around his eyes and mouth, was in need of medical attention, but he stubbornly insisted on remaining at the restaurant until he finished his hard-earned cup of coffee. Several hours later, after someone at Friendship Junior College fetched a first-aid kit, he allowed a friend to place band-aids over the wounds on his face. But throughout the whole ordeal he downplayed his injuries; no bones had been broken, he insisted, displaying the quiet courage for which he would later become famous. Most importantly, he pointed out, no pledges had been violated: the Freedom Riders had passed their first major test, refusing to strike back against an unprovoked assault.

The Trailways Riders who arrived later in the afternoon faced a similarly threatening situation but were able to avoid a violent confrontation, thanks to the intervention of the Reverend C. A. Ivory, the courageous leader of the Rock Hill movement. At the mass meeting held at Friendship Junior College that night, Ivory and others praised the courage and restraint of the bloodied but unbowed Freedom Riders. Confined to a wheelchair and in poor health, Ivory himself was no stranger to threats of violence or acts of courage. For four years— ever since he had led a successful boycott of Rock Hill's local bus company—the outspoken minister had been a primary target of militant segregationists who hoped to drive him out the community. But nothing seemed to faze him—not hate mail, not death threats, not even a recent phone call that pledged to bomb his home and family. "The other night the person on the other end threatened to plant a bomb under my house," he told the Riders. "'Why don't you plant two while you're at it?' I asked. Nothing ever came of it." Six months later, Ivory would die of natural causes, but those who knew him well placed part of the blame on the extraordinary burden of leadership he had agreed to bear.

John Lewis, meanwhile, faced a dilemma. Within minutes of his arrival at the college, he had received a telegram from the American Friends Service Committee notifying him that he been selected as a finalist for a two-year foreign service internship—the same internship that his mentor Jim Lawson had held in the mid-1950s. It had taken the American Friends Service Committee some time to track him down, but there was still enough time for him to make the required final interview in Philadelphia. Accompanying the telegram was a money order that would buy him a plane ticket, but if he wanted to pursue the internship he would have to leave the Freedom Ride almost immediately. Following a long night of soul-searching, Lewis decided to fly to Philadelphia for three days, after which he planned to rejoin the Ride. Barring any unforeseen problems, he would be back on the bus by Monday, May 15, the day the Riders were scheduled to leave Birmingham, Alabama.

The next morning, as the rest of the Riders prepared to head south toward Chester and Winnsboro, a Friendship Junior College student drove Lewis to the Charlotte airport, where he caught a plane to Philadelphia. The seat of hilly Fairfield County, Winnsboro was a conservative community with a deep

Confederate heritage. As the Freedom Riders rolled into the sand hills of central South Carolina on the morning of the tenth—which happened to be Confederate Memorial Day—newspapers all across the nation ran a wire story describing the beatings of the previous day. Many people in South Carolina, not to mention the rest of the South, now knew that Riders were coming their way. Officially CORE welcomed the publicity, but from this point on the Riders would have to deal with an awakened white South.

In Winnsboro, the first sign of trouble came when Hank Thomas, the young Howard student from St. Augustine, sat down at a whites-only lunch counter. Accompanied by Peck, who later recalled that they had hardly settled in their seats when "the restaurant owner dashed away from the counter to call the police," Thomas soon found himself in a conversation with a brawny "police officer who was a stereotype for such a role in Hollywood." "Come with me, boy," the officer drawled. At this point Peck tried to explain that Thomas had a constitutional right to eat lunch wherever he pleased. This didn't seem to faze the policeman, who promptly arrested both men. Within minutes, the two Freedom Riders were behind bars in the city jail—in separate Jim Crow cells. After several hours of confusion and indecision, local officials charged Thomas with trespassing and Peck with "interfering with arrest." By this time the rest of the Riders—with the exception of Frances Bergman, the designated observer for the Winnsboro lunch counter test—had gone on to Sumter, where they were scheduled to spend the night. For several hours, Bergman, as a grateful Peck later put it, "braved the hate-filled town alone trying to find out what the authorities intended to do" with the two arrestees. She got little cooperation from the local police, who seemed pleased that Winnsboro's unwelcome visitors had gotten more than they had bargained for in the heart of Dixie. One officer, after calling her a "nigger lover" and an "outside agitator," told her "to get out of town," adding "We have no use for your kind here."

Following a CORE policy agreed upon at the beginning of the Ride, Farmer left Thomas, Peck, and Bergman behind, hoping that they would be able to rejoin the Ride in Sumter. But he did so reluctantly. Farmer knew from his conversations with field secretary Jim McCain that Winnsboro—like Rock Hill—was a dangerous town, especially for an assertive young black man like Thomas. As a white woman, Bergman, despite her lack of experience in the South, would probably be all right, and Peck—a veteran civil disobedient who had served three years in prison as a young man—could probably take care of himself. Thomas, though, was young and full of pent-up emotion left over from a troubled boyhood. Fortunately, while Farmer was still mulling over his options, the Winnsboro police dropped all charges against Thomas, releasing him around midnight.

While Peck was still languishing in his cell, two policemen drove Thomas to Winnsboro's partially closed and virtually empty bus station. As the police sped off, Thomas noticed several white men standing in the parking lot, looking to his eyes very much like a potential lynch mob. One of the men, upon seeing him, ordered him to "go in the nigger waiting room." Somehow the young Freedom Rider summoned up enough courage to enter the white waiting room, purchase a candy bar, and stroll past "gaping segregationists" who seemed stunned by his defiance. Before the whites could react, a local black minister whom Frances Bergman had called earlier in the day drove up to the waiting room entrance and literally screamed at Thomas to "get in the car and stay down." After the rescue, the minister drove Thomas twenty-five miles south to Columbia, where the Freedom Rider found refuge in the home of a local NAACP leader. The next day Thomas took a bus to Sumter to rejoin the other Riders—including Peck, who had his own tale to tell.

The Winnsboro police had planned to release Peck and Thomas at roughly the same time, but after dropping the original arrest-interference charge against Peck, local officials immediately rearrested him for violating a state liquor law. As Peck was about to be released from the jail, a police officer spied a bottle of whiskey and proudly informed his superiors that the bottle lacked the required South Carolina state liquor stamp. Within minutes Peck was back in jail, charged with illegal possession of untaxed alcohol. Upon learning of Peck's second arrest, Farmer and a carload of CORE supporters—including Jim McCain and a local black attorney, Ernest Finney Jr.—drove from Sumter to Winnsboro, arriving just before dawn. Securing Peck's release with a $50 bail bond, Farmer and McCain whisked their old friend back to Sumter, knowing full well that they could not afford to wait for his day in court.

The safe return of Thomas, Peck, and Bergman buoyed the spirits of the Riders, all of whom were thankful that the schedule called for two days of rest in Sumter. At a mass meeting on Thursday evening at the Emmanuel A. M. E. Church, Farmer talked about the significance of the Freedom Ride, and Peck and Thomas recounted their harrowing experiences in Winnsboro. But the highlight of the meeting was a testimonial by Frances Bergman, who "hushed" the audience with a moving account of her rude introduction to the Deep South. "For the first time I felt that I had a glimpse of what it would be like to be colored," she confessed, "This thing made me realize what it is to be scorned, humiliated and made to feel like dirt . . . The whole thing was such an eye-opener for me . . . It left me so filled with admiration for the colored people who have to live with this all their lives. It seems to me that anything I can do now, day or night, would not be enough . . . Somehow you feel there is a new urgency at this time. You see the courage all about you." Rededicating herself to the cause of racial justice, she praised the activism of young black students but warned that "older persons" should not "sit back and wait for them to do it." Despite its hint of presumption, this admonition struck a responsive chord in the crowd, which included a number of students from nearby Morris College, a black Baptist institution that had been a hot bed of sit-in and boycott activity since the establishment of a campus CORE chapter in March 1960.

Soon after the Riders' arrival in Sumter, Ben Cox took a leave of absence to return to High Point, where he was obliged to deliver a Mother's Day sermon on Sunday morning. Thus, with Lewis already gone, the number of Riders was suddenly down to eleven, only five of whom were black. Both Lewis and Cox planned to rejoin the Ride in Birmingham on Monday morning, but CORE needed at least two substitute Riders for the pivotal three-day journey from Sumter to Birmingham. Fortunately, with McCain's help, Farmer not only found replacements for Lewis and Cox but also added two extra recruits for good measure. One of the four new Freedom Riders was Ike Reynolds, a twenty-seven-year-old black CORE activist and Wayne State University sophomore who had been awakened on Wednesday morning by a 7 a.m. phone call from Gordon Carey. The next thing Reynolds knew, he was on a mid-morning plane from Detroit to Atlanta, where he was picked up and driven to Sumter. The other recruits—Ivor "Jerry" Moore, Herman Harris, and Mae Francis Moultrie—were students at Morris College. Moultrie was a twenty-five-year old senior from Dillon, South Carolina, and Harris and Moore, both twenty-one, were Northern transplants—Harris from Englewood, New Jersey, and Moore from the Bronx. Harris was president of the local CORE chapter and a campus football star, and Moultrie and Moore had been actively involved in several sit-ins and marches. Trained by McCain, all three were seasoned veterans of the Southern freedom struggle.

With the new recruits in hand, Farmer, McCain, and the other CORE staff members spent most of the second day in Sumter assessing the experiences of the previous week and refining the plan for the remainder of the Ride. In gauging the future, they had to deal with a number of unknowns, including the attitudes of black leaders and citizens in Deep South communities that would inevitably be affected by the Ride. Would the Freedom Riders be welcomed as liberators? Or would they just as likely be shunned as foolhardy provocateurs by black Southerners who knew how dangerous it was to provoke the forces of white supremacy? How many black adults were ready to embrace the direct action movement that their children had initiated? And how would the student activists themselves respond to an initiative directed by an organization associated with white Northern intellectuals and an exotic and secular nonviolent philosophy? CORE leaders were hopeful, but after a week on the road they still regarded the black South as something of a puzzle.

Equally perplexing, and far more threatening, was the unpredictability of white officials in the Deep South—and in Washington. What would the police do if the Freedom Riders were physically attacked by segregationist thugs?

Would the mayors of cities like Augusta, Birmingham, and Montgomery set aside their avowed segregationist beliefs and instruct their police chiefs to uphold the law? Perhaps most important, what would the Kennedy administration do if white Southerners brazenly violated the law as interpreted by the Supreme Court? How far would the Justice Department go to protect the Freedom Riders' constitutional rights, knowing that direct intervention would be politically costly for the new administration? While the probable answers to all of these questions remained somewhat murky as the Riders set out on the second week of their southward journey, they did have the benefit of a remarkable and illuminating civil rights address delivered earlier in the week by Attorney General Robert Kennedy.

On Saturday, May 6, in a Law Day speech at the University of Georgia, Robert Kennedy issued the first major policy statement of his attorney generalship. Since no prior attorney general in the post-*Brown* era had dared to speak about civil rights in the Deep South, Kennedy's appearance attracted considerable press attention, as well as an overflow crowd of students, faculty, and invited guests. Noticeably absent from the gathering in Athens were the state's leading politicians, including Georgia's governor, Ernest Vandiver. Kennedy knew, as he reminded the audience, that Georgia had given his brother the second largest electoral majority in the nation during the recent election. But he also knew that most of his listeners were segregationists who would bristle at even the slightest suggestion that the Justice Department planned to force the white South to desegregate any time soon. Of the sixteen hundred persons present, only one—Charlayne Hunter, one of two students who had desegregated the university the previous January—was black. It was in this context that Kennedy faced the ominous task of convincing white Southerners that he intended to enforce the law in a firm but conciliatory manner. Knowing that he had to choose his words carefully, he and his staff had been working on the speech for more than a month.

The result was a clever blend of disarming humor, patriotic rhetoric, and well-placed candor. After reminding the audience that "Southerners have a special respect for candor and plain talk," he got right to the point. "Will we enforce the civil rights statutes?" he asked rhetorically. "The answer is yes, yes we will." His motivation for upholding the civil rights of all Americans was rooted in his commitment to equal justice, he told the crowd, but he was also concerned about the realities of the Cold War: "We, the American people, must avoid another Little Rock or another New Orleans. We cannot afford them . . . Such incidents hurt our country in the eyes of the world." Later in the speech he endorsed the *Brown* decision, condemned the closing of Prince Edward County's schools, hailed the first two black students at the University of Georgia as courageous freedom fighters, and, with an eye to Southern sensitivity to Northern hypocrisy, promised to put his own house in order by hiring black staff members at the Justice Department. He also made it clear that he had no intention of following the lead of the Eisenhower administration's passive approach to civil rights. "We will not stand by and be aloof," he assured the crowd. "We will move."

After a few closing remarks, he sat down, hoping that the crowd would accord him at least a smattering of polite applause. To his surprise, a moment of awkward silence soon gave way to a long and loud ovation. Whether the audience was applauding the substance of his remarks or just his courage was unclear, but most observers judged the speech to be a diplomatic triumph. According to Ralph McGill, the liberal editor of the *Atlanta Constitution*, "Never before, in all its travail of by-gone years, has the South heard so honest and understandable a speech from any Cabinet member." While other Southern editors were somewhat more restrained in their enthusiasm, there was little negative reaction, even among hide-bound conservatives. In the civil rights community, the speech drew rave reviews; congratulations poured in from every major civil rights leader, including Roy Wilkins who expressed the NAACP's "profound appreciation" for the attorney general's forthright stand.

CORE, too, sent a congratulatory note to Attorney General Kennedy. But, in truth, Farmer and other CORE staff members harbored serious reservations about the tone and content of the speech. They were disappointed that he had failed to mention CORE or the Freedom Ride. But even more troubling was his avowed determination "to achieve amicable, voluntary solutions without going to court." Far too often, in their experience, the word "voluntary" had served as a codeword for foot-dragging non-compliance. For Kennedy to say, as he did in the speech, that "the hardest problems of all in law enforcement are those involving a conflict of law and custom" seemed tantamount to saying that continued segregationist resistance was inevitable and even legitimate. They wanted the Kennedy administration to take an unequivocal stand on the immediate and uncompromising enforcement of the law. Nothing less would satisfy the freedom fighters of CORE, especially those who were about to test the waters of resistance in the Deep South.

The Freedom Riders' uneasy feeling about the Kennedy administration's position on civil rights deepened on Tuesday morning, May 9, when a White House press release distanced the president from two civil rights bills that he had previously promised to support. Later the same day, Governor Vandiver issued a statement claiming that during the recent campaign Senator Kennedy had promised that his administration would never use federal troops to enforce desegregation in Georgia. When the expected White House denial failed to materialize, civil rights leaders began to worry that the Kennedy brothers were talking out of both sides of their mouths. At the very least, the Freedom Riders had renewed cause for concern as they said their good-byes to McCain and boarded the buses to Augusta on the morning of the twelfth.

Augusta—where the Freedom Riders were scheduled to spend Friday night—fancied itself as a genteel enclave epitomizing the finest traditions of the Old South. Situated on the west bank of the river, the city exuded an aura of stolid confidence that matched the graceful Victorian homes lining its streets. Earlier in the year the Augusta police had arrested a black soldier for trying to desegregate one of the city's terminal lunch counters, but the Riders encountered no such resistance at either terminal. One thing the Riders had learned during their first week on the road was that each community had its own peculiarities where matters of race and segregation were concerned. Regional and even statewide generalizations, it appeared, were untrustworthy and often misleading. This revelation was not altogether reassuring, since it suggested that the struggle for civil rights would have to be waged in a bewildering array of settings. But the variability of Jim Crow culture across time and space certainly added to the adventure of the Freedom Ride, which was turning out to be far less predictable than expected.

On Saturday morning, May 13, the Freedom Riders set out for Atlanta by way of Athens, the college town that had recently hosted Attorney General Kennedy. The surprisingly warm reception accorded to the attorney general indicated that Athens was a fairly progressive community compared with Rock Hill or Winnsboro. But as the Freedom Riders pulled into Athens for a short rest stop, they could not help remembering the news reports of the ugly scenes that had accompanied the desegregation of the University of Georgia in January. Charlayne Hunter and Hamilton Holmes had gained admission, but only after braving a mob of angry whites and overcoming the machinations of university administrators and politicians. To their relief, the Freedom Riders encountered no such problems when they sat down at the Athens lunch counter. Noting that "there were no gapers," Peck marveled that "a person viewing the Athens desegregated lunch counter and waiting room during our fifteen-minute rest stop might have imagined himself at a rest stop up North rather than deep in Georgia." Later in the day the Riders enjoyed a similar episode in Atlanta, leading Peck to conclude that "our experiences traveling in Georgia were clear proof of how desegregation can come peacefully in a Deep South state, providing there is no deliberate incitement to hatred and violence by local or state political leaders." Civil rights activists who lived in Georgia knew all too well that this sanguine observation gave their state far too much credit, but Peck's appreciation for the importance of political leadership was clearly on the mark, as events in Alabama and Mississippi would later confirm.

The welcoming scenes at the Atlanta bus stations provided a moving affirmation of the civil rights movement's rising spirit. As the Trailways Riders stepped off the bus, a large gathering of students—nearly all veterans of lunch counter sit-ins and picketing campaigns—broke into applause. Rushing forward, the students greeted the road-weary Riders as conquering heroes. The reception in Atlanta could hardly have been better, though the Riders were disappointed to learn that Dr. King was in Montgomery attending an SCLC board meeting. Fortunately, he and SCLC executive director Wyatt Tee Walker were expected back in Atlanta late in the afternoon.

To the Riders' delight, King and Walker returned to Atlanta in time to join them for dinner. Having just received a surprisingly glowing report on SCLC's financial situation, King was in a celebratory mood. Accompanied by several aides, he met the Riders at one of Atlanta's most popular black-owned restaurants. During the dinner, the SCLC leader was at his gracious best, repeatedly praising the Freedom Riders for their courage and offering to help in any way he could.

Some of the Riders were so moved by King's show of support and affection that they began to hope that he might join them on the bus the following morning, but they soon learned that King had no intention of becoming a Freedom Rider. At one point during the dinner, King privately confided in Simeon Booker, the reporter covering the Freedom Ride for *Jet* and *Ebony*, warning him that SCLC's sources had uncovered evidence of a plot to disrupt the Ride with violence. "You will never make it through Alabama," the SCLC leader predicted, obviously worried. Booker did his best to laugh off the threat, facetiously assuring King that he could always hide behind Farmer, who presented attackers with a large and slow-moving target. Later, when Booker told Farmer what King had said, he discovered that the CORE leader had already been apprised of the situation. Unnerved by what he had learned earlier in the evening, Farmer took both Jimmy McDonald and Genevieve Hughes aside and tried to convince them to leave the Ride in Atlanta. He did not want McDonald in Alabama because he did not think he could trust the young folk singer to remain nonviolent, and he did not want Hughes along because he feared that the presence of a young white woman might provoke additional violence among white supremacists obsessed with the threat of miscegenation. To Farmer's dismay, both adamantly refused to leave the Ride, and Hughes even vowed to buy her own ticket to Birmingham if she had to.

Farmer's growing sense of apprehension became clear when the Freedom Riders gathered for a late-night briefing at their Atlanta University dormitory. The Riders were accustomed to Farmer's assertive style of leadership, but they had never seen him quite so solemn or peremptory. He alone would "lead the testings" for the Greyhound group, and Jim Peck would do the same for the trailing Trailways group. They were entering "the most ominous leg of the journey," and there was no room for error. "Discipline had to be tight," he told them, and "strict compliance" with Gandhian philosophy would have to be maintained. The coming journey through Alabama would pose daunting challenges, but it would also give them the opportunity to prove to the world that nonviolent resistance was an idea whose time had come.

Later that night, a dormitory counselor awakened Farmer from a deep sleep. His mother was on the phone, and he rushed down to the first floor to receive what he knew was bad news. Prior to leaving Washington, he had paid a tearful visit to his father's bedside at Freedman's Hospital. Suffering from acute diabetes and recovering from a recent cancer operation, James Farmer Sr. was near death when his son first told him about the Freedom Ride. Realizing that it was unlikely that he would ever see his son again, the old man offered his blessing, plus a few words of warning: "Son, I wish you wouldn't go. But at the same time, I am more proud than I've ever been in my life, because you are going. Please try to survive . . . I think you'll be all right through Virginia, North Carolina, South Carolina, and maybe even Georgia. But in 'Bama, they will doubtless take a potshot at you. With all my heart, I hope they miss." As Farmer's mother informed him of his father's passing, these final words came flooding back to him. He knew that his father would want him to finish the Ride, but he also knew that his distraught mother expected him to return for the funeral. As Farmer later confessed, in making the choice to return to Washington he had to overcome an almost unbearable "confusion of emotions." "There was, of course, the incomparable sorrow and pain," he recalled. "But, frankly, there was also a sense of reprieve, for which I hated myself. Like everyone else, I was afraid of what lay in store for us in Alabama, and now that I was to be spared participation in it, I was relieved, which embarrassed me to tears."

During and after the funeral, Pearl Farmer insisted that her husband had actually "willed the timing of his death" in order to save his son from the coming ordeal in Alabama. But no explanation, real or imagined, made it any easier for Farmer to tell his fellow Riders that he was abandoning them. As they gathered around the breakfast table on Sunday morning, May 14, the embarrassed and emotionally drained leader stunned his charges with the news that his father's death required him to fly to Washington later in the morning. He would rejoin the Ride as soon as possible, he assured them, probably within two or three days. Until then, they could communicate with him by phone, and Joe Perkins would take over his duties as "captain" of the Greyhound group.

Farmer was the third Rider to take leave of the group, following John Lewis and Ben Cox, who was in High Point polishing his Mother's Day sermon. Lewis had been gone the longest—four days—and a great deal had happened since his departure. The trip to Philadelphia—his first journey to the Northeast—was a qualified success. He weathered the American Friends Service Committee interview with ease and even passed the physical, despite the cuts and bruises received during the Rock Hill beating. On Friday, while the other Riders were en route from Sumter to Augusta, he learned that he had won a fellowship. But the overseas assignment, which would begin in the late summer, was to India, not to Tanganyika, where he had hoped to explore his African roots. Though somewhat disappointed, he accepted the India fellowship, which would allow him to follow in the footsteps of Jim Lawson—and Gandhi.

On Saturday he caught a plane to Nashville, with the hope that he could find a ride to Birmingham on Sunday evening. Arriving in Nashville on Saturday night, he had just enough time to spend a few hours with Bernard Lafayette, Jim Bevel, and his other friends in the Nashville movement. Earlier in the weekend, Nashville's civil rights leaders had received word that the city's white theater owners had agreed to desegregate. For fourteen weeks the Nashville movement had applied almost constant pressure in the form of stand-ins and picketing campaigns, vowing to continue the protests until every black activist in the city was in jail if necessary. The theater owners' surrender represented a great victory, and movement leaders planned to celebrate their triumph with a "big picnic" on Sunday afternoon. Against all odds, Lewis was there to help his friends celebrate, but not even a victory of this magnitude could take his mind off his fellow Freedom Riders for very long. "The Freedom Ride," he later confessed, "was once again all I was thinking about."

Although Lewis did not know it at the time, he was not the only person fixated on the Freedom Ride. While he was in Nashville, the leaders of the Alabama Knights of the Ku Klux Klan were finalizing plans of their own. The Klansmen had known about the Freedom Ride since mid-April, thanks to a series of FBI memos forwarded to the Birmingham Police Department. Police Sergeant Tom Cook—an avid Klan supporter and anti-Communist zealot who worked closely with Eugene "Bull" Connor, Birmingham's ultra-segregationist sixty-three-year-old commissioner of public safety—provided the organization with detailed information on the Ride, including a city-by-city itinerary.

On April 17, more than two weeks before the Freedom Ride began, Sergeant Cook met with Gary Thomas Rowe, a member of the Eastview Klavern 13, the most violent Klan enclave in Alabama. W. W. "Red" Self, a police detective and Eastview collaborator who had befriended Rowe while moonlighting as a bouncer at a local VFW hall, arranged the meeting. A rough-edged, loud-talking bully from Savannah, Georgia, Rowe was a dairy worker whose fixation with guns and power sometimes led him to pose as a police officer. Unbeknownst to Cook and Self, Rowe also happened to be an FBI informer, having been recruited by Special Agent Barrett Kemp in April 1960. Unaware that Rowe planned to relay his words to the Birmingham FBI office, Cook laid out an elaborate plot to bring the Freedom Ride to a halt in Birmingham. He assured Rowe that other members of the Birmingham Police Department, as well as officials of the Alabama Highway Patrol, were privy to the plan and could be counted on to cooperate. "You will work with me, and I will work with you on the Freedom Riders," he promised. "We're going to allow you fifteen minutes . . . You can beat 'em, bomb 'em, maim 'em, kill 'em. I don't give a shit. There will be absolutely no arrests. You can assure every Klansman in the country that no one will be arrested in Alabama for that fifteen minutes."

On Thursday night, May 4, while the Freedom Riders were at Virginia Union in Richmond, several Alabama klaverns conducted closed discussions of the Freedom Riders. At the Warrior klavern meeting, an FBI informant learned that when the Riders headed west out of Atlanta, they would be accompanied by "three unidentified Klansmen." At the meeting of the Eastview Klavern 13, which Rowe attended, Grand Titan Hubert Page placed local Klan leaders on special alert in preparation for the Freedom Riders' arrival. Rowe promptly relayed all of this to the FBI, including Page's comment that "the best way to handle the situation was to get all of the CORE representatives out of Alabama, as soon as possible." The FBI informer also told the Birmingham field office that Imperial Wizard Bobby Shelton had drafted a press release claiming that "it was up to the constituted authorities of Alabama to stop any demonstrations by CORE, but if state authorities did not do their duty, the Alabama Knights, KKK, Inc. would do all they could to force the CORE representatives to leave Alabama."

On May 5 the Birmingham field office wired a summary of Rowe's assessment of Shelton's plans to FBI Director J. Edgar Hoover, who forwarded some, though apparently not all, of this information to Attorney General Kennedy, Deputy Attorney General Byron White, and other Justice Department officials four days later. The field office also sent word of the plot to Birmingham police chief Jamie Moore, even though they suspected that Moore was a Klan sympathizer who already knew more about the plot than they did. However, as the circle of informed parties widened, no one said a word to the Freedom Riders themselves.

On Thursday, May 11, Rowe attended a meeting in Birmingham during which Klan leaders assigned individual duties and responsibilities and advised their troops "to bring ball bats and clubs with them to greet the Freedom Riders." The next day the Eastview klavern entertained Bobby Shelton, who presided over a special meeting of Klan leaders—including Page and Eastview's Exalted Cyclops, Robert Thomas, one of Alabama's most rabid white supremacists. Though excited by the prospect of a bloodletting, Shelton insisted that the Birmingham assault force would be limited to sixty handpicked men, thirty assigned to the bus depots and thirty waiting in reserve at a nearby hotel. This limitation disappointed some members of the Eastview klavern who were afraid that they would miss out on the chance of a lifetime, but Page and Thomas had no choice but to obey Shelton's order. With this taken care of, Shelton and the Alabama Klan's board of directors held a Saturday meeting in Tuscaloosa, where they ratified the plot to attack the "outside agitators" from CORE.

The final plan, which resembled a full-scale military operation, called for an initial assault in Anniston, the Riders' first scheduled stop in Alabama, followed by a mop-up action in Birmingham. As an FBI informant reported to the Birmingham field office, the Anniston klavern was responsible for blocking the Riders' access to the local bus stations; but Birmingham Klansmen, working in conjunction with Connor and Cook, were calling most of the shots. Led by Kenneth Adams, a notorious bigot who had ordered the beating of black singer Nat King Cole at the Birmingham Municipal Auditorium in 1956, the Anniston klavern did not belong to Shelton's Alabama Knights, KKK confederation. But Adams and his boys needed little encouragement when Shelton asked them to help out with the welcoming party. No one in Birmingham trusted Adams; and on Friday, the day before the Tuscaloosa meeting, Connor dispatched Cook to Anniston to make sure that everything was in order. From there Cook went on to Atlanta to survey the bus stations where the unsuspecting Freedom Riders were scheduled to arrive the following afternoon.

Connor, of course, was primarily concerned with what was about to happen in his own city, and he left few details unattended as the hour of the Freedom Riders' arrival approached. "If the Negroes go into the restaurant of the depot," he told a Klan contact, "the Klansmen should start an incident of some sort, such as a Klansman pouring coffee on himself and blaming it on the Negro, thus starting a fight. Also, if the Negroes attempt to use the restroom in the depot, Klansmen are to beat them in the restroom and 'make them look like a bulldog got a hold of them'; then remove the clothing of the victim and carry the clothing away. If the nude individual attempts to leave the restroom, he will be immediately arrested and it will be seen that this person is sent to the penitentiary." This particular bit of advice did not merit much attention, since neither Connor nor the Klan had any intention of allowing the Freedom Riders to see the inside of an Alabama bus station, or at least not for very long. Mother's Day or not, the loyal sons of Alabama would show their weak sisters in Virginia, Georgia, and the Carolinas how to deal with outside agitators who challenged the Southern way of life. If the Klansmen did their duty on Sunday afternoon, the Freedom Riders and others would be forced to recognize the power and passion of men who regarded massive resistance as something more than idle talk.

4

Alabama Bound

We had most trouble, it turned into a struggle,
Half way 'cross Alabam,
And that 'hound broke down, and left us all stranded,
In downtown Birmingham.
—Chuck Berry

Jim Farmer's unexpected departure placed a heavy burden on Jim Peck, who suddenly found himself in charge of the Freedom Ride. As Farmer left for the Atlanta airport, Peck could not help wondering if he would ever see his old friend again. They had been through a lot together—surviving the depths of the Cold War and CORE's lean years. Now, Peck had to go on alone, perhaps to glory, but more likely to an untimely rendezvous with violence, or even death. When Peck phoned Fred Shuttlesworth, the outspoken pastor of Birmingham's Bethel Baptist Church and the leader of the Alabama Christian Movement for Human Rights, to give him the exact arrival times of the two "Freedom Buses," the normally unflappable minister offered an alarming picture of what the Freedom Riders could expect once they reached Birmingham. The city was alive with rumors that a white mob planned to greet the Riders at the downtown bus stations. Shuttlesworth was not privy to FBI surveillance and did not know any of the details, but he urged Peck to be careful. Peck, trying to avoid a last-minute panic, calmly relayed Shuttlesworth's warning to the group. He also repeated Tom Gaither's warning about Anniston, a rest stop on the bus route to Birmingham.

Faced with staggered bus schedules, the two groups of Freedom Riders left Atlanta an hour apart. The Greyhound group, with Joe Perkins in charge, was the first to leave, at 11 a.m. Fourteen passengers were on board: five regular passengers, seven Freedom Riders—Genevieve Hughes, Bert Bigelow, Hank Thomas,

Jimmy McDonald, Mae Frances Moultrie, Joe Perkins, Ed Blankenheim—and two journalists, Charlotte Devree and Moses Newson. Among the "regular" passengers were Roy Robinson, the manager of the Atlanta Greyhound station, and two undercover plainclothes agents of the Alabama Highway Patrol, Corporals Ell Cowling and Harry Sims. Both Cowling and Sims sat in the back of the bus, several rows behind the scattered Freedom Riders, who had no inkling of who these two seemingly innocuous white men actually were. Following the orders of Floyd Mann, the director of the Alabama Highway Patrol, Cowling carried a hidden microphone designed to eavesdrop on the Riders.

During the ninety-minute trip to Tallapoosa, the last stop in Georgia, on Highway 78, none of the passengers said very much. Around 1 p.m. the bus crossed the Alabama line and followed the road in a southwesterly arc to Heflin, a small country town on the edge of the Talladega National Forest. After a brief rest stop in Heflin, the Greyhound continued west through De Armanville and Oxford before turning north on Highway 21 toward Anniston. The largest city in Calhoun County and the second largest in east-central Alabama, Anniston was a no-nonsense army town that depended on nearby Fort McClellan and a sprawling ordnance depot for much of its livelihood. Known for its hard-edged race relations, Anniston boasted a relatively large black population (approximately 30 percent in 1961), a well-established NAACP branch, and some of the most aggressive and violent Klansmen in Alabama.

Just south of Anniston, the driver of a southbound Greyhound motioned to the driver of the Freedom Riders' bus, O. T. Jones, to pull over to the side of the road. A white man then ran across the road and yelled to Jones through the window: "There's an angry and unruly crowd gathered at Anniston. There's a rumor that some people on this bus are going to stage a sit-in. The terminal has been closed. Be careful." With this message the Riders' worst fears seemed to be confirmed, but Joe Perkins—hoping that the warning was a bluff, or at least an exaggeration—urged the driver to keep going. A minute or two later, as the bus passed the city limits, several of the Riders couldn't help but notice that Anniston's sidewalks were lined with people, an unusual sight on a Sunday afternoon in a Deep South town. "It seemed that everyone in the town was out to greet us," Genevieve Hughes later commented.

Hank Thomas did not recall seeing anyone on the streets, but he did remember the strange feeling that he and the other Riders experienced as the bus eased into the station parking lot just after 1 p.m. The station was locked shut, and there was silence—and then suddenly, as if out of nowhere, a screaming mob led by Anniston Klan leader William Chappell rushed the bus. As the crowd of about fifty surrounded the bus, an eighteen-year-old Klansman and ex-convict named Roger Couch stretched out on the pavement in front of the bus to block any attempt to leave, while the rest—carrying metal pipes, clubs, and chains—milled around menacingly, some screaming, "Dirty Communists" and "*Sieg heil!*"

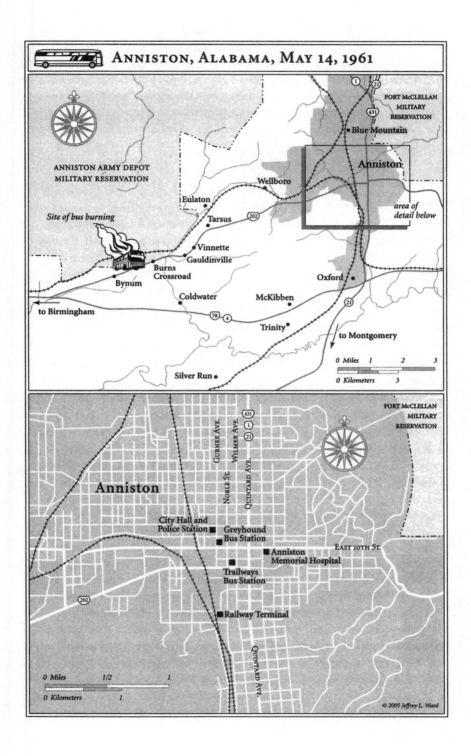

There was no sign of any police, even though Herman Glass, the manager of the Anniston Greyhound station, had warned local officials earlier in the day that a potentially violent mob had gathered around the station. After the driver opened the door, Cowling and Sims hurried to the front to prevent anyone from entering. Leaning on the door lever, the two unarmed investigators managed to close the door and seal the bus, but they could not stop several of the most frenzied attackers from smashing windows, denting the sides of the bus, and slashing tires. "One man stood on the steps, yelling, and calling us cowards," Hughes noticed, but her attention soon turned to a second man who "walked by the side of the bus, slipped a pistol from his pocket and stared at me for some minutes." When she heard a loud noise and shattering glass, she yelled, "Duck, down everyone," thinking that a bullet had hit one of the windows. The projectile turned out to be a rock, but another assailant soon cracked the window above her seat with a fist full of brass knuckles. Joe Perkins's window later suffered a similar fate, as the siege continued for almost twenty minutes. By the time the Anniston police arrived on the scene, the bus looked like it had been in a serious collision. Swaggering through the crowd with billy clubs in hand, the police officers examined the broken windows and slashed tires but showed no interest in arresting anyone. After a few minutes of friendly banter with members of the crowd, the officers suddenly cleared a path and motioned for the bus to exit the parking lot.

A police car escorted the battered Greyhound to the city limits but then turned back, once again leaving the bus to the mercy of the mob. A long line of cars and pickup trucks, plus one car carrying a news reporter and a photographer, had followed the police escort from the station and was ready to resume the assault. Once the entourage reached an isolated stretch of Highway 202 east of Bynum, two of the cars (one of which was driven by Roger Couch's older brother Jerome) raced around the front of the bus and then slowed to a crawl, forcing the bus driver to slow down. Trailing behind were thirty or forty cars and trucks jammed with shrieking whites. Many, like Chappell and the Couches, were Klansmen, though none wore hoods or robes. Some, having just come from church, were dressed in their Sunday best—coats and ties and polished shoes—and a few even had children with them.

The whole scene was darkly surreal and became even more so when a pair of flat tires forced the bus driver to pull over to the side of the road in front of the Forsyth and Son grocery store six miles southwest of town, only a few hundred yards from the Anniston Army Depot. Flinging open the door, the driver, with Robinson trailing close behind, ran into the grocery store and began calling local garages in what turned out to be a futile effort to find replacement tires for the bus. In the meantime, the passengers were left vulnerable to a swarm of onrushing vigilantes. Cowling had just enough time to retrieve his revolver from the baggage compartment before the mob surrounded the bus. The first to reach the Greyhound was a teenage boy who smashed a crowbar through one of the side windows. While one group of men and boys rocked the bus in a vain attempt to turn the vehicle on its side, a second tried to enter through the front door. With gun in hand, Cowling stood in the doorway to block the intruders, but he soon retreated, locking the door behind him. For the next twenty minutes Chappell and other Klansmen pounded on the bus demanding that the Freedom Riders come out to take what was coming to them, but they stayed in their seats, even after the arrival of two highway patrolmen. When neither patrolman made any effort to disperse the crowd, Cowling, Sims, and the Riders decided to stay put.

Eventually, however, two members of the mob, Roger Couch and Cecil "Goober" Lewallyn, decided that they had waited long enough. After returning to his car, which was parked a few yards behind the disabled Greyhound, Lewallyn suddenly ran toward the bus and tossed a flaming bundle of rags through a broken window. Within seconds the bundle exploded, sending dark gray smoke throughout the bus. At first, Genevieve Hughes, seated only a few feet away from the explosion, thought the bomb-thrower was just trying to scare the Freedom Riders with a smoke bomb, but as the smoke got blacker and blacker and as flames began to engulf several of the upholstered seats, she realized that she and the other passengers were in serious trouble. Crouching down in the middle of the bus, she screamed out, "Is there any air up front?" When no one answered, she began to panic. "Oh, my God, they're going to burn us up!" she yelled to the others, who were lost in a dense cloud of smoke. Making her way forward, she finally found an open window six rows from the front and thrust her head out, gasping for air. As she looked out, she saw the outstretched necks of Jimmy McDonald and Charlotte Devree, who had also found open windows. Seconds later, all three squeezed through the windows and dropped to the ground. Still choking from the smoke and fumes, they staggered across the street. Gazing back at the burning bus, they feared that the other passengers were still trapped inside, but they soon caught sight of several passengers who had escaped through the front door on the other side.

They were all lucky to be alive. Several members of the mob had pressed against the door screaming, "Burn them alive" and "Fry the goddamn niggers," and the Freedom Riders had been all but doomed until an exploding fuel tank convinced the mob that the whole bus was about to explode. As the frightened whites retreated, Cowling pried open the door, allowing the rest of the choking passengers to escape. When Hank Thomas, the first Rider to exit the front of the bus, crawled away from the doorway, a white man rushed toward him and asked, "Are you all OK?" Before Thomas could answer, the man's concerned look turned into a sneer as he struck the astonished student in the head with a baseball bat. Thomas fell to the ground and was barely conscious as the rest of the exiting Riders spilled out onto the grass.

By this time, several of the white families living in the surrounding Bynum neighborhood had formed a small crowd in front of the grocery store. Most of the onlookers remained safely in the background, but a few stepped forward to offer assistance to the Riders. One little girl, twelve-year-old Janie Forsyth, supplied the choking victims with water, filling and refilling a five-gallon bucket while braving the insults and taunts of Klansmen. Later ostracized and threatened for this act of kindness, she and her family found it impossible to remain in Anniston in the aftermath of the bus bombing. Even though city leaders were quick to condemn the bombing, there was little sympathy for the Riders among local whites. Indeed, while Forsyth was coming to the Riders' aid, some of her neighbors were urging the marauding Klansmen on.

At one point, with the Riders lying "on the ground around the bus, coughing and bleeding," the mob surged forward. But Cowling's pistol, the heat of the fire, and the acrid fumes wafting from the burning upholstery kept them away. Moments later a second fuel tank explosion drove them back even farther, and eventually a couple of warning shots fired into the air by the highway patrolmen on the scene signaled that the would-be lynching party was over. As the disappointed vigilantes slipped away, Cowling, Sims, and the patrolmen stood guard over the Riders, most of whom were lying or sitting in a daze a few yards from the burned-out shell of the bus. But no one in a position of authority showed any interest in identifying or arresting those responsible for the assault. No one wrote down the license numbers of the Klansmen's cars and pickup trucks, and no one seemed in any hurry to call an ambulance.

Several of the Riders had inhaled smoke and fumes and were in serious need of medical attention, but it would be some time before any of them saw a doctor. One sympathetic white couple who lived nearby allowed Hughes to use their phone to call for an ambulance, and when no one answered, they drove her to the hospital. For the rest of the stricken Riders, getting to the hospital proved to be a bit more complicated. When the ambulance called by one of the state troopers finally arrived, the driver refused to transport any of the injured black Riders. After a few moments of awkward silence, the white Riders, already loaded into the ambulance, began to exit, insisting they could not leave their black friends behind. With this gesture—and a few stern words from Cowling—the driver's resolve weakened, and before long the integrated band was on its way to Anniston Memorial Hospital.

Unfortunately, the scene at the hospital offered the Riders little solace. The first to arrive, Hughes found the medical care in Anniston almost as frightening as the burning bus:

> There was no doctor at the hospital, only a nurse. They had me breathe pure oxygen but that only burned my throat and did not relieve the coughing. I was burning hot and my clothes were a wet mess. After awhile Ed and Bert were brought in, choking. We all lay on our beds and

coughed. Finally a woman doctor came in—she had to look up smoke poisoning before treating us. They brought in the Negro man who had been in the back of the bus with me. I pointed to him and told them to take care of him. But they did not bring him into our emergency room. I understand that they did not do anything at all for Hank. Thirteen in all were brought in, and three were admitted: Ed, the Negro man, and myself. They gave me a room, and I slept. When I woke up the nurse asked me if I could talk with the FBI. The FBI man did not care about us, but only the bombing.

Hughes's general distrust of the FBI's attitude toward civil rights activists was clearly warranted, but—unbeknownst to her—the FBI agent on the scene had actually intervened on the Freedom Riders' behalf. At his urging, the medical staff agreed to treat all of the injured passengers, black and white, though in the end they failed to do so. When the ambulance full of Freedom Riders arrived at the hospital, a group of Klansmen made an unsuccessful attempt to block the entrance to the emergency room. Later, as the crowd outside the hospital grew to menacing proportions, hospital officials began to panic, especially after several Klansmen threatened to burn the building to the ground. With nightfall approaching and with no prospect of adequate police protection, the superintendent ordered the Riders to leave the hospital as soon as possible.

Hughes and several other Riders were in no shape to leave, but Joe Perkins, the leader of the Greyhound group, had no choice but to comply with the evacuation order. Struggling to conceal his rage, he told the Riders to be ready to leave in twenty minutes, though it actually took him well over an hour to arrange safe passage out of the hospital. After both the state troopers and the local police refused to provide the Riders with transportation—or even an escort—Bert Bigelow called friends in Washington in a vain effort to get help from the federal government. A few minutes later Perkins placed a frantic call to Fred Shuttlesworth in Birmingham. A native of the Alabama Black Belt, Shuttlesworth knew enough about towns like Anniston to know that the Freedom Riders were in serious danger. Mobilizing a fleet of eight cars, he planned to lead the rescue mission himself until his longtime bodyguard, Colonel Stone "Buck" Johnson, persuaded him to remain in Birmingham with the Trailways Riders, who had arrived in the city earlier in the afternoon. Just before the cars left for Anniston, Shuttlesworth reminded Johnson and the other volunteers that this was a nonviolent operation. "Gentlemen, this is dangerous," he admitted, "but . . . you mustn't carry any weapons. You must trust God and have faith." All of the "deacons" nodded in assent, but as soon as they were safely out of sight, several of the faithful pulled out shotguns from beneath their seats. Checking triggers and ammunition, they made sure they would be able to defend themselves if the going got rough.

While the Riders waited for Shuttlesworth's deacons to make their way across the back roads of the Alabama hill country, the Anniston hospital superintendent grew impatient and reminded Perkins that the interracial group would not be allowed to spend the night in the hospital. Perhaps, he suggested with a wry smile, they could find refuge in the bus station. Fortunately, the superintendent's mean-spirited suggestion became moot a few minutes later when the rescue mission pulled into the hospital parking lot. With the police holding back the jeering crowd, and with the deacons openly displaying their weapons, the weary but relieved Riders piled into the cars, which promptly drove off into the gathering dusk. "We walked right between those Ku Klux," Buck Johnson later recalled. "Some of them had clubs. There were some deputies too. You couldn't tell the deputies from the Ku Klux."

As the convoy raced toward Birmingham, the Riders peppered their rescuers with questions about the fate of the Trailways group. Perkins's conversation with Shuttlesworth earlier in the afternoon had revealed that the other bus had also run into trouble, but few details had been available. The deacons themselves knew only part of the story, but even the barest outline was enough to confirm the Riders' worst fears: The attack on the bus in Anniston could not be dismissed as the work of an unorganized mob. As the deacons described what had happened to the Trailways group, the true nature of the Riders' predicament came into focus: With the apparent connivance of law enforcement officials, the organized defenders of white supremacy in Alabama had decided to smash the Freedom Ride with violence, in effect announcing to the world that they had no intention of letting the law, the U.S. Constitution, or anything else interfere with the preservation of racial segregation in their sovereign state.

The Trailways Riders' ordeal began even before the group left Atlanta. As Peck and the other Riders waited in line to purchase their tickets, they couldn't help noticing that several regular passengers had disappeared from the line after being approached by a group of white men. The white men themselves—later identified as Alabama Klansmen—eventually boarded the bus, but only a handful of other regular passengers joined them. The Klansmen were beefy, rough-looking characters, mostly in their twenties or thirties, and their hulking presence gave the Riders an uneasy feeling as the bus pulled out. There were seven Freedom Riders scattered throughout the bus: the Bergmans, Jim Peck, Charles Person, Herman Harris, Jerry Moore, and Ike Reynolds. Simeon Booker and his *Jet* magazine colleague, photographer Ted Gaffney, were also on board. Seated in the rear of the bus, the two journalists had a close-up view of the entire harrowing journey from Atlanta to Birmingham. "It was a frightening experience," Booker later reported, "the worst encountered in almost 20 years of journalism."

He was not exaggerating. The bus was barely out of the Atlanta terminal when the Klansmen began to make threatening remarks. "You niggers will be taken care of once you get in Alabama," one Klansman sneered. Once the bus passed the state line, the comments intensified, giving the Riders the distinct impression that something might be brewing in Anniston. Arriving at the Anniston Trailways station approximately an hour after the other Riders had pulled into the Greyhound station, Peck and the Trailways Riders looked around warily before leaving the bus. The waiting room was eerily quiet, and several whites looked away as the unwelcome visitors walked up to the lunch counter. After purchasing a few sandwiches, the Riders walked back to the bus. Later, while waiting nervously to leave, they heard an ambulance siren but didn't think much of it until the bus driver, John Olan Patterson, who had been talking to several Anniston police officers, vaulted up the steps. Flanked by eight "hoodlums," as Peck later called them, Patterson gave them the news about the Greyhound riot. "We have received word that a bus has been burned to the ground and passengers are being carried to the hospital by the carloads," he declared, with no hint of compassion or regret. "A mob is waiting for our bus and will do the same to us unless we get these niggers off the front seats." His bus wasn't going anywhere until the black Freedom Riders retreated to the back of the bus where they belonged.

After a few moments of silence, one of the Riders reminded Patterson that they were interstate passengers who had the right to sit wherever they pleased. Shaking his head in disgust, he exited the bus without a word. But one of the white "hoodlums" soon answered for him: "Niggers get back. You ain't up north. You're in Alabama, and niggers ain't nothing here." To prove his point, he suddenly lunged toward Person, punching him in the face. A second Klansman then struck Harris, who was sitting next to Person in the front section of the bus. Both black Freedom Riders adhered to Gandhian discipline and refused to fight back, but this only encouraged their attackers. Dragging the defenseless students into the aisle, the Klansmen started pummeling them with their fists and kicking them again and again. At this point Peck and Walter Bergman rushed forward from the back to object. As soon as Peck reached the front, one of the attackers turned on him, striking a blow that sent the frail, middle-aged activist reeling across two rows of seats. Within seconds Bergman, the oldest of the Freedom Riders at sixty-one, suffered a similar blow, falling to the floor with a thud. As blood spurted from their faces, both men tried to shield themselves from further attack, but the Klansmen, enraged by the white Riders' attempt to protect their "nigger" collaborators, proceeded to pound them into a bloody mass. While a pair of Klansmen lifted Peck's head, others punched him in the face until he lost consciousness. By this time Bergman was out cold on the floor, but one frenzied assailant continued to stomp on his chest. When Frances Bergman begged the Klansman to stop beating her husband, he ignored her plea and called her a "nigger lover." Fortunately, one of the other Klansmen—realizing that the defenseless Freedom Rider was about to be killed—eventually called a halt to the beating. "Don't kill him," he said coolly, making sure that no one on the bus mistook self-interested restraint for compassion.

Although Walter Bergman's motionless body blocked the aisle, several Klansmen managed to drag Person and Harris, both barely conscious, to the back of the bus, draping them over the passengers sitting in the backseat. A few seconds later, they did the same to Peck and Bergman, creating a pile of bleeding and bruised humanity that left the rest of the passengers in a momentary state of shock. Content with their brutal handiwork, the Klansmen then sat down in the middle of the bus to block any further attempts to violate the color line. At this point a black woman riding as a regular passenger begged to be let off the bus, but the Klansmen forced her to stay. "Shut up, you black bitch," one of them snarled. "Ain't nobody but whites sitting up here. And them nigger lovers . . . can just sit back there with their nigger friends."

Moments later, Patterson, who had left during the melee, returned to the bus, accompanied by a police officer. After surveying the scene, both men appeared satisfied with the restoration of Jim Crow seating arrangements. Turning toward the Klansmen, the police officer grinned and assured them that Alabama justice was on their side: "Don't worry about no lawsuits. I ain't seen a thing." The officer then exited the bus and motioned to Patterson to head out onto the highway. Realizing that there was a mob waiting on the main road to Birmingham, the driver kept to the back roads as he headed west. When none of the Klansmen objected to this detour, the Freedom Riders were puzzled but relieved, thinking that perhaps there were limits to the savagery of the segregationists after all, even in the wilds of eastern Alabama. What they did not know, of course, was that the Klansmen were simply saving them for the welcoming party already gathering in the shadows of downtown Birmingham.

During the next two hours, as the bus rolled toward Birmingham, the Klansmen continued to taunt and torment the Riders. One man brandished a pistol, a second threatened the Riders with a steel pipe, and three others served as "sentries," blocking access to the middle and front sections of the bus. As Booker recalled the scene, one of the sentries was "a pop-eyed fellow who kept taunting: 'Just tell Bobby [Kennedy] and we'll do him in, too.'" When one of the Klansmen approached Booker threateningly, the journalist nervously handed him a copy of *Jet* that featured an advance story on CORE's sponsorship of the Freedom Ride. Over the next few minutes, as the article was passed from Klansman to Klansman, the atmosphere became increasingly tense. "I'd like to choke all of them," one Klansman confessed, while others assured the Riders that they would get what was coming to them when they arrived in Birmingham. By the time the bus reached the outskirts of the city, Peck and the other injured Riders had regained consciousness, but since the Klansmen would not allow any of the Riders to leave their seats or talk among themselves, there was no opportunity for Peck to prepare the group for the impending onslaught.

Though battered and bleeding, and barely able to walk, Peck was determined to set an example for his fellow Freedom Riders. As the designated testers at the Birmingham stop, he and Person would be the first to confront the fully assembled power of Alabama segregationists. The terror-filled ride from Atlanta was a clear indication that they could expect some measure of violence in Birmingham, but at this point Peck and the other Trailways Riders had no detailed knowledge of what had happened to the Greyhound group in Anniston two hours earlier. They thought they were prepared for the worst. In actuality, however, they had no reliable way of gauging what they were up against, no way of appreciating the full implications of challenging Alabama's segregationist institutions, and no inkling of how far Birmingham's ultra-segregationists would go to protect the sanctity of Jim Crow. This was not just the Deep South—it was Birmingham, where close collaboration between the Ku Klux Klan and law enforcement officials was a fact of life. The special agents in the Birmingham FBI field office, as well as their superiors in Washington, possessed detailed information on this collaboration and could have warned the Freedom Riders. But they chose to remain silent.

The dire consequences of the bureau's refusal to intervene were compounded by the active involvement of FBI informant Gary Thomas Rowe. In the final minutes before the Trailways group's arrival, Rowe helped ensure that the plot to "welcome" the Freedom Riders would actually be carried out. The plan called for Rowe and the other Klansmen to initiate the attack at the Greyhound station, where the first group of Freedom Riders was expected to arrive, but news of the Anniston bombing did not reach Birmingham until midafternoon, just minutes before the arrival of the Trailways bus. A frantic call from police headquarters to Rowe, who quickly spread the word, alerted the Klansmen waiting near the Greyhound station that a bus of Freedom Riders was about to arrive at the Trailways station, three blocks away. The "welcoming committee" had just enough time to regroup at the Trailways station. Years later Rowe recalled the mad rush across downtown Birmingham: "We made an astounding sight . . . men running and walking down the streets of Birmingham on Sunday afternoon carrying chains, sticks, and clubs. Everything was deserted; no police officers were to be seen except one on a street corner. He stepped off and let us go by, and we barged into the bus station and took it over like an army of occupation. There were Klansmen in the waiting room, in the rest rooms, in the parking area."

By the time Peck and company arrived, the Klansmen and their police allies were all in place, armed and ready. Police dispatchers, following the agreed-upon plan, had cleared the "target" area: For the next fifteen minutes there would be

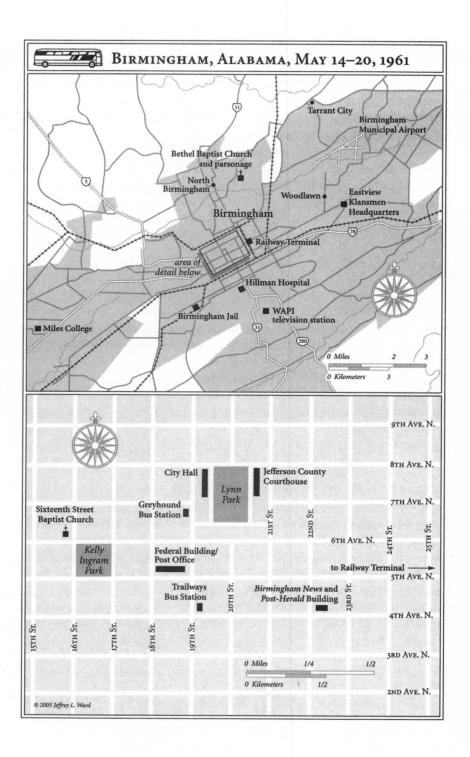

BIRMINGHAM, ALABAMA, MAY 14–20, 1961

Tarrant City

Birmingham Municipal Airport

Bethel Baptist Church and parsonage

North Birmingham

Woodlawn

Eastview Klansmen Headquarters

Birmingham

Railway Terminal

area of detail below

Hillman Hospital

Miles College

Birmingham Jail

WAPI television station

0 Miles 2 3

0 Kilometers 3

9TH AVE. N.

8TH AVE. N.

City Hall

Lynn Park

Jefferson County Courthouse

7TH AVE. N.

Sixteenth Street Baptist Church

Greyhound Bus Station

21ST ST.

22ND ST.

24TH ST.

25TH ST.

6TH AVE. N.

Kelly Ingram Park

Federal Building/ Post Office

to Railway Terminal

5TH AVE. N.

Trailways Bus Station

20TH ST.

Birmingham News and *Post-Herald* Building

23RD ST.

4TH AVE. N.

15TH ST.

16TH ST.

17TH ST.

18TH ST.

19TH ST.

3RD AVE. N.

0 Miles 1/4 1/2

0 Kilometers 1/2

2ND AVE. N.

© 2005 Jeffrey L. Ward

no police presence in or near the Trailways station. The only exceptions were two plainclothes detectives who were in the crowd to monitor the situation and to make sure that the Klansmen left the station before the police arrived. Since it was Sunday, and Mother's Day, there were few bystanders, aside from a handful of news reporters who had been tipped off that something big was about to happen at the Trailways station. Despite the semisecret nature of the operation, the organizers could not resist the temptation to let the outside world catch a glimpse of Alabama manhood in action.

One of the reporters on hand was Howard K. Smith, a national correspondent for CBS News who was in Birmingham working on a television documentary titled *Who Speaks for Birmingham?* Smith and his CBS colleagues were investigating *New York Times* columnist Harrison Salisbury's charges that Alabama's largest city was consumed by lawlessness and racial oppression. "Every channel of communication, every medium of mutual interest, every reasoned approach, every inch of middle ground," wrote Salisbury in April 1960, "has been fragmented by the emotional dynamite of racism, reinforced by the whip, the razor, the gun, the bomb, the torch, the club, the knife, the mob, the police and many branches of the state's apparatus." After several days of interviews, Smith was still trying to decide if Salisbury's claims were exaggerated. A Louisiana native with considerable experience in the Deep South, Smith was more than intrigued when he received a Saturday night call from Dr. Edward R. Fields, the president of the ultra-conservative National States Rights Party (NSRP), an organization known to promote a virulent strain of white supremacist and anti-Semitic extremism. Identifying himself simply as "Fields," the arch segregationist urged Smith to hang around the downtown bus stations "if he wanted to see some real action."

A gun-toting Birmingham chiropractor with close ties to the infamous Georgia extremist J. B. Stoner, Fields himself had every intention of taking part in the action. Along with Stoner, who had driven over from Atlanta for the occasion, and several other NSRP stalwarts, Fields showed up at the Greyhound station on Sunday afternoon armed and ready for the bloodletting—even though Klan leader Hubert Page warned him to stay away. Page and his police accomplices were having enough trouble controlling their own forces without having to worry about Fields and his crew of professional troublemakers. With Police Chief Jamie Moore out of the city and Connor lying low in an effort to distance himself from the impending violence, Detective Tom Cook was in charge of the operation, but Cook did not share Page's concern. When Rowe called Cook to complain that the NSRP was complicating the Klan's plans, the detective told him to relax. "You boys should work together," Cook suggested.

Connor was probably the only man in Birmingham with the power to call the whole thing off. But he was not about to do so. Resisting the entreaties of several friends, including his Methodist pastor, John Rutland, who warned him that joining forces with the Klan was a big mistake, he cast his lot with the extremists. He knew that the welcoming party might backfire—that it could complicate the mayoral campaign of his political ally Art Hanes, that Birmingham might even become a second Little Rock, a city besieged by federal troops—but he simply could not bring himself to let the Freedom Riders off the hook. He had been waiting too long for an opportunity to confront the Yankee agitators on his own turf.

At 4:15 on Sunday afternoon, Connor got all the blood he wanted—and then some. As soon as the bus pulled into the Trailways terminal, the Klansmen on board raced down the aisle to be near the front door. Following a few parting taunts—one man screamed, "You damn Communists, why don't you go back to Russia. You're a shame to the white race"—they hustled down the steps and disappeared into the crowd. They had done their job; the rest was up to their Klan brethren, several of whom were waiting expectantly in front of the terminal. The Klansmen's hurried exit was a bit unnerving, but as Peck and the other Freedom Riders peered out at the crowd there was no sign of any weapons.

One by one, the Riders filed off the bus and onto the unloading platform, where they began to retrieve their luggage. Although there were several rough-looking men standing a few feet from the platform, there was no clear indication that an attack was imminent. After a few moments of hesitation, Peck and Person walked toward the white waiting room to begin testing the terminal's facilities. In his 1962 memoir, Peck recalled the intensity of the scene, especially his concern for the safety of his black colleague. "I did not want to put Person in a position of being forced to proceed if he thought the situation was too dangerous," he remembered, but "when I looked at him, he responded by saying simply, 'Let's go.'" This bravery was not born of ignorance: Person had grown up in the Deep South; he had recently served sixteen days in jail for his part in the Atlanta sit-ins, and he had already been beaten up earlier in the day. Nevertheless, neither he nor Peck was fully prepared for what was about to happen.

Moments after the two Freedom Riders entered the waiting room and approached the whites-only lunch counter, one of the waiting Klansmen pointed to the cuts on Peck's face and the caked blood on his shirt and screamed out that Person, who was walking in front of Peck, deserved to die for attacking a white man. At this point, Peck tried to explain that Person was not the man who had attacked him, adding: "You'll have to kill me before you hurt him." This blatant breach of racial solidarity only served to incite the crowd of Klansmen blocking their path. After an Eastview Klansman named Gene Reeves pushed Person toward the colored waiting room, the young black Freedom Rider gamely continued walking toward the white lunch counter but was unable to sidestep a second Klansman who shoved him up against a concrete wall. Standing nearby, NSRP leader Edward Fields pointed toward Peck and yelled: "Get that son of a bitch." Several burly white men then began to pummel Person with their fists, bloodying his face and mouth and dropping him to his knees. When Peck rushed over to help Person to his feet, several Klansmen grabbed both men by the shoulders and pushed them into a dimly lit corridor leading to a loading platform. In the corridor more than a dozen whites, some armed with lead or iron pipes and others with oversized key rings, pounced on the two Riders, punching and kicking them repeatedly. Before long, the assault turned into a chaotic free-for-all with "fists and arms . . . flying everywhere." In the ensuing confusion, Person managed to escape. Running into the street, he staggered onto a city bus and eventually found his way to Fred Shuttlesworth's parsonage. In the meantime Peck bore the brunt of the attack, eventually losing consciousness and slumping to the floor in a pool of blood.

The fracas had been moved to the back corridor in an effort to avoid the reporters and news photographers roaming the white waiting room, but several newsmen, including Howard K. Smith, witnessed at least part of the attack. Smith, who had only been in Birmingham for a few days, could hardly believe his eyes as the rampaging Klansmen and NSRP "storm troopers" swarmed over the two Freedom Riders. But he soon discovered that this was only the beginning of one of the bloodiest afternoons in Birmingham's history.

While Peck and Person were being assaulted in the corridor, the other Riders searched for a refuge. Jerry Moore and Herman Harris avoided detection by losing themselves in the crowd and slipping away just before the assaults began. Frances Bergman, at her husband's insistence, boarded a city bus moments after their arrival, but Walter himself was unable to escape the mob's fury. Still woozy from his earlier beating, with blood still caked on his clothing, he bravely followed Peck and Person into the white waiting room. After witnessing the initial assault on his two colleagues, he searched in vain for a policeman who could help them, but soon he too was knocked to the floor by an enraged Klansman. When Simeon Booker entered the terminal a few seconds later, he saw the bloodied and defenseless professor crawling on his hands and knees. Recoiling from the grisly scene, Booker retreated to the street, where he found a black cabdriver who agreed to whisk him and Ted Gaffney away to safety.

Others were less fortunate. Several white men attacked Ike Reynolds, kicking and stomping him before heaving his semiconscious body into a curbside trash bin. In the confusion, the mob also attacked a number of bystanders misidentified as Freedom Riders. One of the victims was actually a Klansman named L. B. Earle, who had the misfortune of coming out of the men's room at the wrong time. Attacked by fellow Klansmen who failed to recognize him, Earle suffered several deep head gashes and ended up in the hospital. Another victim of the mob, a twenty-nine-year-old black laborer named George Webb, was assaulted after he entered the baggage room with his fiancée, Mary Spicer, one of the regular passengers on the freedom bus from Atlanta. The last person to leave the bus, Spicer was unaware of the melee inside the station until she and Webb encountered a group of pipe-wielding rioters in the baggage area.

One of the men, undercover FBI informant Gary Thomas Rowe, told Spicer to "get the hell out of here," and she escaped harm, running into the street for help. But Rowe and three others, including an NSRP member, immediately surrounded Webb and proceeded to pummel him with everything from their fists to a baseball bat. Webb fought back but was soon overwhelmed as several more white men joined in. Dozens of others looked on, some yelling, "Kill the nigger." But moments later the assault was interrupted by Red Self, one of the plainclothes detectives on the scene, who grabbed Rowe by the shoulder and told him it was time to go. "Get the boys out of here," he ordered. "I'm ready to give the signal for the police to move in."

During the allotted fifteen minutes, the violence had spread to the sidewalks and streets surrounding the Trailways station, making it difficult to get the word to all of the Klansmen and NSRP members involved in the riot. But by the time the police moved in to restore order, virtually all of the rioters had left the area. Despite Self's warning, Rowe and those attacking Webb were among the last to leave. "Goddamn it, Tom," Self finally screamed at Rowe, "I told you to get out of here! They're on the way." Rowe and several others, however, were preoccupied with Webb and continued the attack until a news photographer snapped a picture of Rowe and the other Klansmen. As soon as the flashbulb went off, they abandoned Webb and ran after the photographer, Tommy Langston of the *Birmingham Post-Herald*, who made it to the station parking lot before being caught. After one man grabbed Langston's camera and smashed it to the ground, Rowe and several others, including Eastview klavern leader Hubert Page, kicked and punched him and threatened to beat him with the same pipes and baseball bats used on Webb. In the meantime, Webb ran into the loading area, where he was recaptured by a pack of Klansmen led by Gene Reeves. With the police closing in, Webb, like Langston, was released after a few final licks, though by this time both men were bleeding profusely. Stumbling into the parking lot, Webb somehow managed to find the car where his terrified fiancée and aunt had been waiting. As they drove away to safety, Langston, whose life had suddenly become intertwined with the beating of a man whom he had never met, staggered down the street to the *Post-Herald* building, where he collapsed into the arms of a shocked colleague. Later in the afternoon, another *Post-Herald* photographer returned to the scene of the assault and retrieved Langston's broken camera, discovering to his and Langston's amazement that the roll of film inside was undamaged.

The graphic picture of the Webb beating that appeared on the front page of the *Post-Herald* the next morning, though initially misidentified as a photograph of the attack on Peck, turned out to be one of the few pieces of documentary evidence to survive the riot. Immediately following the attack on Langston, Rowe and Page grabbed *Birmingham News* photographers Bud Gordon and Tom Lankford and promptly destroyed all of the unexposed film in their cameras. Neither photographer was beaten, but Clancy Lake, a reporter for WAPI radio, was not so lucky. As Rowe and two other Eastview Klansmen, Billy Holt and Ray Graves, walked toward the Greyhound station parking lot to retrieve their cars, they spied Lake sitting in the front seat of his car broadcasting an eyewitness account of the riot. Convinced that Lake had a camera and had been taking photographs of the scene at the Trailways station, the Klansmen smashed the car's windows with a blackjack, ripped the microphone from the dashboard, and dragged the reporter onto the pavement. Although Lake noticed a passing police car and screamed for help, the officer drove on, leaving him at the mercy of attackers. At one point the three men pushed him into a wall, but after Holt swung at him with a pipe and missed, Lake bolted into the Trailways station, where he was relieved to discover that a squad of police had just arrived. With the police on the scene, the gritty reporter was able to resume his broadcast via telephone, as Rowe and his companions called off the pursuit and once again headed toward their cars.

Along the way, they encountered a smiling Bobby Shelton, who congratulated them for a job well done and offered them a ride to the Greyhound parking lot in his Cadillac. Upon their arrival, the Imperial Wizard and his passengers were shocked to discover several local black men writing down the license plate numbers of the Klansmen's cars. Following a brief struggle—at least one of the overmatched blacks was in his mid-sixties—the Klansmen ripped up the pages with the incriminating numbers before heading to Rowe's house for a victory celebration. Arriving at the house around 5 p.m., they stayed there only a few minutes before a phone call from Sergeant Tom Cook sent them back downtown to intercept another bus full of Freedom Riders. The Greyhound freedom bus, having been burned in Anniston, never actually arrived, but Rowe and Page had too much blood lust to return home without getting some action. Wandering into a black neighborhood on the north side of downtown, they picked a fight with a group of young blacks that gave as good as they got. The battle put one Klansman in the hospital and left Rowe with a knife wound in the neck serious enough to require immediate attention from a doctor. None of this, however, dampened the sense of triumph among the Klansmen and their police collaborators.

At a late-night meeting with Rowe, Red Self suggested that the shedding of a little blood was a small price to pay for what they had accomplished. After weeks of anticipation and careful planning, they had done exactly what they set out to do. Carried out in broad daylight, the assault on the Freedom Riders had turned a bus station into a war zone, and the Klansmen involved had come away with only minor injuries and little likelihood of criminal prosecution. In the coming days and weeks, the publication of Langston's photograph would be a source of concern for those who were identifiable as Webb's attackers—and for Rowe's FBI handlers, who were furious that one of their informants had allowed himself to be captured on film during a criminal assault. But as Self and Rowe congratulated each other in the waning hours of May 14, there was no reason to believe that anything had gone wrong.

The late-afternoon scene at the Trailways station testified to the success of the operation. Within twenty minutes of the Freedom Riders' arrival, the mob had vanished, leaving surprisingly little evidence of the riot and few witnesses with a clear sense of what had just happened. When Peck regained consciousness a few minutes after the assault, he was alone in the corridor. Staggering into the waiting room, he encountered a white soldier who asked if he needed help. Before Peck could answer he was surrounded by smirking policemen who made a mock show of concern for his welfare. Waving them off, he slumped on a bench, where he was soon joined by Walter Bergman, the only other Rider still inside the station. With the help of Howard K. Smith, Bergman tried to hail a cab for himself and Peck, but no driver was willing to take them. Fearing that Peck might bleed to death if he remained at the station much longer, Smith offered to transport the two Riders in the station wagon being used by CBS producer David Lowe and his camera crew. But by the time Smith retrieved the car, Peck and Bergman were gone, having finally found a black cabdriver brave enough to drive them to Shuttlesworth's parsonage.

Minutes later, as he watched the police make a belated show of force outside the station, Smith ran across three injured black men sitting on the curb, "bleeding and uncared for." One was Ike Reynolds, and the other two were bystanders caught in the melee. Though dazed and a bit shaken, they all agreed to talk with the CBS newsman about what they had just seen and experienced. Seizing an opportunity to make television history, Smith promptly "piled them" into the station wagon and took them to his motel for a series of "on-camera interviews." Conducted within an hour of the riot, the interviews would have made for spectacular viewing if Smith had been able to show them to a national audience on Sunday evening. Throughout the afternoon, he issued live hourly radio broadcasts on the riot over his motel telephone, but when he tried to file an eyewitness report for the CBS Evening News that night the WAPI television floor director informed him that "we aren't getting any signals." Technical difficulties aside, Smith suspected that the real problem was the ultra-conservative politics of Vincent Townsend, the influential owner of the Birmingham News, WAPI radio, and WAPI television, which served as the local television affiliate for both CBS and NBC. But at the time, neither he nor the disappointed anchorman of the CBS Evening News—Troy, Alabama, native Douglas Edwards—could do anything about it.

Following the late-afternoon interviews, one of Smith's cameramen delivered Reynolds to the Bethel Baptist Church parsonage, where the rest of the Riders had already gathered. An hour or so earlier, a bleeding and battered Charles Person had arrived on Shuttlesworth's doorstep, followed a few minutes later by Bergman and Peck, who stumbled out of a cab looking "as bloody as a slaughtered hog." Peck's condition, in particular, was cause for considerable alarm. Shuttlesworth, who had already spent several minutes frantically trying to find a doctor to tend to Person's wounds, called for an ambulance. It took nearly an hour to locate an ambulance company willing to have anything to do with the Freedom Rides, and during the delay Peck was moved to the parsonage guest room, where he and the other Riders had a brief reunion. Doubled up with pain, Peck struggled to find the right words to buoy their spirits. He wanted to tell them that the Freedom Ride would continue no matter what, that they couldn't give up. But as he drifted in and out of semiconsciousness, it became clear that such serious talk would have to wait. Before long the blood from his wounds saturated a white bedspread, prompting a worried Shuttlesworth to wonder if his injured guest would even make it to the hospital.

To make matters worse, several police cars soon descended on the parsonage. After surveying the interracial group, one of the officers threatened to arrest the Freedom Riders for violating local segregation laws. But Shuttlesworth stood his ground. "You can't arrest these men. They are sick!" he told the officer, who seemed unnerved by the minister's bravado. "They are going to the hospital, or they can stay at my house." A few minutes later, Bull Connor himself phoned to repeat the threat, but once again Shuttlesworth refused to be intimidated. "If you provide them a hotel downtown, I will be glad to release them," he insisted. "Otherwise, they stay here." Realizing that news reporters would have a field day when they learned that the commissioner of public safety had cast the injured Freedom Riders into the street, Connor relented, but he never forgave Shuttlesworth for this act of impertinence.

Within minutes of the police's departure, an ambulance arrived to take Peck to Carraway Methodist Hospital, but the injured Freedom Rider's ordeal was far from over. After Carraway officials refused to treat him, Peck was taken to Jefferson Hillman Hospital, where he underwent emergency surgery to repair several deep gashes in his head. As soon as the press discovered that he was at Hillman, curious reporters swarmed around his bedside, snapping pictures of his wounds—which required fifty-three stitches—and asking him what it felt like to be a martyr. Despite considerable grogginess and weakness, Peck did his best to field the reporters' questions. Speaking almost in a whisper, he told the press—and the nation—exactly what had happened in the mean streets of Birmingham and Anniston. When asked about his plans for the future, he raised his voice just enough to make sure that everyone in the room heard his pledge. "The going is getting rougher," he admitted, "but I'll be on that bus tomorrow headed for Montgomery." With this declaration, he clearly surprised the reporters, nearly all of whom had expected CORE to throw in the towel. As they ran to the phones to file their stories, some may have doubted Peck's sanity, but none doubted his courage.

While Peck was holding his remarkable impromptu press conference, the rest of the Freedom Riders were huddling at the parsonage. In the early evening the convoy from Anniston had finally arrived, prompting a joyous reunion of the Trailways and Greyhound survivors. Though some of the Riders were still in a state of shock, there were handshakes and embraces all around. As they swapped tales of narrow escapes and close encounters with rampaging white bigots, the bonds of common struggle became apparent. All had been battered by the events of the day, and all were fearful of the future. But somehow they had survived, psychologically as well as physically. No one had collapsed under the pressures of the moment, and no one had broken or dishonored the nonviolent code they had pledged to uphold. Although the Freedom Ride itself was clearly in jeopardy, they were still hopeful that their willingness to put their bodies on the line would inspire others to do the same.

At a mass meeting held at Bethel Baptist Church that evening, several of the Freedom Riders spoke in emotional tones about what they had experienced during ten days on the road. Sitting in chairs placed alongside the altar, looking like an array of accident victims in a hospital waiting room, they told their stories one by one. Although fear of the police and the suspicion that the violence was not yet over kept the audience small, the fifty or so who were there witnessed an amazing outpouring of movement culture. Despite a badly swollen eye, cracked ribs, and deep facial cuts, Walter Bergman spoke the longest, presenting an eloquent explanation of CORE's philosophy and hopes for the future. He and others pleaded with the crowd to join the nonviolent movement, to redeem the land of Jim Crow with acts of commitment and sacrifice. For more than an hour the sanctuary reverberated with amens and shouts of encouragement, until Shuttlesworth rose to cap off the evening with a brief sermon. "This is the greatest thing that has ever happened to Alabama," he insisted, momentarily puzzling some of his listeners, "and it has been good for the nation. It was a wonderful thing to see these young students—Negro and white—come, even after the mobs and the bus burning. When white and black men are willing to be beaten up together, it is a sure sign they will soon walk together as brothers . . . No matter how many times they beat us up, segregation has still got to go. Others may be beaten up, but freedom is worth anything." As the Freedom Riders and the faithful roared their approval, Shuttlesworth was almost overcome with emotion, but he regained his composure in time to lead a final round of hymns and prayers before ending the meeting. He and the Riders then retired to the parsonage to share a meal and some sober discussion of what to do next.

Peck was released from the hospital in the early morning hours, and when the other Riders awoke a few hours later the sight of his heavily bandaged body reminded them of their predicament. Clearly, they could not continue the Freedom Ride without some form of police protection. But who could provide such protection? The Anniston and Birmingham police had demonstrated that they had no intention of upholding the civil rights of "outside agitators," and, aside from Ell Cowling's individual bravery in Anniston, there was no reason to believe that the state police could be counted on to fill the void. Governor Patterson had already made it clear during a radio broadcast that the Freedom Riders should not expect police protection in Alabama. As early as December 1960, Patterson had predicted that "you're going to have rioting on your hands if they try forced integration" in Alabama, assuring reporters that, while he opposed mob violence, he would have to side with the defenders of segregation if Northern agitators forced a showdown. "I'll be one of the first ones stirring up trouble, any way I can," he declared.

The Riders' only hope, it seemed, was federal intervention. Surely, once they learned about the lawlessness and violence in Alabama, the Kennedy brothers would have no choice but to intervene, either with federal marshals, federalized national guardsmen, or, as Eisenhower had done in Little Rock, federal troops. But such intervention had to be timely—almost immediate, in fact—for the Freedom Riders to have any hope of reaching New Orleans by May 17.

To this end, Simeon Booker, who had established contact with the Justice Department two weeks earlier on the eve of the Ride, tried to call the attorney general's special assistant John Seigenthaler within minutes of the attack at the Birmingham Trailways station. After several failed attempts, Booker finally got Seigenthaler on the phone late Sunday afternoon. Offering a blow-by-blow account of the violence in both Anniston and Birmingham, Booker reminded him of their earlier conversation in Washington. He had warned Justice Department officials that something like this might happen, and no one had believed him. Now there was no longer any question that the Freedom Riders' civil rights had been violated—indeed, their very lives were in danger. A native Tennessean who had earned a considerable reputation as a forward-looking reporter for the liberal *Nashville Tennessean* before joining the Justice Department, Seigenthaler jotted down a few notes and promised to call back after speaking to the attorney general, which he did a few minutes later. By this time early radio reports and FBI communications had confirmed Booker's account, and Seigenthaler knew he had to do something to calm the Freedom Riders' fears. The Justice Department was committed to protecting the Freedom Riders' civil rights, he assured Booker, and department officials would work out the particulars as soon as possible. In the meantime, however, it was essential, according to Seigenthaler, to defuse the situation by keeping the most sensational aspects of the story out of the press. In response, Booker bluntly reminded Seigenthaler that reporters had been among those attacked in Birmingham. No one could or should put a lid on such a story, he insisted. The Freedom Riders needed protection, not a cover-up.

If the Freedom Riders had been privy to the inner workings of the Kennedy administration, their anxiety level would have been even higher. In the White House, and even in the Justice Department, administration leaders viewed civil rights primarily as a political issue, not as a moral imperative. There were exceptions, of course, most notably Harris Wofford, Sargent Shriver, and Louis Martin. Indeed, with the help of the Freedom Riders, the list would soon expand to include several other administration "liberals" who could not resist the spirit of the movement—most obviously Seigenthaler and John Doar, a Minnesota-born attorney hired by the Justice Department's Civil Rights Division in 1959.

In mid-May 1961, though, the political calculus of the administration allowed little room for interracial provocateurs, however well-meaning they might be. To the Kennedy brothers, taking the civil rights movement into the streets, where uncontrolled conflict was inevitable, was an embarrassing luxury that the United States could not afford in the context of the Cold War. The president was first and foremost a Cold Warrior, and his focus on world affairs was never more intense than during the troubled spring following the Bay of Pigs fiasco. In the midst of getting ready for his first presidential trip abroad—to England and France—he had just learned that Soviet premier Nikita Krushchev had agreed to a June summit meeting in Vienna. As the president demanded of Wofford in no uncertain terms after reading the Monday morning headlines: "Can't you get your goddamned friends off those buses? Stop them."

Part of President Kennedy's anger lay in the fact that the Freedom Rider crisis appeared to have come out of nowhere. The FBI, the agency that should have kept him informed about such matters, had detailed information on the Klan plot to disrupt the Freedom Rides, but no one in the bureau saw fit to relay this information to anyone in the Justice Department. Indeed, Robert Kennedy and other department officials suspected that the FBI was partly responsible for the crisis. After all, it was no secret that FBI director J. Edgar Hoover was a racial conservative who firmly believed that the civil rights movement was riddled with Communist sympathizers, or that official FBI policy directed agents to limit their involvement in civil rights crises to observation and note-taking. Thus, when rumors and reports from Alabama suggested that local FBI agents had done little or nothing to avert the present crisis—indeed, when some even suggested FBI complicity—the Kennedy brothers began to worry that they could not depend on the director for assistance in civil rights matters.

At this point, of course, the Kennedys had little time to focus on Hoover and the FBI. As Seigenthaler's Sunday afternoon conversation with Booker indicated, they were more concerned with the press. While there is no reason to doubt the sincerity of Seigenthaler's concern for the Freedom Riders' safety, the administration's primary goal, at least initially, was to downplay the significance of what had happened in Anniston and Birmingham. To the White House's dismay, the first radio reports of the attacks on the Freedom Riders were as sensational as they were unwelcome, especially Howard K. Smith's gripping eyewitness account broadcast over the CBS radio network. "One passenger was knocked down at my feet by twelve of the hoodlums," Smith told the nation, "and his face was beaten and kicked until it was a bloody pulp." Obviously shaken by what he had seen, the veteran reporter insisted that "the riots have not been spontaneous outbursts of anger but carefully planned and susceptible to having been easily prevented or stopped had there been a wish to do so." Later in the broadcast, he talked about a dangerous "confusion in the Southern mind" about the sanctity of law and order and went on to suggest that the "laws of the land and purposes of the nation badly need a basic restatement, perhaps by the one American assured of an intent mass hearing at any time, the president."

Smith's remarkable broadcast opened the floodgates of public reaction. By early Sunday evening, hundreds of thousands, perhaps even millions, of Americans were aware of the violence that had descended upon Alabama only a few hours before. At this point few listeners had ever heard of CORE, and fewer still were familiar with the term "Freedom Rider." But this would change in a matter of minutes. The dramatic words and images of martyrdom coming out of Alabama proved irresistible beyond anything the civil rights struggle had yet produced. Earlier confrontations—in Montgomery, Little Rock, and elsewhere—had pierced the veil of public complacency, and white supremacist violence in the Deep South was hardly news in a nation that had grieved over the battered body of Emmett Till in 1955. But somehow the beating of the Freedom Riders was different. Nothing, it seems, had prepared Americans for the image of the burning bus outside of Anniston, or of the broken bodies in Birmingham. Even those who had little sympathy for the Freedom Riders could not avoid the disturbing power of the photographs and accounts of the assaults. Citizens of all persuasions found themselves pondering the implications of the violence and dealing with the realization that a group of American citizens had knowingly risked their lives to assert the right to sit together on a bus.

Whatever chance the Kennedy administration had of downplaying the events in Alabama ended on Monday morning when hundreds of newspapers, including the *New York Times* and the *Washington Post*, ran front-page stories describing the carnage in Anniston and Birmingham. Later in the day several television news broadcasts featured brief but dramatic interviews with the injured Riders. In a televised interview conducted at the Bethel parsonage by CBS correspondent Robert Schakne, the camera provided shocking close-ups of

Peck's heavily bandaged face as he told the nation of his two beatings by "hood-lums." Many accounts, both in print and on the air, featured a riveting photograph of the burned-out shell of the Greyhound, the newest icon of the civil rights struggle. After gazing at the photograph in the *Post*, Jim Farmer sensed that the Anniston Klansmen had unwittingly given CORE a powerful and potentially useful image of Southern oppression.

Farmer himself was racked with doubt, however. Since being notified of the attacks on Sunday afternoon, he had been an emotional basket case. Dealing with his father's death—and his mother's grief—was difficult enough, but now he had to face the most threatening crisis in the history of CORE, one that involved not only pressing strategic concerns but also the safety of colleagues who looked to him for leadership. He had led the Freedom Riders to a dangerous place, only to abandon them on the eve of their greatest challenge. Now, as he tried to figure out how to salvage the situation, he couldn't help but second-guess the decisions that had placed the Freedom Riders in harm's way.

On Sunday evening he had dispatched Gordon Carey to Birmingham, but the plucky field secretary could not be expected to work miracles in a city that had already demonstrated its contempt for law and order. After his father's funeral on Tuesday, Farmer himself would be in a position to travel to Alabama to resume leadership of the Ride. But, judging from what he had learned from press reports and hurried conversations with Shuttlesworth and others in Birmingham, there was no guarantee that the Riders would be in any condition to continue the journey even if he managed to join them. All of this pushed Farmer toward the reluctant conclusion that it was probably too risky to continue the Ride. While he still held out some hope that the Riders could travel on to New Orleans by bus, he began to consider a retreat to safer ground—to a war of words that CORE had at least some chance of winning.

Ironically, if Farmer had actually been in Birmingham, rather than 750 miles away in Washington, he might have been more hopeful. When the Freedom Riders— including Cox, who flew in from North Carolina to rejoin the Ride—gathered at the parsonage on Monday morning, the situation appeared less desperate than it had only a few hours earlier. Having survived the initial shock of the attacks, the Riders had regained at least some of the spirit that had brought them to the Deep South in the first place. Suffering from severe smoke inhalation, Mae Frances Moultrie had decided to return directly to South Carolina, but the other Riders were more or less ready to travel on to Montgomery. By a vote of eight to four, the group decided to continue the Freedom Ride. While even those in the majority expressed concern about the lack of police protection in Alabama, Peck's resolute determination to carry on seemed to steel their courage. As Peck himself recalled the scene: "I must have looked sick for . . . some of the group insisted that I fly home immediately. I said that for the most severely beaten rider to quit could be interpreted as meaning that violence had triumphed over nonviolence. It might convince the ultra-segregationists that by violence they could stop the Freedom Riders. My point was accepted and we started our meeting to plan the next lap, from Birmingham to Montgomery. We decided to leave in a single contingent on a Greyhound bus leaving at three in the afternoon."

A second source of inspiration was the courage of Shuttlesworth and the local activists of the Alabama Christian Movement for Human Rights. The crusading minister and his deacons had stood by the Riders in their hour of need, refusing to cower in the face of the Klan and its powerful allies in the Birmingham police department. Having placed the local movement at considerable risk, CORE's vanguard could not, in good conscience, turn back now—unless Shuttlesworth himself advised them to do so. When he voiced a cautious optimism that they had a reasonable chance of resuming the Freedom Ride, the determination to finish what they had started gained new life.

Part of the basis for Shuttlesworth's optimism was the surprisingly even-handed response of the local press to the events of the previous day. The city's staunchly segregationist morning newspaper, the *Birmingham Post-Herald*, carried two front-page stories on the attacks, complete with Langston's photograph of Webb's beating and the graphic image of the burned Greyhound. A companion story on page four featured an interview with Charlotte Devree, who recounted her escape from the burning bus, and the editorial page included a biting commentary entitled "Where Were the Police?" Shuttlesworth had no illusions about the meaning of the *Post-Herald*'s criticism of police complicity; the wording in the paper's front-page headline—"Gangs Beat Up Photographer, And Travelers In Bus Clashes"—gave a telling indication of the editors' priorities. But the criticism was encouraging nonetheless, a sign that the segregationist front was cracking ever so slightly. Perhaps this time Bull Connor and his rogue police force had gone too far.

There were many unknowns to ponder that Monday morning, and Shuttlesworth and the Riders were not quite sure what the day would bring. But the mood at the parsonage brightened considerably around 10 a.m. when Booker received a call from Robert Kennedy. The fact that the attorney general himself was on the line was reassuring, the first clear sign that the administration recognized the seriousness of the crisis in Alabama. As the Freedom Riders gathered around the phone, Booker breathlessly told Kennedy that the situation remained critical: Gangs of Klansmen were still roaming the downtown in anticipation of the next attempt to desegregate the bus terminal. "We are trapped," he reported, before passing the phone to a couple of the Riders, who assured the attorney general that Booker was not exaggerating. Finally, Shuttlesworth went on the line to tell Kennedy what had to be done to ensure the Riders' safe passage to

Montgomery and beyond. After the two men agreed that the Riders would continue the Freedom Ride on a single bus, Kennedy offered to arrange police protection and promised to call back with the details. True to his word, he was back
on the line a few minutes later with the news that the local police had agreed to
provide protection. "Mr. Connor is going to protect you at the station and escort
you to the city line," he declared. Alarmed by Kennedy's naïveté, Shuttlesworth
reminded him that a similar police escort had done nothing to stop the mob in
Anniston. The Riders required police protection all the way to the Mississippi
line, he insisted. Though disappointed, Kennedy realized that the Birmingham
preacher was right. Promising to consult with his staff, as well as with local and
state officials in Alabama, he asked Shuttlesworth to hold tight until a proper
escort could be arranged.

During the next two hours, as the Freedom Riders waited nervously at the
parsonage, the attorney general and his staff made a flurry of phone calls, including several to Governor John Patterson in Montgomery. Widely known as an
outspoken segregationist, Patterson was nonetheless a long-standing supporter
of President Kennedy, having boosted his national political ambitions as far back
as 1956. Even before he picked up the phone, Robert Kennedy knew Patterson
well enough to know that the Alabama governor would do everything he could
to avoid the appearance of supporting "outside agitators." He felt confident,
though, that he could convince Patterson that protecting the Freedom Riders
from violent assaults was essential, not only from a legal or moral perspective but
also as a deterrent to federal intervention. Thus, when Patterson stubbornly
refused to cooperate, Kennedy was both surprised and disappointed. In a series
of heated conversations, the governor lectured Kennedy and Burke Marshall on
the realities of Southern politics and blasted the Freedom Riders as meddling
fools. By midday, the best that the Justice Department officials could get out of
the governor was a vague promise to maintain public order.

Early in the afternoon, after being informed that the "personal diplomacy"
between Patterson and the Justice Department was still in progress with no clear
resolution in sight, the Freedom Riders decided to force the issue. At their
morning meeting, they had agreed to board the 3 p.m. Greyhound to Montgomery, and, even in the absence of guaranteed police protection, it was now time to
follow through with their commitment. Although they knew full well that a mob
was waiting for them at the Greyhound terminal, the Riders calculated that city,
and perhaps even state, officials would do whatever was necessary to prevent a
recurrence of the previous afternoon's violence. National publicity and attention
had inoculated them, or so they hoped.

When the Riders arrived at the Greyhound station, they were relieved to see that
both the police and the press were out in force. Although a crowd of menacing-
looking white men tried to block the entrance to the station, the police managed to

keep the protesters at bay. As the Riders filed into the white waiting room, some of the protesters—including a number of Klansmen who had been at the Trailways station the previous afternoon—shouted racial epithets and lunged forward, but all of the Riders made it safely inside, where several reporters were waiting to conduct impromptu interviews. When one reporter asked Peck how he was faring, the veteran activist repeated the refrain from his bedside news conference the night before. "It's been rough," he declared, "but I'm getting on that bus to Montgomery." In the next few minutes, however, whatever chance they had of leaving Birmingham on their own terms slipped away.

As they waited in vain for a boarding announcement, Shuttlesworth, Peck, and the other Riders discovered just how cruel and efficient segregationist politics could be. Suddenly the station was abuzz with a radio report that Governor Patterson had refused to guarantee the Freedom Riders "safe passage." "The citizens of the state are so enraged," claimed Patterson, "that I cannot guarantee protection for this bunch of rabble-rousers." According to the state police, all along the route from Birmingham to Montgomery angry segregationists were lying in wait for the Freedom Riders. The only solution, Patterson declared, was for the Riders to leave the state immediately; he might provide them with an escort to the state line, but certainly not to Montgomery, where they were sure "to continue their rabble-rousing."

As news of the governor's statement spread, panic and confusion set in. Claiming that the Teamsters Union had issued an order prohibiting its members from driving the Freedom Riders to Montgomery or anywhere else, George Cruit, the manager of the Birmingham Greyhound station, canceled the 3 p.m. run. Hearing this, the Riders and Shuttlesworth gathered in a corner of the waiting room to decide what to do. After a few moments of confusion, Shuttlesworth counseled the Riders to be patient and to adopt a wait-and-see approach to their apparent predicament. After all, he reminded them, "now that the station is integrated we can stay here and wait them out. They are bound to put a bus through sooner or later." Peck and the other CORE staff members on the scene agreed, but they also remained convinced that their best hope was federal intervention.

Earlier in the day Attorney General Kennedy had given Shuttlesworth his private number and had urged the minister to contact him if the Freedom Riders found themselves in need of federal assistance. But, as Shuttlesworth stood by the waiting-room pay phone dialing the numbers, he wasn't sure what to expect, or what he would actually say to the attorney general. In the brief conversation that followed, Kennedy tried to put the Birmingham minister at ease, assuring him that the Justice Department would do whatever it took to get the Freedom Riders on the road. Furious at Patterson and determined to keep his promise, Kennedy immediately mobilized his staff. After rousting Burke Marshall, who was still recovering from a two-week bout with the mumps, he made a series of calls to Alabama officials. Unfortunately, during several minutes of frantic activity he and Marshall encountered one frustrating obstacle after another. Governor Patterson was not in his office, and when a call to Floyd Mann, the head of the state police, revealed that Patterson had reneged on a promise to have Mann accompany the bus to Birmingham, Kennedy exploded, vowing to teach the Alabamians not to trifle with the Justice Department.

At 3:15, as Shuttlesworth and the Riders waited anxiously for some sign of progress, the attorney general was on the phone with George Cruit, demanding that Greyhound find a replacement driver. When Cruit insisted that no regular driver was willing to take the assignment, Kennedy suggested that Greyhound could hire "a driver of one of the colored buses" or perhaps "some Negro school bus driver." After Cruit brushed aside the black driver option, Kennedy was incredulous, refusing to believe that the company couldn't find someone to drive the bus. "We've gone to a lot of trouble to see that they [CORE Freedom Riders] get to [take] this trip, and I am most concerned to see that it is accomplished," he explained, using words that would later come back to haunt him. "Do you know how to drive a bus?" Kennedy asked plaintively. "Surely somebody in the damn bus company can drive a bus, can't they? . . . I think you should . . . be getting in touch with Mr. Greyhound or whoever Greyhound is and somebody better give us an answer to this question." Before hanging up in exasperation, he reminded Cruit that "under the law" the Freedom Riders "were entitled to transportation provided by Greyhound." "The government is going to be very much upset if this group does not get to continue their trip," he warned. "Somebody better get in the damn bus and get it going and get these people on their way."

By 4 p.m. it was clear that the Freedom Riders weren't going anywhere by bus anytime soon. For the time being, they appeared to be safe, thanks to the protective custody of Connor's police. But no one, other than perhaps Connor himself, knew what mean-spirited mischief was in the making. In an interview appearing in the Monday afternoon edition of the *Birmingham News*, Connor made no attempt to hide his contempt for the Freedom Riders, who, he insisted, had no one but themselves to blame for their predicament. "I have said for the last twenty years that these out-of-town meddlers were going to cause bloodshed if they kept meddling in the South's business," he declared, adding that surely he and his police force could not be blamed for the outside agitators' foolish decision to arrive on Mother's Day, "when we try to let off as many of our policemen as possible so they can spend Mother's Day at home with their families."

This siege mentality was all too familiar to Shuttlesworth, who feared that Kennedy had little chance of outmaneuvering Connor and Patterson on their own turf. Throughout the afternoon he held out some hope that the combination of federal power and national publicity would force state and local officials to accept a compromise that gave the Freedom Riders much of what they wanted. As the impasse continued into the late afternoon, however, both he and the Freedom Riders began to question the wisdom of prolonging the crisis. By 5 p.m., after several minutes of spirited discussion, the Riders had reached a consensus that it was time to break the stalemate at the Greyhound station. Rather than risk further bloodshed and a complete collapse of the project, they decided to leave Birmingham by plane.

The only remaining question was whether they should fly to Montgomery or directly to New Orleans. Some of the Riders had seen enough of Alabama and had no interest in resuming the Freedom Ride in Montgomery. Others reasoned that it was still possible to finish the trip by bus and reach New Orleans in time to attend the *Brown* commemoration rally on May 17. Since no one could be sure what they would encounter at the Birmingham airport, the choice of destination remained open as the Riders made arrangements to leave the bus station. Many of the Riders suspected that the choice was beyond their control and that in all likelihood they would end up on the first available southbound flight out of the city. Whatever their destination, they were sure to face some criticism for abandoning the struggle in Birmingham, but Shuttlesworth's sympathetic reaction to their decision gave them some hope that their departure from the troubled city would be seen as a strategic retreat and not as a surrender.

Coming at the end of a long and frustrating afternoon, this sudden turn of events elicited sighs of relief from Robert Kennedy and his staff. In addition to resolving the immediate crisis in Birmingham, the decision to bypass the bus link to Montgomery indicated that the Freedom Riders were finally coming to their senses. While they were afraid to wish for too much, Justice Department officials now had some hope that the beleaguered Riders would soon abandon the buses altogether and fly directly to New Orleans. Moving the crisis to Montgomery would buy Kennedy and his staff a little time, but from their perspective the best solution was to get the Freedom Riders to Louisiana as soon as possible, preferably by air. With the very real possibility that more violence was waiting down the road in central Alabama and Mississippi, the prospect of putting the Riders back on the buses represented a frightening scenario for federal officials, who had come to regard CORE's project as a reckless, almost suicidal experiment.

When the Freedom Riders filed out of the Greyhound waiting room a few minutes after five, the idea of resuming the Ride in Montgomery was still very much alive. As the fourteen Riders—plus Carey, Shuttlesworth, Booker, Newson, Gaffney, and Devree—hustled to the curb and into a line of cars, they were relieved to see that the crowd outside the station had thinned. Only later would they discover that part of the crowd, having been tipped off by the police or reporters, was already on its way to the airport. After hours of waiting for a chance to get at the Riders, the Klansmen of the Eastview klavern, along with dozens of other hard-core white supremacists, had no intention of letting them leave the city without a few parting shots. Although the scene at the airport was tense, the police managed to keep the Klansmen in check as the convoy unloaded. Earlier in the afternoon, Police Chief Jamie Moore had assured the FBI that his men would take care of any potential troublemakers who threatened the Freedom Riders, and the large police presence at the airport suggested that he intended to honor his pledge. Shuttlesworth, satisfied that there would be no repeat of the previous day's assaults, led the riders into the terminal before saying goodbye. Scheduled to lead the weekly mass meeting of the Alabama Christian Movement for Human Rights, he only had time for a quick round of embraces before racing back to a crowd waiting patiently at the Kingston Baptist Church.

The first evening flight to Montgomery was scheduled to leave approximately an hour after the Riders arrived at the airport—but in that hour, a bomb threat phoned in by Klan leader Hubert Page effectively ended the Riders' hopes of actually making it to Montgomery. After purchasing a block of seats at the Eastern Airlines ticket counter, Peck led the Riders onto a plane that would remain on the tarmac until the following morning. "No sooner had we boarded it," Peck later recalled, "than an announcement came over the loudspeaker that a bomb threat had been received, and all passengers would have to debark while luggage was inspected. Time dragged on and eventually the flight was canceled."

During the wait, Booker called Robert Kennedy and told him about the developing situation at the airport. "It's pretty bad down here, and we don't think we're going to get out," Booker explained. "Bull Connor and his people are pretty tough." This discouraging report was enough to convince Kennedy that he needed a personal representative on the scene, preferably someone who had some familiarity with the Deep South. Even though it would take several hours to fly from Washington to Alabama, and with any luck the Freedom Riders would be gone by the time his representative arrived, Kennedy immediately dispatched John Seigenthaler to Birmingham. While changing planes in Atlanta, Seigenthaler phoned his boss for an update and learned of the bomb threat, a sobering development that made him wonder what he or anyone else could do in the face of such lawlessness.

Back at Kingston Baptist, Shuttlesworth may have harbored similar thoughts. But he did not reveal such concerns to the congregation. Instead, he reassured the crowd that the courageous Freedom Riders had already won an important victory by exposing Birmingham's Klan-infested police force and forcing the Kennedy administration to pay attention to white supremacist terror in the Deep South. The first Freedom Ride might be ending prematurely, he conceded, but the spirit of nonviolent resistance was alive and well in Birmingham.

While Shuttlesworth was spreading hope at Kingston Baptist, the realities of the siege at the airport were closing in on the Freedom Riders. Despite a vigorous dissent by Joe Perkins, a solid majority of the Riders concluded that flying to Montgomery was no longer a viable option. Following an informal vote that effectively ended the Freedom Ride, Perkins unloaded on his close friend Ed Blankenheim, who had voted with the majority. "You can go back to being white anytime you want to," Perkins complained. "You have no right to make decisions where black people are involved unless you are prepared to go the distance. In this case, stay with the Freedom Ride plan which dictates going to Montgomery even if it means you might lose your life." Although he shared some of Perkins's concerns, Peck promptly booked eighteen seats on a Capital Airlines flight to New Orleans via Mobile. The flight, however, was canceled after an anonymous caller threatened to blow up the plane. It was now past 8 p.m., the increasingly dispirited Riders had suffered through two bomb scares, and the chance of leaving Birmingham before morning seemed to be slipping away. When Seigenthaler arrived on the scene an hour or so later, Perkins was still fuming. But everyone else seemed resigned to the fact that the Freedom Ride was over.

As Seigenthaler introduced himself to the Riders, he could see right away that a long day of indignities and threats had exacted a heavy toll. Their downcast eyes told him that they were fed up with Alabama and its hate-mongering white majority; they just wanted out. At least five of the Riders—Jim Peck, Walter Bergman, Charles Person, Ike Reynolds, and Genevieve Hughes—were still weak from the attacks and had no business being out of bed, but there they were, huddled in a corner trying to cope in the face of both physical and emotional pain. As Seigenthaler listened to Booker's account of the events of the past few hours—the bomb threats, the taunts from the police and passengers, the airport staff's refusal to serve the Freedom Riders food, the threats from the mob outside the terminal—he knew he had to find a way to get the Riders out of Birmingham as soon as possible. Three members of the group, according to Booker, had already cracked under the strain and were acting irrationally. "This is a trap," one panic-stricken Rider had whispered to the reporter. "We'll all be killed." Clearly the situation called for immediate action.

A frantic round of phone conversations with airline officials produced nothing but frustration, even after Seigenthaler reminded them that he was a personal representative of the attorney general. Fortunately—with the help of a police officer who assured him that his boss, Bull Connor, was as anxious as anyone to see the last of the Freedom Riders—he eventually convinced the airport manager to cooperate with a plan to sneak the Riders on board a flight to New Orleans. Many years later, in an interview with journalist David Halberstam, Seigenthaler recalled his instructions to the manager: "Just pick a plane, get the baggage of everyone else on it, then get the Freedom Riders' baggage on it, slip the Freedom Riders on, then at the last minute announce the plane, and from the moment you announce it, don't answer the phone because all you'll do is get a bomb threat." Somehow the plan went off without a hitch, and at 10:38 p.m. an

Eastern Airlines plane carrying Seigenthaler, Carey, fourteen Freedom Riders, and the four accompanying journalists lifted off the runway. One hour later they were in New Orleans—still in the Deep South but far removed from the angry, tormented city that had nearly cost some of them their lives.

At the New Orleans airport, several reporters, photographers, and television cameramen were on hand to document the Freedom Riders' arrival. But the presence of the press did not stop the New Orleans police from putting the unwelcome fugitives from Alabama through a few moments of gratuitous harassment. Forming a cordon along the tarmac, a long line of white police officers dressed in riot gear surrounded the Riders as they walked towards the terminal. When some of the officers shouted racial epithets, Seigenthaler became concerned and more than a little angry. Only after he identified himself as a Justice Department official did the police reluctantly back off, allowing the Riders to make their way to a small but deliriously relieved welcoming committee of CORE volunteers. Several of the Riders, with tears of joy streaming down their faces, looking much like returning prisoners of war, collapsed into the outstretched arms of their comrades. Against all odds they had made it to New Orleans after all. The great CORE Freedom Ride of 1961 was over.

5

Get on Board, Little Children

Get on board, little children, Get on board, little children,
Get on board, little children, Let's fight for human rights.
Can't you see that mob a-comin', Comin' 'round the bend.
If you fight for freedom, They'll try to do you in.
—1960s freedom song

The joyous late-night rendezvous in New Orleans captured the raw emotion of the moment. But the morning conversations among the Riders and their hosts revealed considerable confusion about the implications of what had just happened. At the home of Oretha and Doris Jean Castle—the unofficial headquarters of New Orleans CORE—there was nervous speculation about the future of the nonviolent movement in the Deep South, and at a press briefing held later in the day at Xavier University, Gordon Carey and Ben Cox were bombarded by questions from hostile reporters. When one reporter suggested that the violence-plagued Freedom Ride had failed, Cox countered: "It proved what we set out to prove—that American citizens cannot travel freely in the United States. Laws are on the books, but they are not being enforced."

Before flying home to New York for medical care, Jim Peck tried to reassure his fellow Riders that the Freedom Ride had indeed accomplished much of what it had been designed to do. But, in truth, he too was worried. With much of the CORE staff out of commission due to injuries and with Jim Farmer still in Washington at his father's funeral, the organization was in obvious disarray. Farmer himself was overcome with a jumble of conflicting emotions. He was proud of CORE's partial victory, relieved that his colleagues were safe, a little ashamed that he had not been with them during the hours of crisis, and more than a little concerned about how all of this would play in the national media. To his dismay, most of the press reports on Tuesday morning characterized the decision to end the Ride as a triumph of pragmatic realism over misguided idealism. Although many observers acknowledged and admired the Freedom Riders' courage, virtually everyone expressed serious reservations about a style of protest that courted martyrdom. Even in black America, where the idea of Christian martyrdom had long been a powerful force and where Martin Luther King's image as an American Gandhi had some currency, nonviolent struggle remained a novel idea.

The lone exception was the black student movement that had taken hold in a number of Southern communities. Here there were clear signs that nonviolence was on the verge of becoming a mass movement, especially in Nashville, where Jim Lawson and a growing band of student activists had launched wave after wave of stand-ins, sit-ins, and other acts of nonviolent resistance. Widely regarded as the leading edge of the student movement, the Nashville group had played a pivotal role in the founding of SNCC, producing an extraordinary number of dedicated activists, including the Freedom Rider John Lewis. Thus, when Nashville became the flash point that reignited the Freedom Ride, few close observers of the movement were surprised.

While the rest of the nation breathed a collective sigh of relief that the Freedom Ride was over, the young activists of the Nashville Movement cried out for continued sacrifice and commitment. Indeed, Lewis and his colleagues were already talking about mobilizing reinforcements for the Freedom Ride on Sunday afternoon, a full day before the CORE Riders retreated to New Orleans. It had been four days since Lewis had said good-bye to the Freedom Riders in South Carolina, promising to rejoin the Ride as soon as possible. Now he had to face the possibility that some of his fellow Riders might not even be alive by the end of the day. Fearing the worst, Lewis, Diane Nash, Bernard Lafayette, and several others held a marathon meeting to examine and reexamine every aspect of the situation.

From the outset there was consensus among the Nashville students that the civil rights community could not afford to let the Freedom Ride fail. The nonviolent movement had reached a critical juncture, they insisted, a moment of decision that in all likelihood would affect the pace of change for years to come. If the movement allowed segregationist thugs to destroy the Freedom Ride, white supremacist extremists would gain new life, violent attacks on civil rights activists would multiply, and attracting new recruits to the nonviolent cause would become much more difficult. The violence in Alabama posed a soul-testing challenge: Did those who professed to believe in nonviolent struggle have the moral and physical courage to risk their lives for the cause of simple justice? The original Freedom Riders had done so willingly and without self-pity, Lewis assured his friends. Could the members of the Nashville Movement be satisfied with anything less from themselves? When no one in the room disagreed with the logic of this rhetorical question, the die was cast: The Nashville Movement would do whatever was necessary to sustain the Freedom Ride. At this point they did not know how many Freedom Riders had been injured or disabled, but the situation seemed to call for reinforcements. As soon as possible—perhaps within hours—new Freedom Riders would go to Birmingham to continue the journey.

Nash, one of the Nashville Movement's most effective and respected activists, was entrusted with the task of calling Farmer to let him know of the movement's decision. Born and raised in Chicago, where she grew up in a middle-class Catholic family, Nash was light-skinned and strikingly beautiful. Only twenty-one, she had transferred to Fisk University in the fall of 1959 after spending two years at Howard. By the end of her first semester at Fisk, she had become one of Lawson's most devoted disciples, and when the Nashville sit-in movement took off in February 1960 she quickly emerged as one of the local movement's most visible leaders. In mid-April, at the founding meeting of SNCC in Raleigh, she was the only woman to receive serious consideration as a candidate for SNCC chairperson. Her Nashville colleague Marion Barry got the nod as SNCC's first official leader, but soon after her return from Raleigh she almost single-handedly transformed the local movement by challenging Mayor Ben West during a rally on the courthouse steps. With the press looking on, she extracted a grudging admission from West that he had no personal objection to the desegregation of Nashville's downtown lunch counters. Later seen as a pivotal turning point in the decline of local white resistance, Nash's ability to outmaneuver West into a breach of segregationist solidarity added to her reputation as a rising star in the student movement.

Local or regional stature aside, Nash remained largely unknown outside of SNCC and SCLC circles. When she finally reached Farmer on Monday afternoon, he wasn't quite sure who she was or what to make of the student's offer to help. Clearly caught off guard, he stammered into the phone: "You realize it may be suicide." These words of warning only served to steel her nerves and to confirm her suspicion that Farmer was out of touch with the spirit of the student movement. "We fully realize that," she replied, brushing off his objection, "but we can't let them stop us with violence. If we do, the movement is dead." When it became clear that Nash was undeterred by his prediction that the students faced a probable "massacre" in Alabama, he wished her well and promised that CORE would do what it could to help. He also made it clear that he still considered the Freedom Ride to be a CORE project, regardless of any Nashville student involvement. As soon as his father's funeral was over, he would return to Alabama, presumably to resume control of the Ride. "I'll fly down and join you wherever you are," he vowed.

All of this took on a somewhat hollow ring a few hours later when the CORE Riders actually flew to New Orleans. "I couldn't believe it," Lewis later wrote, "I understood the thinking behind the decision, but it defied one of the most basic tenets of nonviolent action—that is, there can be no surrender in the face of brute force or any form of violent opposition." This and other arguments reinvigorated the ongoing meeting of the central committee, which was moving toward concrete action by Monday evening. As the discussions progressed, the idea of sending a new wave of Freedom Riders to Alabama and beyond took on a seemingly irreversible momentum, especially after a call to Jim Lawson in Ohio drew a ringing endorsement from the one person who could have nixed the students' plan. Far from reining in his disciples, Lawson promised to join the Freedom Ride as soon as he returned to the South.

By early Tuesday morning someone in Nashville, either inside or outside the movement, had contacted the Justice Department in Washington, identifying Nash as the ringleader of a proposed new Freedom Ride. The reaction in the attorney general's office, which less than two hours earlier had learned that Seigenthaler and the CORE Freedom Riders were safely on the ground in Louisiana, was one of shock and dismay. Fearing that the crisis was being resurrected, Robert Kennedy placed a frantic call to Seigenthaler, who had just drifted off to sleep in his New Orleans motel room. A new Freedom Ride was about to be launched, he informed his half-conscious assistant, and something had to be done to stop it. At 4 a.m. Seigenthaler received a second call, this time from Burke Marshall, Kennedy's special deputy for civil rights. After reiterating the seriousness of the situation, Marshall gave Seigenthaler Nash's phone number and a few additional words of advice: "You come from that goddamn town . . . If you can do anything to turn them around, I'd appreciate it."

When Seigenthaler phoned Nash on Tuesday morning, he described the explosive atmosphere in Birmingham and asked her to consider a postponement of the Ride. To his dismay, she refused, insisting that delaying the hour of freedom was out of the question. Exasperated, he shouted into the phone: "You're going to get your people killed." Once again, she was unmoved. If the first wave of Nashville Freedom Riders were to die, she calmly informed him, "then others will follow them."

On Tuesday evening, after securing travel money from the ministerial leaders of the Nashville Christian Leadership Council—the Nashville Movement's sponsoring organization—Nash telephoned Fred Shuttlesworth in Birmingham to let him know that a new batch of Freedom Riders would soon be on their way. Prior to this point, Shuttlesworth had heard only vague rumblings that something was afoot in Nashville, so he was more than a little surprised when Nash informed him that the Freedom Riders might be coming to Birmingham as early as the next morning. "The students have decided that we can't let violence overcome," she declared. "We are going to come into Birmingham to continue the Freedom Ride." Intrigued, but not sure that the Nashville students knew what they were getting themselves into, Shuttlesworth responded sternly: "Young lady, do you know that the Freedom Riders were almost killed here?" Nash assured him that she did, adding: "That's exactly why the ride must not be stopped. If they stop us with violence, the movement is dead. We're coming. We just want to know if you can meet us." After he agreed, she promised to call back with further details.

The next step was to select the students who would actually participate in the Ride. At a late-night meeting, the central committee calculated that it had enough funds to support ten Freedom Riders, but the gathering momentum of the previous two days had produced far more than ten volunteers. While the entire committee discussed the possible choices, it was agreed that Bevel, as the temporary chairman, would have the final say as to who would board the buses on Wednesday morning. Somewhat surprisingly, Bevel's ten choices did not include Nash, who was deemed too crucial to the entire operation to be placed in jeopardy.

The ten volunteers chosen included two whites—Jim Zwerg and Salynn McCollum—and eight blacks: John Lewis, William Barbee, Paul Brooks, Charles Butler, Allen Cason, Bill Harbour, Catherine Burks, and Lucretia Collins. Zwerg was a twenty-one-year-old exchange student from Wisconsin who had joined the Lawson workshops and the theater stand-ins soon after his arrival at Fisk in early 1961; preparing for a career as a Congregational minister, he had grown close to Lewis in the months leading up to the Freedom Ride. McCollum, also twenty-one, was a transplanted upstate New Yorker attending George Peabody College; active in the sit-in movement, she would later work for SNCC in Atlanta. Barbee, nineteen, was a theology student at American Baptist Theological Seminary (ABT), as was Brooks, a twenty-two-year-old East St. Louis, Illinois, native who had become one of Nashville's most outspoken activists.

The remaining five Riders were all students at Tennessee Agricultural and Industrial (A&I) State University, an all-black public institution that had recently gained fame as the home campus of Olympic track star Wilma Rudolph. Tennessee State, as the university was commonly known, had also provided the Nashville Movement with many of its most committed participants. Butler was a twenty-year-old sophomore from Charleston, South Carolina, and Cason was a bookish nineteen-year-old freshman from Orlando, Florida, who insisted on taking his typewriter on the Freedom Ride. Harbour, also nineteen, was from Piedmont, Alabama, where his father worked in a yarn factory. Like fellow Alabamian John Lewis, Harbour was the first member of his family to go to college, and earlier in the year he and Lewis had struck up a friendship during a long bus ride to the jail-in rally in Rock Hill, South Carolina. Burks was an outgoing and vivacious Birmingham native, who, like Nash, had once posed for *Jet* magazine.

A twenty-one-year-old senior, she would marry fellow Freedom Rider Paul Brooks later in the year. Collins, who had lived on an Army base in El Paso, Texas, before coming to Nashville, was also a twenty-one-year old in her last semester at Tennessee State. Tall and strikingly attractive, with a theatrical voice and a steely determination to confront the white supremacist power structure, she always seemed to be on the front lines of the local freedom struggle. While the ten Riders represented a range of personalities and class backgrounds, all were seasoned veterans of the Nashville Movement. None had yet reached the age of twenty-three.

Once the lineup of Freedom Riders was set, Nash placed a call to Shuttlesworth. This time much of their conversation was relayed in a prearranged code. Realizing that his phone had been tapped by local police, the Birmingham minister had worked out a set of coded messages related to, of all things, poultry. "Roosters" substituted for male Freedom Riders, "hens" for female Riders, "pullets" for students, and so on. What the eavesdropping police thought of all this can only be imagined, but when Nash called Shuttlesworth again on Wednesday morning to tell him "the chickens are boxed," he knew that the Freedom Riders were on their way.

Nash also placed calls to SNCC and SCLC leaders in Atlanta and to Justice Department officials in Washington, who pleaded with her to cancel the Ride. Unmoved, she made a final call to Shuttlesworth just before dawn. The shipment of ten "chickens"—seven "roosters" and three "hens"—was scheduled to leave Nashville at 6:45 a.m., she reported, and would arrive in Birmingham by late morning. Responding in code, Shuttlesworth promised that he would be at the bus station to accept the shipment. As Shuttlesworth later explained, the code was designed to hide the details of the operation, not the operation itself. He wanted Bull Connor and the Birmingham police to know that the Riders were coming. Whatever else happened, he did not want a repeat of the Mother's Day massacre, when the absence of police protection nearly got the CORE Freedom Riders killed. Accordingly, he sent an early-morning telegram to Connor informing him that the Birmingham police would soon be given a second chance to protect the constitutional rights of visiting Freedom Riders. Suspecting a trick, Connor asked his daughter Dora Jean to phone Shuttlesworth's house to see if the information in the telegram was true. Pretending to be a sympathetic white liberal, she was able to confirm that a new Freedom Ride was indeed imminent.

Shuttlesworth also alerted the press that the Freedom Riders were coming, but by that time the "freedom bus" had already left the Nashville terminal. When the students boarded the bus there were no reporters present, and neither the bus driver—E. S. Lane—nor any of the other passengers had any idea that a new

Freedom Ride had begun. Nash and Lewis, the designated leader on the bus, had counseled the students to behave like normal passengers and to avoid any overt challenges to Jim Crow during the Nashville-to-Birmingham run. If all went well, the actual Freedom Ride would begin later in the day when they boarded the bus to Montgomery. But all did not go well. Salynn McCollum, the only white female Rider, missed the bus, although after a frantic seventy-mile car chase she managed to join the other Riders when the bus stopped at Pulaski, a small town in south-central Tennessee that had served as the birthplace of the original Ku Klux Klan in 1866. With McCollum safely on board, the bus crossed the Alabama line without incident by midmorning. The only hint of trouble was the impatience of Jim Zwerg and Paul Brooks, who insisted on sitting as a conspicuously interracial duo near the front of the bus. Somewhat surprisingly, according to Lewis, "no one, not the white passengers nor the driver" seemed to object to this seating arrangement. "It was not until we reached the Birmingham city limits, two hundred miles south of Nashville, that the trouble began," he recalled.

Waiting at the city line were several police cars and a boarding party of police officers who promptly arrested Zwerg and Brooks for violating Alabama law. The officers then checked all of the passengers' tickets, revealing that nine passengers held identical tickets marked Nashville–Birmingham–Montgomery–Jackson–New Orleans. The only Freedom Rider to escape the dragnet was McCollum, who had purchased her ticket in Pulaski. Confident that he had apprehended a band of agitators, the officer in charge ordered the driver to head for the Birmingham Greyhound terminal under police escort. The bus arrived at the terminal at 12:15, too late for the Riders to be transferred to the noon bus to Montgomery. But a late arrival was the least of the Riders' problems. At the terminal, the police temporarily sealed the bus, taping newspaper over the windows to conceal what was going on inside. After reexamining each passenger's ticket before letting anyone off, the police maintained an armed guard over the seven remaining "suspects." By this time Zwerg and Brooks had already been carted off to the city jail, and McCollum, avoiding identification as a Freedom Rider, had disembarked with the other passengers. Rushing undetected through the crowd, she called Nash from a pay phone. Trying not to panic, Nash immediately phoned Burke Marshall in Washington. Why, she asked, were the Freedom Riders being forcibly detained by the Birmingham police? Caught off guard, Marshall promised to investigate, but he couldn't resist reminding Nash that she and the Nashville students had been warned that Birmingham was a dangerous place.

As news of the Freedom Riders' arrival spread, a large crowd began to gather at the terminal, providing the police with a rationale for protective custody. The only way to safeguard the Riders' safety, the officer in charge insisted, was to keep them on board. For more than an hour, the Riders pleaded with the police to respect their constitutional rights, but whenever one of them made a move for the door, a billy club-wielding officer blocked the aisle. The only place the Riders were likely to go, one guard suggested, was back to the Tennessee line with a police escort. Outside of the bus, the press was being told that the Riders were being detained so that they could be safely transferred to the 3 p.m. bus to Montgomery. At one point, the police actually allowed the Riders' luggage to be transferred to the Montgomery bus. But a telephoned bomb threat and the driver's insistence that the Montgomery-bound Greyhound would not move from its bay if the Freedom Riders were permitted to board ended any chance that they would actually leave at three.

In the meantime, Shuttlesworth, accompanied by two aides and Emory Jackson of the *Birmingham World*, was trying to find out what was going on. Arriving at the terminal just before noon, he managed to have a few guarded words with McCollum, but there wasn't much he could do until the Riders were allowed to leave the bus. Finally, at five minutes after four, Police Chief Jamie Moore shepherded the Riders through two rows of police officers and into the terminal building. With the crowd straining to get a piece of them, the seven students made their way to the white waiting room, where they were welcomed by McCollum and a relieved and defiant Shuttlesworth. Ignoring Moore's warning that interracial mingling would incite the crowd, Shuttlesworth led the Riders, white and black, to the terminal's whites-only restaurant, but the door was locked. Cordoned off by the police, the Riders retreated to the terminal's white restrooms, which, to their relief, were open. Preoccupied with the surging crowd, the police made no move to prevent this historic desecration of segregated toilets. Later, back in the waiting room, Shuttlesworth and the Riders celebrated their small victory with round after round of freedom songs. Seemingly unfazed by either the police or the protesters, they invited reporters and other onlookers to join them on the next "freedom bus" to Montgomery.

As the drama at the Greyhound station unfolded, the Birmingham police—and Alabama officials in general—found themselves in a delicate position. Simultaneously restraining the crowd and intimidating the Freedom Riders was turning out to be a difficult proposition, especially with the press looking on. Everyone in a position of authority, from Governor Patterson to Chief Moore, had been under intense scrutiny since Sunday afternoon, and it was becoming increasingly obvious in the wake of the Mother's Day riot that neither Birmingham nor Alabama could afford another round of mob violence and bloodshed. Indeed, on Tuesday, in the face of mounting criticism, the Birmingham police had made a show of arresting Melvin Dove, Jesse Thomas Faggard, and his son Jesse Oliver Faggard—three Tarrant City Klansmen involved in the beating of George Webb. Associates of Dr. Edward Fields, the National States Rights Party leader who defied the Birmingham police order to keep his followers away from the terminal area on Sunday afternoon, the three men were clearly identifiable in the Langston photograph that appeared on the front page of the *Birmingham Post-Herald* on Monday morning. Other assailants, including several Birmingham Klansmen, could also be identified from the photograph, but the police conveniently limited the initial arrests to the three suburban "outsiders" from Tarrant City. The token prosecution of Dove and the Faggards, combined with the later arrests of Howard Thurston Edwards, an Irondale Klansman who can be seen wielding a lead pipe in the photograph, and Herschel Acker, a Klansman from Rome, Georgia, took at least some of the pressure off of the Birmingham police, countering the charge that the riot was the result of collusion between local vigilantes and public officials. In the end, the Tarrant City Klansmen escaped with nothing more than misdemeanor disorderly conduct convictions, small fines, and brief jail terms. Acker and Edwards faced the more serious charge of assault with intent to murder, but both men ultimately walked away without serving a day in prison—Acker after being acquitted by an all-white jury in November, and Edwards after three separate trials ended with hung juries.

This calculated blend of defiance and legal pretense was on full display as state and local officials tried to outmaneuver the Nashville Riders on May 17. Ignoring the larger issue of constitutional rights, Alabama authorities restored "law and order" by branding the Tennessee students as troublemakers and criminals. In a midafternoon statement to the press, an exasperated Governor John Patterson declared that no one could "guarantee the safety of fools." And a few minutes later, just as the Riders were contemplating a move to the loading platform where the 5 p.m. bus to Montgomery was scheduled to depart, Bull Connor strode into the terminal waiting room. Lewis later claimed that he knew who Connor was, even "though I'd never seen him before in my life. He was short, heavy with big ears and a fleshy face. He wore a suit, his white hair was slicked straight back above his forehead, and his eyes were framed by a pair of black, horned-rimmed glasses." At first Connor seemed content to mingle with the police guards, but as soon as the Riders began to move toward the loading platform he stepped in and ordered his officers to place the unwanted visitors from Nashville in "protective custody." Pointing to the unruly crowd, he assured the students that he was arresting them for their "own protection." When Shuttlesworth stepped forward to object, Connor directed Chief Moore to arrest him for interfering with and refusing to obey a police officer. All nine "agitators" were then led to a line of waiting paddy wagons that whisked them off to Birmingham's notorious Southside jail.

At the jail, guards separated the detainees by gender. As the only white female, McCollum was placed in a special facility, and Collins and Burks were put in a cell with several other black women. With the exception of Shuttlesworth, all of the men ended up in a dark and crowded cell that Lewis likened to a dungeon: "It had no mattresses or beds, nothing to sit on at all, just a concrete floor." At 10 p.m. Shuttlesworth was released on bond, but the other prisoners remained in jail, even though no formal charges had been brought against them. Isolated from the outside world with no access to the press—or to Nash, who was desperately trying to find out what had happened to them—Lewis and his cellmates adopted a strategy of Gandhian noncooperation. Although they had not eaten since morning, the students defiantly refused to eat or drink anything. And, since sleeping under these conditions was difficult at best, they decided to pass the time singing freedom songs, a morale booster that had served them well during the Nashville sit-ins.

While the Nashville students were singing and shouting their way into Bull's doghouse, CORE was orchestrating a drama of its own in more than a score of cities and college towns across the nation. With the help of the National Student Association and several labor unions, CORE chapters simultaneously commemorated the May 17 anniversary of the *Brown* decision and protested the violence in Alabama by setting up picket lines in front of bus terminals from Boston to Los Angeles. In the South, the demonstrations were limited to small groups of college students in Nashville, Chapel Hill, Austin, and Lynchburg. But in several Northern cities picket lines stretched around the block. The largest demonstration took place in New York, where more than two thousand people gave up their lunch hour to march in front of the Port Authority bus terminal. Walking at the head of the New York picket line were Jim Peck and Hank Thomas, who had flown in from New Orleans the night before.

Wednesday was also an emotional day in New Orleans, where most of the CORE Freedom Riders attended a private banquet followed by a mass meeting at the New Zion Baptist Church. Frances Bergman was still too shaken to attend, Ivor Moore was in New York attending his grandfather's funeral, and Genevieve Hughes was in a Washington hospital ward recovering from smoke inhalation and nervous exhaustion. But Carey and the rest of the Riders, with the exception of the Port Authority picketers Peck and Thomas, were on hand to help their New Orleans hosts commemorate the judicial death of Jim Crow education. With Rudy Lombard, the chair of New Orleans CORE, serving as master of ceremonies, and with CORE stalwart and sit-in leader Jerome Smith making a surprise appearance after his release from jail earlier in the day, the overflow crowd of 1,500 at New Zion listened with rapt attention for more than two hours as, one by one, the "survivors" of the Alabama Freedom Ride came forward to say a few words. After Blankenheim and Bigelow described the bus-burning scene in Anniston, and Person and Bergman described the Birmingham riot, Ben Cox nearly brought down the house when he urged the audience to stage "sit-ins, kneel-ins, vote-ins, ride-ins, motor-ins, swim-ins, bury-ins, and even marry-ins."

Eight hundred miles to the north, the mood was a bit more somber as Justice Department officials puzzled over how to deal with the latest crisis in Alabama. At a Wednesday night dinner party hosted by Birmingham native Louis Oberdorfer, the head of the department's tax division, the conversation inevitably turned to the legal and political dilemmas posed by the new Freedom Ride. Two of Oberdorfer's guests, Birmingham attorney Douglas Arrant and Deputy Attorney General Byron "Whizzer" White, a former classmate of Oberdorfer's at Yale Law School and a future Supreme Court justice, had good reason to turn their attention to the developing situation in Alabama. Arrant voiced concerns that a full-scale race war was brewing in his hometown, and White was scheduled to meet with Burke Marshall on Thursday morning to discuss the Kennedy administration's response to the recent arrests and Governor Patterson's apparent refusal to guarantee the Freedom Riders' safety. When White remarked that the administration had "to get those people out of there and keep them moving somehow," and that the use of federal soldiers might be the only way to do it, Oberdorfer suggested the politically more palatable alternative of a civilian force made up of federal marshals. By relying on a limited number of marshals, the administration could protect the Riders and also continue to disavow any plan of imposing a second military Reconstruction on the South. By the end of the evening, the three men had roughed out a proposal to send several dozen marshals to Alabama.

The next morning, as the Nashville students completed their first night in jail, White met with Marshall and Robert Kennedy, who decided to interrupt his brother's breakfast with an emergency meeting. With the president still in his pajamas, the attorney general launched into an impromptu briefing on the deteriorating situation in Birmingham. A new group of Freedom Riders was in jail and conducting a hunger strike, the bus company was demanding police protection for any bus carrying Freedom Riders, and John Patterson was waffling on his earlier pledge to provide the Riders with safe passage through the state. The reports from John Seigenthaler and John Doar, the most reliable federal officials on the scene in Alabama, were increasingly discouraging. Seigenthaler's plea for the students' release had gotten nowhere.

As the president nodded in agreement, his younger brother proceeded to unveil a tentative plan for federal intervention that stopped short of military engagement. White then filled in the details, describing potential sources of federal paramilitary personnel such as the U.S. Marshal Service, the Border Patrol, the Bureau of Prisons, and the revenue agents of the Bureau of Alcohol, Tobacco, and Firearms. The idea was to create a credible force that would convince Patterson that the threat of federal intervention was real. Once the governor realized that federal marshals and army support staff were poised to invade Alabama, White reasoned, he would have little choice but to use the state's police power to protect the Freedom Riders.

John Kennedy's preference, as he soon made clear, was to avoid the use of even a civilian federal force; somehow Patterson had to be coaxed into doing the right thing and lifting the burden from the Kennedy brothers' shoulders. To this end, he asked the White House operator to call Patterson's office. Confident that his "old friend" and political ally would listen to reason if the personal touch were administered, he was surprised and a bit miffed when Patterson dodged his call. The governor, according to his secretary in Montgomery, was away on a fishing trip in the Gulf of Mexico and could not be reached by phone. Kennedy, who suspected otherwise, now realized what he was up against. Eisenhower had been forced to deal with Orval Faubus during the Little Rock crisis, and now four years later Patterson seemed to be following the same path of states'-rights demagoguery. Reluctantly Kennedy ordered White and Marshall to begin preparations for sending the marshals to Alabama. Still hoping to avoid federal intervention, he counseled his aides to proceed as discreetly as possible without mentioning his involvement. But he was determined to be ready if the crisis in Alabama exploded.

By Thursday afternoon, at least one thing was already clear: Bull Connor had decided to use the Freedom Rider crisis to discredit both Shuttlesworth, now out of jail, and the local civil rights struggle. Brandishing the minister's telegram announcing the arrival of the outside agitators from Nashville, Connor claimed that Shuttlesworth had masterminded a conspiracy to breach the peace. "As early as 9 a.m.," Connor declared, "he began precipitating trouble by making statements to newspapers and radio stations and sending telegrams and otherwise warning people." This was proof, he insisted, that Shuttlesworth was a rabble-rouser who deserved prosecution for inciting a riot. The editors of the *Birmingham News*, among others, agreed, arguing in a special front-page editorial that Shuttlesworth's actions were equivalent to shouting "fire" in a crowded auditorium.

Shuttlesworth already faced charges of interfering with the Freedom Riders' arrests, and in a brief but raucous trial on Thursday evening he was convicted. Connor, on hand to watch his nemesis squirm, appeared smug as Shuttlesworth stood in the dock, but any thought that the troublesome preacher would break under pressure disappeared as soon as he was released on bail. At a post-trial press conference held at the Bethel parsonage, Shuttlesworth was as defiant as ever, repeating his vow that neither he nor the students in the Southside jail would abandon the Freedom Ride. As the students themselves had been telling Chief Moore throughout the day, they were prepared to remain in jail indefinitely.

Moore's concern, like that of many white Birminghamians, was heightened by the broadcast that evening of the CBS documentary *Who Speaks for Birmingham?* Aired at 9 p.m., just as Shuttlesworth's press conference was coming to a close, the program featured a series of interviews with black and white citizens, including Shuttlesworth and John Temple Graves, a columnist for the *Birmingham Post-Herald*. The dean of Birmingham journalists, Graves was a onetime pro–New Deal moderate who had grown conservative in his declining years. On screen, he presented an image of white-haired civility and reason that belied his militant defense of white supremacy and racial and class privilege. With producer David Lowe and reporter Howard K. Smith interjecting questions and occasional commentary, the back-and-forth dialogue continued for nearly an hour. Stories of cultural and educational progress alternated with tales of Klan violence and white supremacist intransigence. But the overall depiction of the city was less than flattering.

Near the end of the broadcast Shuttlesworth had his say, coolly recounting several beatings and two attempts to bomb his church and parsonage, the first on Christmas night 1956. "I have to have somebody guard my home at night . . . ," he explained. "The police won't do it. It causes your family—wife and children—to go through severe strain . . . But we've learned to make out on it. We found out that if you can't take it, you can't make it . . . Life is a struggle, here, for me in Birmingham," he added, "but it's a glorious struggle." When asked about Bull Connor, Shuttlesworth didn't mince words: "He wants the white people to believe that just by his being in office, he can prevent the inevitable, so he has to talk loud, he has to be loud, because when the sound and fury is gone, then there'll be nothing. There'll be emptiness." The program closed with a brief but powerful epilogue on the May 14 beatings. After replaying his eyewitness report from Sunday, Smith—standing in front of a sprawling photograph of Connor—described the Freedom Riders' airborne exodus to New Orleans and ended by quoting from the *Birmingham News* May 15 editorial acknowledging that "fear and hatred did stalk Birmingham's streets yesterday." Smith had wanted to end the broadcast with a quotation from the philosopher Edmund Burke: "The only thing necessary for the triumph of evil is for good men to do nothing." But CBS executives, fearing a barrage of criticism from white Southerners, insisted that he drop it from the script.

Connor never acknowledged that the combination of Shuttlesworth's barbs and Smith's epilogue pushed him into action. But at 11:30 p.m., an hour and a half after the show's sign-off, he appeared at the city jail, grim-faced and barking orders at people on both sides of the bars. Accompanied by five police officers and *Birmingham News* reporters Tom Lankford and Bud Gordon, he announced that he was tired of listening to freedom songs. It was time for the students to go back to Nashville where they belonged. "You people came in here from Tennessee on a bus," he shouted through the bars. "I'm taking you back to Tennessee in five minutes under police protection." Waiting outside were two black unmarked police cars and a hearse-like limousine ready to transport the students out of the state. As the police began rounding up the seven students (Zwerg and Brooks were later released separately, and Salynn McCollum, released into her father's custody, was already on her way back to New York; before boarding an 11:30 p.m. flight, Walter McCollum told reporters: "I sent her to Nashville to get an education, not to get mixed up in this integration mess"), they demanded to speak with their attorney Len Holt but were told he couldn't help them because he wasn't licensed in Alabama.

Eventually the police loaded the students into two of the cars, jamming their luggage into the limousine. With Lankford and Gordon along for the ride as observers, and with Connor riding shotgun next to the driver of the lead car, the convoy headed northward to Highway 31, the same road that the students had traveled by bus on Wednesday morning. As they left the jail, Connor ordered the students to keep all of the windows closed for their own protection, prompting a defiant Lucretia Collins to remind him that the windows might "keep bullets out, but they can't keep God out." Later, after leaving the city lights behind, Connor tried to engage several of the students in friendly small talk but made no effort to reveal his exact plans for them. At first the students feared that they were headed for some sort of staged ambush, but as Connor continued his jovial chatter they began to relax. Most of the conversation was between Connor and the feisty Birmingham native Catherine Burks, who refused to be intimidated by a man she later claimed "was a powerful dictator but didn't have any power over me." After Connor hinted that he planned to take the students all the way back to Nashville, Burks suggested that in the spirit of Christian fellowship he should join them for breakfast before returning to Alabama. At one point she even offered to cook for him.

To Lewis, who was sitting directly behind the driver's seat, this unexpected banter was somewhat reassuring, but the strained joviality came to an abrupt halt when the convoy reached the small border town of Ardmore, Alabama. "This is where you'll be gettin' out," Connor informed them, adding: "There is the Tennessee line. Cross it and save this state and yourself a lot of trouble." While the officers unloaded the luggage, stacking it alongside the road, the seven students climbed out of the cars to an uncertain fate. Before driving off, Connor pointed to a railroad track that led to a nearby depot from which, he assured them with a wry smile, they could catch a train to Nashville. "Or maybe a bus," he said with a laugh.

It was 4 in the morning, and for a while they "just stood there in the dark" wondering whether they were about to be ambushed or even lynched, but before long they headed down the tracks in search of help. Failing to find the railroad depot, they stumbled on a pay phone and placed a collect call to Nash. Stunned that they had been released from the Birmingham jail, she tried to gather her thoughts about what to do next. She could send a car to bring them to Nashville, or she could find some way to send them back to Birmingham. The choice was up to them, she declared, but the situation was complicated by the fact that eleven new Freedom Riders would soon be on their way to Alabama. Since this was the first they had heard of the second wave of Nashville Riders, the weary students decided to seek food and shelter before making any commitments. Promising to call Nash back as soon as they found a safe haven, they resumed their trek down the tracks.

After walking nearly a mile, they approached a cluster of houses that Lewis later described as "broken-down shacks." Reasonably certain that they were in an all-black neighborhood, the students summoned the courage to knock on the front door of one of the houses, awakening an elderly black couple who, after a bit of coaxing, reluctantly let them in. As Lewis recalled: "They had heard about the Freedom Ride and . . . were very frightened, but they put us all in the back room of their house . . . By this time we were very, very hungry, because we didn't eat anything during the hunger strike, and the elderly man went to three different stores to buy food for our breakfast, so that no one would get suspicious." The couple also allowed Lewis to use their phone to call Nash, who was anxiously awaiting their decision. All seven, he assured her, were determined to go on to New Orleans as planned. Relieved but hardly surprised, she promised to send a car that would have them back in Birmingham by midafternoon.

Leo Lillard—a recent graduate of Tennessee State who would later help train and dispatch the scores of Freedom Riders who passed through Nashville—had already volunteered to pick up the Freedom Riders in Ardmore and drive them to Birmingham. By midmorning, Lillard and the Riders were careening southward from the Tennessee line. The car was crowded, and whenever they passed another vehicle they took the precaution of "squeezing ourselves down in the seats, out of sight," just in case the Alabama police or Klan vigilantes were looking for them. During most of the journey, Lillard nervously guided the "freedom car" through the back roads hoping to escape detection. For a time every approaching car seemed menacing, but finally, just a few minutes before three— a mere fifteen hours after being rousted from their jail cells—the students pulled into the driveway of the Bethel parsonage. Back at Ardmore, Burks had promised the departing Connor that she would be back in Birmingham by "high noon," and she had almost done it.

As Shuttlesworth rushed out to greet the lost Riders, other familiar faces began to appear in the background. All eleven of the reinforcements that Nash had mentioned on the phone were at the parsonage. Of the original ten Nashville Riders, only Brooks, Zwerg—who would be released from jail later in the afternoon— and McCollum were missing; and, as the arriving students soon discovered during a rollicking reunion on the lawn, McCollum had already been replaced by Ruby Doris Smith, a Spelman student and SNCC stalwart who had shared a jail cell with Diane Nash in Rock Hill. In all there were nineteen volunteers ready to board the next "freedom bus" to Montgomery. In addition to Smith, the new recruits included Bernard Lafayette and Joe Carter of American Baptist Theological Seminary, seven sit-in veterans from Tennessee State, and two white women: eighteen-year-old Susan Wilbur of George Peabody College and twenty-year-old Susan Hermann of Fisk, an exchange student from Whittier, California. Most had traveled to Birmingham by train, with Lafayette in charge of the group. A few, at Nash's suggestion, had straggled in by other means in an effort to ensure that at least some of the students would avoid interception by Alabama authorities. When Lewis called to tell her that nineteen "pullets" had arrived at Shuttlesworth's coop, she could hardly believe it, though she continued to worry that the police might close in at any minute. Not wishing to press their luck, she and Lewis decided to put the Riders on the first available bus to Montgomery.

Following a hurried lunch, Shuttlesworth organized a car pool to transport the Riders to the Greyhound terminal and once again sent word to law enforcement officials that a new Freedom Ride was about to begin. By late afternoon news of the Ride had spread across town and even to Montgomery and Washington. The reaction at all levels was a combination of surprise and head-shaking frustration. Despite their differences, local, state, and federal officials shared a common resolve to bring the Freedom Rider crisis to a close. In downtown Birmingham, Connor and the police were growing tired of a cat-and-mouse game with troublemakers who didn't seem to respond to the traditional forms of control and intimidation. Under increasing political pressure to maintain law and order, they knew they could not afford another public relations disaster like the Mother's Day riot. And yet they were not about to let the Freedom Riders run roughshod over the hallowed strictures of racial segregation. At the governor's office in Montgomery, Patterson was playing an equally difficult game, trying to extract political capital out of the crisis without having it blow up in his face.

The situation was no less frustrating for the Justice Department officials who spent most of Thursday working out the preliminary organization of a federal peacekeeping force. Faced with a politically unpalatable scenario, Kennedy and his staff continued to search for some means of ending the crisis before the peacekeeping force was actually deployed. Hoping for a miracle, they privately welcomed Connor's attempt to take the situation in hand. Despite the initial fear that Connor had snapped—"Jesus Christ, Bull has kidnapped them. He's going to kill them," a panic-stricken Seigenthaler had reported early Friday morning—Marshall, White, and Kennedy were actually relieved to learn that Connor had driven the jailed Riders back to Tennessee.

For a brief period on Friday morning, Justice Department officials believed that the day of reckoning in Alabama had been postponed. As the morning progressed, however, they were forced to confront the rumor and later the reality that not one but two groups of Freedom Riders were about to invade Birmingham. By early afternoon the vulnerability of the administration's position—not to mention the vulnerability of the Freedom Riders themselves—had become all too clear. With the Freedom Riders mobilizing, Connor raging, Patterson hiding, and crowds of angry whites gathering, the prospects for a timely resolution of the crisis seemed to be slipping away. And with only Seigenthaler and a token force of FBI agents on the ground in Birmingham, there wasn't much that the Justice Department could do about it, at least in the short run. As the federal officials entrusted with the task of resolving the crisis, Kennedy and his lieutenants could only hope that the Nashville Freedom Riders would come to their senses before it was too late. But even this faint hope began to fade later in the afternoon as word spread that a caravan of Riders had left the parsonage heading in the direction of the downtown Greyhound terminal.

By the time Shuttlesworth and the Freedom Riders arrived at the terminal, a dozen police officers, a number of newspaper and television reporters, and several hundred onlookers were already at the scene. For the fourth time in six days a large crowd had gathered to protest the Freedom Riders' presence in Alabama. Later in the day the size of the crowd would grow to three thousand and beyond, and the rising anger of the most militant protesters would eventually force the police to use its new K-9 corps to maintain order. But as the Riders piled out of the cars and headed toward the loading platform to board the 5 p.m. bus to Montgomery, the protesters seemed more stunned than anything else. "They pushed in at us as we entered the terminal," Lewis recalled, "but no one touched us." Although the bus was already idling in preparation for its departure and there were enough empty seats to accommodate all nineteen Freedom Riders, Greyhound officials promptly canceled the run, claiming that no driver was available. With the police holding back the crowd, the Riders retreated to the white waiting room, where they vowed to remain until the bus line found a driver to take them to Montgomery. After waiting for more than an hour, the Riders returned to the loading platform, but once again they were told that no Greyhound driver was willing to take them to Montgomery or anywhere else. Later, back in the waiting room, they sang freedom songs and prayed as the police strained to keep the swell of protesters from getting completely out of hand.

Most of the protesters remained outside the terminal, but the police made a point of allowing some, including several men dressed in Klan robes, to wander around the waiting room with impunity. Standing smugly only a few feet from the Riders was Imperial Wizard Robert Shelton, decked out in a black robe with an embroidered snake on the back. For nearly three hours the police stood by and watched as Shelton's Klansmen indulged in petty acts of provocation, such as "accidentally" stepping on the Riders' feet, spilling drinks on their clothes, and blocking access to the restrooms. But as darkness approached, Chief Moore decided to clear the room of everyone but the Riders. At the same time, in an effort to reassure the crowd that the police were not coddling the outside agitators, Moore—acting upon orders from Connor—also disconnected the waiting room's public telephones, closed the terminal restaurant, and dispatched two officers to the Bethel parsonage to arrest Shuttlesworth, who had returned to the church to lead a mass meeting. The charge, Connor later explained to reporters, was conspiracy to incite a riot. Who else, he asked, had done more to instigate the civil disorder that had plagued the city since Mother's Day?

By nightfall the scene in and around the terminal had taken on an eerie tone. Emboldened by the cover of darkness, the crowd grew increasingly restless as it became clear that the Riders were prepared to spend the night at the terminal. "We could see them through the glass doors and street-side windows," Lewis remembered, "gesturing at us and shouting. Every now and then a rock or a brick would crash through one of the windows near the ceiling. The police brought in dogs and we could see them outside, pulling at their leashes to keep the crowd back." The brusqueness of the police, and the absence of food and working phones, added to the siege-like atmosphere, but the entire group—which swelled to twenty-one when Brooks and Zwerg arrived at the terminal around eight p.m.—was determined to outlast both the mob and local authorities. As the night progressed, the students began to wonder what was happening in the outside world. Did the public know what was going on in downtown Birmingham? Was anyone working to break the stalemate? Shuttlesworth, who rejoined the students after being released on bond, confirmed that federal authorities were well aware of the standoff at the terminal and actively seeking a solution. Although he knew few details, he did know that Seigenthaler had been dispatched to work out a deal with Patterson.

Seigenthaler's mission to Montgomery followed repeated attempts to reach Patterson by phone, including a call from John Kennedy himself. After Patterson declined to take the president's call, this time without resorting to the subterfuge of a fishing trip, Kennedy phoned Lt. Governor Albert Boutwell, but Boutwell, a loyal Patterson crony, pleaded ignorance of the governor's whereabouts and intentions. By midafternoon the Kennedy brothers knew that they had to do something dramatic to force Patterson to the bargaining table. Infuriated by an obvious snub of his brother, Robert Kennedy informed Patterson's aides that the president was now ready to issue a public ultimatum that would lead to federal intervention in Alabama. This threat brought an immediate response from Patterson, who grabbed the phone to explain why he wanted nothing to do with the Freedom Riders. In the long conversation that followed, Kennedy urged Patterson to cooperate and predicted dire consequences if he didn't, but the recalcitrant governor stubbornly resisted making any commitment to protect the

Freedom Riders. At one point, after Patterson indulged in a gratuitous outburst about the sanctity of segregation, Kennedy nearly lost his temper. Regaining his composure, he continued the jawboning effort until Patterson, sensing that he was being boxed into a corner, abruptly ended the conversation with the demand that the Justice Department send someone to Montgomery to discuss the situation with his staff.

By the time Seigenthaler arrived at the state capitol in Montgomery on Friday evening, the Alabama crisis seemed to be spiraling out of control. Flanked by his entire cabinet, Governor Patterson sat stony-faced at the head of a long polished table. When he learned that Seigenthaler was a Southerner from Tennessee, the governor cracked a smile and welcomed his noticeably nervous visitor to Montgomery, but such niceties soon gave way to a long tirade on states' rights and the Southern way of life. "There's nobody in the whole country that's got the spine to stand up to the goddamned niggers except me," he proclaimed, adding that he had a desk full of mail "congratulating me on the stand that I've taken against what's going on in this country." Bragging that he was "more popular in this country today than John Kennedy," he vowed to hold the line "against Martin Luther King and these rabble-rousers" who had breached the peace. "I want you to know," he added, "that if schools in Alabama are integrated, blood's gonna flow in the streets, and you take that message back to the president and you tell the attorney general that."

Seigenthaler, who had heard this kind of political bombast before, politely sidestepped Patterson's demagogic posturing and eventually managed to move the conversation toward a consideration of realistic options. After several false starts, he began to make headway with the argument that it was in Alabama's interest to hand the Freedom Rider problem over to Mississippi as soon as possible. When Patterson insisted that no one could guarantee the Riders' safe passage from Birmingham to the Mississippi border, Floyd Mann, Alabama's director of safety, surprised the governor with the calm assertion that the state highway patrol was up to the task. Over the next few minutes, Mann, with Seigenthaler's encouragement, guided Patterson toward a reluctant acceptance of the responsibility for the Riders' safety. Although many of the details would not be worked out until later in the evening, Mann's plan called for a combined effort of local and state officials: The Birmingham and Montgomery police would protect the Riders within city limits, and the state police would provide protection on the open highways, with Mann himself on the bus as added insurance.

To this end, Patterson and Seigenthaler hammered out a mutually acceptable public statement, and the suddenly cooperative governor even allowed Seigenthaler to use his phone to call Robert Kennedy with the news that an agreement had been reached. With Patterson and the Alabama cabinet listening in the background, Seigenthaler read the agreed-upon statement over the phone: "The

State of Alabama has the will, the force, the men, and the equipment to give full protection to everyone in Alabama, on the highways and elsewhere." When Kennedy asked if the pledge was genuine, Patterson yelled out, "I've given my word as Governor of Alabama." Still skeptical, Kennedy asked if Patterson was willing to repeat the pledge to H. Vance Greenslit, the president of Southern Greyhound. Once again the governor said yes, and moments later he was on the phone assuring Greenslit that there would be no more bus burnings in the state of Alabama.

By late afternoon Seigenthaler was confident that the end of the Freedom Rider crisis was in sight. Even though the situation remained volatile, Patterson's apparent change of heart and Mann's professionalism had convinced him that the Riders could be protected without the direct involvement of federal law enforcement officers. Events would soon prove him wrong, but as he settled into his Montgomery motel room later that evening, he had no way of knowing that Patterson was having second thoughts about the wisdom of letting the Freedom Riders slip from his grasp. While Mann was busy conferring with local and state police commanders in a legitimate effort to live up to the agreement forged earlier in the day, Patterson was effectively undercutting the agreement with some last-minute political maneuvering. Before leaving his office for the night, the governor directed state attorney general MacDonald Gallion to track down Circuit Judge Walter B. Jones. Earlier in the week Gallion had approached Judge Jones about the need for an injunction that would bar the Freedom Riders from traveling in Alabama, and now he and Patterson wanted to make it official. An arch-conservative who had been grousing about civil rights agitators since the days of the Montgomery Bus Boycott, Jones was happy to oblige, though he reminded Gallion that the draft of the injunction that he was being asked to sign named Jim Farmer and the CORE Riders, not the Nashville Riders, as the offending parties to be enjoined. Unfazed, Gallion insisted that he and the governor wanted the injunction anyway. If nothing else, he reasoned, the resulting confusion could be used as a legal delaying mechanism. The longer the Freedom Riders were tied up in court, the longer they could be kept off Alabama's highways.

By Saturday morning Alabama officials essentially had two plans in place, one that tacitly recognized the Freedom Riders' right to travel and another that branded them as outlaws. If the agreement with the feds fell apart or became too costly politically, they could simply revert to hard-line resistance. Seigenthaler, upon learning of the injunction, felt betrayed, but the knowledge that his own department was hedging its bets tempered his indignation. Even though Robert Kennedy had sanctioned the highway patrol's preparations for the Riders' trip to Montgomery, he continued to pressure the Riders to abandon the Freedom Ride altogether. In an early-morning conversation with Shuttlesworth, Kennedy insisted that the students' best option was to follow the CORE Riders' example and fly to New Orleans. Alabama was dangerous enough, but traveling through Mississippi would be even worse, Kennedy declared, facetiously reminding Shuttlesworth that even "the Lord hasn't . . . been to Mississippi in a long time." Never one to miss a preaching opportunity, Shuttlesworth shot back: "But we think the Lord *should* go to Mississippi, and we want to get him there."

These words dredged up Kennedy's worst fear—that Shuttlesworth himself had decided to join the Freedom Ride. When asked directly if he planned to be on the bus, Shuttlesworth did not hesitate: "Mr. Kennedy, would I ask anybody else to do what I wouldn't do? I'm a battlefield general. I lead troops into battle. Yes, sir, I'm goin' to ride the bus. I've got my ticket." After a brief but futile effort to change the minister's mind, Kennedy realized that he was wasting his time. Shuttlesworth and the Riders were about to put themselves—and the well-being of the nation—at risk, and there was nothing he could do to stop them. Even worse, he had been forced to entrust their lives and the civic order to a group of law enforcement officers that in all probability would let him down and embarrass his brother's administration.

Despite his misgivings about the Alabama police, Kennedy believed that it was essential to remove the Freedom Riders from the Birmingham Greyhound terminal as soon as possible. Bull Connor's city, he was now convinced, was every bit as dangerous as Harrison Salisbury had said it was. During the night much of the crowd surrounding the terminal had dispersed, but Kennedy expected it to build up again after daylight. Thus he urged Shuttlesworth to put the Riders on the first available bus to Montgomery. Wasting no time, Shuttlesworth made sure that the students were ready to ride by 6a.m. Though stiff from a night of trying to sleep on the waiting room's hard benches, the Riders gathered at the loading platform, where they, along with several reporters, waited expectantly for a driver to appear. At five minutes after six a uniformed driver named Joe Caverno approached the bus. Turning to the Riders, he asked if any of them were members of CORE or the NAACP. When no one responded affirmatively, he became flustered and seemed to lose his nerve. "I'm supposed to drive this bus to Dothan, Alabama, through Montgomery," he stammered, barely audible over the clamor of the crowd behind the police lines, "but I understand there is a big convoy down the road. And I don't have but one life to give. And I don't intend to give it to CORE or the NAACP." After Caverno walked away, several onlookers yelled out that Greyhound would never find a driver crazy enough to take the Freedom Riders to Montgomery. Though fearing that this was the case, the Riders decided to stay on the loading platform until another driver materialized.

The drama unfolding there was hardly what Justice Department officials had expected following the negotiations with Patterson and Mann on Friday. After

Patterson reassured Southern Greyhound president Greenslit that state and local law enforcement officers were determined to avoid a repeat of the Mother's Day violence, everything seemed set. Connor and the Birmingham police had agreed to escort the bus to the city line, and Mann and the highway patrol would take over from there. Highway patrol cars would surround the bus during the ninety-mile trip to Montgomery, and the Montgomery police would see to it that nothing happened to the bus or the Freedom Riders during what was expected to be a brief stay in the state capital. Once the bus left Montgomery, the highway patrol would resume responsibility during the westward link to the Mississippi state line. What would happen in Mississippi and Louisiana was anybody's guess, but Justice Department officials were hopeful that governors Ross Barnett and Jimmie Davis would provide the Riders with safe passage through Jackson and on to New Orleans. While both Barnett and Davis were outspoken segregationists, neither had given any indication that he would tolerate anything akin to the violent disruptions that had plagued Anniston and Birmingham. All of this seemed to satisfy Greenslit, who assured Justice Department officials that Greyhound was prepared to do its part. Finding a driver for the Birmingham-to-Montgomery run would not be easy, but he was confident that a volunteer could be found by Saturday morning.

Caught off-guard by the early-morning decision to take the first bus, Seigenthaler was still in his motel room when a Birmingham FBI agent called with the alarming news that the Freedom Riders were stranded on the loading platform. Before rushing to a breakfast meeting with John Doar, Seigenthaler placed a frantic call to Greenslit in Atlanta. Professing shock that Caverno had refused to drive the bus, Greenslit vowed to get the bus out of Birmingham "at the earliest possible moment" and "to come over there and drive it myself" if no one else would do it. Greenslit then called George Cruit, the top Greyhound official in Birmingham, demanding to know why the bus was still at the loading platform. When Cruit explained that no driver was willing to take the wheel, Greenslit threatened to fire him if he didn't get the bus on the road. Cruit promised to do what he could, and within minutes Bull Connor strode into the terminal to take personal charge of the situation. Moments later Caverno reappeared on the loading platform, flanked by a dispatcher and a local Teamsters Union leader. Stepping onto the bus, the stone-faced driver settled in behind the wheel and motioned to the Riders to board.

Most of the Riders were too startled to say anything, but as the police closed ranks around the bus Shuttlesworth could not resist commenting on the irony of the situation. "Man, what's this state coming to!" he shouted to the police, "An armed escort to take a bunch of niggers to a bus station so they can break these silly laws." After a few parting taunts directed at the line of officers—including the jibe "we're gonna make a steer out of Bull"—he attempted to board the bus along with the other Riders. But Chief Moore stepped in front of the door and ordered him to go home. Although Shuttlesworth produced a ticket, Moore repeated the order, and when the minister once again failed to back away from the bus he was arrested for refusing to obey a police officer.

As Shuttlesworth was being led away, a phalanx of police cruisers and motorcycles pulled in front of the loading platform, signaling to Caverno that the escort was assembled and ready to leave. Afraid of being left behind, several reporters made a mad dash for their cars, just in time to join the convoy that was soon barreling down the streets of Birmingham. After five days of turmoil and delay, the Freedom Ride was back on track and moving southward toward Montgomery, an historic capital city with a divided heritage. Having served as both "the cradle of the Confederacy" and the unwilling nurturer of nonviolent struggle, Montgomery presented the Freedom Riders with a unique set of challenges no less daunting than those encountered in Bull Connor's Birmingham.

6

If You Miss Me from the Back of the Bus

If you miss me from the back of the bus,
And you can't find me nowhere,
Come on up to the front of the bus,
I'll be riding up there.
—1960s freedom song

The Freedom Riders' departure from Birmingham resembled a staged Hollywood chase scene—but the high-speed drama was all too real. Since none of the Riders had been briefed on the plan to protect them, there was high anxiety on the bus, at least in the early going. When the Greyhound reached the southern edge of the city, there was a moment of panic as the police escort pulled to the side of the road, but within seconds several highway patrol cars appeared in front of the bus. Overhead a low-flying highway patrol plane tracked the bus's progress down Highway 31, with the rest of the convoy—the cars carrying FBI observers, Floyd Mann's plainclothes detectives, and several reporters—following close behind. Additional highway patrol cars were stationed all along the route at intervals of fifteen miles, and at each checkpoint a new patrolman took the lead. All of this was reassuring, and by the time the bus passed over the Shelby County line and approached the town of Jemison, thirty miles south of Birmingham, many of the Riders had begun to relax. State officials had promised the Justice Department that the bus run to Montgomery would include all of the normal stops, so there was some surprise when the bus did not stop in Jemison—or in any of the other towns along the route. No one on the bus, however, voiced any objection to the express-like pace of the trip. For the first time in days the Nashville students felt relatively safe.

The convoy crossed over the Alabama River and entered Montgomery County around 10 a.m. With the capital city of Montgomery lying just a few miles to the southeast, everything seemed set for a safe arrival. When a message from the pilot of the patrol plane confirmed that the bus was only fourteen miles from the city, Mann relayed the news to Montgomery's public safety commissioner, L. B. Sullivan, the local official responsible for the final leg of the Freedom Riders' escort. A notoriously hard-line segregationist, Sullivan had already gained national attention as the plaintiff in an April 1960 libel suit against the *New York Times*, Shuttlesworth, and three other SCLC leaders who had signed an advertisement in that paper condemning Alabama officials for intimidating and persecuting Martin Luther King. Realizing that Sullivan was potentially the weakest link in the chain of security, Mann reminded the commissioner that he and other city officials had promised to protect the Riders inside the city limits of Montgomery. Unruffled, Sullivan calmly assured Mann that a large contingent of police was waiting at the Montgomery Greyhound terminal.

When Seigenthaler and Doar left their motel, they had every reason to believe that state and local officials would provide the Riders with safe passage through Montgomery. Confident that everything was proceeding according to plan, they felt secure enough to enjoy a leisurely breakfast before heading for the Greyhound terminal. Expecting the bus to make several stops, they calculated—incorrectly—that the Riders would arrive at the Montgomery terminal sometime around 11 a.m. In fact, the bus arrived at the station well before Seigenthaler did. When Caverno eased the bus into its arrival bay at 10:23, there were no policemen in sight. A few minutes earlier, at the Montgomery city line, the Riders had discovered that their police escort was limited to a lone patrolman on a motorcycle. Now, as they prepared to leave the bus, there was an unsettling quiet, not unlike the situation that had greeted the CORE Riders in Birmingham the previous Sunday. "The only people I could see," Lewis recalled, "were a couple of taxi drivers sitting in their cabs, a small group of reporters waiting on the platform, and a dozen or so white men standing together over near the terminal door."

In actuality, there were as many as two hundred protesters in the immediate area waiting to strike a blow for segregation. Lookouts in parked cars had been posted in the streets around the terminal since Friday evening, and some of central Alabama's most notorious Klansmen—including more than a dozen of those involved in the Birmingham Mother's Day riot—were on hand to lead the mob. The ringleader of the "welcoming" party was Claude Henley, a local car salesman and former highway patrolman who had served on Montgomery's volunteer reserve police force since 1956. A close friend of Captain Drue Lackey, the commander of the city's patrol division, Henley had been promised that the police would not interfere with his plan to teach the Freedom Riders a lesson.

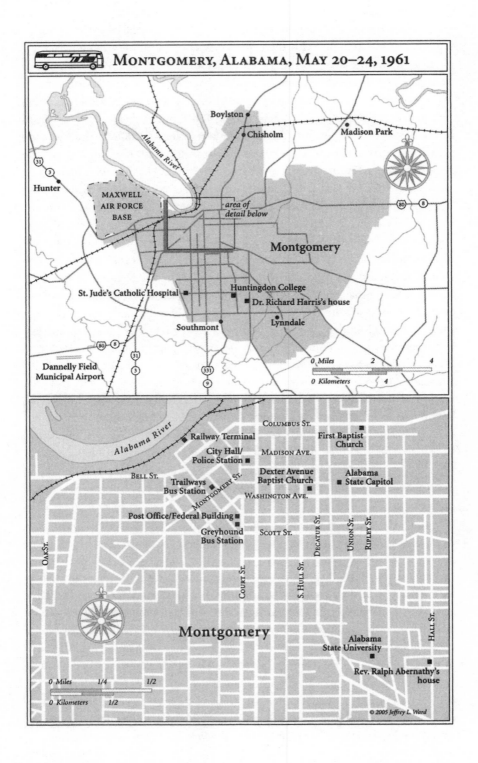

MONTGOMERY, ALABAMA, MAY 20–24, 1961

Boylston

Chisholm

Madison Park

Alabama River

Hunter

MAXWELL
AIR FORCE
BASE

*area of
detail below*

Montgomery

St. Jude's Catholic Hospital

Huntingdon College

Dr. Richard Harris's house

Southmont

Lynndale

Dannelly Field
Municipal Airport

0 Miles 2 4

0 Kilometers 4

Alabama River

Railway Terminal

COLUMBUS ST.

First Baptist
Church

City Hall/
Police Station

MADISON AVE.

BELL ST.

Trailways
Bus Station

MONTGOMERY ST.

Dexter Avenue
Baptist Church

Alabama
State Capitol

WASHINGTON AVE.

Post Office/Federal Building

Greyhound
Bus Station

SCOTT ST.

DECATUR ST.

UNION ST.

RIPLEY ST.

OAK ST.

COURT ST.

S. HULL ST.

Montgomery

Alabama
State University

HALL ST.

Rev. Ralph Abernathy's
house

0 Miles 1/4 1/2

0 Kilometers 1/2

© 2005 Jeffrey L. Ward

After a few moments of hesitation, Lewis, Catherine Burks, Bill Harbour, Jim Zwerg, and several other Riders exited the bus, stepping onto a loading platform where a group of reporters waited with notepads and microphones in hand. Before turning to the reporters to make a statement, Lewis, who had passed through the Montgomery terminal many times before, warned Harbour that things didn't look right. Seconds later, a group of white men armed with lead pipes and baseball bats rushed toward them. Norman Ritter, a writer for *Life* magazine, had just asked the first question, but Lewis, distracted by the advancing mob, never finished his answer. After wheeling around to see what was happening, Ritter attempted to shield the Riders with his outstretched arms. The mob brushed him aside, forcing the Riders to back away toward a low retaining wall that overlooked the post office parking lot eight feet below. For a few moments, the focus of the frenzy was on the reporters, as several attackers clubbed and kicked Ritter, *Life* photographer Don Uhrbrock, Herb Kaplow and Moe Levy of NBC, and *Time* magazine correspondent Calvin Trillin. Other members of the mob began to smash television cameras and sound equipment before turning on the Freedom Riders themselves.

By this time, most of the Riders had left the bus, and several pairs of seatmates had joined hands, forming a human chain on the loading platform. Following nonviolent protocol, Lewis counseled the Riders to hold their ground and "stand together," but the surging mob quickly overwhelmed them. As he remembered the scene: "Out of nowhere, from every direction, came people. White people. Men, women, and children. Dozens of them. Hundreds of them. Out of alleys, out of side streets, around the corners of office buildings, they emerged from everywhere, from all directions, all at once, as if they'd been let out of a gate . . . They carried every makeshift weapon imaginable. Baseball bats, wooden boards, bricks, chains, tire irons, pipes, even garden tools—hoes and rakes. One group had women in front, their faces twisted in anger, screaming, '*Git them niggers, GIT them niggers!*' "

Pressed against the retaining wall, most of the Riders either jumped or were pushed over the railing into the parking lot below. Some landed on the hoods or roofs of cars before scrambling to their feet and staggering toward the street in front of the terminal. With most of the attackers still on the loading platform, the Riders fortunate enough to make it to the lower level gained at least some chance of escape. As the mob concentrated its fury on the reporters and the half-dozen Riders who remained on the platform, the Riders on the street either ran from the area or frantically tried to find someone willing to drive them to Ralph Abernathy's First Baptist Church or some other safe haven. After briefly huddling on the curb, the seven female Riders spied a parked taxicab with a black driver at the wheel. Catherine Burks begged the driver to take them to First Baptist, but he balked—protesting that the law would not allow him to carry more than four passengers, or to carry white passengers at all. Burks, seeing the fear in his face, told him to move over so she could drive the cab herself. Realizing that she meant business, the driver motioned to the five black women to get in, but he wouldn't budge on the segregation issue. Moments later, as the cab pulled away, the two white female Riders, Susan Wilbur and Susan Hermann, found a second cab; once again the driver was black. As the two women climbed into the back-seat, the driver started to object, but before he could press his case a screaming white man grabbed his keys and pulled him out of the car. Other members of the mob, including several women, then dragged Wilbur and Hermann onto the sidewalk and proceeded to beat them with swinging pocketbooks and other makeshift weapons.

Seigenthaler was circling the block looking for a parking place. After slowly steering his way through the throng in front of the terminal, he began to realize that a full-scale riot was in progress. To his amazement and horror, white pro-testers were smashing luggage and tossing it into the street, and several young Freedom Riders appeared to be running for their lives. All of this was bad enough, but as he drew closer to the terminal he saw Susan Wilbur being punched repeatedly by a teenage boy, "a young, skinny kid who looked about fifteen years old . . . facing her and dancing like a boxer and smacking her in the face." On impulse, Seigenthaler jerked the wheel to the right and drove onto the sidewalk. He jumped out of the car and raced over to help but arrived just as Wilbur was slammed against his front fender. Pulling the young woman to her feet, he urged her to get into the car. Not knowing who he was, she pushed him away, screaming: "Mister, this is not your fight! Get away from here! You're gonna get killed!" In the meantime, Hermann had crawled into the backseat, but Seigenthaler hardly noticed her as he pleaded with Wilbur. Suddenly, two rough-looking men dressed in overalls blocked his path to the car door, demanding to know who "the hell" he was. Seigenthaler replied that he was a federal agent and that they had better not challenge his authority. Before he could say any more, a third man struck him in the back of the head with a pipe. Unconscious, he fell to the pavement, where he was kicked in the ribs by other members of the mob. Pushed under the rear bumper of the car, his battered and motionless body remained there until discovered by a reporter twenty-five minutes later.

Somehow Wilbur and Hermann managed to escape their tormentors before being seriously injured. Others were less fortunate. The worst of the carnage was back on the loading platform, where Zwerg, Lewis, and several others found themselves cornered by the mob. The first Rider to be assaulted was Zwerg, who bowed his head in prayer as a group of attackers closed in. Attracting special at-tention as the only white male Rider, he was knocked to the pavement amid screams of "filthy Communists, nigger lovers, you're not going to integrate Montgomery!" According to Fred Leonard, who was standing only a few feet away when Zwerg went down: "It was like those people in the mob were pos-sessed. They couldn't believe that there was a white man who would help us . . . It's like they didn't see the rest of us for about thirty seconds. They didn't see us at all." As the other Riders looked on in horror, Claude Henley and several other Klansmen kicked Zwerg in the back before smashing him in the head with his own suitcase. Dazed and bleeding, Zwerg struggled to get up, but one of the Klansmen promptly pinned the defenseless student's arms back while others punched him repeatedly in the face. To Lucretia Collins, who witnessed the beating from the backseat of a departing taxicab, the savagery of Zwerg's at-tackers was sickening. "Some men held him while white women clawed his face with their nails," she recalled. "And they held up their little children—children who couldn't have been more than a couple years old—to claw his face. I had to turn my head because I just couldn't watch it." Eventually Zwerg's eyes rolled back and his body sagged into unconsciousness. After tossing him over a railing, his attackers went looking for other targets.

Turning to the black Freedom Riders huddled near the railing, several of the Klansmen rushed forward. The first victim in their path was William Barbee, the only Rider who had not traveled to Montgomery on the Greyhound. Sent ahead "to arrange for cars and other necessities," he was at the terminal to welcome his friends when the riot broke out. Standing next to his ABT classmates, Lewis and Lafayette, Barbee had only a moment to shield his face before the advancing Klansmen unleashed a flurry of punches and kicks that dropped him to the pave-ment. While one Klansman held him down, a second jammed a jagged piece of pipe into his ear, and a third bashed him in the skull with a baseball bat, inflicting permanent damage that shortened his life. Moments later, Lewis went down, struck by a large wooden Coca-Cola crate. "I could feel my knees collapse and then nothing," he recalled. "Everything turned white for an instant, then black." Lying unconscious on the pavement, he missed the drama that followed, as Leonard, Lafayette, and Cason escaped from the mob by jumping over the retaining wall and running into the post office, where, to their amazement, postal employees and customers were "carrying on their business, just like nothing was happening outside." As he ran through the mail-sorting room, Lafayette heard the sound of gunfire, which he feared was coming from the Klansmen on the loading platform. "I thought they were shooting Freedom Riders," he recalled years later. The shots actually came from the gun of Floyd Mann, who had ar-rived just in time to protect the three unconscious Freedom Riders from further injury.

Unsure of Sullivan's commitment to protect the Riders, Mann had stationed a force of highway patrolmen a few blocks from the terminal. Although he had no jurisdiction inside the city limits, he was prepared to intervene if the Mont-gomery police abandoned their responsibility. What he was not prepared for, however, was the massive disorder that he encountered at the terminal. Arriving five minutes after the melee began, he wandered helplessly through the chaos until he reached the scene at the loading platform. Moments earlier, a local black man named Miles Davis had tried to rescue Barbee, but by the time Mann arrived both men were under attack. After trying but failing to pull several attackers off of Barbee, he instinctively pulled out his pistol, fired two warning shots, and shouted, "I'll shoot the next man who hits him. Stand back! There'll be no killing here today." To prove that he meant business, Mann then arrested one of the attackers, a Montgomery Klansman named Thurman Ouzts. This seemed to break the spell, and most of the rioters on the loading platform drifted away, though one man continued to attack James Atkins, a Birmingham television reporter, until Mann threatened to shoot him if he didn't stop.

In other areas of the terminal, the rampage continued unabated for several minutes, much of it in full view of reporters, FBI agents, and other witnesses. Looking down from a third-floor window in the Federal Building, John Doar saw enough to make him heartsick. After witnessing the first part of the riot from the street, he had raced upstairs and placed a frantic call to Burke Marshall. "Oh, there are fists punching," the normally soft-spoken attorney shouted into the phone, "A bunch of men led by a guy with a bleeding face are beating them. There are no cops. It's terrible . . . There's not a cop in sight. People are yelling 'Get 'em, get 'em.' It's awful." For several minutes Doar provided Marshall with a running commentary, though he did not witness the attack on Seigenthaler.

Closer to the action on the street, Fred and Anna Gach, a local white couple with liberal views, tried to intervene on the Freedom Riders' behalf. This only seemed to inflame the mob. Later in the day, the Montgomery police arrested the Gaches for disorderly conduct. Eventually fined $300 by a city judge, they were among only a handful of persons arrested that Saturday, even though the police arrived in time to apprehend at least part of the mob. When Commissioner Sullivan and the police appeared on the scene, approximately ten minutes after the bus's arrival, the initial phase of the riot was still in progress. But there was no effort to detain or arrest anyone involved in the beatings. Nor was there any attempt to clear the area, even though the crowd continued to grow. Most of the officers simply stood by and watched as the rioters got in a few more licks. Indeed, according to several observers, the realization that the police were openly sympathetic actually emboldened some members of the crowd, turning gawkers into active rioters. "I saw whites and negroes beaten unmercifully while law officers calmly directed traffic," Tom Lankford of the *Birmingham News* reported, adding: "I was an eye-witness to the mob attack last Sunday on the so-called 'freedom riders' in Birmingham. But with all its terror, it didn't compare with this . . . Saturday was hell in Montgomery."

Although the police were officially on hand to restore order, Sullivan's primary concern was clearly a reassertion of local authority. As soon as he learned that Mann was on the loading platform, he rushed over to take charge. To his dismay, however, he was soon upstaged by the arrival of several state and county officials, including Judge Walter Jones and Attorney General MacDonald Gallion. Walking over to Lewis, who was still lying half-conscious on the pavement, Gallion asked a deputy sheriff to read the injunction that Jones had issued earlier in the morning. The Freedom Riders, Lewis now learned, were outlaws in the state of Alabama.

That the Freedom Riders were also victims of vigilante violence did not seem to trouble Jones and Gallion, or the police officers nearby who made a point of fraternizing with members of the mob. Other than Mann, no one in a position of authority showed any interest in helping the injured Riders. Although Zwerg was bleeding profusely and passing in and out of consciousness, the police refused to call an ambulance. Convinced that Zwerg was near death, Lewis and Barbee, with the help of a reporter, carried the young divinity student over to an empty cab, but the white driver grabbed the keys and stormed off. Still sitting in the back seat but barely conscious, Zwerg soon attracted the attention of the deputy sheriff, who sauntered over to read the injunction for a second time. A few minutes later, Lewis and Barbee found a black cabdriver willing to drive them to a doctor's office, but the police would not allow Zwerg to go with them, insisting that he would have to wait for a white ambulance. When reporters asked Sullivan why no such ambulance had appeared, he claimed that all of the city's white ambulances were in the repair shop. Eventually Mann intervened, ordering one of his young patrolmen, Tommy Giles, to transport Zwerg to St. Jude's Catholic Hospital by car. But Sullivan's intended message was unmistakable: The outside agitators, especially the "nigger loving" white ones, had gotten what they deserved.

By the time Mann and Giles put Zwerg in the car, all of the other Riders had left the bus terminal, and most had found at least a temporary refuge. The five female Riders in the taxicab—all of whom witnessed the beatings of Zwerg, Lewis, and Barbee before leaving—found a phone booth a few blocks from the terminal and called Fred Shuttlesworth, who relayed their whereabouts to Diane Nash. Others called Nash directly, blurting out the shocking news of what had just happened, including the injunction that seemed to make them all fugitives. Fearing that all of the Riders were now subject to arrest, Nash advised them to stay out of sight and away from the police. Unfortunately, this plan had already been compromised by Wilbur and Hermann, who had called the police after fleeing from the terminal area. After retrieving them from a downtown church, police officers promptly made arrangements to send the two women back to Nashville by train. The rest of the Freedom Riders, however, got the word in time to lay low. When he heard about the Riders' plight, the Reverend Solomon S. Seay Sr., one of the heroes of the bus boycott, offered his home as a safe house, and by early afternoon the Riders began to gather there.

Back at the terminal, the crowd hardly seemed to notice that the Freedom Riders were no longer there. With the police making only a token effort to restore order, several of the rioters gathered up the Riders' belongings and constructed a bonfire in the middle of the street. Others continued the attacks on newsmen and anyone else who looked like an outsider. Although the size of the crowd had swelled to several hundred, Sullivan and the handful of officers dispatched to the terminal seemed content to let the riot run its course with a minimum of interference. At 11:30 a disgusted Floyd Mann called in sixty-five highway patrolmen to the scene, and a few minutes later they were joined by several deputy sheriffs on horseback. But the city police did not respond in force until 1 p.m., nearly three hours after the riot had begun. Sensing the reporters' disapproval, Sullivan belatedly ordered his men to make a few arrests and even authorized the use of tear gas to disperse the crowd. Nevertheless, sporadic violence continued for more than two hours as the mob broke up into small gangs that spread the mayhem into surrounding streets. By the time the rioting ended around 4, twenty people had been seriously injured.

Once order was restored, Sullivan held an impromptu press conference in the terminal parking lot. "I really don't know what happened," he told the reporters. "When I got here, all I saw were three men lying in the street. There was two niggers and a white man." Obviously pleased with what had transpired, he made little effort to hide his disregard for the victims, though later in the day he became a bit more cautious as he and other city leaders began to worry about how all of this would play in the press. "We all sincerely regret that this happened here in Montgomery," he declared, insisting "it could have been avoided had outside agitators left us alone . . . Providing police protection for agitators is not our policy, but we would have been ready if we had had definite and positive information they were coming." Federal and state officials would later put Sullivan on the defensive by disputing the claim that he had been unaware of the Freedom Riders' impending arrival. Indeed, many observers, including Judge Richard Rives, eventually concluded that Sullivan had followed the lead of Birmingham's Bull Connor. Several days after the beatings, Rives overheard a local Klansman praise Sullivan for cooperating with the mob. "Sully kept his word," the Klansman chortled. "He said he'd give us half an hour to beat up those God-damned sons of bitches and he did." Even John Patterson, in a 1988 interview, acknowledged that he was fairly certain that Sullivan "had let the Klan know that he'd give them a few minutes to work on the riders a little bit."

Some members of the press suspected as much from the outset, but in the absence of hard evidence of complicity most were content, for the time being at least, to focus on the most sensational episode of the day—the attack on John Seigenthaler. At first Sullivan himself paid little attention to the news that a man claiming to be a personal representative of the president had been beaten by the mob, but the apparent seriousness of Seigenthaler's injuries and the rumor that Sullivan had initially refused to call an ambulance for the stricken federal official made the incident an unavoidable issue by late Saturday afternoon. Following a brief conversation with a police lieutenant, Seigenthaler had lapsed back into unconsciousness before being rushed to a local hospital. Listed in serious condition, he later woke up in an X-ray room as his doctor talked to a stunned Byron White on the phone. Seigenthaler had a fractured skull and several broken ribs, the doctor told White, but with a little luck he would make a full recovery.

Before calling the hospital, White had tracked Robert Kennedy down at an FBI baseball game. Visibly shaken by White's sketchy but graphic report of the riot, Kennedy called an emergency meeting of his senior staff. By late Saturday afternoon he was cloistered with White, Marshall, and several others who were still trying to determine exactly what had happened. When it became clear that the Montgomery police had done little or nothing to protect the Freedom Riders or anybody else who got in the mob's way, Kennedy called John Patterson for an explanation. Patterson, who had not spoken to Kennedy since Thursday evening, dodged the call. For Kennedy this was the final straw. No governor could be allowed to thumb his nose at the federal government while countenancing the wanton disruption of civil order. The force of federal marshals that he and his brother had hoped would never be used, he now realized, was the only available deterrent to continued disorder and disrespect.

After a brief conversation with his brother, who was away on a weekend retreat, the attorney general ordered Marshall and White to activate the mobilization plan. Declaring that he wanted the marshals on the ground in Alabama within twenty-four hours, he asked White to assume operational command of the force and Marshall to handle the legal side of the operation through John Doar. Within minutes Marshall was on the phone with Doar finalizing the language of a proposed federal court injunction prohibiting the Klan and the National States Rights Party from interfering with interstate transit. And within an hour, James McShane, the head of the U.S. Marshal Service, and twenty of his deputies were on their way to National Airport to catch a flight to Montgomery. Other marshals from the various parts of the South and Midwest soon followed, and by midnight more than a hundred had arrived at Montgomery's Maxwell Air Force Base, two miles from the site of the riot.

As the preparations began to take shape on Saturday afternoon, Robert Kennedy called Seigenthaler's hospital room and was pleased to discover that the patient was doing better than expected, despite "a terrible headache." When Kennedy informed him that the marshals were on the way, Seigenthaler expressed regret and apologized for his inability to defuse the crisis. Kennedy assured him that it was not his fault. The federal-state showdown was bound to happen "sooner or later," the attorney general insisted, adding: "Don't feel bad about it, it's just what you had to do, and I'm glad you're all right." Before hanging up, Seigenthaler thanked Kennedy for his understanding, though he couldn't resist offering a few parting words of advice: "Don't run for governor of Alabama; you're not too popular down here." A few minutes later, an unexpected visit from a tearful Floyd Mann reminded Seigenthaler that not all white Alabamians were Kennedy haters. But the hard truth of his quip seemed unassailable as the most harrowing afternoon of his life came to a close.

Robert Kennedy did not like the idea of alienating the voters of a state that had just given his brother five electoral votes, but he was running out of patience—and options. Though politically expedient, relying on state and local officials to preserve civic order was proving too risky. While Kennedy planned to do everything he could to minimize the political damage, he now saw no alternative to a show of federal force in Alabama. With the summit in Vienna less than two weeks away, he simply could not allow the image and moral authority of the United States to be undercut by a mob of racist vigilantes, or, for that matter, by a band of headstrong students determined to provoke them. Like it or not, he had to do something dramatic to bring the Freedom Rider crisis to a close. The decision to send in the marshals was also personal. As several administration insiders later acknowledged, the Kennedy brothers were furious at Patterson. Either out of incompetence or in outright connivance—and the Kennedys suspected the latter—he had presided over a needless escalation of violence that included a shameless attack on federal authority.

Neither the attorney general nor the president would ever trust Patterson again, but by late Saturday afternoon both men had worked through enough of their anger to draft carefully worded public statements outlining the federal government's response to the Montgomery riot. Realizing that the national wire services and radio and television networks were bound to treat a riot that included attacks on newsmen and a presidential envoy as a major news story, the Kennedys hoped to preempt what they feared would be an alarmist press response. The president's brief statement, released directly to the press, conveyed a mixture of concern and reassurance and implicitly criticized Alabama officials as well as the Freedom Riders. He vowed that the federal government would meet its responsibilities to maintain public safety and called upon local officials to do the same.

Longer and more explicit than his brother's effort, the attorney general's statement took the form of a personal telegram to Patterson, the text of which was immediately released to the press. Robert Kennedy wanted the world to know the exact circumstances that had prompted the decision to send a federal peacekeeping force to Alabama. Accordingly, he itemized the governor's failure to live up to his previous assurances. The telegram also informed Patterson that the Justice Department planned to send a team of FBI investigators to Montgomery and to seek an injunction against the Klan and any other groups "interfering with interstate travel by buses."

As it turned out, Kennedy received a call from Patterson a few minutes before the telegram was actually sent. After being assured that "everything seemed to be under control in Alabama," Kennedy read the text of the telegram over the phone. Caught off guard by the announcement that federal intervention was imminent, Patterson insisted that Alabama needed no "outside help," prompting Kennedy to ask him to prove it. "Why don't you call out the National Guard and make it unnecessary for us to take any outside action?" Kennedy asked. Alarmed by this suggestion, Patterson stammered: "This is unnecessary. This will be a matter of embarrassment to me. I will have to take steps to defend myself politically." Kennedy responded, with some sympathy, that he understood the political constraints of Alabama politics, but he added that the Justice Department could not allow political considerations to interfere with a timely resolution of the crisis. "You are going to have to paddle your own boat," he warned.

Later in the evening, Patterson issued a public response to Kennedy's telegram. After claiming that he had "no sympathy for lawbreakers whether they be agitators from outside Alabama or inside-the-state troublemakers," he stated that Alabama law enforcement officials needed "no help—from the federal government, from 'interested citizens,' or anyone else." He then went on to qualify his pledge of protection. "While we will do our utmost to keep the public highways clear and to guard against all disorder," he declared, "we cannot escort busloads or carloads of rabble rousers about our state from city to city for the avowed purpose of disobeying our laws, flouting our customs and traditions, and creating racial incidents. Such unlawful acts serve only to further enrage our populace. I have no use for these agitators or their kind." While acknowledging that Alabama officials had "the duty and the desire to protect human lives no matter who is involved," he insisted that "how we do it is a matter for us to determine."

The full text of the statements, detailed accounts of the riot, and graphic pictures of injured newsmen and Freedom Riders appeared in newspapers across the nation on Sunday morning. What did not appear, however, was any hint of the behind-the-scenes drama being played out among movement activists in Montgomery, Nashville, Atlanta, New Orleans, and Washington. For the Freedom Riders themselves, the biggest story of May 20 was the unreported transformation of a limited project into a full-fledged movement. The seeds of this transformation had been planted the previous Tuesday when the Nashville stu-

dents had stepped in for the CORE Riders, but it was not until Saturday afternoon that a true movement culture began to take hold among the Riders.

As the survivors of the riot gathered at the Reverend Seay's house, the scene
began to resemble a religious revival. Far from scaring the Riders off, the riot
seemed to have forged a renewed sense of common purpose and solidarity. Surviving a trial by fire had somehow dispelled the mystique of massive resistance,
and despite fears of future violence, as well as concern for those who had already
been injured, the importance of sustaining the Freedom Ride was clearer than
ever. Speaking from his hospital bed at St. Jude's, Jim Zwerg assured reporters
that "these beatings cannot deter us from our purpose. We are not martyrs or
publicity-seekers. We want only equality and justice, and we will get it. We will
continue our journey one way or another. We are prepared to die." Lying one
floor below, in St. Jude's black ward, William Barbee echoed Zwerg's pledge: "As
soon as we're recovered from this, we'll start again . . . We'll take all the South has
to throw and still come back for more."

This collective resurrection of the spirit sprang from many sources, some in-
tensely personal, others largely contextual, but no element of the Freedom
Riders' resolve was more important than the network of support sustained by
Nash and the movement volunteers back in Nashville. In the critical hours following the riot, the Nashville office was a beehive of activity, dispensing words
of comfort and encouragement to the Riders and mobilizing a broad coalition of
supporters. Delivered in a flurry of phone calls, Nash's message to the national
civil rights community was unequivocal: The movement could not afford a second failed Freedom Ride. If the white supremacist vigilantes and irresponsible
officials in Alabama got their way, the entire movement would lose momentum
and credibility.

By late afternoon Nash's personal appeals had brought several key organizations and individuals on board. In Nashville, Jim Lawson promptly volunteered
to go to Montgomery to join the Ride, as did Nash herself. In Birmingham, Shuttlesworth, who had tried to join the Ride earlier in the day, also agreed to travel
to Montgomery to help the students regroup. In Atlanta, Ella Baker and other
SNCC leaders promised to recruit a new batch of Freedom Riders if needed;
and in Washington, NAG, the SNCC affiliate that had contributed Hank Thomas
to the original CORE Ride, made a similar pledge. Indeed, several NAG stalwarts, including John Moody and Paul Dietrich, were already on their way to
Alabama. Remorseful about his earlier recalcitrance, Moody was determined to
be in the thick of things this time. Thomas himself was in New York recovering
from his injuries, but as soon as he heard the news reports of the Saturday
morning riot, he too made plans to fly to Montgomery.

All of this support was welcome, but Nash knew that none of it would matter
if she failed to enlist the Southern Christian Leadership Conference and King in

the cause. To this point, King and his advisors had been wary of supporting the second Freedom Ride, as the May 17 SCLC meeting at Shuttlesworth's parsonage had revealed. Thus she was greatly relieved to discover that King agreed with her assessment of the seriousness of the situation. The SCLC president was in Chicago to deliver a speech, but after conferring with Nash, Abernathy, and Walker, he decided to cancel his engagement and return to Atlanta. By late Saturday afternoon Nash and the three SCLC leaders had worked out a plan to hold a mass meeting at Abernathy's church in Montgomery on Sunday evening. King, who had been in Montgomery as recently as May 11, would fly in to deliver the keynote address, and other movement leaders, including Shuttlesworth, would also speak.

Realizing that SCLC's approach to nonviolent direct action was more cautious than SNCC's, Nash had some misgivings about bringing King to Montgomery. Indeed, using his prestige and celebrity to shore up the Freedom Ride was hardly in keeping with SNCC's or the Nashville student movement's democratic ethos. She could only hope that King and other SCLC leaders would come to see the wisdom of SNCC's grassroots philosophy instead of trying to co-opt the students' energies. To some extent, she faced the same problem with Jim Farmer and CORE. When she called Farmer to enlist his support and cooperation, he too promised to fly to Montgomery, adding that he would immediately dispatch additional CORE Riders to Alabama. But, as she suspected, his motives involved more than concern for the future of the Freedom Ride. "Quite frankly," Farmer acknowledged in his autobiography, "although I welcomed the intervention of SNCC, a concern burned within me. I could not let CORE's new program slip from its grasp and be taken over by others."

Robert Kennedy nearly exploded when he received word that King had agreed to lead a rally at First Baptist. The decision to send in the marshals was risky enough, but King's involvement presented Kennedy with a nightmare scenario. Already the subject of intense news coverage, the Montgomery situation would become a media circus if King were allowed to take center stage. Considering the probable threat to King's safety, the federal government would have no choice but to offer him protection, a development that was bound to add fuel to the fire of massive resistance. In an effort to forestall this escalation of the crisis, Kennedy called King in Chicago to plead with him to stay away from Montgomery. To Kennedy's dismay, King refused to change his plans.

The near certainty that King was coming to Montgomery erased any doubts at the Justice Department about the wisdom of mobilizing a force of federal marshals. Convinced that the crisis was deepening, Kennedy summoned his staff, set up a round-the-clock command center in his office, and established an open phone line to his brother's weekend retreat at Glen Ora, Virginia. While the

Kennedys and other administration officials still held out some hope that state authorities—perhaps with the help of the National Guard—could keep things in hand, King's involvement dramatically increased the likelihood that the marshals would actually be used. Even if no actual rioting ensued, marshals would still be needed to escort King to and from the church—an unwelcome development that would provide Alabama segregationists with a convenient symbol of federal encroachment. All of this weighed heavily on Robert Kennedy's staff as they proceeded with the mobilization of the marshals. But by early Saturday evening there was no turning back. White, Oberdorfer, and several other Justice Department officials had already boarded a plane to Montgomery provided by Najeeb Halaby, the head of the Federal Aviation Administration and White and Oberdorfer's former classmate at Yale Law School.

Arriving at Maxwell Air Force Base at 8 p.m., White and his staff set up headquarters in a vacant Quonset hut that soon became a processing center for hundreds of newly deputized marshals. McShane and other experienced marshals from the District of Columbia, who had arrived earlier in the day, provided a core of professionalism, but White soon discovered that most of his makeshift civilian army was a motley assortment of revenue agents, prison guards, and border patrolmen. As Marshall later acknowledged, "the border patrol were the only ones that could shoot . . . Most of them," he admitted, "were the product of senatorial patronage, middle-aged, fat, lethargic people with no law enforcement experience. Many of them came from the South and really thought they were being asked to protect black people whom they considered Communists, or worse. We weren't sure which side they would be on." White himself, of course, was no general, though he had served in the Navy during World War II.

Across town John Doar faced pressure of a different kind. While White and Oberdorfer were busy assembling their peacekeeping force, Doar was running out of time in his efforts to secure a temporary restraining order against the Klan and other groups determined to break the peace. Although he was confident that Judge Frank Johnson would sign the order, Doar had to find him first. Johnson, as it turned out, was spending the weekend at his summer cottage fifty miles north of Montgomery. Fortunately, Lee Dodd, a lifelong friend of Johnson's who also served as his marshal, agreed to guide Doar to the cottage. After driving through the Alabama woods and crossing a small lake by boat, Doar and Dodd finally reached Johnson's cottage a few minutes after midnight. As expected, the judge promptly granted the restraining order, though he surprised Doar by limiting the order's scope to the alleged perpetrators of the Montgomery riot. For the time being, the Klansmen responsible for the previous week's violence in Birmingham were off the hook. Though disappointed, Doar realized that granting even a limited order was an act of courage for an Alabama judge. Accordingly, as soon as he returned to Montgomery he quietly arranged for a band of federal marshals to protect Johnson's life.

Along with the marshals' arrival, the granting of the temporary restraining order set the stage for a dramatic political showdown between state and federal authorities. By Sunday morning Governor Patterson, who seemed to relish his new role as the South's leading defender of states' rights, was fulminating against Washington's unwarranted invasion of Alabama. Pushed into a dangerous but politically promising corner, he demanded a meeting with White in full view of the press. When White arrived at the capitol, the governor was flanked by the entire Alabama cabinet and a gaggle of reporters. Wasting no time, Patterson immediately took the offensive. "We consider you interlopers here," he declared, "and we feel that your presence here will only serve to agitate and provoke the racial situation. We don't need your marshals, we don't want them, and we didn't ask for them. And still the federal government sends them here to help put down a disturbance which it helped create." Declining to take the bait, White remained calm. But Patterson refused to let up, warning White that the federal marshals risked arrest if they challenged state sovereignty. "Make especially certain," he counseled, "that none of your men encroach on any of our state laws, rights, or functions, because we'll arrest them just like anybody else." Patterson went on to grill White about the motives and location of the Freedom Riders, who he claimed were Communist-inspired agitators. After denying that there was any evidence of Communist infiltration into the Freedom Rider movement, White bravely added that "no matter what this group's connection may be, if any, that is no reason why they shouldn't be assured of the right to travel peacefully by bus." Undeterred, Patterson demanded to know if federal marshals were willing to help state authorities enforce Judge Jones's injunction against outside agitators. Caught off guard, White pleaded ignorance of the injunction—and of the Freedom Riders' exact whereabouts. No, he would not arrest the Freedom Riders or even help state authorities to apprehend them. Satisfied with this admission, Patterson allowed the forty-five-minute ordeal to end.

Deeply discouraged by his meeting with Patterson, White took the risky step of bypassing the chain of command with a late-morning call to the White House. Although the attorney general was his immediate superior, he felt more comfortable speaking directly with the president, whom he had known since their navy days in the Pacific. The marshals' presence in Alabama seemed to be making matters worse, he told John Kennedy, adding that it might be prudent to have them withdrawn. Wisely, Kennedy sidestepped White's suggestion with a gentle admonition and a plea for fortitude. But White's momentary crisis of confidence would later prove embarrassing when word of the proposed withdrawal reached Patterson via an eavesdropping telephone operator.

After assuring the president that he would do his best, White steeled his nerves and turned his attention to the crisis of the moment. A plane carrying Martin Luther King was scheduled to arrive around noon, and White had dispatched an armed guard of fifty marshals to the Montgomery airport to make sure that no one got hurt. Fortunately, the scene at the airport was quiet, and the marshals safely escorted King to a brief private meeting with Nash, Lewis, and Lafayette at an outlying black church before proceeding on to Abernathy's downtown parsonage. Later in the afternoon twelve of the marshals returned to the airport to provide an escort for Shuttlesworth, who soon joined the Freedom Riders gathered in the basement library at First Baptist, where they were hiding as fugitives from the injunction issued by Judge Jones.

Although the mass meeting was scheduled to begin at 8 p.m., the faithful began to arrive at First Baptist as early as 5. At that point only a few protesters were in sight of the church, and the early-comers had no trouble making their way to the sanctuary. Outside, a dozen marshals wearing yellow armbands stood quietly by, warily observing the surrounding streets. Then, and for several hours thereafter, the only other law enforcement officers present were a handful of FBI agents and two plainclothes state detectives sent to monitor the situation. Indeed, the most striking aspect of the scene was who was not there. Throughout the day local radio stations had broadcast "the news that Negroes would hold a mass meeting that night at the First Baptist Church," virtually ensuring that a large crowd of white protesters would eventually descend upon the church; and "all day long," according to one observer, "carloads of grim-faced whites converged on Montgomery." Yet there were no city policemen, no uniformed highway patrolmen, and no National Guardsmen on the scene. As events would soon prove, this was a formula for mob violence.

Despite all the rhetoric of the past twenty-four hours, federal authorities in Washington and at Maxwell Field were also reticent to do anything beyond the minimum effort needed to forestall disaster. Even as dusk approached and the crowd outside the church swelled to two thousand and beyond, Justice Department officials stuck to the plan of waiting for Patterson's call for assistance. Unless the situation got completely out of hand, they would not reinforce the small band of marshals at the scene until officially asked to do so. A sense of foreboding dominated the marshals' periodic reports, but so far the crowd outside First Baptist had limited its protests to name-calling and occasional jostling.

By 8 that night fifteen hundred people were inside the sanctuary, and the rising sound of hymns and amens signaled the beginning of the program. The vast majority of the crowd inside the church was black—the only whites being news reporters and television cameramen, plus a few white liberals such as

Jessica Mitford. Many of those present were veterans of the mass meetings that had sustained the bus boycott five years earlier, but nothing quite like this had been seen in Montgomery for a long time.

While Seay presided over the emotional opening of the mass meeting, a drama of a different sort was developing downstairs, where a conclave of ministers—including King and Abernathy—was growing increasingly concerned about the size and mood of the crowd outside. The last few parishioners who had straggled into the church had encountered screamed epithets and a shower of rocks, and some protesters were beginning to smash the windows of cars parked along Ripley Street. Even more alarming to King was the rumor that a group of armed black taxicab drivers was planning to confront the white protesters. No one had been hurt, and so far the cab drivers had kept their distance from the mob, but the situation was serious enough to prompt King to venture outside to see for himself. Ignoring the strong objections of his aides, he and a few volunteers spent several minutes circling the church and eyeing the crowd across the street. At first the protesters seemed stunned by the scouting party's audacity, but eventually someone recognized the famous Atlanta preacher and began screaming, "Nigger King!" Before long, rocks and other missiles were being thrown in King's direction—including a metal canister that one of his aides feared was a bomb. As the aide tossed aside what turned out to be an empty tear gas canister, King and the others scurried back inside the church.

A few minutes later Shuttlesworth had his own brush with the mob. Earlier in the evening, before the crowd had grown unruly, he had volunteered to pick up Farmer at the airport. Now, as he and Farmer approached the church, the scene was much more menacing. Surrounded by a group of angry whites who began to rock their car, the two men fled on foot through a nearby cemetery. Before reaching the church, they encountered an even larger mass of protesters. To Farmer's amazement, Shuttlesworth simply plowed through them, screaming, "Out of the way! Come on! Let him through! Out of the way!"—as if he were escorting a visiting dignitary. With Shuttlesworth waving his arms wildly above his head, the protesters in front of him stepped aside just long enough to allow the two civil rights leaders to make it to the church's basement door.

Once inside, Farmer and Shuttlesworth were taken upstairs to the sanctuary, where King introduced the CORE leader to a congregation that was growing increasingly concerned about what was going on outside. Following his encounter with the tear gas canister, King had tried to reassure the men, women, and children inside the church that the marshals had everything under control; and now the safe arrival of Shuttlesworth and Farmer served as proof that all was well. As Farmer embraced Lewis, whom he had grown fond of during the first week of the original Freedom Ride, and Nash, whom he had never met, a rush of amens filled the sanctuary. Farmer then stepped to the pulpit for a few salutary words before retiring to the basement to join King, Abernathy, and the other movement leaders, who were busily assessing the situation.

It was now a few minutes past 8, and the crisis of the moment was an overturned car. The car, it was later discovered, had been driven by author Jessica Mitford, who was in the city observing events. As King and others watched through a half-open window, the crowd torched the car's gas tank, causing an explosion that seemed to signal an assault on the church itself. Up to this point, the marshals had managed to keep the protesters off of church property and on the far side of Ripley Street, but now the mob was closing in amid screams of "Let's clean the niggers out of here!" Regrouping along the near side of Ripley Street, the marshals, with the encouragement of Mann's two detectives, used their nightsticks to keep the mob at bay. But, as they soon informed White by radio, it was only a matter of time before the thin shield of marshals was pushed aside. White immediately relayed this alarming message to Robert Kennedy, who reluctantly gave the go-ahead for the deployment of the nearly four hundred marshals at Maxwell Field. Within minutes James McShane, an ex–New York cop who had served as John Kennedy's bodyguard and chauffeur during the 1960 campaign, was back on the road, this time leading a convoy of postal trucks and air force vehicles toward First Baptist.

While McShane and the reinforcements were en route, the situation outside the church grew increasingly ominous. As rocks, bricks, and Molotov cocktails rained down on the church grounds, the hopelessly outnumbered marshals— led by William Behen, a revenue agent from Florida—bought a few minutes of time by firing several rounds of tear gas into the crowd of protesters, some of whom waved Confederate flags in defiance. With each round the crowd fell back for a moment, only to advance again as soon as the air cleared. Inside the church, the Reverend Seay led the congregation through several rousing choruses of "Love Lifted Me" in a spirited attempt to stem a full-scale panic. "I want to hear everybody sing," Seay roared from the pulpit, "and mean every word of it." Sing they did, but the stanzas of faith and hope did not stop them from preparing to defend themselves and their families. Anticipating trouble, many of the men— and some of the women—had come to the church armed with knives and pistols, and there was little doubt that they would use them against the white mob if necessary. "We riders were nonviolent, steeped and trained in the teachings of Gandhi," Lewis later explained, "but most of the people of Montgomery were not."

All of this, plus the news that some members of the mob had broken through the line of marshals and were banging on the church door, prompted King to ask Wyatt Tee Walker to call Robert Kennedy in Washington. Seconds earlier Kennedy had received an ominous report from White, who had been monitoring the assault via an open radio line, so he was not surprised when Walker, and then King, described the situation as desperate. Dispensing with formalities, Kennedy immediately assured King that a large contingent of marshals was on its way. After Walker and Abernathy rushed upstairs to deliver the good news, King pressed Kennedy for details. Unsure of the marshals' exact location, Kennedy responded that they would be there soon. When King pressed him again a few seconds later, Kennedy tried to change the subject. Wasn't it time to call off or at least postpone the Freedom Ride? he asked. Would the Freedom Riders agree to some sort of "cooling-off period" that would give federal and state authorities the opportunity to work out a solution? Not quite sure how to respond to this request, King explained that he could not speak for the Freedom Riders; he would, however, broach the idea with Jim Farmer and Diane Nash. Satisfied that he had at least planted the idea of a cooling-off period, Kennedy tried to ease the tension with a nervous quip: "As long as you're in church, Reverend King, and our men are down there, you might as well say a prayer for us." Unimpressed with this strained attempt at gallows humor, King respectfully reminded Kennedy that the mob was closing in. If the marshals "don't get here immediately," King exclaimed, "we're going to have a bloody confrontation." Fortunately, the marshals' arrival soon brought what was becoming an awkward conversation to a close. Before signing off, a greatly relieved King thanked Kennedy for his intervention and promised to call back as soon as the crisis had subsided. They would not talk again until 12:10 a.m. Montgomery time, three long hours later.

Before making his way upstairs, King quickly briefed Abernathy, Nash, and Farmer on the essentials of his conversation with Kennedy. Turning first to Farmer, the organizer of the original Freedom Ride, King relayed the suggestion about the cooling-off period. Though obviously pleased to be consulted, Farmer did not think much of Kennedy's suggestion. "I won't stop it now," he replied. "If I do, we'll just get words and promises." After King hinted that he was inclined to agree with the attorney general's conclusion that "the Freedom Ride has already made its point and now should be called off," Farmer asked Nash what she thought of the idea. "No," she responded, with a flash of irritation. "The Nashville Student Movement wants to go on. We can't stop it now right after we've been clobbered." Buoyed by her certainty, Farmer gave King a definitive answer. "Please tell the attorney general that we've been cooling off for 350 years," he declared in a voice loud enough to be heard throughout the basement. "If we cool off any more, we will be in a deep freeze. The Freedom Ride will go on." Nash was relieved when King agreed to deliver the message, but as the group of leaders walked upstairs to see what was happening, she couldn't help wondering what might have happened if the decision had been left to the great men of the movement. In the days ahead, she and other members of the Nashville

Movement would have to keep vigilant watch over their nervous elders, or so she feared.

King and his colleagues had no idea how many marshals had been dispatched, but as they peered out the church windows, the situation seemed to be improving. After pushing part of the mob back with their nightsticks, the marshals lobbed a massive round of tear gas that momentarily cleared the church grounds. Unfortunately, the retreat proved to be short-lived, and several members of the mob were soon back pounding on the church's front door. To make matters worse, the besieged congregation had to contend with a cloud of tear gas that had drifted into the sanctuary. The marshals, most without gas masks, also found themselves gasping for air. Forced to withdraw from the area in front of the church, they temporarily lost whatever tactical advantage they might have enjoyed. Suddenly an aroused vanguard of protesters was on the verge of breaking into the front of the church. Cutting through the church basement, a rescue squad of marshals managed to block the intruders with nightsticks and an additional round of tear gas, but not before one of the rioters shattered a large stained-glass window with a brick. The brick also struck the forehead of an elderly parishioner, who was soon being attended by several nurses. Most of the congregation, however, sought refuge on the sanctuary floor. At Seay's urgent request, the children were evacuated to the basement, just in time to escape a volley of rocks that broke several windows. Before long, however, no one in the church, not even those in the basement, could avoid the sickening fumes of the tear gas that had seeped through the building's exterior. Despite the marshals' good intentions, the rescue was turning into a fiasco.

Even so, there was no wholesale panic in the church. Over the next thirty minutes, as the outnumbered marshals struggled to keep the mob at bay, the besieged parishioners at First Baptist continued to tap an inner strength that defied the logic of their precarious position. Even in the face of tear gas and surging rioters, freedom songs reverberated through the sanctuary. Earlier the mood had dictated the singing of traditional hymns of hope and praise, But now the hymns were interspersed with the "music of the movement"—songs such as "Ain't Gonna Let Nobody Turn Me 'Round" and "We Shall Overcome." In some cases the Freedom Riders themselves led the singing, as the fear of being arrested was overwhelmed by the emotion of the moment.

To federal authorities, few of whom shared the Riders' faith in direct action, the consequences of standing up for freedom in a Montgomery church seemed very grave indeed. By 9:30, with the crisis at First Baptist showing no signs of letting up, Justice Department officials were preparing for the worst. After releasing a public statement urging "all citizens of Alabama and all travelers in Alabama to consider their actions carefully and to refrain from doing anything which will cause increased tension or provoke violence or resistance," Robert

Kennedy began to contemplate the previously unthinkable. Moved by the force of his own words, he asked the Pentagon to place army units at Fort Benning, ninety-five miles east of Montgomery, on high alert. The troops would only be used as a last resort, he assured White, but the inability of the marshals to disperse the mob and the lack of response from state officials left the federal government with few options.

Unbeknownst to Kennedy and White, Patterson, with the help of a Maxwell telephone operator, was listening in on this and other Justice Department conversations. Officially, though, Patterson was out of the loop. After several futile attempts to contact the governor, Kennedy and White turned to Floyd Mann as the only reachable—and reasonable—state official. A native of Alexander City, Alabama, Mann considered himself a segregationist, but not to the point of countenancing violence or disrespect for the Constitution or the law. "He was Southern," Bernard Lafayette recalled years later, "but I don't think he had the same kind of passion for preserving segregation at any cost as some of his colleagues. I think he was . . . caught in a system where he had to perform certain duties, but he wanted to do it in the most humane way." Although there was little Mann could do without firm authorization from Patterson, he took it upon himself to urge White to send in additional marshals. White, interpreting this request as the first indication that state officials were beginning to recognize the seriousness of the situation, offered to place the marshals already on the scene at Mann's disposal, but he had to confess that he had no additional marshals in reserve. This admission was not what Mann wanted to hear, although, as he later admitted, he secretly hoped that the marshals' weakness would force Patterson's hand.

Meanwhile, the violence in the streets around First Baptist was intensifying. Marshals were being attacked by brick-throwing rioters, and some of the federal peacekeepers were too scared to get out of their vehicles. There were reports of guns being fired randomly into black homes in the vicinity of the church, and a Molotov cocktail had nearly set the church roof on fire. Gangs of marauding whites were roaming the streets at will and appeared to be converging on the church for a massive, coordinated assault. At one point things looked so bleak that Abernathy and King suggested that they and the other high-profile ministers should consider surrendering themselves to the mob in order to save the men, women, and children in the sanctuary. But no one actually moved toward the door. Fortunately, events beyond the ministers' control soon rendered martyrdom unnecessary.

After McShane informed White that he was not sure that his marshals could hold out much longer, the bad news was relayed to the attorney general, who finally had heard enough. Following a brief consultation with Marshall, he decided to ask the president to sign a proclamation authorizing the immediate deployment of the soldiers at Fort Benning. As it turned out, however, the attorney general was not the only one who had heard enough. While Justice Department staff members puzzled over the logistics of acquiring the vacationing president's signature (he was a helicopter ride away in northern Virginia), Patterson, who had been eavesdropping on the phone communications between Washington and White's office at Maxwell Field, decided to act. At 10 p.m., he placed the city of Montgomery under what he called "qualified martial rule." Almost immediately, a swarm of city policemen rushed down Ripley Street, closely followed by fifteen helmeted members of the Alabama National Guard. Within five minutes, more than a hundred Guardsmen had formed a protective shield in front of the church. By that time, the police, with Commissioner Sullivan making a show of his authority, had cleared the immediate area of rioters. Nearby a greatly relieved McShane, with White's approval, offered to place his marshals under the command of the National Guard. Accepting McShane's offer, the colonel in charge of the Guardsmen promptly ordered the marshals to leave the scene. As the overall commander of the Guard, Adjutant General Henry Graham announced a few minutes later that the sovereign state of Alabama had everything under control and needed no further help from federal authorities.

In actuality, dispersing the mob proved more difficult than Graham or anyone else had anticipated. While the worst of the mayhem was over by 10:15, sporadic violence continued for several hours. Indeed, for the besieged gathering inside the sanctuary the joyous news of the soldiers' arrival was soon tempered by the realization that their rescuers were Alabama segregationists, not federal troops. This disappointment did not stop them from proceeding with the mass meeting, however. Despite lingering fumes and frazzled nerves, the celebration of freedom went forward almost as if nothing had happened.

King and others did not mince words that evening. As the television cameras whirred, one speaker after another juxtaposed praise for the Freedom Riders with condemnation of the state and local authorities who had incited a week of lawlessness. After urging the audience to launch "a full scale nonviolent assault on the system of segregation in Alabama," King insisted that "the law may not be able to make a man love me, but it can keep him from lynching me . . . Unless the federal government acts forthrightly in the South to assure every citizen his constitutional rights, we will be plunged into a dark abyss of chaos." Departing from his prepared text, he placed much of the blame on Patterson, who bore the "ultimate responsibility for the hideous action in Alabama." "His consistent preaching of defiance of the law," King claimed, "his vitriolic public pronouncements, and his irresponsible actions created the atmosphere in which violence could thrive. Alabama has sunk to a level of barbarity comparable to the tragic days of Hitler's Germany." Shuttlesworth agreed. "It's a sin and a shame before

God," he declared, "that these people who govern us would let things come to such a sad state. But God is not dead. The most guilty man in this state tonight is Governor Patterson." For nearly two hours expressions of outrage alternated with impassioned calls for continued struggle and sacrifice until everyone in the sanctuary, as Farmer put it, "was ready at that moment to board buses and ride into the Promised Land." Following a final hymn and an emotional benediction, the exhausted preachers dismissed the congregation a few minutes before midnight.

Despite some concern about what they would encounter outside the church, most of the audience wasted no time in heading for the exits. Some had been in the sanctuary since late afternoon, and even those who had arrived late were eager to get home to reassure friends and family that they were safe. To their surprise, however, the exits were blocked by National Guardsmen with drawn bayonets. The only person allowed outside the church was King, who demanded an explanation from General Graham. Moments earlier Graham had received word that Robert Kennedy had officially sanctioned the placing of federal marshals under state control, and he was in no mood to relinquish any of his expanded authority, especially to a meddling black preacher from Georgia. An arch-segregationist who worked as a Birmingham real estate agent in his civilian life, Graham turned a deaf ear to King's appeal for compassion. Some members of the congregation were at the breaking point and desperately needed to go home, King explained. But Graham would not relent, insisting that the situation outside the church was too unstable. Though disappointed, King urged Graham to deliver this message directly to the men and women inside the sanctuary. After some hesitation, he agreed.

Marching into the church with several of his aides, Graham presided over a formal reading of Patterson's declaration of martial law, which predictably began with the hostile phrase "Whereas, as a result of outside agitators coming into Alabama to violate our laws and customs." Farther down, the proclamation claimed that the federal government had "by its actions encouraged these agitators to come into Alabama to foment disorders and breaches of the peace." As a murmur of indignation spread through the sanctuary, Graham stepped forward to inform the crowd that the siege was not over, that in all likelihood they would have to remain in the church and under the protection of the National Guard until morning. Technically it was already morning, but the meaning of his words was clear: Liberation had turned into protective custody.

To the Freedom Riders, who had already experienced the protective custody provided by Bull Connor, the scene was all too familiar. "Those soldiers didn't look like protectors now," Lewis later commented. "Their rifles were pointed our way. They looked like the enemy." From the perspective of those in the sanctuary, martial law looked a lot like continued intimidation and harassment, especially after they realized that the forces surrounding the church were all controlled by Patterson, a governor who had branded the Freedom Riders as outlaws. King, in particular, felt betrayed by the federal government's apparent abdication of authority. In a fit of anger, he called Robert Kennedy to complain, but Kennedy, who had just come from an upbeat interview with a magazine reporter, was not interested in listening to King's lament. "Now, Reverend," he retorted, "don't tell me that. You know just as well as I do that if it hadn't been for the United States marshals, you'd be as dead as Kelsey's nuts right now!" The allusion to Kelsey's nuts—an old Boston Irish aphorism—meant nothing to King, but the tone of Kennedy's voice gave him pause. Before hanging up, King handed the phone to Shuttlesworth, who echoed his colleague's complaint about the marshals' withdrawal. Kennedy would have none of it. "You look after your end, Reverend, and I'll look after mine," he scolded. Clearly, on this night at least, the attorney general had done about all that he was going to do on behalf of the Freedom Riders. As King and Shuttlesworth explained to Seay a few moments later, they now had no choice but to make the best of a bad situation.

While King and others reluctantly turned First Baptist into a makeshift dormitory, the National Guard, aided by Sullivan's police and Mann's highway patrolmen, conducted a mopping-up operation in the surrounding streets. By this time almost all of the marshals had returned to Maxwell, leaving the downtown battleground in the hands of state and local forces. After Graham assured Patterson that everything was under control, the formerly recalcitrant governor called Robert Kennedy to vent his anger. Patterson's tone was abusive from the start, as the pent-up hostilities and emotions of the past week burst forth. "Now you've got what you want," Patterson literally shouted over the phone, "You got yourself a fight. And you've got the National Guard called out, and martial law, and that's what you wanted. We'll take charge of it now with the troops, and you can get out and leave it alone." Kennedy protested that he had only sent in the marshals reluctantly after state and local officials had abrogated their responsibilities, but Patterson refused to accept this or any other explanation that let the federal government off the hook.

It was now 1 in the morning, and back at First Baptist the exhausted congregation was reluctantly settling in for the night. Some were still lined up to use the church's only phone, but most had sprawled out among the pews in an attempt to get some sleep. As Frank Holloway, a SNCC volunteer from Atlanta, described the scene, there "were three or four times as many people as the church was supposed to hold, and it was very hot and uncomfortable. Some people were trying to sleep, but there was hardly room for anybody to turn around. Dr. King, other leaders, and the Freedom Riders were circulating through the church talking to people and trying to keep their spirits up." Fortunately, there was room in the basement to accommodate the children, and most of the reporters had already slipped out of the church to file their stories. But the air inside the sanctuary, still smelling of tear gas, made the quarters seem even tighter than they actually were. Even so, many inside the church were grateful to be alive, having survived what Jessica Mitford called "the most terrifying evening of my life."

Adding to the terror was the sullen presence of Graham and the National Guardsmen—many of whom made no secret of their contempt for the outside agitators who had provoked the Montgomery crisis—and the gnawing uncertainty about what was going on outside the church. As the long night of protective custody stretched on, the gathering at First Baptist was kept in the dark literally and figuratively about the implications of state authority. Only later did they learn that White and other Justice Department officials were engaged in frantic behind-the-scenes negotiations with the National Guard to end the siege once and for all. By 4 a.m. White's growing frustration with Graham had prompted him to send William Orrick to the National Guard armory to see what could be done to get the church evacuated sometime before dawn. What followed was an almost surreal combination of Southern Gothic and Cold War drama. As Orrick recalled the scene: "I was treated like I might have been treated in Russia and taken over to Dixie division . . . where there wasn't a sign of an American flag . . . just the Confederate flags."

After being escorted to Graham's office, Orrick declared that he had been sent by the Justice Department to "negotiate" a timely evacuation of First Baptist. "We want to know whether your troops are going to leave that church and let the people go home," Orrick explained, "and whether they're going to keep the peace here tomorrow." Busy polishing his boots, Graham raised his eyes slowly and grunted: "Well, I'm not about to decide either matter." When Orrick pressed him further, Graham claimed he couldn't make any commitments without talking to the governor first. Only after an exasperated Orrick threatened to send the marshals back to the church did Graham begin to come around. Despite the suspicion that Orrick was bluffing and speaking without clear authority, Graham eventually agreed to begin the evacuation as soon as he could arrange a proper escort. Within minutes a convoy of National Guard trucks and jeeps pulled up in front of the church, and over the next hour the Freedom Riders and the faithful parishioners of First Baptist finally left the scene of a confrontation that none of them would ever forget.

By that time the morning newspapers were already hitting the streets of New York and other eastern cities, as the nation awoke to the news that Montgomery had once again been plunged into chaos. To the relief of both federal and state officials, most of the initial press coverage gave the impression that, as bad as it was, the situation in Montgomery could have been much worse. Despite the threat of mass violence, the damage to people and property apparently had been kept to a minimum. Accounts differed as to the relative contributions of federal, state, and local law enforcement, with conservative and Southern papers emphasizing the latter two. But the dominant story line was cooperation.

For the Kennedy administration, political damage control called for an uplifting cover story of intergovernmental harmony that downplayed the specter of constitutional crisis. White and others denied that the administration had been on the verge of sending in the army, and Robert Kennedy made a point of praising Floyd Mann as an exemplary law enforcement officer who put professionalism ahead of personal interest. If there was a villain in the official account of the Montgomery crisis—other than the mob itself—it was Patterson, but even he got off fairly lightly considering the hard feelings of the night before. While still angry at Patterson for flouting federal authority, Kennedy did not want to provoke another war of words with a member of his own party. The administration was already on shaky political ground in the Deep South, and turning Patterson into another Orval Faubus would only make matters worse.

For federal officials, the public mood in Alabama was only one of several unpredictable factors complicating the situation in the immediate aftermath of the Sunday night siege. Despite Judge Johnson's temporary restraining order, the legal position of the Freedom Riders remained in doubt. Under martial law, the warrants issued by Judge Jones had been turned over to Colonel Herman Price of the Alabama National Guard, but as yet Price had made no arrests. During a tense afternoon press conference at Maxwell Field, White deflected questions about the Freedom Riders' whereabouts and denied that federal officials were working in close cooperation with local "Negro groups or Negro leaders." White's statement to the press reflected the administration's growing misgivings about the decision to use federal marshals to protect the Freedom Riders. Earlier in the day Robert Kennedy had spent forty-five minutes at the White House briefing his brother on the events of the weekend and the political and legal dilemmas posed by the Freedom Riders' unexpected persistence. Despite public pronouncements to the contrary, many of the marshals had not performed well under pressure, the attorney general confessed, and the events of the weekend had cast serious doubt on their reliability as peacekeepers in the Deep South.

The task at hand, the Kennedy brothers concluded, was to arrange for a graceful retreat without weakening the integrity of federal authority or appearing to abandon the Freedom Riders. The latter challenge was especially acute in view of the Freedom Riders' continuing vulnerability to arrest and intimidation by state and local officials. Robert Kennedy, in particular, agonized over the prospect of standing by while Alabama authorities carted the Freedom Riders off to jail. But by late Monday afternoon no one in the White House or the Justice Department had come up with a plan that would get both the marshals and the Freedom Riders safely out of Alabama.

One of the most frustrating aspects of the administration's unenviable position had been the ambiguous role of the FBI in Alabama. In the week since the initial riots in Anniston and Birmingham, FBI officials at all levels had kept a respectful distance from the developing crisis. At this point no one outside of the bureau was aware of Gary Thomas Rowe's involvement in the Birmingham riot, but the inevitable grousing in the attorney general's office about the FBI's apparent failure to keep tabs on the Alabama Klan had already pushed J. Edgar Hoover into preemptive action. On Monday morning, May 15, Hoover informed Burke Marshall and Robert Kennedy that the Birmingham office of the FBI had begun an investigation of the Anniston bus-burning incident. Given the code name FREEBUS, the investigation initially drew plaudits from both Marshall and Kennedy, who made a point of thanking the notoriously thin-skinned Hoover for giving the matter prompt attention. As the week progressed, however, it became clear to Seigenthaler, Doar, and other Justice Department officials in Alabama that Hoover and his agents were more interested in enhancing the bureau's public image than in protecting the Freedom Riders' constitutional rights. Although there were several special agents at the Montgomery riot scene on Saturday morning, none made any attempt to intervene on behalf of the men and women under attack.

Later that morning, around 9:30, Robert Kennedy received an uncharacteristically solicitous call from Hoover himself. After pledging his cooperation, the director delivered the welcome news that the bureau had just arrested four of the men responsible for the Anniston bus burning. All four, including an unemployed teenager, were active members of the Klan. To Kennedy, who had just returned to his office after a few hours of fitful sleep, the arrests could not have been more timely. After thanking Hoover for the bureau's good work, he immediately issued a press release declaring that the case against the four Klansmen would "be pursued with utmost vigor."

Hoover was also pleased, having relieved some of the pressure on the bureau. After hanging up, though, he complained to his staff that he wasn't sure that the attorney general understood the nature of the real danger in Alabama. Outside agitators like King and the Freedom Riders, he was convinced, were actually more dangerous than the Klan. As radical provocateurs and Communist fellow-travelers, they represented a serious threat to civic order and national security, and they were certainly not the kind of people who deserved a special FBI escort, which he feared was part of the Justice Department's plan. Throughout the Freedom Rider crisis, Hoover reiterated his long-standing insistence that the FBI was an investigative agency and "not a protection agency," but he wasn't sure that he could trust the new attorney general to respect its time-honored prerogatives. Realizing that he might need hard evidence of Communist infiltration to head off such an unpleasant assignment, Hoover ordered an immediate investigation of King, the one agitator he was fairly certain had close ties to subversive groups. Later in the day, he received a preliminary report that noted several suspicious connections, including King's ties to the Highlander Folk School, which was described as a "Communist Party training school." Intrigued, Hoover urged his staff to dig deeper into what he suspected was a sinkhole of subversion and unsavory activity.

Back in Montgomery, King and the Freedom Riders had no way of knowing that Hoover and the FBI had launched an investigation that would become an important part of a decade-long effort to discredit the civil rights movement. But they had few illusions about the support that federal officials were prepared to offer. King's early morning conversation with Robert Kennedy about the danger of placing the marshals under state control had ended badly, and nothing had happened since to indicate that the Justice Department was ready to provide the kind of protection that would guarantee the Freedom Riders' safe passage to New Orleans. In the early morning confusion, the Riders had scattered throughout Montgomery's black community, but by late Monday afternoon virtually the entire contingent had regrouped at the home of Dr. Richard Harris, a prominent black pharmacist and former neighbor of King's. Joined by an array of movement leaders—including King, Abernathy, Walker, Farmer, CORE attorney Len Holt, Diane Nash, and Ed King of SNCC—the Riders turned Harris's luxurious two-story brick home into a combination refuge and command center.

During the next two days, Harris's sprawling den became the backdrop for a marathon discussion of the future of the Freedom Ride. The conversation ultimately touched on all aspects of the Freedom Riders' situation, from narrow logistical details to broad philosophical considerations of nonviolent struggle. The first order of business was finding a solution to the Riders' legal problems. A state court had enjoined them from conducting Freedom Rides anywhere in Alabama. But on Monday federal district Judge Frank Johnson vacated the injunction as an unconstitutional infringement on federal law. The Freedom Riders were no longer fugitives, Johnson declared, though he could not help questioning the wisdom of continuing the Ride at the risk of civic disorder.

With the immediate threat of arrest eliminated by Judge Johnson's ruling, the Riders and their advisors began to consider an expanded range of options. While virtually all of the Riders spoke out in favor of resuming the Freedom Ride, there was the challenge of recruitment. Fortunately, Nash had already enlisted additional reinforcements from other movement centers, some from Atlanta and New Orleans and others from as far away as Washington and New York. Although several were still en route as late as Tuesday evening, she expected to have at least twenty volunteers in Montgomery by Wednesday morning.

Before anyone could actually board the buses, however, there were a number of important matters to attend to, including working out clear lines of organizational authority and responsibility. Complicated by generational and ideological divisions, the ongoing discussion among students and older movement leaders took several unexpected turns on Monday evening. Ignoring the democratic sensibilities of the students, Farmer took immediate charge of the meeting, to the obvious consternation of Nash, Lewis, and others. Farmer, Lewis recalled years later, began and ended with self-serving pronouncements on CORE's centrality. Nevertheless, the meeting soon turned away from Farmer and CORE to the subject of King's personal participation in direct action.

Earlier in the week Nash had broached the subject during a phone conversation with King, suggesting that his presence on one of the freedom buses was essential to the movement. But prior to the Monday night meeting there was no organized or collective effort to persuade him to join the Freedom Ride. Though discouraged by King's noncommittal response to her initial entreaties, Nash decided to try again in the more public setting in Montgomery. After consulting with SNCC advisor Ella Baker, who encouraged her to press King on the matter of his joining the ride, Nash steeled her courage and asked King directly if he were willing to join the coming ride to Mississippi. By setting a personal example of commitment, she explained, he could advance the cause of nonviolent struggle to a new level. Momentarily caught off guard, King responded that Nash was probably right, but he needed time to think about it. As several other students seconded Nash's suggestion, Walker, Abernathy, and Bernard Lee—a young SCLC staff member from Montgomery who had been active in the student movement at Alabama State—moved to quash the idea with a series of objections: King was too valuable a leader and too critical to the overall movement to be put at risk. He had already put his body on the line at First Baptist and elsewhere, they argued, and did not need to prove his courage by engaging in a reckless show of solidarity. When it became clear that King was uncomfortable with this line of reasoning, Walker offered a more specific objection, reformulating a legal argument that SCLC attorneys had advanced in anticipation of such a debate. Since King was still on probation for a 1960 Georgia traffic citation, Walker declared, he could not risk an additional arrest, which might put him in prison for as much as six months.

For a moment, this seemed to provide King with a graceful means of deflecting Nash's suggestion. But several of the students quickly pointed out that they too were on probation. With King wavering, Nash and others pressed for an answer. King's response, tempered by his obvious discomfort with being put on the spot, was a qualified "no." As much as he would like to join them on the Ride, he informed the students, he could not allow himself to be forced into a commitment that threatened the broader interests of the movement. Resorting to a Biblical allusion to Christ's martyrdom, he brought the discussion to an abrupt end with the insistence that only he could decide the "time and place" of his "Golgotha."

He then left the room for a private conversation with Walker, who returned a few minutes later with the word that further discussion of the matter was off limits. For the moment, at least, the face-to-face tension was broken, though many in the room resented Walker's admonition as a violation of movement democracy. While virtually all of the students recognized King's dilemma, the abrupt suspension of debate was a rude jolt, especially to those inclined to reject the stated rationale for the SCLC leader's decision. As the meeting broke up, one disappointed student muttered "De Lawd," a mocking reference to King's assumption of Christ-like status, and others were visibly upset by what they had witnessed.

With martial law still in effect and with the resumption of the Freedom Ride scheduled for Wednesday morning, Tuesday was a time for public posturing and behind-the-scenes negotiation. All through the day there were signs of rising apprehension and mobilization, especially in Mississippi. In a morning telegram to Robert Kennedy, Governor Ross Barnett warned: "You will do a great disservice to the agitators and the people of the United States if you do not advise the agitators to stay out of Mississippi." At the same time, Barnett—an outspoken sixty-three-year-old white supremacist with close ties to the White Citizens' Councils—assured the attorney general that the Magnolia State would not tolerate the kind of mob violence that had erupted in Alabama. "The people of Mississippi are capable of handling all violations of law and keeping peace in Mississippi," he insisted. "We . . . do not want any police aid from Washington, either marshals or federal troops."

To prove his point, Barnett placed the Mississippi National Guard on alert and authorized state troopers to search for Freedom Riders at checkpoints along the Alabama-Mississippi border. Later in the day, Barnett's plan of action received the endorsement of John Wright, the head of the Jackson White Citizens' Councils, who declared: "Mississippi is ready . . . Our Governor, the Mayor of Jackson, and other state and city officials have already stated plainly that these outside agitators will not be permitted to stir up trouble in Mississippi." Pointing out that "the vast majority of our public officials are Citizens' Council members," Wright urged his fellow Mississippians to let "our Highway Patrolmen, policemen and other peace officers handle any situation which may arise . . . You and I can help by letting our public officials and police officers know that we're behind them all the way—and by not adding to their problems in time of crisis."

Such calls for restraint buoyed the spirits of Justice Department officials and others who had worried that Mississippi segregationists were even more prone to vigilantism and violence than their Alabama cousins. Earlier in the week former Mississippi governor James Coleman had warned Burke Marshall that he feared that the Freedom Riders would "all be killed" if they tried to cross the state without a military escort, and other sources had confirmed the seriousness of the threat. Thus Barnett's call for law and order was a welcome sign.

Determined to sustain the momentum of the Freedom Ride and eager to demonstrate the solidarity of the coalition that had formed over the past week, King and several other movement leaders abandoned the security of Dr. Harris's house on Tuesday morning to brief the press on their plans. Surrounded by federal marshals and a crush of local, national, and international reporters, Farmer, Abernathy, and Lewis explained why they and their organizations— CORE, SCLC, and SNCC—were committed to resuming the Freedom Ride. King then read a joint declaration vowing that the Freedom Riders would soon board buses for Mississippi, with or without guarantees of police protection. Prior to their departure the Freedom Riders would participate in a nonviolent workshop led by Nashville movement leader Jim Lawson, King announced. And to make sure that the reporters understood the implications of extending the nonviolent movement into Mississippi, he put down the prepared text and spoke from the heart. "Freedom Riders must develop the quiet courage of dying for a cause," he declared, his voice cracking with emotion. "We would not like to see anyone die . . . We all love life, and there are no martyrs here—but we are well aware that we may have some casualties . . . I'm sure these students are willing to face death if necessary."

King's dramatic statement cleared the air and clarified the Freedom Riders' sense of purpose. But it also reinforced the public misconception that he was the supreme leader and chief architect of the Freedom Rides. In truth, he had never been a central figure in the Freedom Rider saga, and his refusal to join the Mississippi Ride had further marginalized his position among the student activists in Montgomery. That evening, when they gathered to finalize preparations for Wednesday morning, the question of King's participation in the Mississippi Freedom Ride came up again. This time the discussion included Jim Bevel— who had driven down from Nashville earlier in the day with three new recruits, Rip Patton of Tennessee State, and LeRoy Wright and Matthew Walker Jr. of Fisk. Lawson was also on hand, having arrived a few hours later in a second carload of NCLC reinforcements. Before leaving Nashville, Lawson dismissed the importance of his role as workshop coordinator, graciously insisting to reporters that King was "in overall charge" of the Montgomery gathering. And during the discussion of King's proper role in the Freedom Rides, he and Bevel, among others, defended the SCLC leader's decision to serve as a spokesperson and fund-raiser rather than as an actual Freedom Rider. Though well-intentioned, the campaign to enlist King as a Freedom Rider had become problematic in their eyes.

For several hours, Lawson led the Riders through a reprise of the sessions that had been instrumental to the Nashville movement. Nearly half of the Riders were from Nashville and had seen Lawson work his magic before, but others were encountering his quiet intensity for the first time. While everyone in the room had practical experience with sit-ins and other forms of direct action, Lawson's presentation of nonviolence as an all-encompassing way of life provided some with a new philosophical grounding for their activism. By the time the gathering broke up around midnight, the number of potential Freedom Riders had risen to almost thirty, enough for two freedom buses, one Greyhound and one Trailways. While no one knew exactly how many Riders would actually board the buses in the morning, the stage was set for the nonviolent movement's first major project in Mississippi.

The nonviolent workshop and the camaraderie that surrounded it produced moments of exhilaration and renewal. But, as several of the Riders later acknowledged, the final hours in Montgomery also brought feelings of dread, including fearful thoughts of what might actually happen in Mississippi. Making an interracial foray into Mississippi had always been a frightening prospect, but earlier in the day the Riders learned that even Medgar Evers, the Mississippi NAACP's state field secretary, had confessed to reporters that he hoped the Freedom Riders would postpone their trip to Jackson. In his words, under the present circumstances it was simply "too dangerous" to force a confrontation with Mississippi segregationists. During the workshop, Lawson, Holt, and others urged the Riders to ignore Evers's warning. But they did not deny the seriousness of the situation.

While they were warned repeatedly about the peril of protest in Mississippi, the Riders also had to face the possibility that they might not make it out of Montgomery. Indeed, much of their discussion focused on the likelihood of more mob violence at the local bus stations. Federal and state officials had promised to protect them from white vigilantes, but few of the Riders were confident that these promises would be kept. Considering the events of the past week and the continuing public banter about state sovereignty, the intentions of law enforcement officials at all levels were open to question. As the Sunday night siege had demonstrated, there was even some doubt about the federal government's *ability* to protect the Riders. None of the Riders could be sure, since, aside from a few general and mildly comforting assurances, the details of the government's plans were unknown to them. Many of the Riders had decided to go to Mississippi no matter what the risk, but, as several of them sat down to write wills and final letters to loved ones before drifting off to bed, the uncertainties of the situation tested their already frayed nerves.

Had the Freedom Riders been privy to the government's planned security measures, they might have slept a little easier. Although some of the details were still being worked out on Tuesday evening—and even into the morning hours— several days of close collaboration between federal and state authorities in

Mississippi and Alabama had produced a consensus that a massive show of force was needed to forestall any chance of violence. In a final flurry of phone calls, Byron White and Governor Ross Barnett put the finishing touches on a military operation "worthy of a NATO war game," as one historian later put it. Unfortunately, the close collaboration also produced a tacit understanding that once the Freedom Riders arrived in Jackson there would be no federal interference with local law enforcement. Earlier in the week Barnett had promised "nonstop rides" for the Freedom Riders. Now it appeared that Barnett was contemplating mass arrests and a declaration of martial law. Unbeknownst to White and other federal officials, the governor was even considering an alternate and more extreme plan that would put the Freedom Riders in a state mental hospital.

While White stated emphatically that the Justice Department hoped that the Freedom Riders would be allowed to travel on to New Orleans, he did not insist upon it—in part because his superiors at the Justice Department and the White House had decided that it was too risky to use federal marshals or military personnel in Mississippi, but also because Robert Kennedy had already struck a deal with the state's senior senator, James O. Eastland. After ex-governor James P. Coleman warned Marshall that Barnett was a rank demagogue who "could not be trusted," Kennedy turned to Eastland, whom he considered to be a political and even personal friend. Despite his unwavering commitment to segregation, Eastland promised Kennedy that no harm would come to the Freedom Riders in Mississippi; however, he could not guarantee that they would escape arrest. Indeed, Eastland hinted that any attempt to violate Mississippi's segregation laws would result in mass arrests. Though hardly pleased with the prospect of jailed Freedom Riders, Kennedy assured Eastland that the federal government's "primary interest was that they weren't beaten up."

Kennedy knew all too well that he was in no position to press Eastland on this point. If the Jackson police chose to put the Freedom Riders in jail, there wasn't much that he or any other federal official could do about it. In effect, the rioting in Alabama had convinced the Kennedy brothers, along with White and Marshall, that almost anything was preferable to mob violence—including unconstitutional arrests of interstate travelers. Ironically, a tentative show of force in one state had undercut federal authority in a second. As events would soon demonstrate, the situation was made to order for Barnett, a militant segregationist eager to cement his ties to the White Citizens' Councils. Realizing that he had been handed a scenario that would allow him to take credit for maintaining both order and segregation, he was almost giddy by the time the arrangements were complete. Inviting White to accompany the Freedom Riders to Jackson, Barnett promised that the Mississippi Highway Patrol would see to it that he had "the nicest ride." "You'll be just as safe as you were in your baby crib," Barnett added with a chuckle.

In later years, some members of the administration—prompted by civil rights leaders and historians who condemned the negotiations with Eastland as a betrayal of democratic ideals—would acknowledge that the agreement to defer to state authorities was a mistake. But under the current conditions of Cold War politics, administration leaders did not feel that they could afford a prolonged crisis that would almost certainly weaken the Democratic Party and embarrass the nation in front of the world. As the government official shouldering the ultimate responsibility for the Freedom Riders' arrests, John Kennedy could take comfort in the knowledge that he was following a long tradition of presidential pragmatism. Like many presidents before him, including Thomas Jefferson and Abraham Lincoln, he could claim that he was simply doing the best he could with a difficult situation.

In late May 1961, Kennedy could not avoid the Lincolnesque challenge of opening a road to freedom in the Deep South. Indeed, by sending federal marshals to Alabama and affirming the constitutionally protected rights of all Americans, he had already taken an important first step toward the implementation of racial justice. But on the morning of the twenty-fourth, as the Freedom Riders prepared to hack out a path of progress through the magnolia jungle of Mississippi, no one could be quite sure how far or fast the young president was willing to travel.

7

Freedom's Coming and It Won't Be Long

We took a trip on a Greyhound bus,
Freedom's coming and it won't be long.
To fight segregation where we must,
Freedom's coming and it won't be long.
Freedom, give us freedom,
Freedom's coming and it won't be long.
—1961 "calypso" freedom song

The federal presence in Alabama and Mississippi was both everywhere and nowhere on Wednesday morning, May 24. Having asserted the power and authority of the national government, the Kennedy administration had withdrawn, at least temporarily, to the sidelines. The short-term, if not the ultimate, fate of the Freedom Ride had been placed in the hands of state officials who, paradoxically, had promised to protect both the safety of the Riders and the sanctity of segregation. When the Trailways group of Freedom Riders left Dr. Harris's house at 6:15 a.m., they were escorted by a half-dozen jeeps driven by Alabama National Guardsmen. This unimpressive show of force raised a few eyebrows among the Riders, who knew next to nothing about the details of the plan to protect them. But as the convoy approached the downtown Trailways terminal, the familiar outline of steel-helmeted soldiers came into view. In and around the terminal, more than five hundred heavily armed Guardsmen stood watch over several clusters of white bystanders. Although the Freedom Riders did not know it, there were also several FBI agents and plainclothes detectives nervously wandering through the crowd.

As the Freedom Riders filed out of their cars, the scene was tense but quiet until the crowd spotted King, who, along with Abernathy, Shuttlesworth, and

Walker, had agreed to accompany the Riders to the terminal. Still uncomfortable with his refusal to join the Ride, King was determined to provide the disappointed students with as much visible support as possible. During an early-morning prayer meeting at Harris's house, he and Abernathy had blessed the Riders; and in a show of solidarity his brother, A. D., had flown in from Atlanta to help desegregate the Montgomery terminal's snack bar. With some members of the crowd screaming words of indignation, King led the combined SCLC–Freedom Rider entourage through the white waiting room and up to the counter, where he and the others ordered coffee and rolls. As several reporters and cameramen pressed forward to record the moment, "the white waitresses removed their aprons and stepped back," but, with the approval of the terminal's manager, black waitresses from the "Negro lunch counter stepped up and took the orders," thus breaking a half-century-old local color bar. Local and state officials, it seemed, had put out the word that nothing—not even the sanctity of Jim Crow dining—was to get in the way of the Freedom Riders' timely departure from Montgomery. Pleased, but wary of this unexpected politeness, some of the Riders began to wonder what other surprises were in the offing. They did not have to wait for long to find out.

Upon arriving at the Trailways loading bay, the Freedom Riders discovered that there were no regular passengers waiting for the morning bus to Jackson. Alabama Guardsmen, on orders from General Graham, were only allowing Freedom Riders and credentialed reporters to enter the bus. More than a dozen reporters were already on board, and several others soon joined them, as the Riders sized up the situation. Not all of the Riders were comfortable with the prospect of traveling to Jackson under such artificial conditions, and others were simply scared to death, but eventually all twelve of the Trailways Riders agreed to board the bus. Each, according to David Dennis, a twenty-year-old Louisiana CORE activist and student at Dillard College, "was prepared to die." In addition to Dennis, the group included two Southern University students from New Orleans, Julia Aaron and Jean Thompson; Harold Andrews, a student at Atlanta's Morehouse College; Paul Dietrich of NAG; and seven members of the Nashville Movement—Jim Lawson, Jim Bevel, C. T. Vivian, Bernard Lafayette, Joseph Carter, Alex Anderson, and Matthew Walker Jr. Three of the Nashville Riders—Lawson, Vivian, and Anderson—were practicing ministers, and three others—Bevel, Lafayette, and Carter—were divinity students. Dietrich was the only white. Walker and Thompson were the youngest at age nineteen, and Vivian was the oldest at thirty-six. Lawson, the third oldest at thirty-two, was the consensus choice as the group's designated leader and spokesperson.

Soon after the twelve Freedom Riders took their seats, General Graham, the movement anti-hero of the Sunday night siege, stepped onto the bus to say a few words. Flanked by several Guardsmen, he warned the Riders—and the newsmen scattered throughout the bus—that they were about to embark on "a hazardous journey." Seconds later, however, speaking in a reassuring voice, he insisted that "we have taken every precaution to protect you," adding: "I sincerely wish you all a safe journey." After Graham departed, six Guardsmen remained on board, as an array of jeeps, patrol cars, and police motorcycles prepared to escort the bus northward to the city limits, where a massive convoy of vehicles was waiting. Once the bus reached the city line, the magnitude of the effort to get the Freedom Riders out of Alabama without any additional violence became apparent. In addition to several dozen highway patrol cars, there were two helicopters and three U.S. Border Patrol planes flying overhead, plus a huge contingent of press cars jammed with reporters and photographers. As the Riders would soon discover, nearly a thousand Guardsmen were stationed along the 140-mile route to the Mississippi border. Less obtrusively, there were also several FBI surveillance units placed at various points along Highways 14 and 80.

Leaving Montgomery a few minutes before eight, the convoy headed west toward Selma, the first scheduled stop on the 258-mile trip to Jackson. During the hour-long, fifty-mile journey to Selma, the Riders chatted amiably with reporters, but when the bus arrived in the town that four years later would become the site of the movement's most celebrated voting rights march, the National Guard colonel in charge of the bus announced that there would be no rest stops on the journey to Jackson. Motioning to the crowds lining the streets of Selma, the colonel did not have to explain why. But Lawson and several of the other Riders made it clear that they did not appreciate the heavy-handed style of protection being imposed on a Freedom Ride that was supposed to test the constitutional right to travel freely from place to place. "This isn't a Freedom Ride, it's a military operation," Bevel yelled out, a sentiment echoed by Lafayette, who confessed: "I feel like I'm going to war." At the same time, they couldn't help wondering what kind of specific threats had precipitated such extreme caution.

As the bus passed through Uniontown, thirty miles west of Selma, the sight of fist-shaking whites on the side of the road was unnerving, but the first sign of serious trouble came near Demopolis, where three cars of screaming teenagers started weaving through the convoy in an attempt to chase down the bus. After a brief stop, during which a nauseated Alex Anderson momentarily left the bus to vomit on the side of the road, the teenagers were detained long enough to allow the convoy to continue unimpeded to the state line. The bus did not stop again until it reached the tiny border town of Scratch Hill, Alabama. Just after reaching Scratch Hill, the bus passed through the slightly larger town of Cuba, prompting several of the Riders to serenade their companions with what one reporter called "impromptu calypso rhythms." One of the songs, improvised by the Riders earlier in the journey, was an adaptation of Harry Belafonte's popular calypso ballad *The Banana Boat Song*, sometimes known as *Day-O*. "We took a trip on

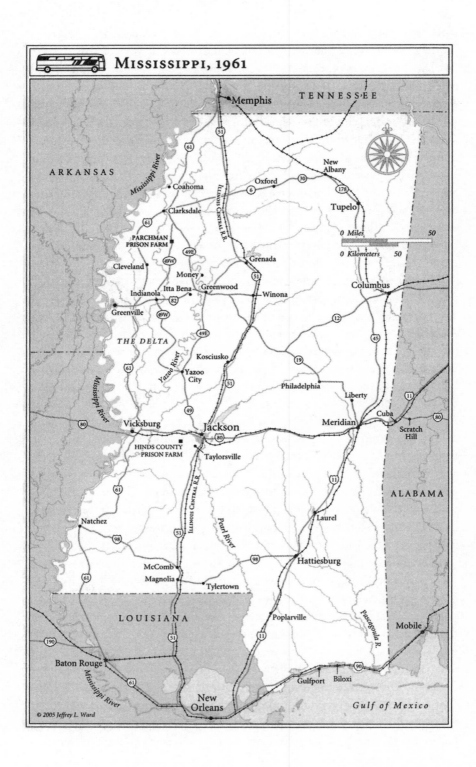

the Greyhound bus, freedom's coming and it won't be long. To fight segregation where we must, freedom's coming and it won't be long. Freedom, give us freedom, freedom's coming and it won't be long," the Freedom Rider chorus sang over and over again, as waves of laughter rippled through the bus. Moments later, however, both the music and the laughter gave way to the sobering reality of the martial spectacle at the state line.

Matching their Alabama cousins, Mississippi authorities had assembled a small army of National Guardsmen and highway patrolmen, enough to escort half a dozen freedom buses into the state. If this was not bracing enough, word soon came that Mississippi authorities had uncovered a plot to dynamite the bus as soon as it crossed the state line. This and other unconfirmed threats caused an hour's delay, during which Mississippi Guardsmen searched the nearby woods and General Graham and his Mississippi counterpart, Adj. General Pat Wilson, assessed the situation. While Wilson and Graham worked out the details of the transfer, an impatient Jim Lawson decided to hold an impromptu press briefing. To the amazement of the reporters encountering Lawson for the first time, the young minister complained that the Freedom Riders had not asked to go to Mississippi in the equivalent of an armored vehicle. As disciples of nonviolence, they "would rather risk violence and be able to travel like ordinary passengers" than cower in the shadow of protectors who neither understood nor respected their philosophy of countering "violence and hate" by "absorbing it without returning it in kind." With the reporters still puzzling over what seemed to be a foolhardy embrace of martyrdom, the bus resumed its journey around 11:30 A.M., nearly four hours after leaving Montgomery.

As soon as the bus crossed over the state line, Graham turned over control of the convoy to Mississippi's commissioner of public safety, T. B. Birdsong, and General Wilson, who promptly replaced the Alabama Guardsmen on board with six Mississippi Guardsmen under the command of Lt. Colonel and future congressman G. V. "Sonny" Montgomery. After Wilson informed the Freedom Riders and reporters on the bus there would be no rest stops on the one-hundred-mile trip to Jackson, C. T. Vivian complained to Montgomery that this decision was "degrading and inhumane," considering that there was no restroom on the bus. But Montgomery's only response was to order Vivian to sit down and be quiet. Stunned by this curt dismissal, Vivian was unable to restrain himself. "Have you no soul?" he plaintively asked Montgomery. "What do you say to your wife and children when you go home at night? Do you ever get on your knees and pray for your inhumanity to your fellow man? May God have mercy on you." Staring ahead, Montgomery did not answer. While Vivian and others seethed, Birdsong directed the motorcade towards Meridian, where the bus stopped briefly for an exchange of drivers. A colorful character who sported dark glasses, a plaid shirt, and a matching plaid-banded hat that made him look like he had just come from the racetrack—Birdsong planned to lead the convoy all the way to Jackson. However, after learning that a second and unexpected band of Freedom Riders had just left Montgomery, he peeled off from the caravan a few miles outside of Meridian and headed back to the Alabama line.

Among the Freedom Riders themselves the decision to send a second group to Mississippi on Wednesday morning was a simple one in keeping with CORE's original plan to conduct bus desegregation tests on both major carriers. But among officials in Montgomery there was considerable surprise when fifteen Freedom Riders purchased tickets for the late-morning Greyhound run to Jackson. While rumors were rampant that hordes of Freedom Riders were descending upon the Deep South, the governmental arrangements for the group that had congregated at Dr. Harris's house had assumed that the Wednesday morning Freedom Ride would involve only one bus. The second group, like the first, included only one white Rider—Peter Ackerberg, a student at Antioch College in Yellow Springs, Ohio—and only two women: Lucretia Collins and Doris Castle. Six of the male Riders—John Lewis, Rip Patton, John Lee Copeland, Grady Donald, Clarence Thomas, and LeRoy Wright—were veterans of the Nashville Movement, and three—Hank Thomas, John Moody, and Dion Diamond—were Howard students and members of NAG. The remaining three Riders were Frank Holloway, representing the Atlanta chapter of SNCC, Jerome Smith of New Orleans CORE, and Jim Farmer. Copeland was the oldest at age forty-four, and Castle the youngest at eighteen.

The Greyhound group bypassed the most obvious choices and selected Collins as their designated leader. Farmer, despite his prominence, was not considered because no one was quite sure if he actually intended to join the Ride. Indeed, as he later acknowledged, he had no intention of going to Jackson until Castle shamed him into it. "I was frankly terrified with the knowledge that the trip to Jackson might be the last trip any of us would ever take," he wrote in 1985. "I was not ready for that. Who, indeed, ever is? . . . It was only the pleading eyes and words of the teenage Doris Castle that persuaded me to get on that bus at the last minute."

With Farmer finally on board, the bus left the terminal at 11:25 amid the jeers of a crowd that had swelled to more than two thousand. Before the bus pulled out, several National Guardsmen and reporters rushed forward to fill some of the unoccupied seats near the Riders, as a much larger force of Guardsmen strained to control the crowd. Out on the highway, a hastily organized escort of highway patrol cruisers and helicopters shadowed the bus's westward track, and the National Guardsmen along the route were once again put on full alert. But, in general, the carefully arranged military procession that had accompanied the first bus was missing. Though hardly on their own, the Greyhound Riders knew nothing of the fate of the first bus and were clearly more vulnerable to assault, or at least to feelings of insecurity, than the Trailways Riders. "There was a lot of tension on the ride to Jackson," Collins recalled, "We didn't know what would happen when we got to the Mississippi line. Whether they were going to implement federal and Alabama 'state' protection or turn us over to the Mississippi state police."

When the bus reached the border and stopped for an exchange of drivers and Guardsmen, a rumor of an impending ambush convinced all but one of the reporters to travel the rest of the way by car. But Mississippi officials waved the bus onward anyway. As the bus rolled westward, Hank Thomas began singing a new version of the 1947 freedom song "Hallelujah! I'm a-Travelin'"—creating an instant anthem by inserting the words "I'm taking a ride on the Greyhound bus line, I'm a-riding the front seat to Jackson this time." By the time the Greyhound pulled into the Jackson terminal, every Rider on the bus was singing about traveling "down freedom's main line," convincing even the most skeptical among them that somehow the journey to Mississippi would turn out all right.

Officials in Montgomery and Washington, not surprisingly, saw things differently. From the perspective of those concerned about civil order and national or regional image, the spirit that propelled the Riders onward looked a lot like misguided fanaticism. For Robert Kennedy, in particular, the news of a second bus inspired feelings of rage, betrayal, and even denial. The supposed leaders of the Freedom Rider movement had said nothing about a second bus, and Kennedy initially claimed that the Greyhound group had "nothing to do with the Freedom Riders." A few minutes later, when it became clear to everyone that this was patently false, he issued a formal statement praising the law enforcement efforts of Alabama and Mississippi authorities and warning potential Freedom Riders that they would not be accorded federal protection. No federal marshals had accompanied the Freedom Riders, he declared, and there were no plans to deploy marshals in the future. After reiterating that "our obligation is to protect interstate travelers and maintain law and order only when local authorities are unable or unwilling to do so," he claimed that "there is no basis at this time to assume that the people of Mississippi will be lawless or that the responsible state and local officials in Mississippi will not maintain law and order with respect to interstate travel."

By noon Kennedy's hopes for a quick resolution to the crisis had all but disappeared, and the reports from the Deep South only got worse as the afternoon progressed. Five minutes after the second bus left the Montgomery terminal, a third group of Freedom Riders departed from Atlanta. The leader of the group was Yale University chaplain William Sloane Coffin Jr., a thirty-six-year-old graduate of Union Theological Seminary who had served as a military liaison to the Russian army during World War II and as a CIA operative during the

Korean War. A nephew of the distinguished theologian Henry Sloane Coffin and a member of the Peace Corps Advisory Council, the Reverend Coffin represented the leftward-leaning wing of the Northeastern intellectual elite.

While Robert Kennedy and others were speculating about the implications of the Connecticut-based Freedom Ride, word came that the first bus had reached Jackson. To Kennedy's relief, the Freedom Riders had arrived safely a few minutes before two. But otherwise the news was not good. As soon as the bus arrived at the Jackson Trailways terminal, the Riders, black and white, filed into the white waiting room. Several also used the white restroom, but when the Riders ignored police captain J. L. Ray's order to "move on," all twelve were placed under arrest. As several reporters, a contingent of National Guardsmen, and a small but cheering crowd of protesters looked on, the police jammed the Riders into a paddy wagon and hauled them off to the city jail. To make matters worse, Kennedy soon learned that the arrested Riders had refused an offer by NAACP attorneys to post a $1,000 bond for each defendant. The Riders would remain in jail at least until their scheduled trial on Thursday afternoon. The formal charges against the Riders were inciting to riot, breach of the peace, and failure to obey a police officer, not violation of state or local segregation laws.

Later in the day the Jackson police dropped the riot incitement charge, but that was cold comfort for federal officials who, despite fair warning from Senator Eastland that the Freedom Riders would be arrested, had continued to hope for an uninterrupted and uneventful journey to New Orleans. In a 1964 interview, Robert Kennedy reluctantly acknowledged his complicity, conceding that he had, in effect, "concurred to the fact that they were going to be arrested." Eastland, he recalled, had told him "what was going to happen: that they'd get there, they'd be protected, and then they'd be locked up." But for some reason the near certainty of the arrests escaped him and others in May 1961.

While the Trailways Riders were settling in at the Jackson city jail, rumors of an impending invasion from the east were precipitating a volatile situation at the downtown Montgomery Greyhound terminal. By the time Coffin's group arrived, a crowd of unruly protesters—some of whom had been at the scene since early morning—was ready for a fight. As Wyatt Tee Walker and Fred Shuttlesworth stepped forward to welcome the seven new recruits, the crowd began pelting them with rocks and bottles. For twenty minutes a cordon of National Guardsmen strained to keep the protesters at bay, as officials puzzled over how to get the nine civil rights activists out of harm's way. Fortunately, the siege was broken when the Guardsmen cleared a path through the crowd large enough to accommodate two cars, one of which was driven by Ralph Abernathy. With the Guardsmen holding back the crowd, the grateful Riders and their hosts climbed into the cars, though it took a minute or two to find a safe exit. In the meantime, several reporters approached the cars to get a statement from Abernathy. Asked

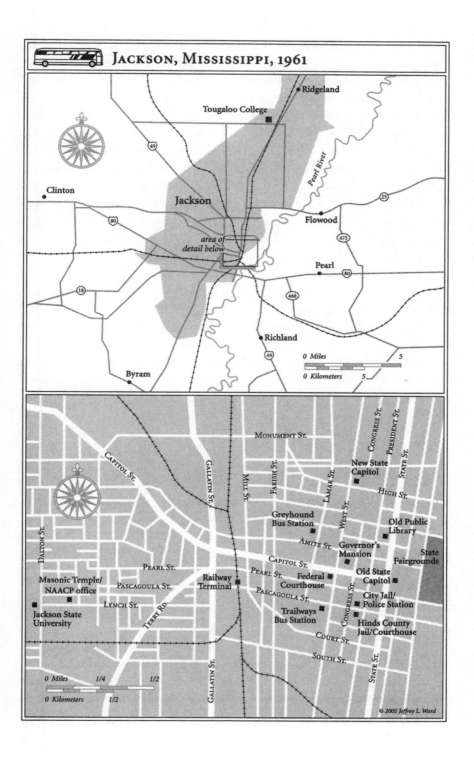

JACKSON, MISSISSIPPI, 1961

Ridgeland

Tougaloo College

Pearl River

Clinton

Jackson

area of detail below

Flowood

Pearl

Richland

Byram

0 Miles 5
0 Kilometers 5

MONUMENT ST.

CAPITOL ST.

GALLATIN ST.

MILL ST.

FARISH ST.

CONGRESS ST.

PRESIDENT ST.

STATE ST.

New State Capitol

HIGH ST.

LAMAR ST.

Greyhound Bus Station

WEST ST.

AMITE ST.

Old Public Library

DALTON ST.

Governor's Mansion

State Fairgrounds

CAPITOL ST.

Masonic Temple/ NAACP office

PEARL ST.

PASCAGOULA ST.

Railway Terminal

PEARL ST.

Federal Courthouse

Old State Capitol

LYNCH ST.

PASCAGOULA ST.

CONGRESS ST.

City Jail/ Police Station

Jackson State University

TERRY RD.

Trailways Bus Station

Hinds County Jail/Courthouse

COURT ST.

GALLATIN ST.

SOUTH ST.

STATE ST.

0 Miles 1/4 1/2
0 Kilometers 1/2

© 2005 Jeffrey L. Ward

what he thought about Robert Kennedy's complaint that the Freedom Riders were embarrassing the nation in front of the world, Abernathy responded tartly: "Well, doesn't the attorney general know we've been embarrassed all our lives?"

What the attorney general knew, or did not know, about black life would ultimately have a profound bearing on the evolution of the Freedom Rider crisis. But on the afternoon of May 24—in Washington no less than in Montgomery and Jackson—pure emotion seemed to be driving much of the official reaction to the Freedom Riders' exasperating commitment to nonviolent direct action. Although Robert Kennedy was angry at Ross Barnett for allowing the Jackson police to put the Trailways group in jail, he was even angrier at the obstinacy of the Riders themselves. Mostly he was worried about the apparent widening of the crisis, and he said so in blunt terms in a late afternoon press release. In a thinly veiled reference to Coffin's group and others contemplating the mobilization of Northern sympathizers, he condemned "curiosity seekers, publicity seekers, and others who are seeking to serve their own causes." Considering the "confused situation" in Alabama and Mississippi, travel in these states was inadvisable, according to Kennedy.

Kennedy knew that movement leaders, not to mention the Freedom Riders themselves, were unlikely to respond favorably to his request for what amounted to a moratorium on activism. Indeed, he was disappointed but not surprised when one of the first responses, a telegram from the Reverend Uriah J. Fields, representing the Montgomery Improvement Association, chastised him for ignoring a century of delayed justice. "Had there not been a cooling-off period following the Civil War," Fields insisted, "the Negro would be free today. Isn't 99 years long enough to cool off, Mr. Attorney General?" Nevertheless, with the crisis deepening, Kennedy felt that he little choice but to put the Freedom Riders on the moral defensive. If they were unwilling to listen to reason, they would have to suffer the consequences of abandoning the sensible restraint of Cold War liberalism. While he had considerable and rising sympathy for their goals, he could not understand their stubborn adherence to a means of protest that put themselves and the nation at risk. Indeed, with nothing less than the national image at stake, he had few if any qualms about pointing out their lack of patriotism. And he was hardly the only one who felt that way.

Speaking on NBC television's evening news broadcast, commentator David Brinkley, a native of North Carolina, editorialized that the Freedom Riders "are accomplishing nothing whatsoever and, on the contrary, are doing positive harm." While acknowledging that the "bus riders are, of course, within their legal rights in riding buses where they like," he maintained that "the result of these expeditions are of no benefit to anyone, white or Negro, the North or the South, nor the United States in general. We think they should stop it." Robert Kennedy was heartened by Brinkley's commentary, and the subsequent arrest of the second group of Freedom Riders following their late-afternoon arrival in Jackson only reinforced his willingness to sacrifice immediate justice in the interests of national security. The second round of arrests followed the same pattern as the first, with the Jackson police swooping in and apprehending all fifteen Riders within three minutes of their arrival.

Kennedy's mood was such that only a full-scale beating, which the Jackson police were careful to avoid, would have garnered any sympathy. His patience with the Freedom Riders was growing thin, especially after he learned that the second group, like the first, had refused bail and was even talking about remaining in jail following their expected convictions on Friday. If Kennedy had thought that having the Freedom Riders in jail would put an end to the crisis, he would have been all for it. But he knew better, realizing that in the upside-down world of movement culture the incarceration of twenty-seven activists would only encourage others to put their bodies on the line. While he admired their courage, he questioned their sanity. He could only hope that a few hours in a Mississippi jail cell would change their minds. To this end, he asked Marshall and White to see if any of the jailed Riders would reconsider the decision to remain behind bars. When they could not find anyone willing to discuss the matter, much less agree to an early release, Kennedy decided to call King directly to see if he could be persuaded to intervene on behalf of a more reasonable approach to nonviolent protest.

The resultant exchange between the two young leaders did not go well. Transcribed by Kennedy's aides, the conversation testified to the wide ideological gap between nonviolent activists and federal officials—even those who had considerable sympathy for the cause of civil rights:

> *King*: It's a matter of conscience and morality. They must use their lives
> and bodies to right a wrong. Our conscience tells us that the law is
> wrong and we must resist, but we have a moral obligation to accept the
> penalty.
> *Kennedy*: That is not going to have the slightest effect on what the
> government is going to do in this field or any other. The fact that they
> stay in jail is not going to have the slightest effect on me.
> *King*: Perhaps it would help if students came down here by the
> hundreds—by the hundreds of thousands.
> *Kennedy*: The country belongs to you as much as to me. You can
> determine what's best just as well as I can, but don't make statements
> that sound like a threat. That's not the way to deal with us. [a pause]
> *King*: It's difficult to understand the position of oppressed people. Ours
> is a way out—creative, moral, and nonviolent. It is not tied to black
> supremacy or Communism, but to the plight of the oppressed. It can

save the soul of America. You must understand that we've made no
gains without pressure, and I hope that pressure will always be moral,
legal, and peaceful.

Kennedy: But the problem won't be settled in Jackson, but by strong
federal action.

King: I'm deeply appreciative of what the Administration is doing. I see a
ray of hope, but I am different from my father. I feel the need of being
free now.

Kennedy: Well, it all depends on what you and the people in jail decide. If
they want to get out, we can get them out.

King: They'll stay.

The call left both men shaken and angry. After hanging up, King complained
to Coffin and others who had gathered in Abernathy's living room: "You know,
they don't understand the social revolution going on in the world, and therefore
they don't understand what we're doing." Kennedy, meanwhile, feeling that he
knew all too well what was going in Montgomery and Jackson, immediately
called Harris Wofford, the only administration official with close ties to the nonviolent movement. "This is too much," an exasperated Kennedy told Wofford, "I
wonder whether they have the best interest of their country at heart. Do you
know that one of them is against the atom bomb—yes, he even picketed against
it in jail. The President is going abroad, and this is all embarrassing him."

Back at Abernathy's house, the postmortem on the Kennedy call was evolving
into a long and wrenching discussion of whether the group should go on to Jackson in the morning. Stung by the suggestion that joining a Freedom Ride was
unpatriotic, Coffin and the others asked King for guidance. Should they go on in
the face of Kennedy's plea for a moratorium? King answered the question by
leading them in prayer, after which a vote was taken by secret ballot. Despite
considerable anguish, the vote was unanimous. All agreed that they had come
too far to turn back.

There were many reasons for the Kennedy brothers' determination to keep the
Freedom Rider movement from spreading. But one of their most pressing
concerns was the apparent polarization of the struggle over racial segregation.
The Freedom Rides had attracted the attention of extremists at both ends of the
political spectrum, including the Arlington, Virginia-based American Nazi Party.
On Wednesday evening, just minutes before Kennedy's emotional call to King,
George Lincoln Rockwell, the Fuehrer of the American Nazi Party, and nine of
his uniformed storm troopers were arrested outside of a New Orleans movie
theater where the pro-Israeli film *Exodus* was playing. Earlier in the evening they
had tried to disrupt a local NAACP membership rally, but the New Orleans

police had ordered them to leave the area. Rockwell and his bodyguard had flown to New Orleans from Washington on Tuesday afternoon, but the rest of the troopers had traveled south in a two-vehicle caravan that included a blue and white Volkswagen van dubbed the "Hate Bus." Signs emblazoned on the van advertised "LINCOLN ROCKWELL's HATE BUS" and slogans such as "WE DO HATE RACE MIXING" and "WE HATE JEW-COMMUNISM." Pledging solidarity with the Klansmen who had attacked the Freedom Riders in Alabama, Rockwell hoped to confront the Riders when they arrived in New Orleans. "Anybody that doesn't hate communism and doesn't hate race-mixers," he explained to reporters, "there's something wrong with them." On Tuesday the Hate Bus stopped briefly in Montgomery, but National Guardsmen promptly escorted it out of town. In New Orleans, Rockwell and the troopers carried signs with the words "America for Whites, Africa for Blacks" and "Gas Chamber for Traitors," which they made clear included the "Communist, nigger-loving" Freedom Riders.

Not wanting to call attention to Rockwell's grotesque parody of the Freedom Ride, administration officials at first tried to downplay the significance of the hate bus. But on Wednesday evening Rockwell's antics became entwined in a senatorial discussion of the wisdom of the Freedom Rides. Already embroiled in a battle over the advisability of attaching an anti-segregation rider to the administration's aid-to-education bill, liberals and conservatives squared off in a fight over the civil and moral equivalency of Rockwell and the Freedom Riders. After Senator John Stennis of Mississippi insisted that by employing "the same reason and logic as the Freedom Riders," Rockwell's neo-Nazis "could well claim they are merely exercising their constitutional rights," Senator Jacob Javits, a liberal Republican from New York, called for a full Senate debate on his colleague's outrageous defamation of the civil rights movement. Ignoring the fact that the administration had already taken a public position that, while not going as far as Stennis's equivalency argument, had implicitly challenged the moral authority of the Freedom Riders, Javits also announced plans to offer a Senate resolution supporting the president's intervention in the South. Despite Javits's good intentions, none of this pleased the president or any of the other administration officials who just wanted the crisis to pass quietly from the scene.

The Freedom Riders would later appreciate Javits's effort to mobilize bipartisan support for racial justice and desegregation. But at the moment they were more concerned with the challenge of surviving their first night in a Mississippi jail. Of the twenty-seven incarcerated Riders, only Bevel, a native of Itta Bena, had significant first-hand experience with Mississippi's special brand of segregation. Prior to their arrival on Wednesday afternoon, the others could only imagine what indignities awaited them. For black Americans, and even for many white Americans, the Mississippi of myth and legend was a terrifying place.

Lewis, for example, was unnerved on the road to Jackson by the sight of Mississippi Guardsmen who "wore big bushy beards that made them look like Confederate soldiers." Only later did he discover that the menacing looking Guardsmen were actually Confederate reenactors suitably groomed for upcoming participation in a Civil War Centennial celebration. And even this discovery was only mildly reassuring in a state where blacks had good reason to fear the worst.

As the state with the highest concentration of black population (42.3 percent in 1960), Mississippi boasted a rich tradition of African-American folk culture, including the artistry of down-home blues. But among white Mississippians, both inside and outside the Black Belt Delta region, an unforgiving and often brutal form of white supremacist repression held sway. In 1890, the state legislature had spearheaded a region-wide trend toward codification of black disfranchisement and Jim Crow with the so-called "Mississippi Plan." And in the seventy years since disfranchisement the state had not relinquished its reputation as the home of the South's most vigilant defenders of racial control and white privilege. Noting that Mississippi led the nation in lynching, poverty, political demagoguery, and social backwardness, the pundit H. L. Mencken dubbed it "the worst American state" in the 1920s. Sadly, in 1961, there was little reason to challenge this unenviable designation; indeed, the recent lynchings of Emmett Till (1955) and Mack Charles Parker (1959) seemed to confirm Mississippi's benighted status as a land apart.

As the Freedom Riders would soon discover, many white Mississippians were uncomfortable with the state's image as a lawless home of Negrophobic vigilantes. There was much talk of a new Mississippi, still proudly segregated but dedicated to the peaceful coexistence and well-being of all of its citizens. Many white Mississippians were proud that, unlike Klan-infested Alabama, Mississippi was a White Citizens' Council (WCC) state. Founded in the Mississippi Delta town of Indianola in 1954, the White Citizens' Councils advocated economic and political pressure, not violence, as the best means to preserve segregation and white supremacy. Even though critics sometimes referred to the councils as "the Klan in the grey flannel suit," most WCC chapters in Mississippi and elsewhere were determined to counter the Deep South's reputation for violent repression. It was in this spirit that Mississippi officials, virtually all of whom were WCC members, accorded the Freedom Riders a firm but polite reception.

Even so, the reality at the Jackson city jail was less pleasant than the carefully crafted public image implied. From the outset, most of the jailed Riders refused to cooperate with their jailers. In an effort to boost morale, Bevel, blessed with a beautiful voice, led round after round of freedom songs, an irritant that nearly drove the guards to distraction. Others—though not Bevel—engaged in a hunger strike that caused considerable controversy among the Riders. Still others infuriated police interrogators by refusing to end their "yes" and "no" answers with the word "sir." Just after his arrival at the city jail, Vivian admonished a guard for calling him "boy." "My church generally ordains *men*, not boys," Vivian informed him, whereupon the guard, with billy club in hand, screamed: "I'll knock yo' fuckin' black nappy head through that goddamn wall if you don't shut yo' goddamn mouth, nigger." Vivian escaped this particular encounter without injury, but not everyone agreed that such symbolic challenges to authority were a good idea. Nor was there any consensus on the proper limits of noncooperation or on the best means of expressing the nonviolent creed. Indeed, many of the Riders—even some of those who had spent time in Tennessee and Alabama jails—had difficult moments either dealing with their fears or maintaining a composure that reconciled protest with common decency. There was, however, solid agreement that as many of the Riders as possible should remain in jail. When Len Holt, who had flown to Jackson with Diane Nash, visited the Riders on Wednesday evening, the commitment to the "jail—no bail" policy was still strong.

Back in Montgomery, where Coffin's group was preparing to depart for Jackson, there was also an unmistakable spirit of movement solidarity. Accompanied to the Trailways terminal by four SCLC leaders—Shuttlesworth, Walker, Abernathy, and Bernard Lee, the former sit-in leader at Montgomery's Alabama State College—Coffin and his six colleagues held a pre-boarding press conference to explain why they had decided to travel on to Mississippi against the Kennedy administration's wishes. Rejecting the argument that the Freedom Rides were embarrassing the nation in front of the world and endangering President Kennedy's stature on the eve of a critical summit meeting, Coffin declared: "We can't drag the name of the United States in the mud. The name of the United States is already in the mud. It is up to us to get it out."

Following the press conference, the seven Riders and their SCLC hosts moved to the Trailways lunch counter for a brief breakfast—the same counter that the Lawson group had desegregated the day before. This time, however, on orders from Governor Patterson, the Montgomery County sheriff, Mac Sim Butler, arrested all eleven of the offending activists for disorderly conduct and conspiring to breach the peace. Although General Graham had agreed to provide the Coffin group with an armed escort of fifty National Guardsmen and thirty-two highway patrolmen, he did not interfere with the arrests. Indeed, he seemed relieved that the escort to the Mississippi border was no longer necessary. "Now everyone is happy," he told reporters, "This is what they wanted, and we have accommodated them. They've been arrested quietly, like they wanted to be, and now I'm happy too."

Graham's not-so-subtle suggestion that this new batch of Freedom Riders was a band of publicity seekers who did not really want to travel on to Mississippi reflected a deliberate strategy to delegitimize the hordes of outside agitators that he and others feared were about to descend upon the Deep South. Based on a combination of misinformation and wishful thinking, it was a strategy that appealed to a wide variety of government leaders, including officials at the Justice Department and the White House. In his initial reaction to the Greyhound group on Wednesday morning, Robert Kennedy had drawn a sharp distinction between real and phony Freedom Riders, and in desperation he returned to this specious line of reasoning on Thursday afternoon. This time, however, he distinguished between the original CORE Freedom Riders and the pretenders that followed. "It took a lot of courage for the first group to go," he told a Washington reporter, "but not much for the others." He even suggested that the Freedom Riders who insisted on remaining in a Mississippi jail should be shunned for irresponsibly producing "good propaganda for America's enemies." Earlier in the afternoon, he had ordered the demobilization of all but one hundred of the federal marshals in Alabama, and now he appeared to be assuming a position of constitutional neutrality with respect to the Freedom Riders' right to travel.

Emboldened by this turn of events, Mississippi's senior senator, James O. Eastland, immediately went on the attack, claiming that the Freedom Rides were "Communist-inspired" and "devised deliberately . . . as a propaganda method to embarrass the president and the United States." Reaching back to the original CORE Ride, he denounced Jim Peck as "a Communist agitator and organizer of the most dangerous kind" and CORE as a subversive organization whose "creed has been lawlessness" and whose "tactics have followed the pattern set by Communist agitators the world over."

Eastland's unrestrained Red-baiting played better in Jackson than in Washington, and the Kennedy administration quickly distanced itself from this and other intemperate attacks on the Freedom Riders. Clearly, the position of the defiant white South provided no refuge for administration officials, who had received an even more telling reminder of this fact earlier in the day when a carload of gun-toting white teenagers wounded the Reverend Solomon Seay outside of his parsonage. Fortunately, Seay escaped with only a wrist wound, but the drive-by incident reminded the Kennedy brothers of why they had sent the marshals to Alabama. If administration officials were somewhat uncomfortable with associating with the Freedom Riders, they were even more uncomfortable tying themselves to the antics and attitudes of cowardly gunmen or white supremacist zealots like Eastland. Even so, when John Kennedy delivered a special state of the union address to Congress on Thursday evening, he avoided any reference to the Freedom Riders or the domestic civil rights struggle. After declaring that he had come to the Capitol "to promote the freedom doctrine," he identified "the whole southern half of the globe" as "the great battleground for the expansion of freedom today." But the more immediate battleground in the southern half of the United States received no mention. Most of the speech focused on foreign aid, national defense, and the space program, and the most memorable line was the president's daring pledge to put a man on the moon by the end of the decade. This implicit slight to the cause of civil rights did not go unnoticed in movement circles, prompting one New York rabbi to comment that "it seems strange to discuss trips to the moon when it is impossible for white and colored Americans to travel together on a bus and use the same facilities in 'the land of the free and the home of the brave.'"

Politically speaking, Kennedy's omission of the domestic freedom struggle may have made sense. But neither his silence nor Eastland's bombast did anything to slow the momentum of the Freedom Rider movement. On Thursday afternoon, several hours before the state of the union address, Pauline Knight, speaking for the Nashville Movement, announced that there was no shortage of available reinforcements for the Riders arrested in Jackson. "If the people there have to stay in jail—if they are convicted," Knight promised, "then there will be another busload from Nashville." Not to be outdone, the CORE office in New York issued a field order expanding its nonviolent campaign to railroad and airline terminals. Written by Farmer earlier in the week, the order declared that "the time to act is now." On Friday morning the *New York Times* reported that the CORE office "had the appearance of a combat field headquarters," as more than a dozen staff members and volunteers "frantically answered batteries of telephones, dispatched telegrams and mimeographed statements and bulletins." According to CORE spokesperson Marvin Rich, "more than 100 Freedom Riders" were "standing by at strategic locations in the South to train others in nonviolent techniques or to take places on buses themselves." When reporters pressed him for a statement on where all this was headed, Rich suggested that the movement was poised to "end segregation by the end of this year."

Rich's heady prediction was part hyperbole, but it also reflected a growing confidence that the entire civil rights movement was lining up behind the Freedom Riders. On Thursday even the leaders of the NAACP and the National Urban League, two organizations that generally steered clear of direct action, summarily rejected the attorney general's plea for a cooling-off period. "There can be no cooling-off period in the effort to obtain one's citizenship rights," Roy Wilkins declared. Accordingly, he urged the student members of the NAACP's 123 college chapters to insist on nonsegregated travel when they returned home at the end of the spring semester.

On Friday morning the Freedom Rider movement received another unexpected boost when Jim Peck was interviewed by Dave Garroway on the NBC network's *Today Show*. Speaking in a calm and reasoned voice and looking much like an ordinary citizen, Peck defended the Freedom Rides in front of a national audience, a good part of which had seen pictures of his bandaged head ten days earlier. Although Peck's television appearance triggered a storm of protest in the Deep South—especially in Mississippi, where editors characterized the CORE leader as "Garroway's latest anti-Southern hero"—for many Americans it matched a sympathetic human face with a movement that sometimes seemed too abstract and exotic to comprehend.

Perhaps even more important, Friday morning also marked an organizational milestone in the brief history of the Freedom Rider movement. At Ebenezer Baptist Church in Atlanta, King convened an organizational meeting of the Freedom Ride Coordinating Committee (FRCC). On hand were representatives of five organizations interested in sustaining and expanding the Freedom Rider movement: King and Bernard Lee of SCLC; Gordon Carey of CORE; Ed King of SNCC; two preachers representing the NCLC in the absence of the arrested Freedom Riders Bevel and Lawson; and a delegate from the National Student Association. At the founding meeting, the group agreed to establish recruitment centers in Nashville, Atlanta, New Orleans, and Jackson; to coordinate fund-raising for an all-out assault on Jim Crow transportation; to seek a meeting with the president; and to push for unambiguous endorsements of desegregated travel from both the Justice Department and the Interstate Commerce Commission. This was a tall order for a movement that had seen a majority of its leaders arrested in the preceding forty-eight hours, but the founding members of the FRCC were determined to make a statement, both to themselves and the world, that the Freedom Rider movement could not be broken by arrests, demagogic Red-baiting, or even federal equivocation.

On Friday afternoon, while administration officials and Southern liberals continued to tiptoe across the minefield of Cold War politics and public opinion, the focus of movement and media attention shifted to the Freedom Riders' pending legal problems. In Montgomery, five members of Coffin's group, including Coffin himself, after deciding that one night in a Southern jail was enough, posted bond and prepared to return to Connecticut. Before boarding a plane for New York, Coffin condemned the arrest and confinement of the eleven movement activists as "blatantly illegal" and "a travesty of justice." Earlier in the afternoon General Graham, on hand to arrange a National Guard escort for the departing professors, had condemned the plan to send in additional Freedom Riders as "immoral, stupid, and criminal." Infuriated by a hunger strike being staged by the five activists still in jail, Graham and other Alabama officials insisted that Abernathy and his fellow inmates were being treated well and in accordance with the law. Indeed, if anyone wanted proof of Montgomery's commitment to equal justice, he only had to visit the county courthouse, where earlier in the day five white men had been convicted and sentenced for their involvement in the rioting of May 20 and 21.

In Jackson, Mississippi officials were making similar claims as twenty-seven jailed Freedom Riders were brought before Municipal Judge James L. Spencer.

As several national reporters later acknowledged, the overall mood in the court-room was unexpectedly civil. Following Spencer's lead, the local prosecutor, Jack Travis, began with a gesture of compassion by dropping the second charge of disobeying a police officer. City officials did not want to "be harsh," he explained. Nodding his head in approval, Judge Spencer then asked the defendants to enter a plea to the remaining charge of breaching the peace. When all twenty-seven defendants pleaded not guilty and defense attorneys followed with a request for a directed verdict of acquittal, both Travis and Spencer seemed a bit miffed, but, realizing that Mississippi justice was also on trial, they made a concerted effort to keep their composure.

The city's first and only prosecution witness was J. L. Ray, the police captain who had rounded up both groups of Riders on Wednesday. After acknowledging that he had been given a standing order to arrest the Riders if they tried to enter the terminal's white waiting room, Ray explained that he and his superiors were aware of "what happened in Montgomery" and "didn't want a similar incident to happen here." The defense then called three of the defendants to the stand as witnesses. The first was Jim Lawson, who, after describing his background as a pacifist and conscientious objector, proceeded to excoriate Mississippi authorities for escorting the Freedom Riders to Jackson against their will. Taking Lawson's testimony as a cue, defense lawyer Wiley Branton interjected the assertion that the state of Mississippi was guilty of "entrapment," having "deliberately brought these defendants from the state line to Jackson to arrest them."

After nearly two hours of listening to Travis's warnings and the Freedom Riders' apostasy, Judge Spencer had heard enough. Within seconds of Branton's closing statement—which reminded the judge that he and other Mississippi officials had taken an oath to uphold the U.S. Constitution—Spencer found all twenty-seven defendants guilty as charged. After informing the audience that "we're not here trying any segregation laws or the rights of these people to sit on any buses or to eat in any place," he scolded the Freedom Riders for seeking recourse in the streets instead of the courts. "Their avowed purpose," he insisted, "was to inflame the public." Finding them "in open defiance of the laws of Mississippi," he sentenced each defendant to a $200 fine and a suspended sixty-day jail term.

Prior to the trial, the Freedom Riders had announced their intention to remain in jail until Mississippi authorities agreed to recognize the legality of desegregated interstate transit, but Spencer and other Mississippi officials held out some hope that at least some of the Riders were bluffing. In truth, there were those among the Riders who questioned the strategy of "jail—no bail." For some, spending sixty days, or even one more night, in a Mississippi jail was a frightening prospect. Nevertheless, when the convicted Freedom Riders met with their attorneys on Friday evening, no one spoke in favor of a mass bail-out. Some, like Lucretia Collins, who had promised to return to Nashville for the

May 29 graduation exercises at Tennessee State, had personal reasons for paying her $200 fine and accepting a suspended sentence, and CORE officials decided that the four Freedom Riders from Louisiana—David Dennis, Jerome Smith, Doris Castle, and Julia Aaron—were needed in New Orleans to set up an FRCC recruitment and training center. But there was general agreement that the rest of the Riders could serve the cause best by remaining in jail.

On Friday afternoon, following the organizational meeting of the FRCC, King had told reporters that there would be a "temporary lull" in the Freedom Rides while movement organizers set up recruiting and training centers around the South. But the predicted lull did not last long. Hoping to sustain the movement's momentum, Diane Nash returned to Nashville on Saturday morning to help Leo Lillard and Pauline Knight finalize the arrangements for a new round of Rides. By Saturday afternoon, thirteen new Freedom Riders were ready to go. Just after lunch, Knight, Allen Cason (who had narrowly escaped serious injury in Montgomery the previous Saturday), and two other Riders boarded a bus for Montgomery, with plans to travel on to Jackson. At 5:15 a second group of nine Riders—all students at Tennessee State—boarded a Greyhound headed for Jackson via Memphis. Like Cason, seven of the nine Tennessee State Riders had participated in the recent Birmingham to Montgomery Freedom Ride, and even though they had returned to Nashville earlier in the week to take their final exams, all still faced the possibility of expulsion for their participation in the Freedom Rides.

By the time the Trailways group arrived in Jackson, the Greyhound group was already in jail. After a late-night stop in Memphis, the Greyhound departed for Mississippi around 1:15 in the morning and arrived in Jackson just before dawn. Although the Greyhound Riders, unlike the Trailways Riders, traveled without a police escort, local authorities were waiting for them at the terminal. As soon as they walked into the white waiting room, the nine students were arrested for breaching the peace and led to a waiting paddy wagon. Before entering the wagon, one of the students handed a pile of pamphlets on "Fellowship and Human Rights in America" to a detective who jokingly promised to distribute them. Otherwise the arrests followed the same pattern as those of the previous Wednesday. "They passed us right on through the white terminal, into the paddy wagon, and into jail," Fred Leonard recalled. "There was no violence in Mississippi." Eight hours later, Knight and the Trailways group suffered a similar fate, bringing the total number of arrested Mississippi Freedom Riders to forty-four. Arresting Freedom Riders, as one local editor complained on Monday morning, was becoming "monotonous."

He was not alone in his feelings. Even before news of the latest arrests hit the papers, there were signs that many Americans—and not only white Mississippians—were growing tired of the Freedom Riders. In a stinging Sunday morning editorial, the *New York Times* declared: "The battle against segregation will not be won overnight nor by any one dramatic strategy. The Freedom Riders, for all their idealism, now may be overreaching themselves. There is a danger that if their offensive is continued at the present pace, exacerbated feelings on both sides could lead to tragic results in which the extremists could overwhelm the men of moderation on whom the real solution will ultimately depend . . . the Freedom Riders have made their point. Now is the time for restraint, relaxation of tension and a cessation of their courageous, legal, peaceful but nonetheless provocative action in the South." The *Times* certainly did not speak for all white Americans, and there were still many voices urging the Freedom Riders to press their case, including an unrepentant William Sloane Coffin who reminded his Sunday morning congregation at Yale that "any return to normalcy means a return to injustice." But in the nation as a whole the tide of public opinion seemed to be running against the Riders. Many Americans, particularly outside the South, felt conflicted, as sympathy for civil rights vied with disapproval of the Freedom Riders' tactics. But even among those who were strongly sympathetic to the civil rights movement there seemed to be a rising wave of sentiment in favor of a moratorium or cooling-off period. Indeed, with the president's departure for Paris scheduled for Tuesday evening, the argument for national solidarity seemed especially compelling.

On Monday, May 29, the prospects for a cooling-off period did not look good. On the contrary, the situation appeared to be heating up on all fronts. In Jackson, the day began with the pre-dawn transfer of twenty-two Freedom Riders to the Hinds County Penal Farm, seventeen miles south of the city. Judging by the smiles on the faces of their guards, the Riders had good reason to fear the move. As one black inmate at the county jail told Farmer: "That's where they're gonna try to break you. They're gonna try to whip your ass." After Jack Young seconded the inmate's warning—"That place is rough. You're going to have trouble there," he predicted—Farmer asked him to let the FBI know what was going on.

The actual scene at the penal farm turned out to be even worse than the Riders had anticipated. "When we got there," Frank Holloway recalled, "we met several men in ten-gallon hats, looking like something out of an old Western, with rifles in their hands, staring at us as if we were desperate killers about to escape." This sight drew a sardonic smile from Holloway, but what happened next was anything but humorous. As he described the scene: "Soon they took us out to a room, boys on one side and girls on the other. One by one they took us into another room for questioning before they gave us their black and white stripes. There were about eight guards with sticks in their hands in the second room, and the Freedom Rider being questioned was surrounded by these men. Outside we could hear the questions, and the thumps and whacks, and sometimes a quick groan or cry when their questions weren't answered to their satisfaction. They beat several Riders who didn't say 'Yes, sir,' but none of them would Uncle-Tom the guards. Rev. C. T. Vivian . . . was beaten pretty bad. When he came out he had blood streaming from his head."

This was more than enough to convince Holloway, Harold Andrews (Holloway's classmate at Morehouse), and Peter Ackerberg, the white Freedom Rider from Antioch College, to post bond and accept a police escort to the Jackson airport. However, nineteen of the Riders decided to stick it out, to the obvious satisfaction of farm superintendent Max Thomas and his boss, Sheriff J. R. Gilfoy. "We are not going to coddle them," promised Gilfoy. "When they go to work on the county roads this afternoon they are going to work just like anyone else here." The Freedom Riders would also wear "black and white striped prison uniforms," just like the other prisoners, though he couldn't resist pointing out that so far the regular inmates had refused to "have anything to do with them." This would not be the last time that a Mississippi official would suggest that outside agitators were the lowest of the low, deserving the contempt of even hardened criminals. Despite his pledge to treat the Riders like the other prisoners, Gilfoy soon decided that it was too risky to put them to work on the roads or in the fields, where they might encounter meddling journalists. Instead he kept them confined to their cells, which many of the Riders came to view as a greater hardship than anything that might have awaited them beyond the bars.

Meanwhile, on Wednesday, May 24, the Justice Department had filed a request to expand the injunction against Alabama Klansmen and other vigilantes to include local police officials in Birmingham and Montgomery, and Judge Johnson had agreed to begin hearings on the matter on Monday. With John Doar handling the government's case and federal marshals standing guard, and with L. B. Sullivan, Jamie Moore, Bull Connor, riot leader Claude Henley, and Imperial Wizard Robert Shelton in the audience, the scene in Johnson's courtroom was one of the most dramatic in the city's history.

The opening witness, a Tennessee State student named Patricia Jenkins, identified Henley as one of the leading assailants during the May 20 riot and testified that she had seen a policeman leave the scene as soon as the bus arrived at the terminal. Other witnesses—including Fred Gach, FBI Special Agent Spender Robb, and John McCloud, a black postal employee—confirmed the general absence of police protection and the refusal of sheriff's deputies and other local authorities to intervene on behalf of reporters and Freedom Riders under attack. Even more damning was the testimony of Stuart Culpepper, a reporter for the *Montgomery Advertiser*, who testified that Jack Shows, a local police detective, had told him before the riot began that the police "would not lift a finger" to protect the Freedom Riders. By the time the hearing recessed just after 6 p.m., the government's case for an expanded injunction appeared to be a lock. But there were still more witnesses waiting to testify, and Johnson had yet to hear from the defense. To the dismay of those who had hoped to put the episode behind them, the hearing would go on for three more days.

Racial tensions were also rising in Washington, where there was a lot of tough talk on both sides of the Freedom Rider issue on the Monday following the Mississippi arrests. One militant segregationist, Senator Olin D. Johnston of South Carolina, even sent a public letter to his constituents insisting that the Freedom Riders "should be stopped in their tracks at the place of origin and not allowed to prey upon the religious, racial, and social differences of our people." The biggest political story to come out of the nation's capital on May 29, however, was Robert Kennedy's decision to file a petition asking the Interstate Commerce Commission to adopt "stringent regulations" prohibiting segregation in interstate bus travel. Citing the recent experiences of the Freedom Riders, he declared that ICC action was needed to end the legal confusion that had contributed to mob violence in the South.

Six years earlier the ICC had issued an order mandating the desegregation of interstate train travel, including terminal restaurants, waiting rooms, and restrooms. The November 1955 order had also directed interstate bus companies to discontinue the practice of segregating passengers, but said nothing about segregated bus terminals. Even more confusing was the commission's subsequent decision to forego any real effort to enforce the order. When the ICC won a judgment against Southern Stages Inc. in April 1961, it was the first instance of even token enforcement of bus desegregation. And in the Southern Stages case, which involved the segregation of a black interstate passenger in Georgia in the summer of 1960, the $100 fines levied against the company and a driver represented little more than a slap on the wrist. While a number of other cases were pending, the ICC's overall record of enforcement was, in the words of one historian, "a sorry one," thanks in part to the willingness of Justice Department officials to look the other way.

In submitting a detailed, seven-section petition to the ICC, Kennedy was attempting to end the confusion. He was also sending a clear signal that his own department would no longer tolerate nonenforcement of the law. Why he waited so long to do so is something of a mystery, but there is no evidence that he thought much about the ICC's potential role until the Freedom Ride Coordinating Committee called for the commission's involvement on May 26. As he surely knew, the ICC had enjoyed jurisdiction over interstate buses since the passage of the Motor Carrier Act of 1935, yet had done next to nothing to combat discrimination; but he also knew that, as a newly appointed attorney general still adjusting to the realities of bureaucratic life, he had little hope of summarily countermanding decades of inaction and neglect. Considering the ICC's notorious reputation for political conservatism and glacial deliberation, his lack of confidence was well founded, which suggests that his decision to turn to the ICC on May 29 was more an act of desperation than the result of a carefully rendered strategy.

When Kennedy first broached the subject with Burke Marshall and others on Friday, there was no hint that he actually planned to follow through with a formal appeal to the ICC. But on Monday morning, after a weekend of alarming reports about impending Freedom Rides and racial polarization, he could think of nothing else, ordering his staff to produce a fully developed document by the end of the day. The resulting "petition," a novel form of appeal suggested by Justice Department attorney Robert Saloscin, was a hodgepodge of legal and legislative citations mixed with moral and political imperatives. Nevertheless, the message to the lumbering ICC was clear. "Just as our Constitution is color blind, and neither knows nor tolerates classes among citizens" the petition advised, "so too is the Interstate Commerce Act. The time has come for this commission, in administering that act, to declare unequivocally by regulation that a Negro passenger is free to travel the length and breadth of this country in the same manner as any other passenger."

Kennedy's enthusiasm for the egalitarian platitudes in the petition confirmed what many on his staff already knew: Despite his growing impatience with the Freedom Riders' confrontational tactics and his lack of experience in civil rights matters, the attorney general was ideologically and emotionally committed to racial equality. Even when concern for his brother's vulnerability on the world stage pushed him to lash out at the Freedom Riders' intransigence, he could not bring himself to abandon the basic principle of equal justice. On Friday afternoon, while he was still fuming over the civil rights community's rejection of a cooling-off period, he delivered an apparently unscripted Voice of America radio address that trumpeted the nation's commitment to equality. Speaking to an international audience spread across sixty countries, he attempted to put the recent troubles in Alabama and Mississippi in the context of a nation that was trying to overcome the violent and white supremacist excesses of a lawless minority.

Most of his speech was a predictable rejoinder to Communist insinuations that the mobs in Alabama represented the interests and attitudes of a racially repressive capitalist regime, but at times he went much farther down the freedom road than Cold War rhetoric or political discretion dictated, even suggesting the possibility that the American electorate would elect a black president before the end of the century, a prediction that proved to be only eight years off. Pointing out the contrast between his brother's status as an Irish-Catholic president and the anti-Irish discrimination that his grandfather had faced in the early twentieth century, he insisted that a similar transformation would soon come to black America. Such talk was no substitute for action, as several liberal commentators pointed out. In the politically and racially constrained atmosphere of May 1961, though, even a single moment of idealistic indiscretion was newsworthy.

None of this, of course, proves or even suggests that idealism was the driving force behind Kennedy's decision to petition the ICC on May 29. On the contrary, all available evidence indicates that he embraced the petition as a pragmatic solution to a short-term political problem. Although he knew that it would take weeks and even months to obtain a definitive ICC ruling on the regulations themselves, he recognized the immediate symbolic value of the petition. Having failed in his jawboning effort to convince the Freedom Riders to accept a cooling-off period, he hoped that the petition would at least take some of the steam out of the movement. That it did not do so was a profound disappointment for him and his staff, not to mention a clear sign that, for all his good intentions, the attorney general did not yet understand the depth of feeling that was driving young Americans, black and white, onto the freedom buses.

By Tuesday evening—with the exception of eight white Riders incarcerated in the city jail—five groups of Riders were all packed into a county jail that was Spartan even by Mississippi standards. Even without the overcrowding, the county jail was a miserable place, as Frank Holloway's experience earlier in the week had demonstrated. "When we went in," Holloway recalled, "we were met by some of the meanest looking, tobacco-chewing lawmen I have ever seen. They ordered us around like a bunch of dogs, and I really began to feel like I was in a Mississippi jail. Our cell was nasty, and the beds were harder than the city jail beds, hardly sleepable, but the eight of us in our cell had to lie down somewhere." Later, after Holloway and others disobeyed an order to stop singing freedom songs, several Riders were put in a sweat box; and when even that didn't stop the singing, at least one jailer warned them that he "could get rid of a nigger in Mississippi, and nobody could do anything about it."

The wretched conditions at the Hinds County Jail should have been enough to force at least some of the Freedom Riders to reconsider their commitment to the "jail—no bail" policy. Most observers, including government officials at all levels, certainly expected the policy to unravel as the Freedom Riders began to realize what it was actually like to spend hard time in a Mississippi jail. Even among movement supporters, there was a common expectation that sooner or later most of the Riders would agree to be released on bond. Only among the Freedom Riders themselves, it seems, was there a full appreciation of the strange but powerful seductiveness of meaningful sacrifice and unmerited suffering. The greater the hardship, the more committed they seemed to be, a dynamic that could not be explained away as a mere manifestation of peer pressure or youthful illusions of invulnerability. Something deeper was at work, something that remained hidden from all but the most perceptive observers.

One of the first to detect the special character of the Freedom Rider experience was the veteran journalist Walter Lippmann. "It would be vain for anyone to expect that there can be a quick and easy end to the kind of courage and determination which has been shown in the bus rides and in the lunch-counter sit-ins," he wrote on May 25. "No one should expect this kind of thing to disappear." A second observer who shared Lippmann's viewpoint was Leslie Dunbar, the executive director of the Southern Regional Council and the author of a special Freedom Ride report authorized by the council and released on Tuesday, May 30. "The Freedom Ride will continue," Dunbar predicted, "If not in its present form, in some other similar style, and soon. There is in it momentum too great to be held back. The South and the nation are now critically dependent on the quality of Negro leadership, and its ability to direct that momentum and not be overrun by it." Nevertheless, in keeping with the traditions of white Southern liberalism, Dunbar went on to insist that "the big problems . . . can be tackled only by the South itself: by white Southerners coming to deserve the trust of Negro Southerners . . . There would be no Freedom Ride if there were compliance with law and decency in the South."

The overlapping issues of legal compliance and public decency were also the focus of attention in Montgomery on Tuesday morning. In one courtroom, the Alabama Court of Appeals upheld the conviction of twelve Birmingham blacks arrested during a series of sit-ins in March 1960. Ten of those arrested were students, and two, including Shuttlesworth, were leaders charged with inciting the sit-ins. Just down the street, in a second courtroom, Judge Johnson was presiding over the second day of the injunction hearing. Throughout the day Doar grilled a series of witnesses, including Imperial Wizard Shelton and Cecil "Goober" Lewallyn, the Klansman suspected of tossing the firebomb into the Trailways bus outside of Anniston. The star witness for the defense of Alabama's sovereignty was George Cruit, the Birmingham Greyhound superintendent who had haggled with the attorney general by phone on May 15 and again on May 20. Reading from a transcript of the first conversation, Cruit quoted Kennedy's declaration that the "Government is going to be very much upset if this group does not get to continue their trip." To Cruit, to most of the white Southerners in the courtroom, and to thousands of others who read the attorney general's words in news accounts, this declaration was proof that the federal government had conspired with the Freedom Riders to attack the Southern way of life. Even more damning for some was Kennedy's insistence that Cruit recruit a black driver after white bus drivers refused to drive to Montgomery.

On Thursday, June 1, seven white Freedom Riders at the Jackson city jail initiated a hunger strike that soon spread to the black Riders incarcerated in the county jail across the street. Later in the day, in Chicago, seven former Freedom Riders—Walter and Frances Bergman, Ike Reynolds, Jerome Smith, Dave Dennis, Doris Castle, and Julia Aaron—announced a drive to recruit "hundreds or thousands" of new Freedom Riders. Dismissing the call for a cooling-off period, Bergman urged his fellow activists to strike "while the iron is hot." "American students are going to strike, strike, strike and ride, ride, ride," he predicted, "until we achieve our goal of an open country." In Ithaca, New York, a group of Cornell students promised to reinforce the student Riders already arrested in Mississippi; in Cambridge, Massachusetts, Harvard students formed an Emergency Public Integration Committee (EPIC) that sponsored end-of-the-semester "freedom parties" as a means of raising funds for CORE; and in New Haven, Connecticut, a petition of support for the Freedom Riders signed by 307 members of the Yale faculty and administration, including Yale Law School dean Eugene Rostow, was on its way to the White House. Farther afield, in San Francisco, a group of clergymen announced the founding of "Freedom Writers," an organization pledged to gather funds and a million signatures in support of the Freedom Rides. To the dismay of those who had hoped for an early resolution of the crisis, the Freedom Rider movement was becoming national in scope.

Nevertheless, on Friday morning the focus of attention returned to Montgomery, where Judge Johnson issued an unexpectedly sweeping set of injunctive rulings. As expected, Johnson formally enjoined Alabama Klansmen from interfering with interstate travel and ordered the Montgomery police to protect all interstate travelers regardless of race. Citing Klan-inspired violence and the "willful and deliberate failure" of Montgomery police officials to do their duty, he issued a preliminary injunction against Robert Shelton's Alabama Knights of the Ku Klux Klan, Alvin Horn's Talladega-based U.S. Klans, Montgomery Klansmen Claude Henley and Thurman Ouzts, Commissioner Sullivan, Police Chief Ruppenthal, and "their officers, agents, employees, members, and all persons acting in concert with them." But he did not stop there. To the surprise of almost everyone in the courtroom, he also granted a temporary restraining order prohibiting CORE, SNCC, SCLC, and the Montgomery City Jail Council from "sponsoring, financing, assisting or encouraging any individual or group of individuals in traveling in interstate commerce through or in Alabama for the purpose of testing the state or local laws as those laws relate to racial segregation." The order also specifically restrained the activities of several movement leaders, including King, Abernathy, Walker, and Shuttlesworth. In effect, he had placed at least a temporary ban on future Freedom Rides in the state of Alabama. On June 12 he would convene a hearing to determine whether the order should be vacated or turned into a full-fledged injunction. Until then, he warned, the anti–Freedom Ride ruling, like the injunction against the Klan and the Montgomery police, would be rigidly enforced. "If there are any such incidents as this again," he declared, "I am going to put some Klansmen, some city officials, and some Negro preachers in the federal penitentiary."

In a lengthy, fifteen-page preamble and in a stern-voiced statement from the bench, Johnson surveyed the evidence of incitement and dereliction of duty and explained the logic of his double-edged ruling. "Those who sponsor, finance, and encourage groups to come into this area, with the knowledge that such trips will foment violence," he argued, "are just as effective in causing an obstruction to interstate travel as mobs themselves." Even though he conceded that the sponsoring organizations and individuals had engaged "in agitation within the law of the United States," he maintained that such agitation constituted "an undue burden upon the free flow of interstate commerce at this particular time and under the circumstances that exist." While acknowledging that organizing bands of Freedom Riders "may be a legal right," he insisted that "the right of the public to be protected from the evils of their conduct is a greater and more important right." Anticipating legal and constitutional objections, he reminded potential critics that "the right of the public to be protected from evils of conduct, even though the constitutional rights of certain persons or groups are thereby in some manner infringed, has received frequent and consistent recognition from the courts of the United States." Individuals traveling through Alabama "on bona-fide trips" deserved full constitutional protection, but civil rights activists, at least in the short run, would have to sacrifice some of their freedom for the greater good.

Predictably, Johnson's bold ruling elicited a wide range of reactions. In Alabama, the mainstream white press hailed the paired injunctions as an even-handed rebuke to violent Klan-led extremists and provocative outside agitators "With one stroke of the pen," one Montgomery editor wrote, the "upstart Republican" judge from Winston County "ceased to be the villain and became the hero of the hour." James Free, a columnist with the *Birmingham News*, agreed, pointing out that Johnson was "the first federal official of real stature and influence to crack down on both sides of the freedom rider hullabaloo."

Most civil rights activists, of course, felt otherwise. From the perspective of those who saw the Freedom Rides as a necessary step down the road to desegregation, Johnson's ruling was an unexpected slap in the face. Within minutes of Johnson's injunctive decree, Marvin Rich announced that CORE had asked Montgomery attorney Solomon Seay Jr., the son of one of the leaders named in the restraining order, to seek a stay in federal court. In Atlanta, Martin Luther King initially refused to comment on Johnson's decision to include the names of specific civil rights leaders in the order, but he expressed serious doubt that the ruling would halt the Freedom Rides. "I think we have revealed through many experiences," King reminded Johnson and the nation, "that we have no fear of going to jail and staying to serve time when necessary. We have transformed jails and prisons from dungeons of shame to havens of freedom and justice." Others voiced their objections more bluntly, and some even put their words into action.

At 11:30 A.M., a little more than an hour after Johnson issued his injunction, eight Freedom Riders left the Montgomery Trailways terminal on a bus bound for Jackson. Before leaving, the eight "post-injunction" Riders tested the station's restrooms and waiting rooms. Even after a bomb threat delayed their departure, local authorities did not attempt to stop them from boarding the bus (as a federal district court spokesman later explained, the injunction did not apply to anyone who did not have prior knowledge of it). When the bus stopped near Selma, Sheriff Jim Clark, who would achieve national notoriety in 1965 for his persecution of civil rights demonstrators, arrested one of the white Riders, Ralph Fertig of Chicago, for allegedly bothering a white female passenger. But the other seven Riders made it safely to Jackson, where they were promptly arrested for trying to desegregate the Trailways terminal.

The first Freedom Riders to leave Montgomery after the injunction, they were actually the second group to be arrested in Jackson on June 2. At 7:30 a.m., two and a half hours *before* Johnson's ruling, another group of Mississippi-bound Freedom Riders had departed from the Montgomery Trailways terminal. Led by SNCC veteran and Montgomery-riot survivor Ruby Doris Smith, the group of six Riders included three white male volunteers from Long Island and two black students from Nashville, Charles Butler and Joy Reagon. On Friday afternoon, when a frightened but defiant Reagon was arrested in Jackson along with Smith and the others, she was taken to the Hinds County Jail. Four hours later her younger brother Cordell joined her there, the sixty-fifth Freedom Rider to enter the strange world of Mississippi justice. With the exception of C. T. Vivian, Hank Thomas, and Jean Thompson—all of whom were struck in the face by penal farm superintendent Max Thomas for failing to address him as "sir"—none of the jailed Riders had yet seen the violent side of that world. But no one could be sure how long the show of restraint would last. Earlier in the day, following a perfunctory investigation, Mississippi authorities had exonerated Max Thomas, ruling that Vivian's injuries had occurred during an assault on the superintendent and not, as Vivian claimed, during a beating. Even more ominously, there were signs that the hunger strikes and freedom songs were beginning to wear on the nerves of the guards, particularly at the overcrowded county jail where the black Riders were imprisoned.

For Justice Department officials in Washington, the increasingly unstable situation in Mississippi was a matter of great concern, but on Friday afternoon and on through the weekend their most pressing problem was formulating a response to Judge Johnson's temporary restraining order. From the outset Marshall, Doar, and others expressed grave doubts about the constitutionality of the order. Earlier in the week, after the local prosecutor had requested the order, Doar had presented Johnson with a memorandum explaining why the Justice Department opposed such an extreme measure. In the wake of the Friday morning ruling, department officials publicly reiterated their objections, pointing out that the Supreme Court had already closed the option of restoring civil order through constitutionally questionable judicial orders. In the 1958 Little Rock case, the court had ruled that no such shortcuts would be allowed, and the department had no interest in reopening the question three years later. Privately, however, many department officials welcomed the order as a judicial substitute for the voluntary cooling-off period requested by the attorney general. While they felt compelled to challenge the order in court, they were pleased that the ban on Alabama Freedom Rides would be in effect for at least two weeks, and perhaps even longer if the Fifth Circuit Court of Appeals took its time to rule on a motion to vacate the order.

Of course, no one in the Justice Department could be sure how the FRCC would react to Johnson's high-handed judicial intervention. As an act of faith, the department went ahead with its withdrawal of the marshals at Maxwell Field, announcing on Friday that the remaining fifty marshals had received demobilization orders. Even so, the likelihood of additional Freedom Rides was a continuing concern. On Saturday King announced that the FRCC planned to sidestep Judge Johnson's improper ruling by sending Freedom Riders into Mississippi through states other than Alabama, and he even hinted that the present plan to comply with the order might change in the future. "There are legal remedies to the order," he declared, "and we intend to exhaust them all." But he also warned that the option of civil disobedience was still open. "If a law is unjust," he told reporters, "we have a moral responsibility to disobey the unjust law."

This kind of talk made Justice Department officials, and many other observers, very nervous. While editorial and public opinion outside of the South was sharply divided on the question of the restraining order's legality, there was widespread agreement that mass disorder offered no solution to the problem of racial discrimination. On Friday, during a visit to New York City, former president Harry Truman took time out from his morning walk to excoriate "meddlesome intruders" from the North. "They stir up trouble," he declared, " . . . they ought to stay here and attend to their own business." Likening the Freedom Riders to William Lloyd Garrison, Harriet Beecher Stowe, and other Abolitionists who provoked a bloody civil war, Truman argued that the nation should let the South solve its own problems. "Goodwill and common sense," not agitation or civil disobedience, he insisted, represented the best approach to social change. In upbraiding the Freedom Riders, Truman undoubtedly spoke for many, if not most, white Americans. But there were some, perhaps even a growing number, who were willing to speak out for a broader vision of participatory democracy. One such voice was that of Rabbi David Seligson, whose Saturday sermon on

June 3 applauded the Freedom Riders' commitment to nonviolent direct action. "The Gandhian spirit is written all over them . . . ," he told his midtown Manhattan congregation, "while the faces of the whites are distorted with hatred and rage, the Negroes radiate a kind of spiritual dignity and inner peace, a quality of the soul that is slowly and surely teaching Americans a moral lesson . . . The world of Gandhi and that of the segregated South may be worlds apart. But the confrontation between physical force and the power of the spirit, between evil and good, is essentially the same."

Although Rabbi Seligson did not mention him by name, the example set by William Barbee in a Montgomery courtroom on Friday morning testified to the integrity and raw moral courage described in the sermon. Brought back to Montgomery to sign a warrant against Thurman Ouzts, one of the Klansmen who had nearly beaten him to death on May 20, Barbee decided that signing the warrant violated "the principles of nonviolence." "I feel that the violence perpetrated against me was prompted by the general evil of segregation to our society," he later explained. "Therefore, no one person should be punished." One month after the original CORE Freedom Riders boarded a bus to destiny, the message of hope and redemption was still alive.

8

Ain't Gonna Let No Jail House Turn Me 'Round

Ain't gonna let no jail house, Lordy, turn me 'round,
I'm gonna keep on a-walkin,' Lord, keep on a-talkin,' Lord,
Marching up to freedom land.
—1960s freedom song

Delivering the message of hope and redemption required a sustained campaign of personal commitment and nonviolent fortitude. But, in and of themselves, the actions and experiences of the Freedom Riders could not topple or even seriously challenge the Jim Crow regime. To be an effective agent of historical change, the moral drama of the Freedom Rides needed a broad and attentive audience—an audience that could only be reached through the mass media. Without widespread press coverage, the 1961 Freedom Rides would have suffered the same obscure fate as the 1947 Journey of Reconciliation. In the early going, as we have seen, the 1961 CORE Ride garnered few headlines. But the situation changed dramatically in the wake of the May 14 riots in Anniston and Birmingham. During the second half of May, the Freedom Rider crisis was front-page news in newspapers across the nation and throughout much of the world, and a source of riveting images for local and network television reporters. Indeed, following the formation of the FRCC on May 26, nourishing and sustaining press interest in the Freedom Rides was a key element of movement strategy.

In early June maintaining the Freedom Rides' status as a media event became more challenging as President Kennedy's visit to Paris and Vienna overshadowed all other news stories. But FRCC leaders did their best to keep the movement in the public eye, resorting to press conferences, television and radio interviews, and even staged publicity stunts. On June 5, for example, Jim Peck interrupted Harry Truman's Monday morning walk in an effort to obtain a retraction of Friday's anti-Freedom Rider remarks. Although Truman refused to oblige, the confrontation between the former president and the injured Freedom Rider became a national news story. Later in the day, Martin Luther King, who was also in New York, held a press conference during which he called for a second Emancipation Proclamation. "The time has now come," King declared, "for the President of the United States to issue a firm Executive Order declaring all forms of racial segregation illegal . . . There is a mighty stirring in this land. The sit-ins at lunch counters and Freedom Riders on buses are making it palpably clear that segregation must end and that it must end soon."

King and other FRCC leaders feared that some headline-hunting journalists would lose interest in the Rides as the threat of violence subsided and the daily arrests in Jackson became routine; and the daily coverage of the movement did indeed drop off in early June. Nevertheless, the developing story in the Deep South continued to attract considerable media attention, especially among magazine editors. As the Freedom Rider saga entered its second month, several major magazines ran cover stories or lengthy features on the Rides. For example, the June 5 issue of *Newsweek* presented three captioned photographs on its cover: one of Robert Kennedy accompanied by the quotation "We stand for human liberty"; a second of Martin Luther King with the caption "We must be prepared to suffer . . . even die"; and a third of John Patterson, with the defiant quotation "The Federal government encourages these agitators." The five-page cover story focused on the journey from Montgomery to Jackson, but also included two long sidebars. The first, entitled "A New Breed—The Militant Negro in the South," presented profiles of SNCC, CORE, and the Nashville Movement, plus thumbnail sketches of Lawson, Nash, Ed King, and Wyatt Tee Walker. "The white South has not seen such Negroes before," the sidebar proclaimed. "Impatient at the slow course of racial integration, they are mostly young people who have emerged from the Negro colleges and churches to take up battle with their own complex mystique of religious fervor and Gandhi-like passive resistance—all of it summed up in the word non-violence."

The second sidebar, "How the World Press Viewed the Days of Tension," offered a far-flung sample of international editorial opinion, including comments from editors in Egypt, India, Kenya, France, and the Soviet Union. "As if written on the wind," *Newsweek* concluded, "the Freedom Rider story swept around the globe last week." Noting the Cold War implications of the crisis, the sidebar cited no less of an authority than Edward R. Murrow, the distinguished journalist and newly appointed director of the U. S. Information Agency (USIA), who declared, "There are no more domestic issues." As the reaction to the Freedom Rides had demonstrated, significant events in the United States are inevitably "absorbed, debated, and pondered on all shores of every ocean." Fortunately, according to *Newsweek,* many "overseas editors" had stressed not only the "racial bigotry" of Southern segregationists but also "the complex issues involved and the Federal government's efforts to calm and correct the situation." Predictably, the pro-administration sidebar ended with a summary of Robert Kennedy's May 26 Voice of America broadcast, and at the close of the general article the editors allowed him to have the last word. Recreating the late-night scene at the Justice Department on May 24—the Freedom Riders' first day in Jackson—the editors portrayed a weary but resolute attorney general pouring himself "a nightcap of Old Grand-Dad over ice." "Well, it's still a step forward," Kennedy mused, "But these situations are something we're going to have to live with. This is going on and on."

Kennedy was right, of course. But for a brief period in early June some observers wondered if the Rides would continue. During the weekend of June 3–4, and on Monday the fifth, there were no new Rides in Mississippi or anywhere else. With the attention of the nation and the world focused on the summit in Vienna, it is unlikely that additional Riders would have drawn much media coverage, but the three-day respite had little to do with the public's preoccupation with the Cold War parley between Kennedy and Khrushchev. In movement circles, the matter of greatest concern was Judge Johnson's restraining order. Until Johnson rendered a final injunctive decision on June 12, the FRCC had little choice but to bypass Alabama. Circumventing Johnson's order required an unexpected and complicated rerouting of several planned Freedom Rides, as well as a temporary relocation of FRCC recruiting and training centers. For the time being, at least, Montgomery could no longer serve as a major center of Freedom Rider activity. New Orleans, Nashville, and Atlanta would have to pick up the slack as new travel patterns were developed. Jackson, FRCC leaders agreed, would remain the primary target, but the Freedom Rides would now converge on the city from the north and the south, not the east.

The situation also prompted a partial reorganization of the FRCC. Working in close collaboration but with separate strengths, the four primary participating organizations—CORE, SNCC, SCLC, and the Nashville Movement—divided up the movement's responsibilities along geographical lines. While CORE concentrated its energies in New Orleans and on various recruiting and fund-raising efforts outside the South, SCLC and SNCC volunteers jointly maintained a recruiting and communications command center in Atlanta. At the same time, the Nashville student movement remained the emotional nerve center of the struggle. Despite the persistence of ideological disagreements—especially over the role of religion in the movement—representatives of the four organizations held weekly meetings in an effort to maintain their common commitment to nonviolent struggle. The result was a loose but surprisingly effective coalition that sustained the Freedom Rider movement without stultifying the creativity of an eclectic band of volunteers. Striking a balance between nonviolent discipline and individual freedom was never easy, but as a general rule the Freedom Riders came closer than most movement activists to achieving this ideal.

When a new group of seven Freedom Riders arrived at the Jackson Trailways station on Tuesday, June 6, the arrests followed the same pattern as those of the previous week, with one exception. At a Monday afternoon trial, Judge Spencer had announced that future Freedom Riders would face stiffer penalties than the sentences handed out during the first week of arrests. The new policy, which mandated four-month rather than two-month sentences, was prompted by the discovery that some of the Freedom Riders had "served time in Federal prisons for refusing to bear arms in defense of their country." "Some have discharges other than honorable conditions," Spencer explained. "Some have atheistic beliefs, and three . . . have beliefs, learnings, and ideologies contrary to the principles on which this country was founded." While he didn't elaborate on what those principles were, his message to the press and the Freedom Riders was clear: Mississippi was cracking down on outside agitators. In a brief trial held minutes after their arrival, the seven new Riders received four-month jail terms, two months of which were suspended, and $200 fines. Unfazed, all seven declined to post bond and announced that they planned to join the hunger strikes at the county and city jails.

The onslaught continued on Wednesday as two more groups of Riders converged on the city. By that evening there was no doubt that the Freedom Rides were once again in full swing and gaining momentum. Within the civil rights movement, there were still those who had serious reservations about the use of provocative direct action in the Deep South. Indeed, Roy Wilkins voiced such reservations during a visit to Jackson that evening. Speaking to an overflow crowd of twelve hundred at the Lynch Street Masonic Hall, Wilkins acknowledged that the NAACP believed that the best "way to make progress . . . is to set up a test case, carry it through the courts, and get a determination. We do not believe you can test a law and get it thrown out by staying in jail. After one spends 20 or 60 days in jail, the law is still on the books and still constitutes a support for segregation." Nevertheless, even Wilkins seemed resigned to the reality that the Freedom Riders' tactics had energized the movement. The NAACP does "not sneer at those who choose to stay in jail," he told the crowd, adding that "even though methods may differ there is basic agreement among Negro leaders and organizations in the overall goals and objectives. All methods should be used."

The successful recruitment of local Freedom Riders would rattle the nerves of Mississippi officials in the weeks to come, but in early June their most pressing concern was the daily tide of Riders from other parts of the nation. Virtually every day brought at least one new group of Riders to Jackson. On Thursday, June 8, two groups of Riders descended upon the city. The first—a two-man delegation from New York—arrived on an early-morning plane from Montgomery. Mark Lane, a white New York state assemblyman, and Percy Sutton, a black attorney recently elected president of the Manhattan branch of the NAACP, told reporters that they were "deeply concerned" about recent arrests of New Yorkers visiting Mississippi. Their fact-finding mission took on a new dimension when Sutton tried to use the airport's white restroom. Charged with breaching the peace, both men were behind bars by noon.

For the most part, Mississippi officials denied that the growing number of jailed Riders was putting a strain on the state's police and penal facilities. But there were signs that at least some were beginning to worry about the seemingly endless stream of outside agitators willing to go to jail. On Friday, June 9, several speakers at the annual convention of the Mississippi Municipal Association, meeting in Biloxi, warned that the Freedom Riders represented an unprecedented challenge to the Mississippi way of life. After Lieutenant Governor Paul Johnson told the gathering of municipal leaders that "we in Mississippi and this nation of ours are facing some frightening years," Attorney General Joe Patterson acknowledged that "the very soul and fiber of every city in Mississippi is being tested." They had good reason to worry. Earlier in the day, just before dawn, a new group of Freedom Riders had been arrested at the Illinois Central terminal. After undergoing nonviolence training in Nashville, five white college students—three from Ohio and two from New York—had boarded a train for Jackson determined to demonstrate their solidarity with earlier Riders.

Mississippi officials were also troubled by a sweeping desegregation petition filed with the federal district court in Jackson later in the morning. Presented on behalf of three local blacks by NAACP attorneys R. Jess Brown, Constance Baker Motley, and Derrick Bell, the petition initiated a class action suit to enjoin the police from enforcing state and local transit segregation statutes. Although the petition did not mention the Freedom Riders by name, the NAACP also sought an injunction against the breach-of-peace ordinances used to "arrest, harass, and intimidate" travelers exercising "their federally protected right to use interstate and intrastate facilities and services without segregation or discrimination against them solely because of race or color." Several weeks earlier the NAACP had asked the court to overturn the convictions of several black students arrested for sitting in the front section of a local bus, but the new petition represented a significant escalation of the legal campaign to dismantle the state's Jim Crow transit system. On Saturday the district court forwarded the petition to Judge Elbert P. Tuttle, the chief judge of the Fifth Circuit Court of Appeals in New Orleans. Empowered to convene a three-judge panel to rule on the petition, Tuttle promised to begin hearings on the matter sometime in

July. In the meantime, the Freedom Riders would continue to face arrest and imprisonment.

Despite the obvious fact that the Freedom Rides were disrupting civic order and providing Soviet publicists with propaganda material, the ongoing frontal assault on segregated transit had now achieved a measure of respectability in certain quarters. The noted Broadway theatrical team of Elaine May and Mike Nichols hosted a benefit concert in New York to raise funds for Freedom Riders, and the general board of the National Council of Churches approved a resolution endorsing nonviolent direct action as a legitimate means of attacking racial segregation. Even worse, from the perspective of conservative white supremacists, on Monday, June 12, Judge Frank Johnson allowed the temporary restraining order against the Freedom Riders to lapse. Ruling that there was no justification for a permanent injunction, Johnson, in effect, reopened Alabama and Mississippi's eastern flank to future Freedom Rides. Almost immediately, jubilant FRCC and CORE officials announced plans to open an office in Montgomery where Tom Gaither and Ralph Abernathy would recruit and train Mississippi-bound Freedom Riders.

These and other related developments were more than enough to convince Mississippi authorities that the Freedom Rider onslaught would continue for the foreseeable future. As far as they were concerned, the only good news on the horizon was an FRCC decision to send at least some of the impending Freedom Rides to locations other than Mississippi. During a four-day hiatus, from June 12 to 15, the only Freedom Rider to arrive in the state was Danny Thompson, a white college student from Cleveland, Ohio, who had missed a connecting bus in Memphis. After straggling into Jackson on Wednesday morning and conduct-ing a one-man test of the segregated facilities at the Greyhound terminal, he ended up in the city jail with the other white Riders.

By that time, both the city and county jails were jammed with Freedom Riders, and local officials had already made plans to transfer some of the Riders to the state prison farm at Parchman, 120 miles northwest of Jackson. On Mon-day, June 12, the Hinds County Board of Supervisors authorized Sheriff Gilfoy to transfer as many prisoners to Parchman "as he may deem necessary to relieve and keep relieved the crowded conditions in the county jail." White supremacist leaders immediately hailed the prospect of transferring the Freedom Riders to the dreaded confines of Parchman, where the Riders would finally encounter the full force of Mississippi justice.

As Mississippi officials prepared for the transfer to Parchman, the Freedom Rides also took a new turn in Washington, where CORE field secretary Gene-vieve Hughes held a press conference on Monday, June 12. Still recovering from her harrowing experiences in Alabama, but now flanked by more than thirty volunteers sporting large blue and white buttons identifying themselves as

"Freedom Riders," Hughes announced that two special groups of Riders would depart from the nation's capital within twenty-four hours. The first group, consisting of eighteen clergymen—fourteen Protestant ministers and four rabbis—had agreed to undertake an "Interfaith Freedom Ride" from Washington to Tallahassee, Florida. The second group, numbering fifteen, represented an eclectic assortment of teachers, students, doctors, and representatives of organized labor. Taking a more easterly route than the Interfaith Ride, they planned to conduct tests along the Atlantic seaboard, stopping in Wilmington, North Carolina, Charleston, South Carolina, and Jacksonville, Florida, and ending up in the Gulf coast city of St. Petersburg. It had been more than five weeks since the original CORE Freedom Ride had left Washington, but now the Southeastern states would get a second chance to demonstrate compliance with federal law. Flashing her effervescent smile, Hughes optimistically predicted that the new Riders would "be given service at all stops but Tallahassee and Tampa."

This goal seemed well in reach three days later as the Interfaith Riders headed west toward Tallahassee and the Florida Panhandle on the final leg of their journey. Along the way they ran into a bit of trouble in the county seat town of Lake City, where waitresses at a snack bar refused to serve a racially mixed group of clergymen. But they encountered less hostility than was expected at the Tallahassee Trailways terminal, where they once again shared a meal with the NAACP fact-finders. The situation was tenser later in the day at the Greyhound terminal, where the Riders had to sidestep a crowd of angry protesters, two of whom attacked an interracial testing team trying to desegregate a white restroom. But with the grudging assistance of the Tallahassee police, a second attempt to desegregate the restroom proved successful. In the terminal restaurant, the management saw to it that black Freedom Riders were served by black waiters and white Riders by white waiters. But the fact that all of the Riders were served in the same room took at least some of the sting out of what was clearly a half-hearted effort at compliance with federal law. Satisfied that they had established an integrationist beachhead in the capital of the Sunshine State, the eighteen Interfaith Riders decided to fly home that afternoon.

Accompanied by several local black activists, the Riders arrived at the Tallahassee airport in time to conduct a test at the airport's white restaurant. A relatively new facility constructed with the help of federal funds but managed by a private company, the restaurant had never served black patrons, as a black CORE staff member turned away in April had discovered. That segregated dining was still the rule on June 15 became abundantly clear when local authorities stymied the proposed test by simply closing the restaurant as soon as the Riders arrived at the airport. Tired and disgusted, eight of the Riders soon flew home as planned. The other ten, however, decided to remain at the airport until the restaurant reopened and served them in compliance with federal law. Among the ten were

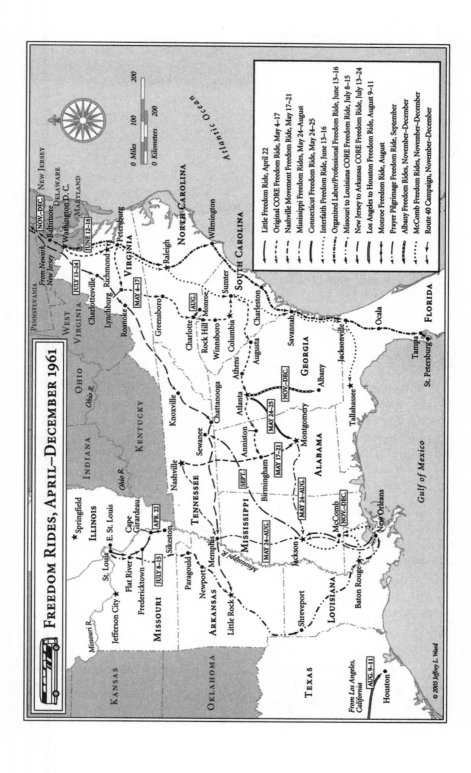

FREEDOM RIDES, APRIL–DECEMBER 1961

Little Freedom Ride, April 22

Original CORE Freedom Ride, May 4–17

Nashville Movement Freedom Ride, May 17–21

Mississippi Freedom Rides, May 24–August

Connecticut Freedom Ride, May 24–25

Interfaith Freedom Ride, June 13–16

Organized Labor/Professional Freedom Ride, June 13–16

Missouri to Louisiana CORE Freedom Ride, July 8–15

New Jersey to Arkansas CORE Freedom Ride, July 13–24

Los Angeles to Houston Freedom Ride, August 9–11

Monroe Freedom Ride, August

Prayer Pilgrimage Freedom Ride, September

Albany Freedom Rides, November–December

McComb Freedom Rides, November–December

Route 40 Campaign, November–December

© 2005 Jeffrey L. Ward

Robert McAfee Brown, a distinguished Presbyterian theologian who held a chaired professorship at Union Theological Seminary; Ralph Roy, a longtime CORE member and pastor of the Grace Methodist Church in New York City; three black ministers, John W. Collier Jr., of Newark, New Jersey, Arthur Hardge of New Britain, Connecticut, and Petty McKinney of Springfield, Massachusetts; and two young reform rabbis from northern New Jersey, Martin Freedman, a friend and protégé of Bayard Rustin's, and Israel "Si" Dresner, an outspoken Brooklyn-born activist later dubbed "the most arrested rabbi in America."

The press initially reported the Riders' action as a hunger strike, but from the outset their common goal was to break the local color bar by eating together at the airport restaurant. Before they were through they discovered just how difficult this seemingly simple task could be. As Burke Marshall had conceded in a lengthy interview on June 11, enforcing desegregation at aviation facilities was a "knotty problem" complicated by clever uses of private funding and the fact "that the Federal Aviation Agency was not a regulatory agency in the sense that the ICC was." But, as several members of the group explained to reporters, such legalisms were of little concern to ten clergymen who knew right from wrong. Even so, they sent a telegram to the chairman of the ICC urging federal intervention. By nightfall their stubborn protest had drawn a large crowd of angry whites, but they refused to budge until the airport itself closed at midnight.

At 7:30 the next morning, they returned to the airport to resume the vigil outside the terminal restaurant. Joined by several local activists and surrounded by police and a bevy of reporters, they remained there for nearly five hours. After nervously monitoring the situation throughout the morning, Governor Farris Bryant called Robert Kennedy to ask for help. "You've got to get these people out of here," Bryant pleaded, "I've done all I can do." Concerned about the Riders' safety and fearful that he had another white supremacist siege on his hands, Kennedy asked Bryant to hold things together for an hour or two while he tried to persuade the Riders to suspend their protest. Minutes later, around 12:30, Burke Marshall was on the phone with John Collier, but their brief conversation ended abruptly when Tallahassee city attorney James Messer ordered the Riders to leave the airport within fifteen seconds. When Collier and the others stood their ground, the police moved in and arrested them for unlawful assembly. The police also arrested three local civil rights leaders, including CORE veteran Priscilla Stephens. By mid-afternoon, all thirteen defendants were ensconced in the city jail, a run-down and overcrowded facility that shocked those who had never seen the inside of a Southern lockup. "The conditions in the jail were foreboding," Ralph Roy wrote later. "Our black colleagues were separated from us, of course, though we could communicate by yelling through a wall dividing us by race."

Meanwhile, other Freedom Riders were running into trouble in the central Florida community of Ocala, Governor Bryant's home town. When several black Riders tried to enter a white cafeteria at the Ocala Greyhound station, two white men shoved them backwards. The police immediately intervened, ordering the Riders to return to the bus. But three of the seven Riders involved—Leslie Smith, a black minister from Albany, New York; Herbert Callender, a black union leader from New Jersey; and James O'Connor, a white economics instructor at Barnard College in Manhattan—refused to comply with the order. Charged with unlawful assembly and failure to obey a police officer, they were released on bond later in the day. By that time their fellow Riders, after successfully desegregating the Ocala terminal's white restrooms, had proceeded southward to Tampa and St. Petersburg, their final destination. Before the day was over the two Gulf Coast cities had weathered desegregation with less difficulty than most local observers had anticipated.

In the early hours of Thursday, June 15, while the Interfaith Riders were still on the road to Florida, a new and dark chapter of the Freedom Rider saga opened in Mississippi. The first transfer of Freedom Riders to Parchman began just after midnight as forty-five male prisoners—twenty-nine blacks and sixteen whites—were loaded into a convoy of trucks. After the Riders were herded into what amounted to "airless, seat-less containers," in John Lewis's words, "the doors were closed, locked, and in utter darkness we were driven away, bracing ourselves against one another, as the trucks lurched around turns, the drivers doing the best they could to slam us into the walls. We had no idea where we were going." As the convoy lurched northward, however, at least some of the Riders began to suspect that they were on Highway 49, the road to the Delta and the dreaded Parchman farm. It was a road that thousands of unfortunate Mississippians had taken since the prison's construction in 1904, and very few had survived the experience without suffering lasting physical and emotional scars. Many, of course, did not survive at all.

When the Riders arrived at the prison at dawn, there was just enough light to see the outlines of their new home—a world bounded by "a barbed-wire fence stretching away in either direction." There were also "armed guards with shotguns," Lewis recalled. "And beyond the guards, inside the fence, a complex of boxy wooden and concrete buildings. And beyond them, nothing but dark, flat Mississippi delta." As the Freedom Riders' eyes adjusted to the light, the imposing figure of Superintendent Fred Jones appeared at the gate. "We have some bad niggers here," Jones drawled. "We have niggers on death row that'll beat you up and cut you as soon as look at you." Moments later the guards began pushing the Riders toward a nearby processing building, but the forced march was soon interrupted by a scuffle in the rear of the line. Terry Sullivan and Felix Singer, two white Freedom Riders who had remained in the back of one of the trucks and then gone limp in defiance of the guards, were being dragged toward the processing center by their feet. "We refuse to cooperate, because we've been unjustly imprisoned," Sullivan cried out. But the guards were unimpressed. "What you actin' like that for?" one guard asked. "Ain't no newspaper men out here."

Taken to the basement of the concrete-block processing center, the Riders soon found themselves under the control of a man who introduced himself as Deputy Tyson. Later described by Stokely Carmichael as "a massive, red-faced, cigar-smoking cracker in cowboy boots," Tyson would become an all too familiar figure to the Riders during their stay at Parchman. Without any explanation other than a smirk, he ordered them to remove all of their clothes. When Sullivan and Singer refused, a guard shocked them with an electric cattle prod. But even this did not bring compliance, forcing the frustrated guards to rip off the resisters' clothes before throwing them into a holding cell. The rest of the Riders remained in the room for more than two hours as a crowd of curious white guards gawked at them through barred basement windows.

The whole scene was both frightening and demeaning, and the Riders did not know what to expect next. "We were consumed by embarrassment," Farmer recalled. "We stood for ages—uncomfortable, dehumanized. Our audience cackled with laughter and obscene comments. They had a fixation about genitals, a preoccupation with size." Finally, they were led, two by two, down a long corridor to a shower room, where they were ordered to shave off all facial hair. To John Lewis, the shower room evoked images of Nazi Germany and concentration camps. "This was 1961 in America," he later reflected, "yet here we were, treated like animals." From the shower room, they marched to their cells in Parchman's maximum security wing, where, still naked, they waited for the distribution of prison clothes. The clothes, when they finally arrived, were meager—a T-shirt and boxer shorts, but no shoes or socks. Understandably some complained, but Bevel, for one, responded philosophically. "What's this hang-up about clothes?" he bellowed, "Gandhi wrapped a rag around his balls and brought the whole British Empire to its knees!"

A few hours later, Governor Ross Barnett and Colonel T. B. Birdsong, the head of the Mississippi Highway Patrol, paid a visit to Parchman to see how the prisoners were doing. In a meeting with the prison staff, Barnett warned that "it will be hard for you men to take what they may say to you," and Birdsong predicted that the Freedom Riders would be "different than any other prisoners you have handled before." Accordingly, Barnett announced, the Freedom Riders would not be put to work in the fields with the other prisoners, at least for the time being. "If they refused to work, what could we do?" he explained. "It would upset the whole prison routine." By keeping the Freedom Riders locked up and isolated, the dual threat of a sit-down strike and unsettling contact between outside agitators and regular inmates could be avoided. As he told reporters before returning to Jackson, everything was under control, and the Freedom Riders whom he had visited had assured him that they had been "well treated." Indeed, they were "resigned to serving their sentences."

The prospect of scores, and eventually hundreds, of Freedom Riders spending the rest of June and July at Parchman was appealing to Barnett and many other white Mississippians. But this scenario held no such charm for federal officials in Washington. A world unto itself, Parchman was almost impossible to monitor; and, while the terrors of the South's most infamous prison might deter some prospective Freedom Riders from actually coming to Mississippi, others almost certainly would be drawn by the lure of real danger and meaningful sacrifice. On Friday, June 16, President Kennedy returned to Washington after ten days in Palm Beach, Florida, where he was vacationing and receiving treatment for a painful back condition. Like his personal ailments, the ongoing Freedom Rider crisis presented him with a seemingly inexhaustible set of irritations. In addition to the Parchman transfers and the arrests in Tallahassee and Ocala, a new set of five Freedom Riders had arrived in Jackson on Friday afternoon. Four of the five were college students, and one, Elizabeth Hirschfeld, was a laboratory technician who worked for the Atomic Energy Commission in Ithaca, New York, adding a new wrinkle to the argument that the Freedom Riders represented a security risk.

In the midst of this turmoil, Robert Kennedy presided over a memorable meeting at the Justice Department. A week earlier, Burke Marshall had met with a small group of civil rights activists during a conference held at a York River plantation house near Capahosic, Virginia. For several weeks, Justice Department officials had been looking for a chance to nudge student activists toward a greater emphasis on voting rights agitation, and the Capahosic conference represented the first opportunity for Marshall to make his pitch. A voter registration campaign, Marshall argued, had distinct advantages over confrontational direct-action campaigns such as sit-ins and Freedom Rides, not the least of which was the administration's willingness to fund the former but not the latter. Among those at the Capahosic conference were several black student leaders favorably disposed to the idea, including incoming SNCC chairman Chuck McDew, Charles Jones of Johnson C. Smith University (and the recent Freedom Ride led by William Sloane Coffin), Charles Sherrod of Virginia Union, and Tim Jenkins, a recent Howard graduate who served as vice president of the National Student Association. Encouraged by their receptiveness, Marshall invited them, along with several FRCC leaders, to a June 16 meeting at the Justice Department.

To Nash, Lawson, Walker, and the other FRCC representatives present, the primary purpose of the meeting was to urge the federal government to intervene on behalf of the Freedom Riders unjustly arrested in Mississippi. But, from the outset, Marshall and Kennedy tried to steer the conversation toward a discussion of voting rights. After making the administration's preferences clear, Kennedy all but promised to provide movement leaders with tax exemptions, foundation grants, and legal and physical protection if they agreed to shift their attention to voting issues. To several of the students, including the voting-rights enthusiast Sherrod, Kennedy's offer sounded too much like a bribe, and the meeting nearly broke up when Sherrod jumped to his feet to scold the attorney general. "You are a public official, sir," Sherrod reminded Kennedy, "It's not your responsibility before God or under the law to tell us how to honor our constitutional rights. It's your job to protect us when we do." At this point, Walker and others interceded to calm Sherrod down, and Kennedy, after a brief pause, continued to press the argument for a voting rights campaign. Ignoring the gathering's emotional ties to direct action, he outlined an ambitious region-wide voter education project similar to one proposed earlier in the year by Stephen Currier of the Taconic Foundation, and Harold Fleming, the founder of the Potomac Institute and the former director of the Southern Regional Council. All of this was food for thought, and by the time the meeting adjourned even the most skeptical of the young leaders had a heightened sense of the attorney general's interest in civil rights. For better or for worse, the Freedom Rides had certainly gotten his attention.

Kennedy left the June 16 meeting with the distinct impression that he had witnessed the beginning of a move toward voting rights and away from direct action. Even though he realized that the Freedom Rider crisis was far from over, the long-term prospects for a less confrontational approach to civil rights activism seemed to be improving. His faith in such a reorientation rested on a rather simplistic dichotomy of orderly voting rights campaigns versus provocative direct-action struggles that would lead inexorably to disorder and violence in the streets. But on June 17, less than twenty-four hours after the meeting with the student leaders, the validity of this dichotomous conception was challenged by Martin Luther King. During a Saturday afternoon press conference at the Los Angeles airport, King predicted that the Freedom Rides would be followed by an all-out nonviolent campaign for black voting rights. "We are going to win the transportation fight through passive resistance," he told reporters. "Then we will tackle the problem of Negro voting in Dixie. We will make a nonviolent assault on all phases of all segregation. But our big move will be to intensify voter registrations through stand-ins at places of registration and polling, and anything else we can do to emphasize the degree to which the negro is denied his right of franchise."

Such an open-ended, multi-faceted approach to voting rights activism was not, of course, what Kennedy or the Taconic Foundation had in mind. And the gap between the movement's view of things and Kennedy's became even more apparent on Sunday when King—followed by Sammy Davis Jr., Mahalia Jackson, Dick Gregory, and a string of other celebrities—reiterated his commitment to direct action during a mass rally at the Los Angeles Sports Arena. The rally, which drew a crowd of nearly twenty thousand and raised a substantial amount of money for Freedom Rides and other civil rights causes, signaled that the restless spirit of grassroots insurgency was still rising. Whether the target was disfranchisement or segregated bus terminals, getting the struggle out of the streets was not going to be easy.

Even so, voting rights remained the strategy of choice at the Justice Department, in most intellectual circles, and for many movement activists. For Robert Kennedy, in particular, the effort to accelerate the transition from protest to politics was a high priority throughout the summer of 1961. On Saturday, June 17, while King was raising funds in Los Angeles, Kennedy interrupted a dinner party to lobby Harry Belafonte on the matter. Even though it was his tenth wedding anniversary, Kennedy found time to urge the singer-activist to use his influence on behalf of political action. Ten days later, Belafonte, in Washington for a series of concerts, met with a select group of SNCC leaders in an effort to convince them to form a political action vanguard within the Freedom Rider movement. At the close of the meeting, the students agreed to do so, and a grateful Belafonte promised to give them $10,000 to initiate the project. Led by Tim Jenkins and Charles Jones, the Harry Belafonte Committee, as the group came to be known, would play a pivotal role in SNCC's turn toward political action later in the summer.

In the meantime, the direct action tactics of the FRCC continued to draw new recruits to the movement. During the week following the Sunday rally in Los Angeles, four groups of Freedom Riders arrived in Jackson. On Monday, June 20, nine more jailed Freedom Riders were transferred from Jackson to Parchman, but later in the day their former cells were filled by fifteen new Riders. Nine more Riders, including Wyatt Tee Walker and his wife, Theresa, arrived from Montgomery on Tuesday and ended up in the same courtroom facing the same unsympathetic judge.

June 21, the day the Freedom Rides resumed along the Montgomery-to-Jackson stretch of Highway 80, was the summer solstice, the official dividing line between spring and summer. Coincidentally, it was also a day of deep contextual change for the Freedom Rider movement. While the Walker group was on the way to Jackson, U.S. District Judge Sidney Mize was presiding over a hearing that would determine the legality of the Freedom Rider arrests by Mississippi authorities. The plaintiff was Elizabeth "Betsy" Wyckoff, a forty-five-year-old freelance writer—and former professor of Greek at Bryn Mawr, Vassar, Wells, and Mount Holyoke colleges—from Greenwich Village. The first white woman to participate in a Mississippi Freedom Ride, she had been arrested for breaching the peace on June 2. Declaring that the arrest was unconstitutional and a "disgrace in the eyes of the rest of the world," her attorney, William Kunstler, a feisty New York civil liberties lawyer, made a plea for a writ of habeas corpus, which if granted would free not only Wyckoff but all of the other jailed Freedom Riders. Opposing the writ was Hinds County prosecutor Jack Travis, who maintained that the arrests had rescued the state from an outbreak of interracial violence. After listening to two hours of testimony, Judge Mize took the matter under advisement and promised to render a decision before the end of the month.

On the same day, there were two other potentially important legal developments. In New Orleans, Judge Elbert Tuttle, the chief judge of the U.S. Fifth Circuit Court of Appeals, ordered a three-judge panel to convene in Jackson on July 10 to consider an NAACP motion challenging transit segregation in Mississippi. Meanwhile, in Nashville, Burke Marshall clarified the federal government's position on the Mississippi arrests in a speech at the annual Fisk University Race Relations Institute. Speaking to more than a hundred race relations specialists from around the nation, Marshall confessed that the Justice Department was "powerless" to prevent the arrest of Freedom Riders by local or state authorities. Describing the government's unfortunate position as "one of the frustrations" of federalism, he nonetheless predicted that segregated transit would soon be a thing of the past. Noting the hearing held in Biloxi earlier in the day, he endorsed Kunstler's habeas corpus motion and expressed hope that Judge Mize would invalidate the Freedom Riders' arrests.

The legal maneuvering in Biloxi, New Orleans, and Nashville was significant and newsworthy, but the day's most important development related to the Freedom Rides did not take place in a courtroom or any other public arena. In a run-down dormitory at Jackson's Tougaloo College, hidden from the gaze of judges and reporters, four black students were plotting a minor revolution. To this point all of the Freedom Riders arrested in Mississippi had come from somewhere else, and many editors and politicians from around the state had boasted that black and white Mississippians shared a common disregard for disruptive outside agitators. Hardly a day passed without an editorial or speech reminding the public that the Freedom Riders were all outsiders, and even the *Jackson Advocate*, the state's most widely read black newspaper, lent its editorial voice to the anti-Freedom Rider campaign. According to *Advocate* columnist Percy Greene, "a vast majority of the rank and file of Jackson Negroes view the Freedom Riders as doing more harm than good in visiting the city . . . Most point to a sharp change in the attitude of their employers, and most noticeable change in the attitude of the white employees with whom and by whose direction they perform the duties of their daily work. A large number of those among the unemployed have been heard to blame the Freedom Riders for their continued unemployment and their failure to find a new job. Many have been heard to express the opinion that Negroes of the city would be better off if the Freedom Riders had never come to Jackson."

Whatever truth there was in Greene's assessment, it did not apply to many of the city's students, including four Tougaloo students who set out to dispel the image of local black complacency. One of the four, Mary Harrison, was a twenty-one-year-old Asian-American from San Antonio, Texas, and another, Joe Ross, was a visiting student from Tennessee State who had helped recruit and train Freedom Riders in Nashville. Along with Elnora Price, a twenty-five-year-old from nearby Raymond, Mississippi, and Tom Armstrong, a nineteen-year-old sophomore from the Delta town of Silver City, Harrison and Ross decided that it was time to organize a home-grown Freedom Ride. Accordingly, on Friday afternoon, June 23, they entered the Jackson Trailways station, bought tickets to New Orleans, and sat down in the white waiting room. Disregarding a police order to leave, they were arrested and carted off to jail, making them the first Freedom Riders to be apprehended while trying to *leave* Mississippi.

While the full implications of the first local Freedom Ride would not become apparent until early July when scores of black Mississippians followed the lead of the "Tougaloo Four," the episode raised deep concerns among local and state authorities. Publicly they dismissed the Tougaloo Four as little more than misguided pranksters, but privately they began to brace themselves for what they feared was an inevitable coupling of local and national movements.

The local support system emerging among black Mississippians was part of a growing national network that boosted the Freedom Rider movement during the critical days of late June and early July. In addition to the substantial financial contributions solicited by CORE, SCLC, and the NAACP, there were numerous expressions of support from a wide range of groups and influential individuals. In many Northern communities, religious authorities were the Freedom Riders' most vocal supporters. But there was also considerable support among secular leaders, especially among labor union officials, academic intellectuals, and liberal politicians such as New York Governor Nelson Rockefeller. Speaking at a CORE rally in Washington in mid-June, United Auto Workers leader Victor Reuther characterized the Freedom Riders as "America's Peace Corps to America," and several other noted speakers, including the novelist James Baldwin, echoed his praise for the young idealists languishing in Mississippi jails. "I don't see how we can blame these young people," Rockefeller reasoned in a conversation with reporters, "In fact, I think we can't help but admire them."

At the same time, however, it was becoming increasingly clear that the public at large remained cool to the idea of nonviolent direct action. According to a June 21 Gallup Poll, only 63 percent of those polled responded that they were familiar with the activities of the Freedom Riders; and of that group, 24 percent approved of the Rides, 64 percent disapproved, and 12 percent had no opinion. By contrast, 70 percent of the respondents to a June 18 poll approved of the Kennedy administration's decision to send federal marshals to Alabama, with only 13 percent expressing disapproval. Among Southern respondents the comparable figures were 50 percent approval and 29 percent disapproval, suggesting that law and order was a powerful national ideal. When asked: "Do you think integration should be brought about gradually or do you think every means should be used to bring it about in the near future?" only 23 percent favored the "near future" option, as opposed to 61 percent favoring "gradually," 7 percent responding "never," and 9 percent with no opinion. Even though a solid majority of Americans supported integrated transportation, Gallup researchers concluded that "many persons had misgivings about the way in which the Freedom Riders were attempting to bring an end to segregation in buses, trains and in waiting rooms, chiefly on the grounds that it was causing too much trouble. The public has also been found to be pessimistic about the racial outlook in the South in the year ahead. As Freedom Riders continue to move into that region Americans are fearful that racial relations in the South will get worse rather than better in the next twelve months." All of this stood in sharp contrast to a June 8 *Jet* magazine reader poll, in which 96 percent of the respondents, presumably almost all black, said "yes" when asked if the Freedom Rides should continue. But this simply underscored the wide gulf between black and white Americans on matters of civil rights strategy.

While the Gallup figures were neither authoritative nor easily interpretable, they reinforced the general impression that many whites continued to resent the Freedom Riders' disruptive tactics long after the mobs in Anniston and Birmingham had dispersed. In late June, as the second month of Freedom Rides drew to a close, the general public's acceptance of nonviolent direct action was still very much in doubt. Indeed, the rift between the attitudes of ordinary citizens and those of movement activists and their religious and intellectual supporters seemed to be widening. Even within the movement some leaders had begun to question the advisability of continuing the Rides indefinitely. For some, the strategy of filling the jails of Mississippi was a dangerous gambit that threatened to monopolize and squander the broader movement's energies and funds. With the Justice Department leaning on the ICC, with the entire administration pressing for a systemic reorientation toward voting rights, and with the national and international press losing interest in the crisis, the need for additional Rides became questionable. As a dramatic construct, the daily arrests in Jackson and elsewhere were still newsworthy and useful to the movement. But the nerve-shattering sense of crisis that had followed the confrontations in Alabama was gone, replaced by the grinding routine of prison life and legal wrangling.

Meanwhile, the Riders kept coming. On June 25, twenty Freedom Riders—the largest single group to date—arrived in Jackson by train. Eleven of the Riders were black, nine were women, and fourteen were from California. Several were Jewish, others were Catholic or Protestant, and still others were completely secular. The oldest, Marian Kendall, a social worker from San Leandro, California, was thirty-five. The youngest, Bob Mason, was a seventeen-year-old high school student from Los Angeles. Among the twenty Riders arrested, there were nine students, two clerks, a housewife, a painter, a civil engineer, a social worker, a freelance writer, a teacher, a secretary, a model, and a professional boxer. In the local press, all were dismissed as cranks and misfits. But, in private, even the most zealous segregationists must have wondered what was unfolding in the hearts and minds of a new generation of Americans. Mississippi, along with much of the nation, was still rigidly segregated. But intrusions such as the June 25 Freedom Ride made many white Mississippians feel that their once comfortable world was shrinking and under siege. And they were right. Despite the misgivings of politicians and public concern about the implications of direct action, an impatient vanguard of young Americans had finally brought the struggle for racial liberation and democratic renewal to the one state widely considered beyond redemption.

Diversity was the hallmark of the Freedom Rides. No previous movement campaign—not even the sit-ins of 1960—had attracted such a variety of participants. Transcending organizational, regional, and racial boundaries, Freedom Riders became emblematic symbols of a movement that extolled the virtues of political inclusion and social equality. While many Freedom Riders were Southern black college students in their late teens or early twenties, others were white, Northern, or middle-aged. While many were deeply religious, others were largely or completely secular. Men were in the majority, but more than a quarter of the Riders were women. This diversity, so fitting for an idealistic cause, was one of the strengths of the Freedom Rider campaign, one of the reasons why so many men and women were willing to join the Rides even after it became clear that they were headed for Parchman. Nevertheless, in the social and political context of Cold War America, diversity was a decidedly mixed blessing. In 1961 the tensions and suspicions that had given rise to McCarthyism, the Red Scare, and consensus ideology were still very much alive in the American mainstream. In many communities, especially in the South, intolerance of difference and unorthodox behavior was a reflexive reality, and anyone who strayed from the common channels of national or regional life was subject to intense criticism and even ostracism. Activists of any kind engendered suspicion, but activists such as the Freedom Riders, many of whom were unconventional even by civil rights movement standards, inevitably provoked the public's deepest fears. Even in the early going, when the campaign was limited to a small vanguard of CORE activists, the Freedom Rides encountered a certain amount of criticism. But once they evolved into a mass movement, the Riders' individual and collective vulnerability to charges of social and political subversion became a serious lia-bility for the entire civil rights movement.

This vulnerability, manifested in both external criticism and internal conflict, was one of the costs of success. As the scope of the Freedom Rides expanded, movement leaders lost a measure of control over the recruiting process and inev-itably faced the problem of maintaining cohesion and focus. Like any movement with hundreds of participants, the Freedom Rides attracted a range of individ-uals representing a wide spectrum of personalities, backgrounds, and ideologies. For the most part, these differences did not pose a serious threat to the common purpose of the Rides. But the personal histories of individual Riders did provide critics with ammunition that could be used to discredit the entire movement. Once the Riders were arrested and identified, investigating and exposing their flawed characters and unsavory backgrounds became a popular pastime among segregationist politicians and law enforcement officers. In Mississippi, and to a lesser extent in other Deep South states, investigators pored over arrest records, college transcripts, and public statements in an effort to uncover patterns of cul-tural and political subversion. Presented in daily press installments, these tales of personal infamy, antisocial behavior, and racial and political conspiracies became an important part of the Freedom Rider story. In the white Southern version of this story—and sometimes even in the version propagated by national colum-nists—the Freedom Riders were social and political misfits. Some were juvenile delinquents, others were beatniks or miscegenationists, and still others were Communist fellow travelers. But the clear implication was that all of the Riders were pathological in some fundamental way.

In Mississippi, the task of uncovering the criminal backgrounds of the Free-dom Riders was delegated to the State Sovereignty Commission, an investiga-tive and propaganda agency established in 1956. Working in close cooperation with the highway patrol and the White Citizens' Councils, the commission was empowered "to do and perform any and all acts and things deemed necessary and proper to protect the sovereignty of the State of Mississippi, and her sister states." Like the Georgia Bureau of Investigation (GBI) and Florida's Legislative Investigation Committee, also known as the Johns Committee, the Sovereignty Commission patterned itself after the FBI, targeting alleged subversives and troublemakers. Even before the first group of Freedom Riders arrived in Missis-sippi, the commission was on the case, compiling information on CORE, SNCC, and movement leaders. Once the rounds of arrests began, investigators moni-tored every aspect of the Freedom Rides, amassing files on each Rider and scru-tinizing anyone who publicly supported the Rides.

Although the stated rationale for this massive effort was the preservation of civic order, the driving force behind the Sovereignty Commission's investigative activities was the deeply held conviction that the civil rights movement, including the Freedom Rides, was connected to an international Communist conspiracy. The sense of panic that spread across much of the Deep South in the summer of 1961 was, first and foremost, a reaction to what appeared to be an impending loss of racial privilege and social control. But the intensity of the resistance to the Freedom Riders had a lot to do with the widespread perception that they were "outside agitators" in the truest sense of the term, that they represented forces alien and hostile to American values. The notion that the Freedom Rides were part of a Communist plot first emerged in Alabama in mid-May when Bull Connor, Attorney General MacDonald Gallion, and others played upon Cold War suspicions of a grand conspiracy to subvert the Southern way of life. Later, after the focus of the Rides moved to Jackson, the Communist linkage became the stock-in-trade of Mississippi politicians and editors attempting to discredit the campaign.

The growing diversity of the Freedom Riders also affected the internal dynamics of the movement. Any movement that involved multiple organizations, hundreds of participants, and thousands of active supporters was bound to have a measure of inconsistency and internal conflict. But this was especially true in a protest movement that faced the emotional and physical challenges of mass incarceration. Beginning in late May, prison life was the dominant reality for most of the Freedom Riders, including many of the movement's leaders. The fact that Farmer, Lawson, Lewis, Bevel, Walker, and hundreds of others shared the Parchman experience provided a certain commonality, a bond of sacrifice and struggle that fostered a sense of solidarity. Yet, at the same time, the intensity and uncertain outcome of the experience sometimes reinforced and even accentuated existing differences of perspective, political ideology, and philosophical conviction. While Parchman often brought people together in ways that they could not have imagined before entering the prison's walls, it sometimes had the opposite effect. Like most closed authoritarian institutions, Parchman exerted a powerful influence over everyone in its grasp. But for a group as diverse and determined as the Freedom Riders it was an imperfect and unpredictable crucible of personal survival, collective engagement, and movement culture.

The depth and variety of the Freedom Riders' prison experiences had a lot do with the special conditions created for them at Parchman. For the Riders, even more than for regular inmates, Parchman was a world unto itself. While beatings and acts of outright brutality were rare, the world of isolation and deprivation mandated by Mississippi authorities tested the limits of the Riders' resilience. By order of Governor Barnett, the Freedom Riders did no prison labor and were confined to their cells "throughout each day, never going outside, even for exercise."

Spread out through the prison's large U-shaped maximum security wing, the Freedom Riders' two-person cells made group conversation and community life extremely difficult. In mid-July, when the number of Freedom Riders in Parchman became too large for the maximum security wing, many of the Riders were transferred to the prison's first offenders' unit, where they lived barracks-style in two large rooms filled with cots. But during the first month there was little or no opportunity for communal living, beloved or otherwise. With a few exceptions, interaction beyond adjoining cells was limited to singing, which became a treasured lifeline for many of the Riders.

"The monotony was tremendous," John Lewis recalled, "We had no reading material other than the Bible, a palm-sized copy of the New Testament, which was given to each of us by the local Salvation Army . . . We each had our own metal-frame bed with a mattress made by the inmates. That, a commode, and a small washbowl completed the cell's furnishings. There were walls between the cells, so we could not see one another. Only when we were taken out to shower, which was twice a week, did we see anyone but our cellmate and the guards. Once a week we could write a letter . . ."

The shower ritual provided a brief respite from the loneliness and isolation of cell life. But the dominant reality for Lewis and hundreds of others was an involuntary personalization of time and space. Cut off from family, friends, and worldly institutions, separated from the regular prisoners, constricted by the limits of cells and cell-mates, and deprived of most of life's chosen pleasures, the Riders had no choice but to fall back upon themselves. Consigned to seemingly endless hours of reflection, introspection, and contemplation, they lived primarily in interior worlds dominated by matters of mind and spirit. Freedom songs, hunger strikes, and other provocations provided a semblance of community life. But for the most part the individual Freedom Riders were on their own.

It was in this context that Farmer, Lewis, and other leaders tried to maintain a modicum of unity and collective purpose. From the beginning of the Freedom Rides few had doubted the difficulty of building the beloved community. But doing so under these conditions was especially daunting, given the wide differences of opinion among the Riders on matters of faith and philosophy. Despite a common commitment to nonviolent direct action, the philosophical distance between secular and religious activists involved persistent and even fundamental disagreements. At one end of the spectrum, the Nashville students led by Bevel, Lewis, and Lafayette pressed for a deep and mystical commitment to a philosophy grounded in the principles of the Christian social gospel and Gandhianism. To them, nonviolent struggle was an all-encompassing way of life, and the challenges of Parchman were a welcome spur to greater sacrifice and commitment. By contrast, at the other end of the spectrum avowedly secular and worldly activists such as the street-wise New Yorker Stokely Carmichael saw the Freedom Riders' predicament primarily in terms of power and political re-alism. To them nonviolent direct action was a tactical initiative that carried no meaning beyond its social and political utility. Many others, of course, fell some-where between these two poles, and with so much time for thought and reflec-tion nearly everyone was engaged in some form of reformulation or reassessment. Consequently, there was more dynamism than order, and for some, more confu-sion than clarity.

In effect, the Freedom Riders turned a prison into an unruly but ultimately enlightening laboratory where competing theories of nonviolent struggle could be discussed and tested. In the darkest corners of Parchman, where prison authorities had hoped to break the Riders' spirit, a remarkable mix of personal and political education became the basis of individual and collective survival. Even though fear and insecurity remained an integral part of the Parchman expe-rience throughout the summer, it did not take long for the Riders to make the best of a bad situation. Once they realized that Mississippi authorities did not dare resort to Parchman's traditional means of intimidation and control—namely, brutal, life-threatening violence—the Riders, despite numerous indig-nities and aggravations, had the upper hand.

If federal officials and the national press had not been hovering over the situ-ation in Mississippi, the guards might have been given the authority to unleash the full force of Parchman's infamous brutality. But political and cultural realities left Barnett and his lieutenants with a limited range of options. They could make the jailed Riders miserable by withholding privileges, restricting movement, or serving inedible food. And, as John Lewis recalled, they could keep the lights on "around the clock, making it difficult to sleep," or keep the windows closed as the Riders "baked in the airless heat." Indeed, they could even spray the Riders with fire hoses, as they did on one occasion, and then bring in giant fans to blow cold air over shivering bodies. But none of this was enough to slow the momentum of a nonviolent movement that embraced unmerited suffering. While a few indi-vidual Riders buckled under the strain and abandoned their "jail—no bail" pledges, the vast majority came to view the Parchman experience as an emi-nently survivable rite of passage. Unwittingly, Mississippi authorities had pro-vided them with a means of achieving a higher stage of Gandhian consciousness, and most of the Riders took full advantage of this ironic situation.

The Riders' ability to turn almost any situation to their advantage also became clear during the so-called "mattress war" that began on June 24. After a week of exuberant singing and preaching, the Riders had pushed their jailers to the limits of endurance, prompting Deputy Tyson, the head of the maximum security unit, to threaten to remove all of the mattresses in the cellblock if the Riders didn't quiet down. Though ultimately a subject of dark humor, the idea of taking away the Riders' mattresses and forcing them to sleep either on a concrete floor or on the cold metal coils of a box spring was hardly a trivial matter at the time. As Jim Farmer recalled, "The mattresses were the only convenience we had in those little cells. They were our link to civilization, so to speak. Everything else was cold and hard, and the mattress was no more than an inch and a half thick and straw, but at least it was something." Already sleep-deprived, many of the Riders soon fell silent in an effort to keep their mattresses. But others could not resist transforming the threatened removal into a test of moral fortitude.

Speaking in his best preacher's voice, Jim Bevel yelled out: "What they're trying to do is take your soul away. It's not the mattress, it's your soul . . . Satan put us in here for forty days and forty nights. To tempt us with the flesh. He's sayin' to us, 'If you'll just stop your singin' and bail outta there, I'll give you anything you want—soft, thick, cotton mattresses and down pillows and everything. Be good boys, and I'll let you keep your mattresses." This call to righteousness elicited a round of concurring amens, especially among Bevel's Nashville colleagues. But the first Rider to turn Bevel's words into action was, surprisingly, Hank Thomas, a predominantly secular activist who loved to sing. After bellowing "Come get my mattress, I'll keep my soul," Thomas propped his mattress up against the cell bars and urged the other Riders to follow suit. Soon all but two had done so.

The only holdouts were cellmates Fred Leonard and Stokely Carmichael. But when the guards and trustees came to collect the mattresses a few minutes later, no exceptions were allowed, and they too lost their bedding. This apparent injustice left Leonard and Carmichael fuming, but the rest of the Riders broke into song, intoning the choruses of "Ain't Gonna Let Nobody Turn Me 'Round" and placing special emphasis on the lines "Ain't gonna let no jail house, Lordy, turn me 'round, I'm gonna keep on a-walkin', Lord, keep on a-talkin', Lord, marching up to freedom land." The forceful singing continued for hours, as the Riders worked their way through a medley of freedom songs before falling asleep on their mattress-less box springs. The next day Deputy Tyson returned the mattresses but warned that he would take them away permanently if the Riders didn't tone down their incessant singing. Accepting the challenge, Thomas and several other Riders were soon singing louder than ever, and Tyson promptly ordered the trustees to retrieve the mattresses, this time for good. As the trustees went through the cellblock, there was little resistance—until they reached Leonard and Carmichael's cell. After a brief struggle Carmichael surrendered his mattress, but Leonard fought on, defying both Deputy Tyson and his fellow Riders, the majority of whom had decided that voluntarily relinquishing the mattresses was the best way to demonstrate moral authority.

After vanquishing Leonard, Deputy Tyson returned to the cell block to gloat and to see if the Riders were ready to acknowledge his authority. But as he strutted along the cell bars he was sorely disappointed by what he heard. Instead of bowing down, the Riders mocked him. "Since those mattresses are so valu-able," Lafayette yelled out, "why don't you auction them off and tell people that the Freedom Riders slept there. In that way, you can get back some of the money the Freedom Rides are costing you. And we'll sing a little song at your auction." Unaccustomed to such insolence from black prisoners, Tyson shot back, "You shut yo' mouth, boy." Realizing that he had struck a nerve, Lafayette couldn't resist following up with a question about the deputy's use of the word "boy." "Deputy Tyson," Lafayette asked, straining to keep a straight face, "do you mean anything derogatory when you call us boy?" Caught off guard, Tyson lost what-ever composure he had left. "I don't know nuthin' 'bout no *'rogatory*," he insisted. "All I know is if you boys don't stop that singin' ya'll gon' be singin' in the rain." What he meant by this was unclear, but within minutes Hank Thomas was singing a new stanza of the old labor song "Which Side Are You On?": "Ole *big* man Deputy Tyson said, I *don'* wanna cause you pain, But *if* you don't stop that singin' now, You'll be singin' in the rain."

Hearing this taunt, Tyson ordered his guards to spray the cellblock with a high-pressure fire hose. Later, as the drenched Riders sat in their cells wondering what other indignities Tyson was planning, the cell block windows were opened and exhaust fans were turned on to confirm the message of intimidation. During the long, cold night that followed, there was more shivering and sniffling than singing in the cell block. But once they dried out, the Riders returned to their singing as if nothing had happened. Indeed, though the mattresses were gone, the struggle had left many of the Riders with a new sense of collective purpose and pride. For a growing number of Riders the mystique of sacrifice and unmer-ited suffering was evolving into an article of faith and a powerful source of indi-vidual and common resolve.

This was not, of course, what Ross Barnett and his lieutenants had intended. But, like the imposed institutionalization of Jim Crow in the early twentieth-century South, the mass incarceration of Freedom Riders at Parchman had unin-tended consequences for a movement that had long suffered from organizational disunity and fragmentation. Not only did the unresolved crisis at Parchman pro-vide a temporary focus for the movement at large, but also the personal dynamics of the drama being played out in the cells and corridors of the prison acted as a unifying force.

Whatever their ultimate significance, the unexpected benefits derived from the gathering at Parchman were not apparent enough at the time to alter the movement's strategy of challenging the constitutionality of the Freedom Riders' arrests and imprisonment. Having already proven that they could mobilize hun-dreds of activists who were willing to go jail for their beliefs, movement leaders saw little advantage in prolonging the struggle. In addition to the obvious injus-tice involved, Mississippi's policy of fining and sentencing Freedom Riders to

long jail terms placed a heavy legal and financial burden on CORE, which continued to bear the primary responsibility for underwriting and sustaining the
Freedom Rider movement. In effect, Mississippi's decision to arrest the Freedom Riders had initiated a war of attrition, a contest between the state's ability to
accommodate wave after wave of Riders and the movement's capacity to sustain
them, financially and otherwise. As of early July, the outcome of this struggle was
still very much in doubt, and Farmer and others worried that the movement's
greatest challenges lay ahead. To this point, much of the financial cost had been
postponed by the Riders' decision to forgo bail. But this favorable situation was
about to end, thanks to a provision of Mississippi's disorderly conduct statute
that required the jailed Riders to post bond within forty days of conviction.
Riders who missed this deadline lost their right of appeal and any alternative to
serving out their entire sentence. In this context, posting bond on the thirty-
ninth day became an essential part of the Riders' legal challenge to Mississippi's
Jim Crow system.

The first mass bail-out took place on July 7, bringing joy and liberation to the
Freedom Riders involved. But it also represented an ominous development for
a movement perpetually short of funds. For each Freedom Rider, bond was set
at $500, but that was only the beginning of the financial burden imposed by
litigation. In addition to the bond payment, CORE had to come up with
enough money to provide each Freedom Rider with a defense attorney, transportation back home, and, at some time later in the summer, transportation
back to Mississippi for an appellate trial. When combined with court costs,
housing costs, the purchase of bus and train tickets for the actual Freedom
Rides, and other miscellaneous outlays, the average cost per Freedom Rider
was well over $1,000 dollars.

At his post-release press conference in Jackson, Farmer was careful to avoid
any mention of CORE's precarious financial situation. And he was equally dis-
creet when he arrived at New York's LaGuardia Airport the next day. The Freedom Rides had unleashed a transcendent feeling of hope and redemption that
was stronger than any force wielded by demagogic politicians or prison wardens,
he told the reporters at La Guardia. Despite the desperate efforts of men like
Ross Barnett and Fred Jones, the nonviolent movement was alive and well and
poised to expand its influence into every corner of the Jim Crow South. Though
undoubtedly genuine, Farmer's lofty rhetoric represented the public face of the
movement. The behind-the-scenes reality at CORE headquarters was, as might
be expected, considerably more complicated. Despite its recent notoriety,
CORE remained a relatively small organization with a limited staff and modest
financial resources. During Farmer's absence, the number of volunteers and
chapters, and the general level of activity, had all increased. But it was a constant
struggle for the organization to keep pace with expanding responsibilities. Even

more troubling, of course, was the continuing uncertainty of the federal government's response to the Freedom Rides.

In the early summer of 1961, no one could be sure how far the Kennedy administration was willing to go to protect the Freedom Riders' constitutional rights, or whether the Riders could gain meaningful access to the federal court system. Ironically, some of this uncertainty stemmed from Robert Kennedy's decision to petition the ICC. Though promising in the abstract, the petition essentially put the administration on the sidelines until the notoriously slow-moving regulatory agency got around to responding to the attorney general's request. On June 19 the ICC announced that it had begun a preliminary investigation of the issues raised by the Justice Department's petition, but it also announced that formal hearings on the matter would not begin until August 15.

In the meantime, movement attorneys were left with limited legal options. In mid-June the filing of a habeas corpus motion on behalf of Betsy Wyckoff, who had been arrested on June 2, held out some hope that all of the Freedom Rider arrests would be nullified. But on June 27 District Judge Sidney Mize ruled against the motion, arguing that the plaintiff had not yet exhausted potential remedies in state courts. Ignoring William Kunstler's insistence that the racially biased Mississippi courts were of no value to Wyckoff or any other Freedom Rider, Mize declared that the federal courts had no valid interest in the case until the state courts rendered a judgment on the legality of the arrests. A week later, Jack Young, Wyckoff's other attorney, asked for a reconsideration of the ruling, but on July 6 Mize denied the appeal. Refusing to give up, Kunstler, backed by the national office of the ACLU, applied for a certificate of probable cause, a document that would allow Wyckoff's case to be heard by the Fifth Circuit Court of Appeals. On July 12, Judge Minor Wisdom, the most racially liberal member of the Fifth Circuit Court, granted the certificate, but ten days later Wisdom and his four colleagues issued a unanimous decision rejecting Kunstler's appeal. The final blow came two weeks later, on July 26, when Associate Justice Hugo Black, speaking for the U.S. Supreme Court, upheld the Fifth Circuit's denial of a writ of habeas corpus. In private, Black, like Wisdom, expressed considerable sympathy for the Riders' precarious legal situation, but as a matter of law he felt compelled to rule against Kunstler's unproven allegation that Wyckoff could not get a fair hearing in the courts of Mississippi.

The Wyckoff case represented a major setback for movement leaders who had hoped to circumvent the costly and potentially debilitating process of appealing the Freedom Riders' convictions in state court. Fortunately for the movement, it was only one of several important legal developments to emerge in late June and July. Most were favorable to the cause of racial equality, and for the first time in years civil rights advocates detected a quickening in the legal assault on Jim Crow. For more than a decade the trajectory of civil rights law and federal policy had been tilting toward desegregation, but now it appeared that both the Justice Department and the federal courts were zeroing in on specific violations of social justice and equal protection. Most obviously, there was a noticeable shift in the Justice Department's approach to enforcement.

The first sign of this shift was the petition sent to the ICC in late May, but the new attitude became even more obvious in mid-June when Robert Kennedy testified before a largely hostile Senate appropriations subcommittee. Asked to justify the funds expended on federal marshals in Alabama, Kennedy was immediately put on the defensive by two ultra-segregationist senators, John McClellan of Arkansas and Allen Ellender of Louisiana. Turning the hearing into a debate on the Freedom Rides, McClellan and Ellender subjected Kennedy to a withering attack. To their surprise, Kennedy not only stood his ground, defending the federal government's actions in Alabama, but also hinted that the Justice Department was gearing up for broader civil rights initiatives in the Deep South. After Ellender insisted that the Freedom Riders "were deserving of their reception and got exactly what was to be expected," the attorney general responded coolly but forcefully: "I have a tough time accepting that this should be determined in the streets and that people should be beaten."

One week later, on June 26, his words took on added significance when Justice Department attorneys filed a suit to end racial discrimination at New Orleans's Moisant International Airport. This was the first time that the federal government had actually gone to court to challenge segregated air terminal facilities. Normally stymied by complicated private leasing arrangements that seemed to place airport restaurants beyond the reach of federal authority, the department's attorneys had decided that, as a new facility, the New Orleans terminal offered a good test case for emerging interpretations of the Federal Aviation Act. Segregation at air terminals was a tough nut to crack, but the Justice Department's new resolve in this difficult area of civil rights law suggested that even here Jim Crow's days were numbered. Less surprising was the department's increased activity on behalf of voting rights. On July 6 the department filed voter registration suits against two Mississippi counties, Forrest and Clarke, and a week later it filed a similar suit against the city of New Orleans.

All of these suits were encouraging, but for the Freedom Riders the most promising legal development in late June and early July was the Justice Department's decision to join an existing NAACP suit seeking a permanent injunction barring the city of Jackson, the state of Mississippi, and several bus and railroad lines from arresting Freedom Riders. Certified by a three-judge federal panel on July 11, the Justice Department's petition to serve as "a friend of the court" declared that "the United States is concerned when Federal civil rights are violated on a massive scale and a continuing basis." Insisting that Mississippi officials had no legal basis to arrest passengers for violating state segregation laws, the petition contended that "the state and its officials are acting beyond the scope of their lawful power if they make such arrests and obtain such convictions." Accepted over the strong objections of the state's attorney, the petition was especially alarming to segregationists because the NAACP's brief made no distinction between interstate and intrastate passengers. For the first time the Justice Department appeared to be sanctioning an all-out assault on segregated transit laws, even laws that did not affect interstate commerce.

The legality of intrastate bus segregation had been successfully challenged as early as 1956, when the Supreme Court had ordered the desegregation of Montgomery's local buses in *Gayle v. Browder*, but the Justice Department had demonstrated little interest in applying *Gayle* to other cities. If the department's attorneys recognized the significance of the unprecedented challenge to states' rights in Mississippi, they did not say so in the petition. Still, everyone involved had some sense that the federal government was sailing into uncharted waters. Whatever their intentions, department attorneys soon discovered that they would have to wait for their day in court. Overruling Judge Elbert Tuttle's objections, the two Mississippi judges on the panel—Sidney Mize of Gulfport and Claude Clayton of Tupelo—voted to postpone hearings on the injunction until August 7, one week before the Freedom Riders' appellate trials were scheduled to begin.

The apparent liberalization of the Justice Department's civil rights policies gave movement leaders a measure of hope, but few observers had any illusions about the source of the change. Like the rest of the Kennedy administration, the leadership of the Justice Department appeared to be more political than ideological, and the department's response to the Freedom Rider crisis still bore all the earmarks of an exercise in political damage control. Despite the recent legal maneuvering, this was the same group of men that had struck a bargain with Ross Barnett and James Eastland, agreeing to stand by while the Mississippi police violated the Freedom Riders' constitutional rights. As a means of resolving the crisis, the bargain had backfired, forcing the department to deal with the politically embarrassing situation at the Hinds County Jail and Parchman. But there was no evidence that the new attitude in Washington represented anything more than a frantic attempt to calm the passions that threatened to overtake the administration's low-key approach to the issue of civil rights.

In this context, continued pressure from the movement was essential. Despite financial difficulties, the FRCC was determined to maintain a steady flow of Freedom Riders into Mississippi. And, for the most part, the recruiting and training centers in Nashville, New Orleans, Atlanta, and Montgomery did just that, drawing a wide range of college students, ministers, labor leaders, and other volunteers into the struggle. The one notable exception was the first week in July when a temporary shortage of recruits dictated a shift in strategy. Faced with a potentially embarrassing lull in movement activity, the FRCC turned to Mississippi's home-grown activists for help. Cultivating Jackson's local movement was nothing new, but the decision to recruit local Freedom Riders represented a significant escalation of the campaign to foment a wide-scale internal rebellion. Even though the vast majority of the state's black citizens remained aloof from the movement, the exceptions had grown too numerous and too vocal to ignore. Despite protestations to the contrary, this was cause for considerable concern among white Mississippians, particularly in Jackson where the connection between the Freedom Rides and the recent upsurge in local activism was obvious. Led by CORE field secretaries Tom Gaither and Richard Haley, the campaign to embolden Jackson's local activists became a significant factor in the larger struggle when it became clear that a number of students at Tougaloo, Jackson State, and several local high schools were eager to become Freedom Riders. Taking advantage of the notoriety surrounding the June 23 arrest of the Tougaloo Four, Gaither and Haley, with the approval of the FRCC, recruited more than a score of local Freedom Riders by the end of the month, setting the stage for a new round of Rides that would soon shake the state to its foundations. Giddy with anticipation, the FRCC authorized Haley to announce the formation of the Jackson Non-Violent Movement, an organization that was sure to arouse the ire of local segregationists.

The sudden upsurge of the Jackson movement was a shocking development for many white Mississippians. Time and again they had been assured by state and local officials that everything was under control and that the Freedom Rides were a temporary annoyance concocted by outside agitators. But now it appeared that the Freedom Rides had tapped a wellspring of dissent inside Mississippi itself. Although many wary segregationists had suspected as much for some time, the events of early July confirmed their worst fears. Buffeted on all sides, they faced the prospect of an ever-widening and seemingly permanent challenge to their authority. Almost every day brought new intrusions, some in the form of perceived breaches of racial etiquette that reflected subtle but disturbing changes in racial behavior.

By midsummer, arresting Freedom Riders in Jackson had become routine, and local and state officials felt that they had developed a firm and effective way of dealing with the almost daily disruptions. Yet, at the same time, they were becoming increasingly concerned about what was happening in the rest of the South. Governor Ross Barnett, in particular, was convinced that an inconsistent response was weakening the South's defense of segregation. Fearful that many Southern officials had let down their guard, he invited the region's governors to a special conference held in Jackson on July 19.

Billed as a wake-up call for the leaders of the segregationist South, the meeting turned out to be a major disappointment, drawing only the governors of

Alabama, Arkansas, South Carolina, and Mississippi, plus lower-level representatives from Florida, Georgia, Louisiana, and Kentucky. Barnett had hoped to demonstrate that the white South constituted a solid bloc, but he accomplished exactly the opposite by convening a rump meeting of extremists. Obviously bitter at being snubbed, he opened the conference with a public complaint against "the lack of unity among the leaders of the South," many of whom he found to be "soft" and "timid" in their defense of the Southern way of life. Several hours of segregationist posturing followed, including suggestions that Barnett was ready to form a third party based on resistance to segregation. But neither he nor any of the other delegates could hide the fact that the conference had failed to rally the region's political elite.

To Barnett's dismay, July 19 was also an unusually busy day in Washington, where a White House press conference revealed the president's newfound determination to use the interstate commerce clause as a guarantor of the right to travel freely from state to state. In his most forceful statement to date, Kennedy insisted that "there is no question of the legal rights of the freedom travelers, freedom riders, that move in interstate commerce." Drawing an analogy with freedom of the press, he reasoned: "We may not like what people print in a paper, but there is no question about their constitutional right to print it. So that follows, in my opinion, for those who move in interstate commerce." While he stopped short of endorsing the Freedom Riders' reason for traveling, he maintained that all Americans, regardless of "the purpose for which they travel [,] ... should enjoy the full constitutional protections given to them by the law and by the Constitution." Alluding to the Justice Department petition awaiting consideration by the ICC, he added that he was "hopeful" that the administration's position would eventually "become the generally accepted view" and that "any legal doubts about the right of people to move in interstate commerce" would soon disappear.

To the editors of the *New York Times*, the president's long-awaited statement on the Freedom Rides "had no precise meaning" and fell far short of "a profile in political courage." But the president's words communicated an entirely different message to the besieged segregationists of the Deep South. To them, Kennedy's oblique language represented a semantic smoke screen for the administration's aggressive advocacy of civil rights and social equality. Earlier in the year, many white Southerners had held out hope that political considerations would force the administration to adopt a cautious approach to civil rights matters, and for a time administration leaders actively reinforced this view through legislative inaction and the appointment of racial conservatives to the federal judiciary. Despite repeated entreaties from civil rights lobbyists, the administration steadfastly refused to introduce any new civil legislation. And as late as June, the president, ignoring the strong objections of virtually every civil rights leader in the nation, appointed W. Harold Cox, one of Mississippi's most outspoken white supremacists, to the federal bench. Yet none of this seemed to matter very much by midsummer. Unable to avoid the constitutional questions posed by the Freedom Rider crisis, the administration, despite its strong political ties to the white South, edged closer and closer to actual enforcement of equal protection under the law.

Politics still mattered, of course, but as the summer progressed the administration's civil rights policy makers seemed to be increasingly concerned with the international politics of the Cold War as opposed to the traditional domestic variety. While the Kennedy brothers did not want to alienate Southern conservatives such as James Eastland and John Patterson, the goal of securing the trust of the Third World often took priority over efforts to maintain existing domestic political arrangements. Clearly, the Kennedys did not want to have to choose between white Southern votes and the approval of the dark-skinned masses of Africa, Asia, and Latin America. But, with the eyes of the world watching, the administration simply could not afford to repudiate the basic principles of racial equality and equal protection affirmed in *Boynton* and other Supreme Court decisions. In this context, the rhetoric, if not the reality, of social justice prevailed, and desegregation took on an air of inevitability. To this point the administration's accomplishments in the field of civil rights had been modest and largely symbolic, but the white supremacists of the South were increasingly fearful that this situation was about to change and that it was only a matter of time before the federal government launched an all-out assault on segregation. Such fears were exacerbated in late July, when administration supporters in the Senate overcame stiff opposition from Southern senators and pushed through the appointment of NAACP attorney and Howard University Law School dean Spottswood Robinson to the Civil Rights Commission. And there were even rumors that the president had decided to appoint Robinson's longtime NAACP colleague Thurgood Marshall to a federal judgeship.

The suspicion that the Kennedy administration was actively encouraging the civil rights movement was especially strong in Alabama, where Governor Patterson and others were still fulminating about the unwarranted federal invasion of Montgomery. In the two months since the confrontation over the use of federal marshals, Patterson had done his best to sustain a running feud with the attorney general, the favorite whipping boy of Alabama politics. But this was not always easy. Unlike the situation in Mississippi, most of the action in Alabama during June and July took place behind the scenes as FBI agents and other investigators gathered evidence against the Anniston bombers and the Birmingham rioters. On June 16, in an obvious attempt to stir things up, Patterson announced that he was prepared to fire any Alabama highway patrolman who cooperated with the FBI, which he depicted as a meddling agency that sympathized with outside agitators. To most civil rights activists, the notion that the FBI was actively working on behalf of the movement was laughable, but this notion was almost an article of faith in Alabama, where many whites were convinced that they were up against a broad federal conspiracy led by the Justice Department.

According to Patterson, the continuing assault on the state's segregation laws reflected a special animus toward Alabama. When the Justice Department filed a discrimination suit against Montgomery's Dannelly Field on July 26, Patterson charged that Robert Kennedy was "picking on Alabama," even though the governor was well aware that the suit was identical to an earlier action brought against airport segregation in New Orleans. "This must be his way of getting even with us for the humiliation which came from his support of the so-called Freedom Riders," Patterson explained. "These rabble rousers really took Mr. Kennedy for a ride, and now he is trying to vent his ire again on the Southern people." Upon hearing this, Kennedy once again vehemently denied that he had encouraged the Freedom Riders to travel through the South, though he could not resist reminding the public that Patterson, not the federal government, was to blame for the breakdown of law and order in Alabama. In predictable fashion, Patterson responded with another round of personal invective, but Kennedy, sensing that he was being used for political purposes, allowed the matter to drop. Faced with a troubling and uncertain situation in Mississippi, where the Freedom Riders' appellate trials were scheduled to begin in three weeks, he saw no advantage in fanning the flames of sectional discord in a state that had already tested the limits of his patience.

9

Woke Up This Morning with
My Mind Stayed on Freedom

> Woke up this morning with my mind stayed on freedom,
> Walkin' and talkin' with my mind stayed on freedom,
> Ain't no harm to keep your mind stayed on freedom,
> Everybody's got his mind stayed on freedom.
> —1960s freedom song

The midsummer exchange between John Patterson and Robert Kennedy drew surprisingly little reaction from the national press, suggesting that the two-month-old Freedom Rider crisis had lost much of its novelty. Despite the periodic arrests in Jackson and the fulminations coming out of Montgomery, the Freedom Rides were no longer front-page news outside of Mississippi and Alabama. For most Americans, the Rides had receded into the background of national life, taking their place alongside school desegregation suits and sit-ins as manifestations of a continuing struggle. With no easy resolution in sight, the controversy surrounding the Rides appeared to be a virtual stalemate. After interviewing representatives of both the Freedom Rider movement and the white supremacist resistance in mid-July, Associated Press staff writer Hugh Mulligan concluded that "oddly enough, in the absence of any racial progress either way both sides are claiming victory in Mississippi. Meanwhile, the buses continue to arrive, the patrol wagon still waits, and the rest of the South, and the country, watches to see how long either philosophy can hold out."

What Mulligan detected, more than anything else, was the willingness of both sides to prolong the struggle indefinitely, regardless of the consequences. "It is now plain to even the few so-called moderates in our midst," insisted White

Citizens' Councils leader William Simmons, "that the integrationists will stop at nothing in their efforts to force the South to integrate. There is now a clearer public understanding of the tactics of the integrationists and of the steps necessary to defeat them. The issue has finally been joined, and the white South has tasted victory. Our appetites are whetted." Speaking for the Freedom Riders, Jim Lawson was no less resolute in his determination to engage the enemy, albeit nonviolently. Acknowledging that he and other nonviolent activists had broken an unjust peace, he warned Mulligan that it was all but impossible "to solve the problem" of racial injustice "without people being hurt." "Only when this hostility comes to the surface," he advised, "as it did in Montgomery and Birmingham, will we begin to see that the system of segregation is an evil which destroys people and teaches them a contempt for life. We are trying to reach the conscience of the South. Brutality must be suffered to show the true character of segregation."

In this combative context, with the result still very much in doubt, momentum was a precious commodity. Neither side could afford to let up or to give even the appearance of weakness or doubt. For the segregationists of Mississippi, the situation dictated an open-ended commitment to the arrest and prosecution of Freedom Riders, while for movement leaders it underscored the necessity of maintaining a steady flow of Riders into Jackson. This calculus tested the human and logistical resources of both sides, but in late July and early August the FRCC and CORE faced the special challenge of rounding up and preparing the released Freedom Riders for trial. Making sure that all of the appellate defendants returned to Mississippi in time for the legal proceedings scheduled to begin in mid-August was an enormous task. Indeed, the staff members and volunteers at the CORE office in New York and at the FRCC recruiting centers in the South soon discovered that they had time for little else. This realization, combined with financial considerations, forced movement leaders to suspend the Mississippi Freedom Rides for the month of August. However, they did so only after orchestrating a burst of new Rides in late July.

Designed to convince Mississippi authorities that there was no shortage of Freedom Riders willing to come to Jackson, the four groups that descended upon the city during an eight-day period raised the total number of Riders arrested since May 24 to nearly three hundred. On Sunday morning, the twenty-third, seven white Riders—six from California and one from New York City—were arrested at the Jackson train depot. And on Monday afternoon four Riders who had flown to Jackson from Montgomery were arrested at the city airport after trying to desegregate the airport restaurant. Three of those arrested were members of the Petway family: the Reverend Matthew Petway, pastor of the AME Zion Church in Montgomery; his sixteen-year-old son, Alphonso; and his twenty-year-old daughter, Kredelle, a student at Florida A&M in Tallahassee.

The fourth was Cecil Thomas, a white college student from Ohio who had spent a year at Fisk. Jailing three Freedom Riders from the same family was a new experience for the Jackson police, but this was only the first of several unusual arrests that punctuated the week.

On Saturday, July 29, the police apprehended ten white Riders at the Greyhound terminal, including Widjonarko Tjokroadisumarto, a graduate student at the University of Washington and the son of the former Indonesian ambassador to Pakistan; and Norma Wagner, a forty-four-year-old blind woman from Rochester, New York. Wary of bad publicity and fearing an international incident, the police refused to arrest Tjokroadisumarto and Wagner. "We're more humane than to arrest a blind woman," Chief of Detectives M. B. Pierce explained, adding that the Indonesian student was accorded special courtesy as "a guest of this country."

Earlier in the week, both the State Department and the Indonesian Embassy had urged Tjokroadisumarto to stay away from the Freedom Rides, either as a participant or as an observer, but the young student ignored their entreaties. In a telegram sent to the embassy, he cited "the Supreme Court decision on interstate travel, and President Kennedy's opinion on the exercise of the individual to travel" as proof that his participation in a Freedom Ride was "neither illegal nor political." Adding to the drama, the Jackson police confessed that they were not sure whether their dark-complexioned visitor was "black" or "white." "I do not intend to change Mississippi customs," Tjokroadisumarto explained with a wink, "That's for Mississippians to do. In my opinion, however, the customs of segregation and discrimination are wrong, ethically and otherwise."

On Sunday morning, while local officials were still pondering the implications of racial ambiguity and international scrutiny, not to mention the special challenges posed by handicapped Riders, the largest single group of Freedom Riders to date arrived at the Jackson railroad. Accompanied by Richard Steward, a Dillard student and New Orleans CORE activist, fourteen Riders from southern California filled several paddy wagons after challenging the terminal's segregated facilities. Most of the California Riders were student activists affiliated with UCLA. Ten were white, and four were black: Lonnie Thurman, a Montgomery native and Alabama State College graduate; Michael Grubbs, the nephew of the noted black historian John Hope Franklin, Helen Singleton, an art student at Santa Monica City College; and her husband, Bob, a twenty-five-year-old graduate student in international economics at UCLA.

The mass arrest of the Los Angeles Riders on July 30 was the last major confrontation between the Jackson police and Freedom Riders prior to the trials. However, the last individual arrest took place the next day when Jim Wahlstrom tried to use the telephone in the "Negro" waiting room at the Greyhound terminal. The arrest and conviction of the white twenty-four-year-old University of

Wisconsin student represented a milestone of sorts, since he was the first Freedom Rider to be rearrested. Originally arrested on June 6, he was out on bond and awaiting his appellate trial when a patrolman apprehended him in the phone booth. Wahlstrom's second arrest caused a considerable stir, not only because it set a precedent but also because state investigators had identified him as a "Soviet trained" Freedom Rider. Having traveled to Havana with the Fair Play for Cuba Committee in 1960, he was especially suspect in the eyes of vigilant Mississippians. In the white South, civil rights and Cold War crises tended to merge into a single confrontation between outside forces and the Southern way of life. For many segregationists the local and regional struggle against Freedom Riders and other "outside agitators" was inextricably bound to the international struggle against Soviet tyranny. And nowhere was the mutual reinforcement of segregationist anxieties and Cold War tensions more obvious than in Jackson, especially in the weeks leading up to the Freedom Rider trials.

With the temporary suspension of the Freedom Rides, Jackson's bus and train terminals entered a period of relative calm in early August. But this hiatus did not extend to the city's courtrooms, where a series of heated legal confrontations created a warlike atmosphere. Fought on segregationist soil, the legal war between local prosecutors and movement attorneys was a decidedly unequal struggle skewed by powerful racial and regional traditions. Initially, Jackson city officials "had agreed to the customary procedure in mass arrests, requiring only one or two typical cases to show for arraignment and trial and applying the findings in those cases to all the others," but in late July, in an obvious attempt to ensnare CORE and the FRCC in a financially burdensome legal tangle, the city's attorneys reneged on the agreement. Instead of a few representative defendants, all of the Freedom Riders out on bail would now be required to return to Jackson by August 14, the designated arraignment date, "on pain of forfeiting the five-hundred-dollar bond CORE had put up on each." City prosecutor Jack Travis and other local officials made no secret of their intentions. "We figure that if we can knock CORE out of the box, we've broken the back of the so-called civil rights movement in Mississippi," Travis informed CORE attorney Jack Young, "and that's what we intend to do." Dragging out the trials, making them as costly as possible, and generally keeping the defendants and their attorneys off balance were all part of a strategy designed to sap the movement's energies and resources.

Bringing nearly two hundred defendants back to Jackson by mid-August was a daunting task, but movement leaders had no other way of avoiding a financially crippling forfeiture of $100,000 dollars or more. At an emergency meeting on Thursday, August 3, the FRCC authorized Carl Rachlin and William Kunstler to meet with Hinds County Judge Russel Moore in the hope that he would overrule the decision to require all of the Riders to appear in court both on the day of arraignment and also on their individual trial dates. On the following Wednesday, during a special conference with Moore, the two attorneys argued that representative proceedings were not only fairer but safer than the proposed mass return. "We are here to try to assure an orderly trial," Rachlin insisted, suggesting that a mass return of Freedom Riders "might spark an 'irresponsible act' by white Mississippians." When Judge Moore turned them down, Rachlin and Kunstler filed an appeal with Circuit Judge Leon Hendrick, urging a compromise that would eliminate the requirement to appear at the August 14 arraignment. "All are ready and willing to come back for their trials as they come up," Kunstler maintained, but "to make them come when the calendar is called and again for their trials is a harassment on the part of the state." Forcing the defendants to appear twice would cost CORE an estimated $20,000 in unnecessary expenses, he explained. Unmoved, Judge Hendrick advised the Freedom Riders to be in court on August 14 or suffer the consequences.

The rebuff on August 10 capped off a week of legal setbacks for the Freedom Riders. Earlier in the week the Justice Department had refused CORE's request for the placement of federal marshals at the upcoming trials in Jackson, and on Monday, August 7, Judge Robert Rives, speaking for a three-judge panel of the Fifth Circuit Court of Appeals, had granted a six-week delay in the NAACP's suit against Jackson's municipal breach-of-peace law. Dismissing the objections of NAACP attorney Constance Baker Motley, who had asked for a temporary injunction that would forestall any further arrests under the law, the court scheduled the next hearing on the matter for September 25. Motley's co-counsel in the suit, Justice Department attorney Robert Owens, was present in the courtroom when the ruling was handed down, but neither he nor any other federal official offered an opinion on the wisdom of the delay. Once again it appeared that the Justice Department was eager to avoid any precipitous or provocative action that might be construed as a challenge to the integrity of the legal process in the Deep South.

FRCC leaders had no such reservations and continued to question the fairness of a legal system that harassed and intimidated anyone who challenged the segregationist order—a system that they hoped would soon disappear. For the time being, however, they had no choice but to comply with the requirements of that system. Although Farmer and other movement leaders were reluctant to say so publicly, much more than money was at stake. The Freedom Riders' public image and the integrity of the nonviolent movement were also on the line. If a substantial number of Freedom Riders failed to return to Mississippi for trial, there would be widespread speculation that the missing Riders were afraid to return, that fear or other personal considerations had outweighed their commitment to the struggle. Whatever the real reasons for the failure to appear, the suspicion that the Freedom Riders lacked faith or courage was potentially devastating to a movement that trafficked in moral capital. No element of the movement's mystique was more compelling than the drama of personal sacrifice, and no aspect of nonviolent direct action was more essential than individual accountability. Thus there was no allowance for excused absences. Realizing this simple truth, Farmer and his colleagues spared no effort in the campaign to retrieve the scattered Freedom Riders. With Marvin Rich skillfully coordinating an emergency fund-raising effort and with the rest of the staff and volunteers focusing on the logistics of contacting and transporting the defendants, CORE was able to retrieve 192 of the released Freedom Riders. Only nine Riders failed to appear for arraignment on August 14, and three of those arrived a day late after being detained by the New Orleans police, leaving only six actual forfeitures. One of the six could not be found, and two others—one in northern Saskatchewan and a second in Turkey—were simply too far away to return to Jackson in time.

On Sunday evening, August 13, the mood in Jackson was calm enough to allow movement leaders to hold a mass "freedom rally" at the same black Masonic Temple where Martin Luther King had spoken five weeks earlier. Sponsored by the Jackson Non-Violent Movement, the rally drew more than a thousand supporters, including virtually all of the returning Freedom Riders. Following an afternoon planning session at Tougaloo, the Riders traveled to the downtown temple in a caravan of cars, avoiding any unnecessary stops, and they were ushered into the hall through a cordon of police officers who kept the surrounding area clear of white demonstrators. Once inside, they were greeted by waves of applause from an overwhelmingly black audience dominated by young student activists, some still in their early teens. During the next two hours the Riders and their hosts "clapped, sang, and shouted" as a series of speakers representing the NAACP, CORE, SCLC, and the Jackson Movement held forth. With several national reporters looking on, Farmer told the crowd that they were part of a growing national movement for freedom and insisted that the Freedom Rides "must continue no matter how much it costs." For the Freedom Riders themselves, the feelings of emotional uplift inspired by Farmer and others would soon be tested by the challenges of a hostile courtroom. And for their local supporters, there would be even greater tests imposed by a rigidly segregated society. But no one present at the Masonic Temple that evening left the hall without at least some appreciation for the rising power of the movement.

The scene at the Hinds County Courthouse on Monday, August 14, was rife with tension, but the soft-spoken Judge Russel Moore did his best to maintain legal decorum and the appearance, if not the reality, of judicial neutrality. Early in the day, he convened a special arraignment for Percy Sutton and Mark Lane, two high-profile Freedom Riders scheduled to return to New York on an early afternoon plane. Both men pleaded not guilty, as did all of the defendants who

later appeared at the regular 2 p.m. arraignment. At the beginning of the afternoon session, Kunstler filed several defense motions, including a declaration
that the local statutes involved in the Freedom Rider arrests "were unconstitutional on their face and a violation of the U.S. Constitution," a call for a "class
action" streamlining of the court's appellate procedures, and a demand for a
change of venue to the "furtherest county in the state from Hinds." After swiftly
rejecting all of Kunstler's motions, Judge Moore brought the defendants forward
in pairs to register their pleas and assign trial dates. Following a prearranged
agreement grudgingly accepted by Kunstler, the judge scheduled two appellate
trials a day, beginning with Hank Thomas and Julia Aaron on August 22. Collectively, the scheduled trials filled twenty-two weeks of the court's docket, stretching into mid-January 1962. By 5 p.m. the mass arraignment was over, bringing
temporary relief to the defendants who now knew when they had to return to
Mississippi. Having seen enough of Mississippi justice for one day, most of the
Riders filed out of the courtroom as quickly as possible, and many left the state
before nightfall.

Judge Moore's rulings set a difficult course for CORE and the Freedom
Riders. In the short term, the scheduled appellate trials would consume virtually
all of CORE's resources, making it all but impossible to extend the Freedom
Rides to other areas of the South. And, with more than a hundred additional
Freedom Riders languishing in Mississippi jails, there would almost certainly be
many more trials to follow. Barring timely intervention by the federal courts, the
legal tangle related to the Jackson arrests would take months, and even years, to
unravel. To CORE stalwarts, this burden was an unfortunate but necessary part
of conducting nonviolent direct action on a mass scale. But to many others, both
inside and outside the movement, the mounting costs and uncertain future of
the Freedom Rides seemed to confirm the wisdom of less disruptive approaches
to social change. Publicly, the leaders of the NAACP and SCLC pledged their
support to the legal battle being waged in Jackson. Privately, however, they
expressed grave doubts about any strategy that placed the fate of the movement
in the hands of segregationist judges.

Officials at the Justice Department were even less sanguine about the legal
situation in Mississippi. Earlier in the summer Robert Kennedy and his colleagues had placed their faith in the Interstate Commerce Commission, and the
events of July and early August had done nothing to alter their belief that the
long-neglected but potentially powerful regulatory agency would eventually
provide a politically and legally palatable solution to the Freedom Rider crisis.

Most movement leaders doubted that the present ICC commissioners had
either the will or the capacity to desegregate public transit facilities. But, whatever their expectations, they recognized the symbolic and political importance
of the ICC hearings that opened in Washington on Tuesday, August 15, less than

twenty-four hours after the mass arraignment in Jackson. On the Sunday afternoon following his speech at the Riverside Church, King challenged the ICC to issue a sweeping ruling that included a "blanket order" against segregation in bus, rail, and air terminals. "The Freedom Rides have already served a great purpose," he told reporters, highlighting "the indignities and injustices that the Negro people still confront as they attempt to do the simple thing of traveling as interstate passengers." He acknowledged, though, that a clear and broad ICC mandate held the power to go even further. If strict compliance were enforced for interstate travelers, all segregated travel would "almost inevitably end," even among intrastate travelers. "This will be the point where Freedom Rides will end," he predicted.

The ICC had already received similar advice from hundreds of CORE supporters who had either signed petitions or submitted letters endorsing the Justice Department's proposal for a comprehensive desegregation order. To make sure that the commissioners realized what was at stake, CORE set up a line of sign-carrying "Freedom Riders" outside the ICC building on the first morning of the hearings. Inside the building, CORE's chief counsel, Carl Rachlin, was one of thirteen witnesses testifying before the commission. Following the lead of Justice Department attorney St. John Barrett, who insisted that the ICC had the power and the duty "to halt discrimination in this field," Rachlin urged the commissioners to "apply a little moral force" to the "wonderful, decent people" of the white South. "You must help them to get rid of a tradition which is morally wrong," he declared, with a wink, "even though they oppose change at the moment."

The oral arguments that began on August 15 initiated the public phase of the ICC's deliberations, but most of the groundwork for the deliberations had already been laid in lengthy behind-the-scenes negotiations held in June, July, and early August. The procedures established by the ICC in mid-June set aside a month for the submission of written briefs and three additional weeks for rebuttal statements. Representing the Justice Department, Burke Marshall urged the commissioners to act with dispatch, and the department's brief filed on July 20 reiterated the comprehensive demands outlined in the attorney general's extraordinary May 29 petition. The attorney general wanted nothing less than a broadly enforceable order that would supersede the indefinite mandates of the Motor Carrier Act of 1935 and the obvious limitations of the *Morgan* and *Boynton* decisions. Historically, the conflicting provisions of state and federal laws on matters of Jim Crow transit had tilted toward segregation, in part because only the state statutes included specific commands. Thus meaningful desegregation would require a detailed and directive order along the lines proposed by the attorney general. Although the opposition of state and local officials to such an order was a given, Justice Department officials hoped to persuade private bus companies and other interstate carriers to support the administration's position. After the briefs submitted in July indicated that the carriers had serious reservations about the scope and coercive nature of the attorney general's plan, Marshall invited several transit industry executives to a closed-door meeting in Washington.

At the meeting the executives listened politely to what Marshall and other Justice Department officials had to say, but in the end they were unwilling to accept a comprehensive plan. The best they could do was to offer to withdraw their opposition if the administration agreed to limit the plan's regulatory power to vehicles and facilities specializing in interstate travel. Leaving most of the Jim Crow transit system intact, this limitation was, as Marshall explained, totally unacceptable to an administration looking for a way to end rather than perpetuate the Freedom Rider crisis.

The failure to convert the transit executives was disappointing, but the most important lobbying effort, the one that really mattered, was directed at the ICC commissioners themselves. Since most of the commissioners were Republicans appointed during the Eisenhower era, and only one—a Massachusetts Democrat named William Tucker—was a Kennedy appointee, the administration faced an uphill political struggle in its dealings with the notoriously prickly commission. Having Tucker on the commission was a plus, but the others had to be approached with great care through essentially nonpolitical channels. Consequently, the administration mounted a broad-gauged appeal that emphasized the national security aspects of the struggle for civil rights. According to Marshall and several other high-ranking members of the administration, the immediate need for a sweeping ICC desegregation order transcended considerations of racial equity or legal precedent. In a letter to the commissioners, Secretary of Defense Robert McNamara argued that the enforcement of segregation on buses and trains posed a serious threat to the morale of black military personnel assigned to Southern bases. A similar letter submitted by Secretary of State Dean Rusk, a native Georgian familiar with Southern laws and customs, insisted that the persistence of segregated transit facilities was a major embarrassment for a nation promoting democracy and freedom in a largely nonwhite world.

Reiterated by other administration officials throughout the summer of 1961, Rusk's point received timely reinforcement from a series of diplomatic incidents related to the recent proliferation of black African envoys to the United States. As recently as 1959, the sub-Saharan diplomatic corps in Washington and New York had consisted of a small number of envoys representing Ethiopia, Liberia, and Ghana. But with the arrival of representatives from more than two dozen newly independent African nations in 1960 and 1961, the treatment of African diplomats by their American hosts became a subject of intense interest and controversy. Most obviously, the racial segregation that dominated the greater

Washington area became an embarrassing reality for the new Kennedy administration. The segregated housing patterns of the District of Columbia, suburban Maryland, and northern Virginia proved to be a major irritant for visiting African families. But the primary flash point was the segregated facilities along the Route 40 corridor between Washington and the New Jersey border. When traveling back and forth between Washington embassies and the United Nations headquarters in New York, black Africans discovered that virtually all of the restaurants and other public accommodations were for whites only.

After receiving a number of complaints from African delegations, the State Department created the Special Service Protocol Section (SPSS) of the Office of Protocol in March 1961. Headed by Pedro Sanjuan, a thirty-year-old Cuban émigré and former Kennedy campaign worker with a Russian studies degree from Harvard, the SPSS initially worked quietly behind the scenes to smooth over any hard feelings. But, following a denial of service to Adam Malik Sow, the new ambassador from Chad, in late June, Sanjuan discussed the Route 40 problem directly with President Kennedy, who authorized an organized effort to convince restaurant owners and Maryland officials that discrimination along Route 40 was harming the national image. By the end of July, several White House aides, including Harris Wofford and Fred Dutton, had been enlisted in the effort to promote the desegregation of Route 40, setting the stage for a major public controversy that would eventually involve CORE and a recalcitrant Maryland legislature. At the time of the August ICC hearings, the public struggle over what was later known as the Route 40 campaign had not yet begun. But it would soon become an important part of the political backdrop that both the ICC and the Justice Department had to take into account.

The increasingly obvious diplomatic implications of segregation provided administration officials with a degree of leverage in the effort to secure an ICC desegregation order. The effort itself, however, was not something that many officials relished. Although Marshall and others would eventually come to appreciate the political and moral growth that the Freedom Rider crisis forced upon them, the usefulness and advisability of nonviolent direct action escaped them at the time. While recognizing the need for social change, they strongly preferred less disruptive forms of civil activism such as bringing test cases before the courts or conducting voter registration drives. Encouraging movement leaders to de-emphasize direct action techniques had been on the administration's agenda since the earliest days of the Kennedy presidency. But the effort to make the civil rights movement more "civil" took on a new urgency after the Freedom Rides provoked massive resistance in the Deep South. As we have already seen, several meetings held in the early summer brought black student leaders, white liberals, and Justice Department representatives together for an ongoing discussion of the prospects for a region-wide voting rights campaign funded by private foundations. Although the discussion angered Diane Nash and other direct-action advocates who suspected that the administration was trying to blunt the radicalism of the student movement with the promise of voting rights funding, a growing number of student activists appeared willing to consider the proposed shift.

As the summer progressed, it became clear that the likelihood of such a shift rested upon the organizational and ideological evolution of SNCC. When SNCC's central committee hired Charles Sherrod as the organization's first field secretary in June, it took an important step towards the actualization of a voting rights project. Even though Sherrod was a strong advocate of direct action, he also believed that SNCC should be actively involved in promoting the registration of black voters. Less than a month after becoming field secretary, he met with Amzie Moore, a veteran NAACP activist who had been calling for a voting rights campaign since the late 1940s, and Bob Moses, a twenty-five-year-old black teacher from Harlem who had befriended Moore the previous summer. Meeting in Moore's home town of Cleveland, Mississippi, in the heart of the Delta, the three men discussed the viability of establishing a pilot voting rights project in Cleveland and nearby black belt communities. After assessing the local situation, they agreed that Cleveland was not quite ready for an infusion of SNCC volunteers, but with Moore's help Sherrod and Moses soon found another site for the project in McComb, two hundred miles to the south.

Aided by several Freedom Riders, Moses soon mobilized the Pike County Nonviolent Movement, a daring initiative that led to more than a hundred arrests and several confrontations during the fall and winter of 1961. Even in the remotest corner of the Delta, the fallout from the arrest and imprisonment of hundreds of committed activists penetrated the previously impenetrable walls of segregationist complacency. Here, as elsewhere, the involvement of Freedom Riders added volatility and confounded traditional patterns of accommodation and compromise. Indeed, wherever the Freedom Riders showed up—from McComb to Albany, Georgia, to Monroe, North Carolina—the spirit of nonviolent direct action empowered and energized local black movements, creating an interlocking chain of movement centers. Both before and after their appellate trials in Jackson, restless Riders offered their services as nonviolent shock troops, confirming the suspicion that the Freedom Rides represented the opening campaign of an all-out assault on the Jim Crow South.

By the end of the year the diffusion of Freedom Riders would help to turn the Mississippi Delta and southwestern Georgia into major civil rights battlegrounds, but nothing demonstrated the widening impact of the Freedom Rides more clearly than the developing situation in the North Carolina Piedmont town of Monroe. Destined to be the most controversial episode of the Freedom Rider saga, the Monroe Freedom Ride involved nineteen Riders who spent the last two weeks of August in Monroe trying to convert a local movement to the philosophy of nonviolence. For more than two years, Robert Williams and the Monroe NAACP had been engaged in an ongoing and high-profile struggle with both local segregationists and national civil rights leaders alarmed by his advocacy of "armed self-reliance." Since his celebrated censure by a large majority of the delegates to the 1959 NAACP national convention, he had grown even more militant, openly challenging the Jim Crow system at every opportunity and roundly condemning moderate leaders for their empty words and lack of resolute action. Refusing to abide by the conventional rules of practical and Cold War politics, he attracted a loyal following among black radicals, especially in Harlem where community activists such as Mae Frances Mallory and black intellectuals such as novelist John Mayfield and historian John Henrik Clarke welcomed his unabashed militance as a refreshing alternative to liberal inaction and caution. In 1960, Williams became a key figure in the radical Fair Play for Cuba Committee, defending Fidel Castro as a visionary exponent of social and racial democracy; and by the spring of 1961 he was punctuating his speeches with revolutionary rhetoric that came dangerously close to a call to arms. "I am going to meet violence with violence," he told a Harlem crowd on May 17, the seventh anniversary of *Brown*, "It is better to live just thirty seconds, walking upright in human dignity, than to live a thousand years crawling at the feet of our oppressors."

By the time the Freedom Riders arrived on August 17, armed conflict between the local movement and Klan-linked law enforcement officials was imminent, and the Riders soon found themselves in the midst of a violent confrontation that forced Williams to flee the country as a fugitive. Williams ended up in Cuba (and later in China), and several of the Riders ended up in jail, charged with various offenses, including aiding and abetting the kidnapping of a white couple that had strayed into the melee. Even though an abundance of trial testimony confirmed the obvious—the Freedom Riders played no role in the alleged kidnapping, and they did everything they could to thwart the violence in Monroe—their association with Williams was "a grievous error," according to one SCLC leader, and a major source of embarrassment for the nonviolent movement. Although CORE, SCLC, and other nonviolent organizations tried to distance themselves from Williams, who remained on the FBI's Most Wanted List for nearly a decade, individual Freedom Riders and some CORE chapters became involved in the various Monroe defense groups that sprang up during the fall of 1961. Dave Morton, an independent-minded Freedom Rider and folk singer from Minnesota, picketed the White House in September before going on to New York to help organize the Committee to Aid the Monroe Defenders (CAMD). And other Freedom Riders, including Journey of Reconciliation veterans Conrad Lynn and William Worthy, later raised funds and spoke at CAMD rallies in New York, Cleveland, and other Northern cities. Part of their concern was the fate of John Lowry, a young Freedom Rider from Queens, New York, who lost several appeals after his accessory to kidnapping conviction and who ultimately served a long jail sentence.

For sheer drama, nothing could match the story of Robert Williams. But as a key episode of the lengthy legal struggle between the Freedom Riders and the state of Mississippi, the trial of Hank Thomas had a special excitement of its own. With both sides anticipating a pivotal contest, the tension began to build in the days leading up to the August 22 trial. Earlier in the month William Kunstler had deliberately muddied the legal waters by filing a special appeal on behalf of five Freedom Riders. By asking that the Riders' cases be remanded from the county court to state court, he automatically triggered an appeal at the federal district level. On Saturday, August 19, the matter went before District Judge Harold Cox, the extreme segregationist who had recently been appointed to a federal judgeship over the strong objections of civil rights leaders. Arguing that the local breach-of-peace statute under which his clients had been convicted was actually "a segregation law—pure and simple," Kunstler hoped to circumvent the county court appellate proceedings scheduled to begin the following Tuesday. Since the Freedom Riders had come to Mississippi "to dramatize the segregation in inter-state commerce," he insisted that 'the federal court is the proper place for these cases." After questioning Kunstler about CORE's motives, Cox promised to issue a ruling on the removal issue, but not before the beginning of the trials in Judge Moore's court. Hank Thomas and the other early defendants would have their day in court, Mississippi style.

On Tuesday morning, August 22, Hank Thomas's trial began at the Hinds County Courthouse. Flanked by four defense attorneys—Rachlin, Kunstler, Jack Young, and Carsie Hall—the strapping nineteen-year-old Freedom Rider stood silently as Judge Moore's bailiff called the court to order. After a few opening remarks from Moore, who acknowledged the reporters in the gallery and noted that this was the only the first of approximately 190 trials to come, the selection of the jury commenced. As expected, the defense attorneys promptly challenged the selection process, which all but guaranteed an all-white jury. Although Mississippi law prohibited women from serving on juries, it was tech-nically possible for black jurymen to be selected from the registered voter list. In this instance, fifty-one of the fifty-three members of the jury pool were white, and with six peremptory challenges the prosecution could easily exclude the two black members of the pool. After Kunstler pointed this out and introduced testi-mony from several longtime black voters who had never been asked to serve on a jury, the prosecution countered with evidence from "several Jackson white city employees and newsmen that they, too, had been registered voters for many years and had never been called for jury duty." Such assurances proved good enough for Judge Moore, who dismissed Kunstler's motion to quash the venire. Later, when Kunstler questioned the impartiality of prospective jurors, asking specifically about their attitudes toward racial integration and CORE, Moore upheld state attorney Jack Travis's objection to this line of questioning. And when Travis himself alluded to the racial implications of the trial, Moore issued a stern reprimand to both sides. "This is not a racial issue," the judge insisted, "it is a breach of the peace trial. CORE is not on trial here."

Despite Moore's protestations, the proceedings quickly turned into a racial show trial on Wednesday afternoon. Parading a string of witnesses in front of the all-white jury, Travis tried to prove that the arrest of Thomas and the other Freedom Riders who had invaded Jackson on May 24 had prevented an outbreak of violence and rioting. Among the dozen witnesses called to confirm both the seriousness of the threat and the Freedom Riders' provocative behavior were Chamber of Commerce officials, Alabama and Mississippi law enforcement officers, and reporters who covered the Freedom Riders' journey from Montgomery to Jackson. The first to take the stand was Ell Cowling, the Alabama Public Safety Commission investigator who had witnessed the assaults on the Freedom Riders in Anniston. Describing the mob that met the bus at the Anniston terminal, Cowling recalled that several angry whites had beaten "on the side of the bus with heavy instruments" and screamed "Communist Niggers" at the Riders. He then went on to describe the roadside bombing of the bus several minutes later. When asked on cross-examination if he had seen Thomas "do anything illegal from Atlanta to Anniston," Cowling said "No." But this admission did nothing to diminish the image of rioting segregationists that Travis hoped to convey to the jury.

An array of white Mississippians followed the Alabama witnesses, and in each case they told the same story: The arrest of the Freedom Riders by the Jackson police had forestalled a riot. The monotonous marathon of examination and cross-examination continued into the evening until Judge Moore finally called a recess a few minutes before midnight. When the trial resumed the next morning, Travis was at it again, bringing the total number of prosecution witnesses to fifteen before resting his case. By the time Travis sat down it was early afternoon, and nearly everyone in the room expected Thomas's attorneys to fill the rest of the day with an examination of defense witnesses. But when Kunstler rose to speak he announced that the defense had decided to rest its case without calling any witnesses of its own. Instead, he offered a motion to place the text of the *Boynton* decision into the trial record, a motion summarily rejected by Judge Moore, who had already ruled that *Boynton* was irrelevant to the case.

Surprised and a bit flustered by Kunstler's maneuver, Travis launched into a rambling closing argument that reminded the members of the jury of their duty to uphold law and order. The police and the prosecution had done their part;

now it was time for the jury to send a clear message to anyone who dared to challenge the laws and customs of Mississippi. Pointing to Thomas, Travis declared: "Turn him loose . . . and blood will flow . . . If you want your property protected from riffraff and subversives, you must return a guilty verdict." In response, Kunstler offered a brief closing statement praising Travis's rhetorical flair but questioning whether the prosecution had presented any proof that the Freedom Riders had breached the peace. Forty-five minutes later a unanimous jury returned the expected guilty verdict. After granting Kunstler's request for an individual poll of the jurors, Judge Moore sentenced Thomas to four months in jail and a $200 fine, a somewhat stiffer penalty than the two-month sentence (plus two months suspended) imposed by the municipal court in May. Kunstler immediately announced that the defense would appeal the verdict to the state courts, and ultimately to the U.S. Supreme Court if necessary. Moments later Thomas was released pending payment of a $2,000 bond, bringing what one observer called "the hardest contested misdemeanor case in the annals of Mississippi jurisprudence" to a close.

In actuality, of course, Thomas's trial involved no real closure. On Friday morning, while he was en route to Washington to discuss his future at Howard University, Julia Aaron became the second Freedom Rider to face Travis and Judge Moore. Like Thomas, Aaron was a college student who had become a movement veteran at a young age. As a student activist at Southern University, she had been a mainstay of New Orleans CORE and one of the first to volunteer for the Mississippi Freedom Rides. Petite and attractive, she did not fit the image of a disruptive subversive. But that did not stop Travis from portraying her as a dangerous "rabble-rouser." "What did she want here?" he asked the jury rhetorically, answering: "The same thing they had in Montgomery—bloodshed. She wouldn't be sitting there today if those policemen hadn't been there. We would have had martial law and lots of other things this city doesn't want if we hadn't had the police protection." This time it took only three witnesses and six hours to bring the case to the jury, which needed only fifteen minutes of deliberation to agree on a guilty verdict. The streamlining of the trial eased the burden on those in the courtroom, but it brought little comfort to movement leaders, who were more concerned with the mounting cost of the appeals process. While Aaron announced that she planned to forgo bail and return to jail, defense attorneys did not expect many of the Freedom Riders to follow her lead. With bail set at $2,000 per defendant, it wouldn't take long to exhaust CORE's coffers. Indeed, there was nothing to stop Judge Moore from raising the bail figure even higher as the trials progressed. Barring intervention by the federal courts or a massive infusion of funds, the state of Mississippi's goal of bankrupting CORE now loomed as a realistic possibility.

The likelihood of federal intervention had never been high, but the slight hope that the appellate trials would be removed to the federal courts disappeared on August 26, the day after Aaron's trial. Refusing to invoke the Reconstruction-era civil rights act cited in Kunstler's request for removal, District Judge Cox ruled that the federal courts had no interest in the breach of peace trials. Prior to his appointment in June, movement leaders had warned the Kennedy administration that Cox was a white supremacist ideologue, and now they saw just how right they had been. Insisting that the Freedom Riders' arrests had nothing to do with "integration or segregation," Cox characterized the statute in question as "a pure and simple peace law enacted by the legislature in good faith to assure peace and tranquility among its people . . . This court may not be regarded as any haven for any counterfeit citizens from other states deliberately seeking to cause trouble here," he declared, using language that might have been appropriate at a White Citizens' Council rally but that seemed unnecessarily harsh in the context of a federal court order. Claiming that the "petitioners heralded their arrival in Jackson from other states for provocative purposes," he argued that "their status as interstate passengers is extremely doubtful." Although most legal observers, including those at the Justice Department, failed to see the logic of this last statement, Cox's intemperate ruling was not subject to a timely legal challenge. For the foreseeable future, the Freedom Riders' legal fate would remain in the hands of white Mississippians who shared the judge's contempt for the civil right struggle.

Coming on the heels of the first two appellate convictions, Cox's ruling gave pause to the Freedom Riders awaiting trial. Even though CORE policy expressly prohibited the paying of fines in cases of unjust prosecution, some of the Riders began to consider the wisdom of dropping their appeals and accepting the option of paying the remainder of their fines plus $3 per day for unserved jail time. The third and fourth trials were scheduled for Monday, August 28, but just prior to the opening of court Judge Moore announced that both defendants—John Moody, Hank Thomas's roommate at Howard, and Matthew Walker Jr., a nineteen-year-old black Freedom Rider from Nashville—had withdrawn their appeals and paid their fines. Speaking for CORE, field secretary Tom Gaither made it clear that the two Riders had done so without organizational approval. "We feel it is an admission of guilt," Gaither explained, pointing out that both Moody and Walker had paid the fines with their own funds.

On Wednesday, New Orleans CORE activists Doris Castle and Jerome Smith became the third and fourth Freedom Riders to drop their appeals, prompting speculation that most or all of the 184 Freedom Riders awaiting trial would soon follow suit. Unlike Moody and Walker, Castle and Smith chose to return to jail rather than pay their fines, an option endorsed by Jim Farmer the next day. At this point, not even Farmer—who was busy preparing for CORE's annual convention scheduled to open in Washington the next day—had a firm sense of the Freedom Riders' willingness to return to jail. But he worried that relatively few would follow the lead of Aaron, Castle, and Smith, the three New Orleans CORE stalwarts who always seemed to put the needs of the movement ahead of personal considerations. With the beginning of the fall semester only days away, many student activists were preparing to return to school, and others had jobs and families to consider. Earlier in the summer, many Freedom Riders had vowed to remain in jail for as long as it took to bring down the walls of segregation. Now, as the long season of sacrifice drew to a close, the harsh realities of Mississippi prison life began to take their toll. During the tumultuous final week of August, seven Freedom Riders, including Jim Wahlstrom and Bob Singleton, posted bond before serving the full thirty-nine days recommended by movement attorneys. On the last day of the month, even CORE field secretary Richard Haley, who had been languishing in the Hinds County Jail since his arrest for picketing Ross Barnett's segregationist governors' conference in late July, accepted bail. For the native Chicagoan, as for many of the Freedom Riders, August in Mississippi had proven to be the cruelest month.

10

Oh, Freedom

Oh, Freedom, Oh, Freedom, No More Jim Crow Over Me.
And before I'll be a slave, I'll be buried in my grave,
And go home to my Lord and be free.
—1960s freedom song

Jim Farmer woke up on the morning of September 1 with a troubled mind. He had been national director of CORE for exactly seven months and was proud of what he and the Freedom Riders had accomplished. But, as he contemplated the mounting challenges to the nonviolent movement, he couldn't escape the thought that Roy Wilkins, Thurgood Marshall, and other critics of the Freedom Rides might be right after all. With the appellate trials in Jackson bogged down in confusion, with the escalation of violence in McComb and Monroe, and with no apparent movement in the Interstate Commerce Commission's deliberations, there was little reason for optimism. Despite all of the sacrifices, and despite many inspiring acts of courage, the Freedom Rides appeared to be headed for failure. After four months of Rides and the mobilization of hundreds of activists, the crisis had evolved into a war of attrition that seemed to favor the defenders of segregation. Having set out to prove the viability of direct action in the Deep South, CORE was in danger of proving exactly the opposite. Confounded by the ambiguous response of the Kennedy administration, a strategy designed to guarantee federal protection of constitutional rights had actually put the Freedom Riders at the mercy of unreconstructed state and local officials. Perhaps worst of all, by inadvertently revealing the movement's financial and legal vulnerability, the Freedom Rides had placed the entire civil rights struggle in jeopardy.

Later that day, as Farmer made his way to a staff planning meeting at a Washington church, several reporters pressed him for a statement on the deteriorating situation in Jackson. With the CORE convention scheduled to open in a few hours, there was widespread speculation that the organization's attorneys had decided to withdraw all of the pending appeals. After insisting that there "will be no definite word" on the matter until after the convention delegates had deliberated in closed session, Farmer hinted that CORE had little choice but to shift tactics. "Our feeling is that the authorities of Mississippi are merely harassing us," he declared, predicting that each Freedom Rider would "receive a maximum sentence in the appeal trial regardless of the sentence previously received." Farmer himself was ready to return to jail if the only alternative was to pay an extortionist fine levied by an all-white Mississippi jury, or so he said as he walked away from the reporters. In truth, Farmer had no desire to serve the remaining twenty-seven days of his sentence and desperately hoped that some force would intervene before he had to make good on his pledge.

Timely intervention by the federal judiciary was Farmer's best hope, but the probability of such intervention was difficult to gauge in the wake of recent district and circuit court decisions. He and other movement leaders had been looking for a clear indication from the federal courts that legal and physical harassment of civil rights activists would no longer be tolerated. Fortunately for Farmer, who was ready for a bit of good news, one of the earliest signs that the federal judiciary was moving in this direction surfaced just hours before the opening of the CORE convention. Speaking at a press conference across town, Attorney General Kennedy announced that a federal grand jury meeting in Birmingham had issued indictments against nine of the men involved in the May 14 Anniston bus burning. Charged with violating section 33 of the U.S. motor vehicle code on two counts—"interfering with the safety and welfare of persons in interstate commerce and with conspiring to interfere with interstate commerce"—the defendants faced a maximum penalty of twenty years imprisonment and a $10,000 fine on the first count and five years and an additional $10,000 fine on the second. All nine were members of the Anniston Klan, including Cecil "Goober" Lewallyn, the twenty-two-year-old hothead who had tossed the firebomb into the bus. Lewallyn was in the Anniston hospital recovering from injuries suffered in an August 13 automobile accident, and a second Klansman, Roger Couch, was already in jail awaiting trial on a burglary charge. The other seven were taken into custody by the FBI and brought before U.S. Commissioner Ruby Price Robinson for arraignment. A tenth conspirator, Dalford Roberts, escaped indictment after agreeing to testify against his fellow Klansmen.

Moments after the CORE conference's closing on Monday, a beaming Farmer told reporters that CORE was not only alive and well but ready to expand the struggle for freedom. After confirming the organization's plan to withdraw the Freedom Rider appeals and after urging all of the defendants to return to Mississippi to serve the remainder of their sentences, he called for a series of new nonviolent initiatives. "It would be easy for us to get bogged down in litigation," he explained, "and that is just what the state of Mississippi would like to see. We have resolved to resume direct nonviolent action instead." Not only would there be new Freedom Rides, but squads of "Freedom Dwellers" would soon fan out across the country to combat racial discrimination in the housing industry. "Negro motorcades" would be sent to housing developments to ensure that "open houses" were truly open; real estate offices refusing to serve blacks could expect sit-ins; and developers who enforced restrictive covenants would be picketed. At the same time, CORE's existing campaign against employment discrimination by chain stores would receive new emphasis. In particular, CORE planned to target the retail giant Sears Roebuck, which generally restricted its black employees to menial positions. Finally, in a gesture that did not go unnoticed at the Justice Department, Farmer also announced an expansion of CORE's involvement in voter registration.

Designed to restore momentum, Farmer's press briefing reflected CORE's continuing commitment to direct action and the Freedom Rides, but it remained to be seen whether the embattled organization could put any of its ambitious plans into operation. Even within the movement there was widespread skepticism about CORE's capacity to sustain a broad program of direct action; and back in Mississippi many local and state officials dismissed Farmer's declarations as empty bluster. Noting that $500 in bail money would be returned to each Freedom Rider who decided to serve out his or her sentence, one assistant city prosecutor claimed that CORE's decision to drop the appeals was a desperate gambit "to get their hands on the appeal bond money." In Jackson, CORE's change in tactics was widely interpreted as a sign of weakness and impending defeat. "Mississippians are beginning to feel they have licked the 'Freedom Rider' movement," an Associated Press story in the *Jackson Daily News* reported on Wednesday, September 6. Quoting unnamed local observers, the story suggested that the Freedom Riders' "prolonged attack" on Mississippi had "backfired." The American public, one observer insisted, had concluded that outside agitators "were taking unfair advantage" of a state that had "bent over backward being fair to them, within the framework of segregation."

Within the civil rights division of the Justice Department, there was considerable sympathy and growing admiration for the Freedom Riders and other student activists challenging the status quo in the Deep South, but in the political context of 1961 these sentiments did not lead to broad-based or sustained legal intervention. Beginning with the first arrests in Jackson in late May, the intimidation of Freedom Riders by state and local officials had drawn little public comment from federal officials. And, despite the civil rights rhetoric that animated the attorney general's ICC petition, there was no indication that the events of the late summer had altered the administration's essentially neutral position on the prosecution of nonviolent dissenters. Detecting little or no political pressure to intervene on behalf of the Freedom Riders and judging public opinion to be sharply divided on the issue, administration leaders from the president on down were unwilling to undertake risky or radical initiatives that might endanger existing political arrangements.

Aside from a few maverick politicians and left-leaning commentators, those who spoke out most forcefully for the right to agitate were either the Freedom Riders themselves, student activists on college campuses, or liberal religious leaders. During the late summer and early fall of 1961, recent veterans of the Freedom Rides delivered lectures and testimonials at scores of churches and colleges across the nation. Virtually all of the original CORE Riders participated in this makeshift speakers bureau, and Ed Blankenheim, Hank Thomas, and Ben Cox—all of whom had joined the CORE staff—were especially active as recruiters and fund-raisers. Almost all of this activity took place in carefully selected venues where a sympathetic audience was guaranteed, namely college lecture halls and chapels. While the vast majority of students and faculty at predominantly white institutions in the North remained too conservative to embrace the Freedom Rides, movement lecturers attracted significant attention and support on campuses from Cornell to UCLA. And even in the South there were signs that at least some white students harbored sympathy for the Riders.

One notable expression of support surfaced on September 8, when several dozen students gathered at the Tennessee state capitol in Nashville to protest the expulsion of fourteen Freedom Riders from Tennessee A&I. While an interracial group of twenty-five picketed outside the capitol, eleven others, including John Lewis, formed a double line in front of Governor Buford Ellington's office. Although Ellington managed to scurry out a side door without confronting the protesters, the boldness of the students' action did not go unnoticed in a nation unaccustomed to such assertive behavior. The sit-ins and the Freedom Rides had involved private businesses and a few public terminals, but now the student invasion had spread to a seat of state government.

Three days after the picketing in Nashville, on Monday, September 11, the arraignment of seventy-eight additional Freedom Rider defendants in Jackson intensified the legal and financial pressure bearing down on CORE. After each defendant pleaded not guilty, the Hinds County court scheduled appellate trials for the spring of 1962, ensuring that the legal struggle in Mississippi would continue for at least nine more months. The movement's prospects for a quick legal victory were no more promising in Alabama, where white officials announced on Tuesday that the U.S. Fifth Circuit Court of Appeals had upheld Judge Frank Johnson's ruling that William Sloane Coffin, Wyatt Tee Walker, Fred Shuttlesworth, Ralph Abernathy, and six other Freedom Riders must stand trial on the breach-of-peace charges filed on May 25. This and other recent developments drew cheers that evening at a raucous White Citizens' Council rally in Montgomery. As more than 800 WCC members looked on, the special guest speaker, Governor Ross Barnett, reported that the "ruthless actions" of the Freedom Riders, the NAACP, and meddlers such as Chief Justice Earl Warren had backfired. Outside agitators were on the run, Barnett declared, and even in the North the integrationist cause was losing ground. Back in Jackson, according to the governor, the Freedom Riders were finally learning the full meaning of Mississippi justice.

On Wednesday morning Barnett's words took on added weight when Jim Bevel went on trial for contributing to the delinquency of a minor. Charged with enticing four local high school students to demonstrate in support of the Freedom Rides, Bevel refused Judge Russel Moore's offer of a light sentence in exchange for a no-contest plea. Acting as his own counsel, the twenty-four-year-old minister was eloquent in defending the young students' right to bear witness against the evil of Jim Crow, but not even Bevel, the most mystical of the Nashville Freedom Riders, could make any headway against the flow of racial tradition. Following a swift conviction, Moore issued the maximum sentence of $2,000 in fines and six months in jail. Bevel, who for the time being chose not to appeal, was behind bars by early afternoon. And he was not alone. Earlier in the day, while Bevel was standing trial, the Jackson police had arrested fifteen new Freedom Riders—all Episcopal priests—at the Trailways terminal. Since six weeks had passed since the last round of arrests on July 31, the priests' arrival at the city jail caused quite a stir, especially after the police and the press discovered that one of the arrested Freedom Riders was Robert L. Pierson, the thirty-five-year-old son-in-law of Nelson Rockefeller, the liberal Republican governor of New York.

On Saturday morning the press reported that the fifteen clergymen were still in the city jail praying "for the segregationists whose policies had led to their imprisonment." In Detroit, where a national Episcopal convention was in session, and in many other Northern cities, there were signs of sympathy for the jailed priests. Locally, however, any feelings of remorse were tempered by a wire service story detailing a pretrial conversation between Mayor Allen Thompson and the Reverend Lee Belford of New York. According to Thompson, Belford told him that the prayer pilgrimage "would have been worth it" even if it had led to violence. "Our church has a history of martyrdom," Belford proudly explained.

The wide philosophical gulf between white Christian segregationists and social gospel activists such as Belford became increasingly clear in the fall of 1961, as segregationist officials demonstrated their willingness to mete out harsh punishment to clergymen who violated the South's racial mores. On September 15, the same day that the fifteen priests faced Judge Spencer in Jackson, the Reverend

William Sloane Coffin and nine other ministerial Freedom Riders charged with breaching the peace were assessed $100 fines and sentenced to jail terms ranging from ten to fifteen days by Montgomery County Judge Alex Marks. The two local defendants, Ralph Abernathy and Bernard Lee, received ten-day sentences, but all the others, including Shuttlesworth, received fifteen days. An eleventh defendant, Wyatt Tee Walker, was actually acquitted on the breach-of-peace charge, but conviction on a related charge of unlawful assembly resulted in a ninety-day sentence. Explaining the severity of Walker's sentence, Judge Marks reasoned that the SCLC executive director's role as a liaison to the press made him especially dangerous. "There would have been very little trouble in Montgomery if there hadn't been so much publicity," Marks insisted. All of the defendants, including Walker, filed immediate appeals and accepted bail. But as they left the courthouse they could not help wondering how far Alabama officials were willing to go in their effort to ensnare the movement in a tangle of legal prosecutions.

Fred Shuttlesworth's effort to extract justice from the courts suggested a measure of faith in American democracy. For more than a decade the Birmingham minister had served as a model of assertive citizenship—a black man undeterred by bombs, beatings, and legal harassment. Encouraged by the *Brown* decision and the promise of a Second Reconstruction, he preached and practiced a gospel of rising expectations for black Americans. During the first eight months of the Kennedy presidency, the expansive rhetoric of the "New Frontier" boosted such expectations, and Shuttlesworth stepped up his demands for a realization of democratic ideals. Nevertheless, as the summer of the Freedom Rides came to a close, he and other movement leaders began to wonder if the new administration was capable of taking an unequivocal stand on matters of racial justice. Repeating the same pattern of mixed signals that had delayed the implementation of school desegregation during the Eisenhower years, the administration had adopted a policy of temporization that unintentionally sustained white supremacist resistance to social change. Indeed, by mid-September some segregationist leaders were declaring victory in the war against the Freedom Riders.

On Monday, September 18, the *Jackson Daily News* smugly trumpeted that local and state officials had rejected a desperate overture from CORE, which had "offered to halt their Freedom Rider program into Jackson" if Mississippi authorities agreed to withhold further prosecutions and let 250 pending appeal cases be adjudicated by the circuit and state supreme court justices. Quoting a weekend television interview with Mayor Allen Thompson, the *Daily News* reported that Jackson officials did not intend "to yield one inch in prosecuting those who violate our local laws." "There will be no letup in a single case," Thompson declared, "nor will we permit any other type of disturbance here which violates our laws. We feel we have completely broken the Freedom Rider movement here." The threat to the Mississippi way of life had been turned back, he insisted, adding: "If anything, things have improved in Jackson since the advent of the first Freedom Rider group here four months ago." Mississippians were allegedly more convinced than ever that "our way of life here is best for us, and for the most part, no one pays any attention to them anymore since our splendid police department is handling the situation."

Thompson's growing confidence rested on a sanguine but credible assessment of the situation. On the surface, at least, the Freedom Riders' prospects appeared to be declining on all fronts, from public opinion and politics to legal decisions and the financial condition of the movement. For several weeks the American public had been preoccupied with the home-run race between two New York Yankees sluggers, Mickey Mantle and Roger Maris. The pursuit of Babe Ruth's record of sixty home runs, set in 1927, had eclipsed all other stories, including the pursuit of freedom in Mississippi and Alabama. As Thompson and others detected, the dominant attitudes among white Americans reflected complacency and a visceral distrust of radical reform. Even among liberals there was a strong preference for gradualism and a hesitance to embrace confrontational activism.

Despite all that had happened during the past four months, there was no groundswell of public support for the Freedom Rides; indeed, the popular basis for altering long-standing political arrangements and legal traditions seemed to be slipping away. Most obviously, the legal strategy had revealed the movement's financial vulnerability. The common assumption that CORE stood on the verge of financial collapse by mid-September was understandable, but the organization's actual financial condition was less grave than Thompson and many other white Mississippians believed. Although Marvin Rich's effort to find a bail bond company willing to underwrite CORE's growing obligations proved futile (one Connecticut company agreed to advance the bond money but withdrew the offer the next day when Mississippi officials threatened to cancel its license to do business in the state), Jim Farmer found an unlikely angel at the NAACP Legal Defense and Educational Fund Inc., commonly known as the "Inc. (or Ink) Fund." Despite his strong misgivings about the wisdom of the Freedom Rides, Thurgood Marshall, who would soon leave his position as head of the fund to take a seat on the U.S. Second Circuit Court of Appeals, magnanimously offered to step into the breach. "What the hell!" he told Farmer, after learning of CORE's plight. "The Ink Fund has about $300,000 in bail-bond money. It's not doing anything but sitting there. You might as well use it as long as it lasts."

Stunned by Marshall's offer, Farmer "could hardly wait" to relay the good news to his CORE colleagues. But at a staff meeting the next morning he was surprised to discover that Rich was reluctant to accept the money. The fear that there would be strings attached to the loan and the suspicion that Marshall's organization planned to take partial credit for the Freedom Rides made Rich more than a little uncomfortable. Indeed, in light of the public criticism of the Rides by Marshall, Wilkins, and other national NAACP leaders, he found the offer galling, if not insulting. Earlier in the summer, one NAACP leader had jibed to reporters that "CORE gets people in jail and we have to get them out," but now for some reason the Inc. Fund was willing to put itself in financial jeopardy to save CORE. Rich smelled a rat. Farmer himself was mindful of the danger of becoming a junior partner to an organization that did not share CORE's commitment to direct action. But, having run out of viable alternatives, he waved off Rich's objections and accepted Marshall's offer.

Whatever Marshall's motivations, acceptance of the offer was, as Rich predicted, only a prelude to even greater Inc. Fund involvement in the Freedom Rider campaign. Following several weeks of discussion and negotiation between Farmer and Marshall, CORE's policy-making body, the National Action Committee, agreed to let the Inc. Fund take over the responsibility of representing the Mississippi Freedom Riders in court. By the end of November the transfer of responsibility was complete, lessening CORE's legal and financial burden but confirming the widespread suspicion among white Southerners that the NAACP had been masterminding the Freedom Rides all along.

Even with this infusion of funds, CORE faced a difficult road ahead. The only real solution to the organization's financial and legal problems was federal intervention on a massive scale, and the probability of such intervention was still in doubt as the summer of 1961 came to an official end on September 22. More than a month had passed since the members of ICC had listened to the oral arguments for and against Attorney General Kennedy's desegregation petition. And it had been almost four months since the filing of the petition itself. "The time has come for this commission to declare unequivocally by regulation," Kennedy had declared on May 29, "that a Negro passenger is free to travel the length and breadth of this country in the same manner as any other passenger." But time, it seemed, was marching on with no unequivocal resolution in sight. Growing increasingly impatient, CORE leaders in New York, as well as SNCC activists in Nashville, began to look for some means of forcing the ICC to issue a favorable ruling.

In early September tentative plans for a mass demonstration known as the "Washington Project" took shape. Patterned after A. Philip Randolph's planned 1941 March on Washington, the project would bring hundreds, perhaps even thousands, of nonviolent demonstrators to the capital city to apply pressure on the ICC and the Kennedy administration. The exact date of the march was yet to be determined, and movement leaders were still working out the logistical details as the summer drew to a close. But among the members of the FRCC there was general agreement that the situation required a "spectacular" demonstration of nonviolent commitment and solidarity. As Farmer declared in a September 5 press release, the Washington project would transfer "the struggle for dignity on the nation's highways from the courts to the conscience of America."

Whether the financially strapped nonviolent movement could have pulled off a march of this magnitude in the fall of 1961 remains an open question. The proposed demonstration that seemed so critical as late as September 21 became moot a day later when the eleven commissioners of the ICC issued a unanimous ruling prohibiting racial discrimination in interstate bus transit. Endorsing virtually every point in the attorney general's petition, the commission announced that, beginning on November 1, 1961, all interstate buses would be required to display a certificate that read: "Seating aboard this vehicle is without regard to race, color, creed, or national origin, by order of the Interstate Commerce Commission." Displaying the signs would be mandatory until January 1, 1963, but the commission reserved the right to extend the requirement indefinitely. Beginning in 1963, federal law would require the same text to be printed on all bus tickets "sold for transportation in interstate or foreign commerce." As of November 1, all terminals serving interstate buses would be required to post and abide by the new ICC regulations. Interstate carriers were forbidden to use racially segregated terminal facilities, which, according to the commissioners, were still common "in a substantial part of the United States." "In many motor passenger terminals," they reported, with a suggestion of feigned surprise, "Negro interstate passengers are compelled to use eating, rest room and other facilities which are segregated."

In an important point of clarification that raised more than a few eyebrows in movement circles, the commissioners indicated that their desegregation order "would not be applicable . . . to every independently operated roadside restaurant at which a bus stops solely to pick up or discharge passengers, or to every independently operated corner drug store which sells tickets for a motor carrier. Where a carrier's ticket agent does nothing more for the benefit of the carrier's passengers than sell tickets and post schedules, we would not consider his place of business to be a terminal facility." However, the commissioners made it clear that the new rules applied to any ticket agent who "offers or provides facilities for the comfort and convenience of passengers, such as a public waiting room, rest room, or eating facilities." The ICC order also required bus operators to report any attempts to interfere with the new regulations and provided fines of up to $500 for each violation. The obligation to report interference within fifteen days of an incident pertained to governmental as well as individual violators, a provision that would prove crucial to enforcement in the months to come.

The ICC ruling applied only to interstate bus transportation and did not extend to air or train travel, but within these limitations the commissioners had gone about as far anyone in the Kennedy administration could have reasonably expected. William Tucker, the Kennedy appointee to the commission, had consulted with Burke Marshall and other Justice Department officials throughout the deliberations, and those same officials had encouraged Tucker to press for a sweeping ruling that would resolve the Freedom Rider crisis and ensure meaningful desegregation. Still, until the ruling was actually announced there was concern within the administration that the conservative bent of the other commissioners would foil Tucker's efforts. Since anything short of a complete endorsement of the attorney general's position would have sustained or even exacerbated the conflict over bus segregation, Marshall and his colleagues regarded the ruling as a major accomplishment.

Whatever its origins, the ICC ruling drew considerable praise from the national press. Even editors who had expressed serious misgivings about the Freedom Rides hailed the ruling as a legal and administrative milestone. Although many expressed surprise at the scope of the ruling, outside of the South there was a strong current of editorial support for the commission's advanced position. Almost everyone credited the attorney general with precipitating the ruling, but there was also widespread recognition that the Freedom Rides had been a crucial factor in both the timing and character of the ICC's deliberations. "Much of the credit for overcoming the inertia and political resistance that hamstrung the I.C.C. before on this issue must obviously go to the Freedom Rider movement of last spring," a New York Times editorial declared two days after the ruling. "Though, as we argued at the time, the movement raised dangers when it continued beyond the realization of its point of focusing attention on the need for integrated interstate bus transportation, nevertheless that demonstration started the chain of events which resulted in the new I.C.C. order."

The notion that the Freedom Rides had catalyzed the ruling was even stronger among white Southern editors, the vast majority of whom rejected the rationale for the commission's newfound activism. Repeating the pattern established in the mid-1950s following the Brown decision, many segregationist editors tried to downplay the significance of the ruling. Some made passing references to a minor adjustment in administrative policy, and others ignored the ruling altogether. But, other than the expected expressions of outrage by Citizens' Council stalwarts, there were few calls for outright defiance or massive resistance.

Among the more thoughtful segregationists, this restraint reflected a spirit of resignation, a sense that desegregation was inevitable. For many others, however, an entirely different set of expectations was at work. To most white Southerners, the ICC ruling appeared to be just another unenforceable edict. In May 1955 the Supreme Court had ordered the implementation of school desegregation "with all deliberate speed," yet six years later all but a handful of Southern schools remained segregated. In November 1955 the ICC had ordered the desegregation of interstate railway travel, yet racial segregation was still the general rule on Southern trains in 1961. Perhaps this time it would be different, but historical experience suggested that there was no reason for segregationists to panic.

Such skepticism was also prevalent among black Americans. In the black press, as in the broader black community, past disappointments tempered the response to the ICC ruling. Virtually all of the editorials and public statements praising the ruling included a word or two of warning. The true value of the ruling, black editors and civil rights leaders pointed out, depended on the degree of enforcement—a condition that would only be revealed in the weeks and months following implementation on November 1. Every major civil rights organization, from CORE to the NAACP, sent telegrams of congratulation to the Justice Department, but in private conversations, and in some cases in press releases, these same organizations expressed concerns about the likelihood of effective enforcement. Farmer went even further, reminding the attorney general that, in and of itself, the ICC ruling did not solve the legal problems of the Freedom Riders convicted in Jackson. Although Farmer promised that "no additional riders would be recruited and sent to Mississippi," he informed Kennedy that "those already in jail would continue serving their forty days." Beginning on November 1, Farmer added, CORE "would send out interracial teams to crisscross the South and test the enforcement of the order." If enforcement proved lacking or haphazard, he warned, the Freedom Rides "would resume immediately."

The ICC ruling had an immediate impact on the Freedom Rider movement. Suspending the preparations for the Washington Project, movement leaders began to plan a new wave of Freedom Rides designed to test enforcement of the ruling. At the CORE office in New York and at the FRCC recruitment centers in the South, the next six weeks would be a time of feverish activity and hopeful speculation about the future. Seven years after *Brown* and fourteen years after *Morgan v. Virginia*, a major federal agency other than the Justice Department had finally weighed in on the side of racial justice, mandating desegregation as something more than an unrealized ideal. Whether the rhetoric of equal treatment could be translated into something tangible remained to be seen. But this time, unlike the "with all deliberate speed" waffling of the 1955 *Brown* implementation decision, there was a firm date for compliance. Government officials had set a date for desegregation, and Farmer and other movement leaders were determined to hold them to it.

The prospects for enforcement depended upon a number of unknowns, including the level of commitment at the Justice Department, the response of local and state officials, and the willingness of white Southerners to obey federal law and to eschew violence. The last of these was perhaps the most difficult to predict, but the initial signs following the ruling were not encouraging, at least as far as John Doar was concerned. Just hours before the announcement of the ICC decision, Doar arrived in Mississippi to conduct an investigation of the situation in Amite, Pike, and Walthall counties. For three days he roamed around McComb and Liberty, gauging both the status of the voting rights campaign and the mood of local white supremacists. By Sunday morning he was convinced that southwestern Mississippi was a racial time bomb that could explode at any time.

The determination of Mississippi's state and local officials to maintain the status quo was on full display in a Jackson courtroom the following week. After a fifteen-week delay, the NAACP's lawsuit challenging the legality of segregated public transportation in Mississippi finally gained a hearing from a three-judge federal panel headed by Circuit Judge Richard Rives of Montgomery. Flanked by two conservative Mississippi jurists, Sidney Mize of Gulfport and Claude Clayton of Tupelo, the liberal Rives made a valiant effort to give the NAACP suit a fair and proper hearing, but no amount of judicial decorum could dampen the tension and hostility that filled the courtroom. A close friend of Justice Hugo Black's, Rives was widely regarded as a traitor to the white South, and Mize and Clayton made no effort to conceal their disdain for his heretical views.

During the four-day hearing, NAACP attorney Constance Baker Motley presented a string of witnesses, including several bus and railway company representatives and NAACP field secretary Medgar Evers. All testified to the pervasiveness of segregated transit in Mississippi, and Evers described a harrowing personal incident that had taken place on a Trailways bus in Meridian in March 1958, when he was physically accosted for not moving to the back of the bus when ordered to do so. Evers, a World War II combat veteran, fought back, forcing his stunned attacker to flee from the bus. With Evers still sitting in the front seat, the bus continued on to Jackson without any additional confrontations.

Evers's testimony was disturbing to white supremacists on several counts, including the suggestions that native black Mississippians were dissatisfied with the present system of racial segregation and that even the police were sometimes uncertain about their authority to enforce Jim Crow laws. Even so, several witnesses for the state did their best to reassure the court that racial separation and social order were still synonymous in Mississippi. "It has been a policy of mine and the city council, the police department and the people," Mayor Allen Thompson of Jackson declared on Tuesday morning, "to maintain what has worked for the past one hundred years to bring happiness, peace and prosperity. That has been to maintain a separation of the races—not segregation, we don't call it segregation—to maintain peace and order and to keep down disturbances . . . Laws can come and laws can go and laws can change. But the policy we have adopted here has been to maintain happiness and contentment between the races and to live together in peace and quiet."

The notion that Mississippi's traditions fostered tranquility—as the state contended—drew a strong objection from Motley, who countered with several witnesses who had been arrested or beaten for challenging Jim Crow transit. Noting that most of the incidents in question occurred outside of Jackson, Attorney General Joe Patterson and city attorneys reiterated an earlier objection to the statewide scope of the NAACP suit. Since the court had already ruled that the attorney general could not be held responsible for the breach-of-peace arrests in Jackson, Motley was in a difficult position, but she continued to press for an injunction that would invalidate segregated transit throughout the state.

Following closing arguments on Thursday morning, the four-day hearing came to an end, though not without a measure of confusion. Catching almost everyone off guard, Judge Rives announced that he was ready to issue a preliminary injunction "removing segregation signs from all waiting rooms," prohibiting the arrest of Freedom Riders under breach-of-peace statutes, and directing the Jackson City Lines to cease enforcement of racial segregation on city buses. While he stopped short of advocating an injunction against Greyhound, Trailways, or Attorney General Patterson, Rives's announcement sent a shudder through the courtroom. Suddenly all eyes turned to Mize and Clayton, either one of whom could turn Rives's revolutionary proposal into a legal mandate. Those familiar with the two Mississippi jurists had no reason to believe that Rives's judgment would be sustained, but some segregationists were disappointed when Clayton refused to comment and Mize offered only a curt statement that he was "not prepared to express any opinion or give any views at this time."

In the days following Rives's announcement, there was considerable speculation about the likelihood and implications of a preliminary injunction. In Nashville, where SCLC was wrapping up its annual three-day convention, even a slight chance that such an injunction might be granted was greeted as welcome news. Three days earlier, on the eve of the convention, Martin Luther King had hailed the ICC ruling as proof that the Freedom Riders' struggle "had not been in vain." The desegregation of buses and terminals was imminent, he insisted, and the nonviolent movement would soon move on to other challenges, including the goal of doubling the number of black voters in the South by the end of the year. "We are willing to suffer, sacrifice and die, if necessary, to make that freedom a reality," he declared, adding that the struggle for racial equality was actually a fight "to save the soul of the nation."

How the nation as a whole would respond to nonviolent activity of this magnitude was a subject of considerable debate in civil rights circles during the fall of 1961. But movement leaders had already learned valuable lessons about what to expect in the Deep South. In McComb, for example, they had discovered that voting rights agitation was just as dangerous as other forms of direct action. Contrary to the expectations of Justice Department officials, most white segregationists seemed to put black voter registration efforts in the same category as sit-ins and freedom rides. Regardless of the specific issue at hand, a fixation on a broad-based conspiracy of "outside agitators" invalidated the claim to legitimate dissent. Later in the decade—following the 1963 March on Washington, the Civil Rights Acts of 1964 and 1965, and other expressions of movement strength and solidarity—the notion of the civil rights movement's legitimacy would become a grudgingly accepted fact of life among white Southerners. But in 1961 such acceptance was rare, especially in the Deep South where racial demography and the dictates of caste and class kept open dissent to a minimum. Unbeknownst to all but a few whites, and to many blacks as well, there were untapped sources of movement strength, even in the most remote black communities. But the conditions had to be right, as they were in the wake of the Freedom Rides, for this unrealized potential to become a meaningful part of the political landscape.

The movement that emerged in Albany, Georgia, during the fall of 1961 demonstrated just how quickly an external provocation could energize internal dissent. Within days of their arrival in a seemingly placid community of sixty thousand, SNCC activists Charles Sherrod and Cordell Reagon turned a series of church prayer meetings at Shiloh Baptist Church into an insurgent revolt against racial complacency. With the black proportion of the local population hovering around 40 percent and a tradition of nonconfrontational race relations, Albany supported a struggling NAACP branch with a declining membership. At the height of its influence, in the years following World War II, the Albany branch had mounted a successful voter registration drive that produced an expectation of black participation in local public life. But a decade and a half later the city remained rigidly segregated.

In May 1961, Tom Chatmon, a local black businessman, organized an NAACP Youth Council with the intention of nudging white officials towards gradual reform. Like Martin Luther King, Chatmon had attended Morehouse College during the late 1940s, but he did not share King's faith in militant direct action. Instead, he counseled Albany's black youth to be patient and ever-mindful of their elders' vulnerability. Alarmed by rumors of SNCC's growing influence among the Youth Council members who were reportedly enthralled by tales of Freedom Rides and sit-ins, Chatmon warned local and regional NAACP leaders that Sherrod and Reagon were playing with fire. Though not unmindful of Chatmon's limitations, Vernon Jordan, Georgia's NAACP field secretary, shared the Youth Council leader's concerns and did what he could to discourage any further SNCC interference. In mid-October, several local NAACP leaders informed the two troublesome SNCC workers that they were no longer welcome in the city. But Sherrod and Reagon, confident that something significant was stirring among their young followers, had no intention of leaving. Indeed, several of the most adventurous Youth Council members had already informed Chatmon that they planned to participate in a desegregation test at the Albany Trailways terminal on November 1.

Fearing that he was about to lose all credibility with his charges, Chatmon reluctantly agreed to consider the idea, and in late October he met with Sherrod and Reagon to work out a compromise that would protect both the students and the local reputation of the NAACP. All agreed that there would be no mention of NAACP involvement and that the students would suspend the test if and when arrests became imminent. Though somewhat uncomfortable with the latter restriction, Sherrod and Reagon decided not to force the issue. Despite the NAACP's foot-dragging, their organizational efforts were progressing much faster than they had hoped, and they were eager to share the good news with their colleagues in Mississippi. On October 30, they boarded a bus for a whirlwind trip to McComb, where they planned to discuss the situation in Albany and to attend the trial of three SNCC colleagues. Two days later, if all went well, they would return to Albany as Freedom Riders testing the ICC order. The students, Chatmon promised, would meet them in the white waiting room of the Trailways station for a joint test.

Sherrod and Reagon returned to Albany via the SNCC office in Atlanta, where they met with James Forman and Charles Jones on Halloween night. Forman and Jones were busy making final preparations for their own ICC test—an early morning visit to Jake's Fine Foods Restaurant at the downtown Atlanta Trailways station. But they offered Sherrod and Reagon an official observer for the four-hour bus run to Albany. Salynn McCollum, the veteran Freedom Rider from Nashville's Peabody College who had been hired as one of SNCC's first white staff members, was eager to go along, and when the morning bus to Albany left the Trailways station she was on it. Avoiding any direct contact with Sherrod and Reagon, she sat quietly among the white passengers as the drama of Georgia's first compliance test unfolded. Halfway along the route, the bus was pulled over to the side of the road by Georgia state troopers who walked up and down the aisle before waving the driver on. Although Sherrod and Reagon were sitting in the front section behind the driver, there were no arrests. But it was clear that authorities in Atlanta and Albany knew that a Freedom Ride was in progress.

Arriving at the Albany Trailways station at 6:30 in the morning, Sherrod and Reagon, with McCollum trailing well behind, strolled into the waiting room expecting to see the familiar faces of the Youth Council volunteers. To their surprise and dismay, however, not a single volunteer was there to greet them. Fearing that the students were already in jail and after looking warily at the police patrolling the waiting room, they quietly exited the station in search of their missing disciples. After a few frantic phone calls, they learned that there had been no arrests and no attempt to desegregate the station. The students had stayed away because they had become convinced that local white supremacists planned to beat or even kill them if they tried to test compliance with the ICC order.

In actuality, Albany's police chief, Laurie Pritchett, had convinced Mayor Asa Kelley and the city commission that the best way to handle Freedom Riders was to avoid violence at all costs. At a special closed meeting of the city commission on October 30, Pritchett had outlined a strategy patterned after that of the Jackson police: vigilante violence would be preempted by timely arrests, and the basis for all Freedom Rider arrests would be the maintenance of public order, not the violation of segregation laws. That the rumor mill in the black community suggested just the opposite spoke volumes about the underlying insecurities and fears that dominated race relations in the city. How Sherrod and Reagon were able to quiet such fears is not altogether clear, but by mid-afternoon they had convinced nine Youth Council members to violate the sanctity of the same white waiting room that they had been afraid to enter only hours before.

With the two SNCC workers watching from a nearby street corner, and with McCollum observing from an even closer vantage point, the nine students walked into the waiting room to confront the unjust power of the white establishment. "The bus station was full of men in blue," Sherrod later wrote, "but up through the mass of people, past the men with guns and billies ready, into the terminal they marched, quiet and clean. They were allowed to buy tickets to Florida but after sitting in the waiting room they were asked to leave under threat of arrest.

Although they did so immediately, the significance of what they had already accomplished soon became apparent. By standing up for their constitutional rights, however briefly, they had broken the spell of unchallenged dominance. As Sherrod put it, "From that moment on, segregation was dead." In the aftermath of the November 1 confrontation, the black community in Albany seemed to take on a new spirit of assertiveness and pride. Indeed, despite persistent disputes over organizational authority and the advisability of outside involvement in the local struggle, the expectation of direct and even militant action would soon become a widely accepted fact of life in Albany.

By the end of the year the gathering movement in Albany would become one of the freedom struggle's most visible manifestations. But in early November it was still a minor sideshow in the larger drama prompted by the implementation and testing of the ICC order. At the CORE and NAACP offices in New York, at SCLC's headquarters in Atlanta, and at the FRCC recruiting stations around the South, the focus of attention by November was the systematic testing of the ICC's order by several hundred volunteers. After weeks of careful preparation, CORE, acting on behalf of the FRCC, dispatched several dozen bands of Freedom Riders during the first week of November. With Gordon Carey and Marvin Rich serving as the primary coordinators, teams of testers traveled designated routes in sixteen states, from the Deep South to the border regions of Oklahoma, Kentucky, Maryland, and Delaware. The goal was to get a comprehensive picture of compliance and noncompliance that could be reported to the press and forwarded to the ICC and the Justice Department.

Publicly CORE and other FRCC leaders predicted near universal compliance, but privately they conceded that there was no way of knowing how the white South would respond to the ICC order. In truth, they expected a mixed response, ranging from gracious acceptance to grudging acknowledgment to outright resistance. Since the mass testing represented the most ambitious short-term project ever attempted by CORE or any other civil rights organization, there were also concerns about logistical shortcomings and possible lapses in nonviolent discipline. While some of the testers were veterans of earlier Freedom Rides, most were new and untested volunteers—a less than ideal situation for a movement that could ill afford a misstep. Since CORE wanted the tests to replicate the experiences of normal travelers, local volunteers were essential, but this strategy carried obvious risks. Whatever the degree of compliance, getting to the end of the day without suffering an embarrassing incident or losing anyone along the way would be an accomplishment in itself.

Fortunately for CORE, as the reports trickled in during the first week of testing, it became clear that even the unseasoned testers were living up to the high standards of poise and discipline that had characterized the Freedom Rider movement since early May. Perhaps even more important, the reports indicated that most of the testers were encountering less resistance than expected. The best news came out of Virginia, Kentucky, Texas, and West Virginia, where the tests found total compliance. In Florida, where tests were conducted at bus stations in Jacksonville and the Panhandle communities of Tallahassee and Marianna, there was compliance but no sign of the required ICC postings; the same was true in Arkansas, where Freedom Riders were served at bus stations in six cities. In Tennessee there was compliance in four of the five bus stations tested, with mandated segregation persisting only in the small town of Linden. In North Carolina the only community to enforce transit segregation on the first day of the new order was the tiny Piedmont town of Wadesboro, just down the road from Monroe. And in Oklahoma noncompliance was limited to McAlester, a remote hill town in the southeastern part of the state.

The reports from the Deep South, though decidedly mixed, were more troubling. In South Carolina testers were served without incident in Charleston, Columbia, Greenville, Rock Hill, Spartanburg, and Sumter, but segregated facilities persisted in Camden, Florence, and Lancaster. In some South Carolina communities—in Camden, where a follow-up test revealed compliance, and in Greenville, where the manager of the Trailways station endorsed compliance but insisted that many black passengers were confused by the ICC order and "didn't know where to sit"—the situation was difficult to evaluate. Similar inconsistencies appeared in Louisiana, where compliance was generally limited to New Orleans and the southern Cajun parishes. When a group of Freedom Riders arrived in the southwest Louisiana town of Crowley, they were greeted by "policemen armed with sawed-off shotguns and tear gas guns." Though fearing the worst, the Riders soon learned that the somewhat over-zealous local sheriff simply "wanted to avoid an Alabama or Mississippi incident." Adding to the confusion, the waiting room at the Crowley Greyhound terminal complied with the ICC order, but the adjacent terminal restaurant remained closed to black patrons. There was more consistency in the northern and central part of the state, where Freedom Riders encountered stiff resistance from police determined to maintain segregated facilities. In Shreveport, Monroe, Alexandria, and Lafayette, black Riders were barred from entering white waiting rooms, and in Baton Rouge a terminal restaurant was closed. When the manager of the Shreveport Trailways terminal defied a police order and removed several "whites only" signs, he ended up in jail. And when Trailways officials removed segregation signs in Alexandria, a state judge immediately ordered the installation of new signs.

The situation was no less confusing in Georgia, where state officials had taken preliminary steps to challenge the legality of the ICC order in federal court but where Freedom Riders also found compliance in a number of communities, including Thomasville, Valdosta, Macon, and Augusta. At this point the only sign of active noncompliance outside of Albany was an ugly incident at the Atlanta Trailways station, where Jim Forman, Charles Jones, Bernard Lafayette, and Jim Bevel were arrested after trying to desegregate the whites-only lunch counter at Jake's Fine Foods. The Atlanta arrests surprised some movement observers who had expected more from a city that had taken the first steps toward school desegregation earlier in the year. But no one was surprised by the turmoil that ensued when CORE testers attempted to desegregate bus station facilities in Birmingham, Alabama.

Hoping to avoid violence, CORE leaders scheduled a minimal number of tests in Alabama. The symbolic importance of Birmingham, however, was impossible to ignore, and Freedom Riders were sent into the city on November 3. Two days earlier, on the day the ICC order went into effect, the trial of the Anniston bus burners had opened in the courtroom of U.S. District Judge H. Hobart Grooms, an unfortunate coincidence that concerned both government and movement observers. Almost simultaneously Grooms's colleague in Montgomery, Judge Frank Johnson, had issued an injunction enjoining Trailways and Greyhound officials, as well as state and local officials, from maintaining segregation among interstate passengers at any of the terminals located in the twenty-three counties of the Middle District of Alabama. Unfortunately, this injunction did not apply to Birmingham or Bull Connor, who promised to arrest anyone who violated the city's segregation ordinances. Though somewhat less specific, Governor Patterson appeared to endorse Connor's threat, labeling Johnson's ruling an "insult to every citizen of Alabama." If the Freedom Riders "continue to invade our state and continue to try to run over us," Patterson warned, "we want to serve notice that we are going to defend ourselves, and we are not going to take it lying down." This bluster did not prevent compliance in several Alabama towns and cities, including Anniston, where CORE testers successfully desegregated the lunch counters at both of the city's bus terminals. But Connor's Birmingham was another matter.

When the testers arrived at the Birmingham Greyhound station, the required ICC posting was, predictably, nowhere in sight. But Ralph Sizemore, the thirty-four-year-old manager of the Greyhound cafeteria, agreed to serve the testers anyway. Moments later, a Birmingham policeman stepped forward to arrest Sizemore for violating a city ordinance outlawing mixed dining. While the Freedom Riders themselves escaped arrest, Sizemore was carted off to jail before being released on a $100 bond. On November 5, when Freedom Riders made a second attempt to desegregate the cafeteria, Sizemore was rearrested along with two waitresses. And over the next three days the plucky manager was arrested two more times. Caught in the middle, Greyhound officials urged the Justice Department to intervene, but department officials in Washington were reluctant to do so, fearing that a precipitous attempt to enforce the ICC order would only make matters worse.

The only "official" response from the federal government came from Malcolm Weaver, the U.S. attorney in Birmingham, who worked out a tentative compromise with city attorney John Breckinridge. If the city called a halt to the arrests, Weaver promised, the Justice Department would not contest state court jurisdiction over the Sizemore case. Summarily rejected by Bull Connor, the proposed agreement had little discernible effect on a legal impasse that would bedevil lawyers and politicians for several months. But the Justice Department's timidity did not go unnoticed among movement leaders awaiting confirmation of the department's determination to enforce the ICC order.

Judging by the early reports from Mississippi, the ICC was going to need all the help it could get. Although there was an encouraging report from the Delta town of Greenville, where a group of interracial testers was served without incident, Mississippi Freedom Riders met stiff resistance everywhere else. In Hamilton and Tupelo testers were told that the local bus stations had been closed "for repairs," and in a dozen other communities the ICC order was simply ignored. In Grenada city officials challenged the order with a new ordinance prohibiting race mixing in all public facilities, and in Meridian the police installed new signs directing passengers to separate waiting rooms. In the Vicksburg station the ICC order was prominently displayed, but that did not stop the local police from escorting two black Freedom Riders out of the white waiting room.

Although the Vicksburg testers avoided arrest, three Freedom Riders who tried to desegregate the Jackson Trailways terminal were not so fortunate. The first tester arrested was the Reverend Charles Jones, dean of Campbell Junior College, the institution that had welcomed the McComb students expelled from Burgland High School. Entering the white waiting room at the Trailways terminal just after dawn, Jones was promptly arrested for breaching the peace. An hour later a policeman patrolling the same waiting room arrested Levert Taylor and Glenda Jackson, two veterans of Shreveport CORE who had just arrived on an overnight bus. In Jackson, as in McComb, bus company officials had posted the ICC order and had even painted over the "white" and "colored" door signs that identified separate waiting rooms. But just before the order went into effect, city officials in both cities countermanded these actions by placing temporary Jim Crow signs on the sidewalks adjacent to the cities' bus and railway stations. When asked to explain this apparent inconsistency, Mayor Thompson told reporters that he had consented to the ICC posting and the sign removal because he "didn't want to embarrass the bus and train people." Denying that the arrests at the Trailways station constituted a violation of the ICC order, he repeated the familiar refrain that he was simply trying to keep the peace. "We're going to see that there's no violence from these agitators coming from the outside," he declared with a hint of a smile, "even if we have to have policemen for each one."

Though not unexpected, the situation in Mississippi posed a difficult problem for movement leaders, who did not want to give the impression that white Southerners were defying the ICC order with impunity. Allowing stories of resistance to overshadow evidence of compliance would not serve the interests of the movement, but neither would ignoring or glossing over outright acts of defiance. Somehow Farmer, Carey, and Rich had to find a way to accentuate the positive while simultaneously pointing out the need for continued pressure from activists and governmental officials. CORE leaders adopted a similar strategy in early November when they forwarded a systematic report to the Justice Department and the ICC. In this and other communications, the message was clear: Timely enforcement of the ICC order was crucial. Straightforward and prescriptive, the order presented a welcome alternative to the "all deliberate speed" syndrome that had slowed the pace of school desegregation. But it also carried a sobering responsibility to assert the authority and legitimacy of federal law. If the Justice Department allowed a defiant minority to ignore the order, the consequences could be catastrophic, not only for the cause of desegregation but also for the broader interests of the Kennedy administration. After six months of involuntary zigzagging across the political landscape, the Freedom Rider crisis had finally brought the administration to a crossroads. Like it or not, federal authorities entrusted with enforcement of the ICC order faced a clear choice that would influence the course of American democracy for months or even years to come.

Despite the foot-dragging in Birmingham, proof of federal resolve came almost immediately. In fact, the Justice Department's first request for an injunction enjoining local officials from obstructing compliance actually preceded the ICC order by several hours. On October 31 department attorneys asked District Judge Claude Clayton to overrule a state circuit court order forbidding the removal of Jim Crow signs at the Greenwood, Mississippi, bus station. Clayton refused to grant an immediate restraining order, but he scheduled a November 20 hearing to discuss the matter. Though disappointed with Clayton's response, Justice officials decided to take even bolder action three days later. Responding to both the Greenwood situation and the obstructionist actions of city officials in McComb, a suit filed with the federal district court in Jackson requested the convening of a three-judge federal panel that could rule on the constitutionality of Mississippi's bus segregation laws. The suit targeted McComb and named Mayor C. H. Douglas and Police Chief George Guy as defendants. On November 3 a similar suit was filed against officials in Monroe, Louisiana, and department officials promised additional actions would be forthcoming in other non-compliant communities. Almost simultaneously, the ICC district office announced that it had opened an investigation of complaints by Levert Taylor and Glenda Jackson, the two Louisiana Freedom Riders arrested in Jackson on November 1.

The balance sheet at the end of the first week of implementation was mixed but generally encouraging. Although several Deep South communities were resisting the order, there were signs of hope almost everywhere—even in Birmingham. On November 7 an unidentified high-level official at the Justice Department hinted to one Birmingham reporter that additional arrests at the Trailways café would force the government to seek relief in the federal courts. The attorney general, the official was careful to add, preferred to avoid such action, but the department was ready to add Birmingham to the growing list of communities under a court order to desegregate. Adding force to this threat, on the following day Judge Grooms issued an injunction prohibiting the city of Birmingham from enforcing segregation in public parks, theaters, and auditoriums.

Despite these promising developments, CORE and other movement leaders were wary of putting too much faith in federal power. Even though outright defiance of the ICC order was limited to the Deep South, resistance to the spirit of the law clearly extended to all parts of the segregated South. Segregation in intrastate transit and other public accommodations remained almost universal across the region, and even in the border states the color line was, with few exceptions, still in force. The extent and persistence of discrimination became painfully clear during the second week of November when CORE activists stepped up the pressure along Route 40 in an action designed to complement an ongoing federal desegregation initiative. Seven weeks earlier, on September 13, State Department protocol officer Richard Sanjuan had addressed the Maryland legislature on the importance of eliminating segregation along the diplomatic corridor from Washington to New York. Couched in the rhetoric of Cold War patriotism, Sanjuan's appeal stressed the international implications of discrimination. "When an American citizen humiliates a foreign representative or another American citizen for racial reasons," he insisted, "the results can be just as damaging to his country as the passing of secret information to the enemy." Stunned by the bluntness of Sanjuan's words, and more incensed than chastened, the Maryland legislators promptly dug in their heels on the Route 40 desegregation issue. CORE, however, seized upon the Sanjuan episode as a rationale for organizing a formal campaign to desegregate Route 40.

In mid-October Washington CORE leader Julius Hobson announced plans for a massive Freedom Ride to be held on Saturday, November 11. Hoping to dramatize the issue in a way that would force Maryland governor Millard Tawes to call a special legislative session for the purpose of passing an equal access public accommodations law, CORE recruited a large number of Riders willing to stage sit-ins at restaurants along the route. Behind the scenes, Hobson and others, including Sanjuan, tried to persuade the restaurant owners to desegregate voluntarily. But there were few signs of cooperation until early November, when the ICC order gave added force to the effort. On November 8, just three days before the scheduled sit-ins, forty-seven restaurants (thirty-five in Maryland and twelve in Delaware) agreed to desegregate. Although this left approximately half of the restaurants outside of the agreement, CORE leaders decided to suspend the scheduled protest. Declaring a partial victory, Hobson congratulated the compliant restaurant owners and managers but warned that CORE would conduct a series of desegregation tests later in the month.

Though the Route 40 campaign was far from over, its trajectory provided movement leaders with a measure of encouragement. While no one expected limited progress in the borderlands to resolve the impasse in the Deep South, the State Department's unofficial alliance with Maryland CORE reinforced the expectation that the Justice Department would do whatever was necessary to enforce the ICC order. Reaching beyond bus terminals and the ICC mandate, the Route 40 campaign also demonstrated the broadening sweep of the Freedom Rider movement. Even universal compliance with the ICC order, it now seemed, would not bring the crisis to a close. As many segregationists had feared, partial desegregation had unleashed a revolution of rising expectations that virtually ensured a recurring cycle of movement and resistance. For movement activists, the Freedom Rides, along with sit-ins and other forms of nonviolent direct action, had confirmed the power of public protest, signaling the emergence of a new democratic ethos. Thus, even though the desegregation of interstate transportation was far from complete in November 1961 and federal officials remained reluctant to force the issue in the absence of outright violence, observers close to the action were confident that the ICC order was propelling the Freedom Riders towards the Promised Land.

As the year of the Freedom Rides drew to a close, crises in such hardened places as McComb, Mississippi, and Albany, Georgia, confirmed that, despite a general pattern of compliance with the ICC order, there was a great deal of desegregation work left to be done in the Deep South. "A well-advertised group of Freedom Riders may receive police protection," columnist Anthony Lewis wrote in the *New York Times* on December 3, "but it would probably still be a brave, indeed foolhardy local Negro who sat down at the 'white' restaurant in an Alabama or Mississippi bus terminal." While he predicted "that acceptance of Federal law is only a matter of time—in short, inevitable," Lewis warned his readers that "ending the deep-seated tradition of racial discrimination will be a long and difficult process," especially in places like Mississippi where "one should beware of false optimism." Indeed, even in the Upper South and border states, where virtually all terminals, buses, and trains were desegregated, there were pockets of dogged segregationist resistance, as a series of arrests at several Route 40 restaurants demonstrated on December 16.

For the most part, however, movement leaders and administration officials were pleased with the overall response to implementation of transit desegregation. In most areas outright resistance had been replaced by a spirit of resignation, and evidence of real progress could be seen in some of the South's toughest white supremacist strongholds. Even in Birmingham, where Bull Connor sustained a spirited rear-guard political action against desegregation of bus terminal restaurants, there was some grudging movement toward compliance by mid-December. After Connor urged the city commission to revoke the Trailways restaurant's license because it violated the city's segregated dining ordinance, an influential local businessmen's group countered with a call for compliance with federal law. On December 14 the Justice Department tried to preempt Connor's action by seeking a federal injunction against any further interference with the ICC order in Birmingham. But five days later—following a public hearing—the city commission voted unanimously to revoke the license, all but forcing the federal courts to intervene. In early January 1962 Federal District Judge Seybourn H. Lynne, a conservative segregationist, surprised many local observers by issuing a temporary injunction that nullified the commission's action. Left with no legal alternative, Connor and the commissioners conceded defeat on the narrow issue of segregated transit facilities and transferred their energies to other fronts in the war against desegregation and federal encroachment. While the broader struggle to preserve Alabama's white supremacist traditions went on, the battle of the Birmingham bus terminals was over.

The prospects for compliance with the ICC order were also improving in Mississippi, though here the situation was muddled by mixed signals from the federal courts and by continued reliance on local breach-of-peace ordinances. Even though the traditional Jim Crow signs had been removed from the bus and rail terminals in Jackson and other cities, the threat of arrest remained for anyone who attempted to desegregate white waiting rooms and lunch counters. Lacking Chief Laurie Pritchett's political and diplomatic skills, and burdened with the stigma of the Freedom Rider trials, Jackson officials made little effort to conceal their segregationist intentions. Consequently, on December 14, the Justice Department joined the NAACP's appeal of the federal district court's refusal to grant an injunction enjoining the use of segregationist breach-of-peace statutes in Mississippi. In a written brief filed with the U.S. Supreme Court Associate Justice Hugo Black, Solicitor General Archibald Cox complained that "hundreds of American citizens" had been "arrested and convicted for merely claiming their constitutional rights."

Two days later, a long-awaited Supreme Court ruling on a Baton Rouge sit-in case that involved similar misuse of breach-of-peace statutes temporarily raised hopes that the court would grant at least a temporary stay of the ongoing prosecution of more than three hundred Mississippi Freedom Riders. Reversing the convictions of sixteen blacks arrested for causing civil disorder in Baton Rouge, the court's reasoning seemed to open the door for the ultimate dismissal of charges against all of the Riders convicted in Jackson. But on Monday, December 18, the court stunned NAACP attorneys and Justice Department officials with a unanimous ruling rejecting the request for a stay. Although the stated basis of the rejection was narrow and hinged on a technical interpretation of legal standing—the three defendants representing the class action had not been arrested for breach of peace—the court's ruling sent a chill through movement and government leaders already weary from several months of seemingly unnecessary and gratuitous complications.

"It is important not to read too much into the Supreme Court's refusal," a New York Times editorial counseled. But among those who had grown accustomed to victory at the highest level of judicial review, this was not easy advice to follow. Coming one week before the most cherished day of the Christian faith, the unexpected twist of legal defeat provided yet another reminder that unmerited suffering was the chosen fate of those who embraced the philosophy of nonviolence. For many of the Freedom Riders, the trials and tests of tolerance would continue, literally and figuratively, for years to come. And for some, even legal triumph and racial desegregation would bring little satisfaction as long as the beloved community remained an unrealized ideal.

Epilogue: Glory Bound

> Yes, we are the Freedom Riders,
> And we ride a long Greyhound.
> White or black, we know no difference, Lord,
> For we are Glory bound.
> —1960s freedom song

During the winter of 1961–62, the Freedom Riders exited from the center stage of American public life. But they did not go quietly. If 1961 was the year of the Freedom Rides, encompassing the heart of the drama, 1962 was the denouement. For the movement, and for the Freedom Riders themselves, the weeks and months following the initial implementation of the ICC order were filled with legal, tactical, and other matters related to the Rides. Indeed, for much of the nation—especially for white Southerners—1962 proved to be a challenging period of adaptation and adjustment, a transitional era that saw the passing of old myths and the birth of new realities of race, region, and democracy. In Washington, Justice Department officials spent much of the year scrambling to meet—or in some cases deflect—the rising expectations of movement activists, while the president and other administration leaders dealt with the political fall-out from the federal government's recent tilt toward constitutional enforcement and social justice. And in New York and Atlanta, civil rights leaders faced similar challenges as they strained to maintain momentum and a spirit of cooperation in the face of new organizational realities—chiefly, the enhanced power and vitality of CORE and SNCC.

The Freedom Rides had compounded and accelerated the changes initiated by the 1960 sit-ins, and the reconfigured world of civil rights activism—in which students generally took the lead while lawyers, ministers, and other elders struggled to keep up—looked radically different from the late-1950s movement led by the NAACP and SCLC. By the end of 1962 virtually all matters related to the movement—from generational and organizational lines of authority to ideological considerations of nonviolence and interracialism—were in flux or undergoing serious reexamination. Not all of this could be attributed to the success of the Freedom Rides, of course. But, as Diane McWhorter later put it, the Rides seemed to be "one of history's rare alchemical phenomena, altering the structural makeup of everything they touched."

The aftershocks from the Freedom Rides could be felt everywhere, but the most obvious seismic shifts were in the Deep South, where the active phase of the crisis lasted the longest. This was especially true in Mississippi, where the weekly Freedom Rider appellate trials continued until late May 1962, and where the rumblings of black unrest and white resistance were amplified by the unsettling influence of student activists affiliated with SNCC and CORE.

Despite the removal of Jim Crow signs across the state, compliance with the ICC order was haphazard at best, and in many Mississippi communities anyone asserting the constitutional right to equal access to transit facilities risked arrest for breach of peace. NAACP attorney and future Harvard Law School professor Derrick Bell discovered this on January 10, when he was arrested for loitering in the white waiting room of the Jackson railroad terminal, and three weeks later the police arrested Ernest McBride, a black soldier from Los Angeles, for a similar infraction at the Jackson Greyhound station.

Such arrests became less common after February 26, when the U.S. Supreme Court issued a unanimous and definitive ruling in *Bailey v. Patterson*, the NAACP class-action desegregation case filed by the NAACP on behalf of Samuel Bailey and three other Jackson blacks in June 1961. Annulling the two-to-one decision of the three-judge federal district panel, the court stated plainly: "We have settled beyond question that no state may require racial segregation of interstate or intrastate transportation facilities." Once again, however, the situation was muddied by the court's refusal to issue an injunction staying the prosecution of the Freedom Riders arrested in Jackson. According to the court, since the plaintiffs were not actually Freedom Riders and had never been arrested as such, Bailey and the others had no standing to enjoin the prosecutions. Though technically correct, this decision created confusion and ensured continued resistance on the part of Mississippi segregationists interested in preserving Jim Crow transit.

Part of the problem was a poisonous statewide political atmosphere that implicitly sanctioned vigilante and extralegal enforcement of segregated mores. Emboldened by defiant White Citizens' Council leaders and demagogic politicians, individual bus drivers, station agents, and police officers routinely ignored federal mandates, dismissing them as illegitimate infringements of local control and states' rights. Believing that intimidation and even violence were acceptable means of maintaining segregation, many white Mississippians felt empowered to do whatever was necessary to counter the efforts of perceived troublemakers. On April 26, for example, a policeman in the southern Mississippi town of Taylorsville shot and killed Corporal Roman Duckworth after the young black soldier failed to move to the back of a bus. Although Duckworth was unarmed and had the legal right to sit wherever he pleased, there were no legal consequences for the policeman, and the local and state press all but ignored the incident. The fact that Duckworth was a Mississippi native returning home to visit a sick wife did not seem to evoke much sympathy among white segregationists, who saw him as just another good Negro gone bad. In the wake of the Freedom Rides, any black Mississippian with experience outside the state was suspect, and Duckworth's violation of segregationist traditions simply confirmed the suspicion that virtually all of the state's racial problems could be attributed to outside influences.

During the weeks and months following the Rides, Mississippi segregationists felt that they were still under siege from outside agitators, and to some extent they were right. Even though the vast majority of Freedom Riders had long since left the state, the dozen or so who remained were part of a growing movement presence in Mississippi. Though modest in comparison to Freedom Summer 1964, when nearly a thousand student activists descended upon the state, the rising spirit of the "Move on Mississippi," as SNCC called it, was palpable in 1962. Even in Jackson, where the concentration of visiting activists was greatest and where CORE field secretary Tom Gaither returned in January to reorganize the Jackson Non-Violent Movement, the number of those involved was small. But the mere presence of "professional agitators" such as Gaither was unnerving to white Mississippians, many of whom were beginning to realize that the state was no longer off-limits to the national movement. Martin Luther King drove this point home in early February when he chose Clarksdale, Mississippi, in the heart of the Delta, as the first stop in a region-wide "People to People" tour aimed at recruiting a "nonviolent army" known as the SCLC "Freedom Corps." Visiting seven communities and delivering a dozen speeches in three days, King served notice that the local activists who had been struggling for years to bring change to the Delta were no longer alone.

SCLC's profile in Mississippi never quite matched the promise of King's speeches. But an emerging alliance of SNCC, CORE, and the NAACP picked up at least some of the slack, crafting an umbrella organization, the Council of Federated Organizations (COFO), to coordinate voter registration projects and other movement initiatives across the state. All of the COFO projects involved collaboration between local and visiting student activists, and several were staffed by former Freedom Riders, including Lester McKinnie in Laurel, Hollis Watkins in Hattiesburg, and the newly married Jim and Diane Nash Bevel in Cleveland. Even when Freedom Riders were not involved, many local whites and blacks assumed otherwise. In Greenwood, for example, project leader Sam Block was routinely misidentified as a Freedom Rider, a mistake that compounded the difficulty of organizing fearful black citizens. "People would just get afraid of me," Block later explained to Jim Forman. "They said, 'He's a Freedom Rider.'" They didn't want "to have anything to do with me . . . because I was a Freedom Rider. I was there to stir up trouble, that's all." As Block and many others discovered, being identified as—or even associating with—an outside agitator could have severe consequences in Mississippi. Arrested seven times during his first eight months in Greenwood, Block suffered several beatings at the hands of white vigilantes or policemen, one of whom characterized him as "the most dangerous nigger in Mississippi."

At one time or another, similar characterizations were applied to other militant activists, including Bob Moses, Medgar Evers, and David Dennis, who became CORE's Mississippi field secretary in the summer of 1962. But for many white Mississippians the most unsettling and confounding activists of them all were the Bevels, a husband and wife team that symbolized the continuing influence of the Freedom Rides. Indeed, Diane Nash Bevel's status as the most visible female "agitator" in the state was especially perplexing to white supremacists unaccustomed to tongue-lashings and moral challenges from twenty-one-year-old pregnant women. After spending several frustrating weeks in Jackson and Laurel and facing an upcoming appellate trial for her alleged corruption of underage activists the previous summer, she confounded prosecutors and other white officials on April 30 by abandoning her appeal. Surrendering herself to authorities, who promptly arrested her for sitting in the white section of the Hinds County courtroom, she released a public statement explaining why she was ready to begin serving a two-year term in jail:

> To appeal further would necessitate my sitting through another court trial in a Mississippi court, and I have reached the conclusion that I can no longer cooperate with the evil and unjust court system of this state. I subscribe to the philosophy of nonviolence; thus to one of the basic tenets of nonviolence—that you refuse to cooperate with evil. The only condition under which I will leave jail will be if the unjust and untrue charges against me are completely dropped. Some people have asked me how I can do this when I am expecting my first child in September. I have searched my soul about this and considered it in prayer. I have reached the conclusion that in the long run this will be the best thing I can do for my child. Since my child will be a black child, born in

Mississippi, whether I am in jail or not, he will be born in prison. I
believe that if I go to jail now it may help hasten that day when my child
and all children will be free, not only on the day of their birth, but for
all of their lives.

In truth, the ICC mandate yielded relatively little in the way of actual desegregation in Mississippi by the end of 1962. Here, more than anywhere else,
movement leaders had to deal with a ferocious form of white supremacist resistance paradoxically fueled by a combination of outside intervention and the
apparent futility of that intervention. In the long run the ICC order would lead
to grudging desegregation and ultimately to new social mores, but in the short
run, the perceived emptiness of the Freedom Riders' victory encouraged continued resistance on all fronts, including voting rights and school desegregation.
With the help of meddling federal officials, outside agitators had invaded the
state, yet the Mississippi way of life remained intact. Among white Mississippians in 1962, this was the primary lesson conveyed by the Freedom Rides.

For some, this delusional sense of invulnerability to fundamental change
began to fade in the fall of 1962 following the court-ordered integration of the
University of Mississippi by James Meredith, a plucky Air Force veteran and
Jackson State student who had enlisted the support of the NAACP Legal
Defense Fund during a long legal struggle to breach the barriers of Mississippi's
most hallowed bastion of white privilege. For many others, though, the fact that
Meredith's arrival at Ole Miss precipitated a major riot later known as the Battle
of Oxford—that the enrollment of a single black student required the deployment of more than three thousand federal troops—simply reinforced the notion
that Mississippi was a land apart and beyond the reach of effective outside intervention. With military guards shadowing his every move, Meredith remained at
Ole Miss for a full academic year, graduating in the spring of 1963. But the Battle
of Oxford and its aftermath left a legacy of racial polarization and distrust that
heightened white Mississippi's sense of alienation. Most tragically, as the historian John Dittmer has observed, the backlash from the Meredith crisis struck
the disfranchised and dispossessed blacks living in "movement" communities
such as Greenwood with special force. Economically and physically vulnerable,
without the benefit of political power or constitutional protection, they "would
bear the brunt of white rage over the defeat suffered at the hands of the federal
government."

At the close of 1962, the same could have been said of the Freedom Rides,
which seemingly had produced more resistance than progress, leaving local
blacks in a precarious position once the mass of Freedom Riders had left the
state. In the case of transit desegregation, however, the balance sheet soon shifted
toward compliance and genuine progress, providing even Mississippi blacks

with tangible gains that justified the provocations and intrusions of 1961. Despite the federal government's continuing reluctance to interfere in other areas of public life, the combined efforts of the Justice Department, the ICC, and the federal courts to desegregate the state's bus, rail, and air terminals proved successful by the summer of 1963.

Early in the year the Justice Department filed lawsuits against the police departments of Greenwood and Winona, which had persisted in enforcing segregation at local terminals, but in June the department reported that its investigators "knew of no rail, bus, or airline facility still maintaining segregation," in Mississippi or anywhere else. While de facto and self-segregation remained common, especially in communities where unmarked but duplicate waiting rooms and other facilities survived, and many Mississippi blacks were still wary of asserting the right to sit where they pleased, the age of systemic, legally enforced transit segregation was over. Nearly two years after the Mississippi Freedom Rides, the results could be seen as a civil rights milestone, despite a rear-guard legal action to punish the individuals and organizations involved. For at least some of the Riders arrested in Jackson and McComb, and for the attorneys who represented them, the legal ordeal of appeals, continuances, and court appearances continued until 1965. But by that time the first major civil rights victory in the nation's most hidebound state was secure, suggesting that the Rides were only a prelude to further struggle and ultimate triumph.

No other state matched Mississippi's general and persistent pattern of defiance and delay in the aftermath of the Freedom Rides. However, for a time there were pockets of determined resistance in the nearby states of Louisiana, Alabama, and Georgia. In the heart of the Deep South, the Freedom Rides inadvertently spawned an era of racial polarization and political resistance. Here, with the notable exception of metropolitan Atlanta, the pace of social change actually slowed for a time, and the quality of life for many blacks got worse before it got better, triggering widespread disillusionment and despair. Indeed, if the situation in Mississippi, Louisiana, Alabama, and southwestern Georgia had been the only measure of the Freedom Rides' impact, the nonviolent movement's claim to victory would have been in some jeopardy.

Fortunately for the movement, this pattern of reactionary defiance did not hold in other areas of the South and its borderlands. While there was plenty of grousing about black militants, outside agitators, and federal meddling in local affairs, the dominant reality in most of the region was slow but steady progress toward desegregation. Not only was compliance with the ICC order all but universal outside the Deep South by early 1962, but also the suddenness of transit desegregation, however grudging or involuntary, seemed to foster a growing resignation that desegregation of other institutions was inevitable and even imminent. Unlike the Deep South, where the threat of massive and even violent resistance remained an integral part of regional culture, the rest of the area below the Mason-Dixon line seemed to be moving toward political moderation and away from the sectionalist siege mentality associated with the "Solid South." As early as November 1961 public opinion polls revealed that, outside of Mississippi and Alabama, an overwhelming majority of Southern whites had concluded that it was only a matter of time before all public accommodations were desegregated. And the proportion of Southern respondents who felt this way continued to rise in 1962.

This was especially true in border states such as Missouri, Kentucky, and Maryland, where two-party political dynamics and racial demographics promoted a more open atmosphere, and where both school desegregation and black voting had proceeded beyond the stage of tokenism. But even in the so-called Rim South states of Florida, Texas, and Arkansas, as well as in the Upper South states of Virginia, North Carolina, and Tennessee—all states where the dual school system was still intact and black voting was still rare—the Freedom Rides failed to produce the kind of backlash that forestalled progress. In South Carolina, a state often accorded Deep South status, the situation was less promising, especially in communities such as Rock Hill and Winnsboro, where the Freedom Riders had encountered stiff resistance in 1961. Yet, in general, the Palmetto State did not live up to its longstanding reputation for sectionalist defiance. Movement activity in the state quickened noticeably in 1962, as Jim McCain spearheaded an ambitious Voter Education Project that registered 3,700 new black voters by the end of the year. And both CORE and an increasingly active NAACP led by state field secretary I. DeQuincey Newman organized a series of desegregation campaigns that extracted significant gains without provoking widespread violence. While segregated institutions remained in force throughout most of the state, the tone of public reaction and political discourse suggested something less than massive resistance.

The ability of McCain to operate in the open, despite his close association with the Freedom Rides, and his continuing success in recruiting local volunteers were welcome signs that encouraged CORE to expand its operations in neighboring states, especially in North Carolina. During the spring of 1962 the organization launched an ambitious campaign to create "Freedom Highways" all along the southeastern seaboard. Conceived as "a natural southward extension of the Route 40" campaign," which was still active in Maryland, the Freedom Highways project targeted the popular but segregated Howard Johnson's restaurants that dotted tourist routes from Baltimore to Miami.

The campaign attracted a number of veteran activists, including Jim Peck and Bayard Rustin, and by the end of May almost all of the chain's restaurants in Maryland and Florida had capitulated to CORE's pressure. Some locally owned franchises in other states resisted, however, prompting the organization to refine its strategy. Concentrating its efforts on North Carolina, CORE dispatched field secretaries and former Freedom Riders Ben Cox and Jerome Smith to the state to organize local chapters and mobilize demonstrators in several key cities. Aided by many of the same local activists who had hosted and supported the original Freedom Riders in May 1961, Cox and Smith developed strong CORE chapters in Greensboro, Raleigh, and Burlington that initiated mass protests at several Howard Johnson's restaurants in August and September.

During four weeks of sit-ins and marches, more than two thousand demonstrators participated and nearly one hundred were arrested. After an initial round of arrests in Durham, Farmer, Peck, and Roy Wilkins flew in from New York to lead a protest march, and at a subsequent march in Statesville, Farmer and a local minister spoke to more than six hundred supporters in the town square amidst "a thick fog of insecticide laid by the police." In other communities, the police were more restrained, and Peck—whose gripping memoir, *Freedom Ride*, would soon be published by Harper and Row—came away from the Durham march with the sense that both official intimidation and white resistance were diminishing. Comparing his recent experience with his first visit to Durham in 1947, he concluded that "this type of protest in a place like Durham would have been inconceivable fifteen years ago."

Perhaps even more telling was the successful desegregation of more than half of the state's Howard Johnson's restaurants by the end of August, along with Governor Terry Sanford's willingness to meet with Farmer and other movement leaders to discuss ways of accelerating the pace of desegregation in North Carolina. Desegregating the remaining restaurants would require eight more months of negotiation and mass protest. But, as Peck observed, North Carolina officials, unlike their Mississippi and Alabama counterparts, seemed to be embracing a more tolerant attitude toward dissent.

Many observers, however, viewed the Freedom Riders' victory either as an anomaly or as confirmation that governmentally administered gradualism was the key to civil order and social progress. Emphasizing the Kennedy's administration's capacity to respond to the crisis, while downplaying the catalyzing role of the Freedom Riders themselves, the mainstream viewpoint tended to focus on the ICC order, not on the provocations that brought it about. Predictably, this perspective became stronger over time. While detailed memories of the Rides inevitably faded, the effects of the order became clearer and more tangible, especially after the official validation of the order's importance by administration and supporting media sources.

Reformulated to fit both the general myths of reformist politics and the more specific conditions of an election year, the story of the Freedom Rides became the story of transit desegregation in 1962. Among nonviolent activists and in some black communities, particularly along the route of the Freedom Rides, there was consternation that recent history was being recast to serve the interests of the centrist Kennedy administration. But most Americans, then and later, had little appreciation for the clash between movement and establishment lore.

Even though it had great difficulty resolving the Freedom Rider crisis, the Kennedy administration demonstrated its ability to put a self-serving spin on the Rides as early as May 1961, during the immediate aftermath of the Anniston and Birmingham riots. And this effort continued off and on for the better part of a year. In December an official press release summarizing "the Administration's accomplishments in the civil rights field" hailed the ICC order and the government's role in bringing about "substantial progress" in transit desegregation but barely mentioned the Freedom Riders. Indeed, at a press conference held in January 1962, the president failed to mention the Freedom Riders at all in a statement citing the order as one of three significant civil rights achievements accomplished during his first year in office.

Whether this particular statement represented a failure of understanding or a deliberate misappropriation of credit is unclear, but one suspects that such slights often reflected a purposeful political or ideological strategy. For a variety of reasons, administration officials did not want to encourage or legitimize direct action, especially by naive and radical provocateurs who operated outside the bounds of political consensus. Later in the decade, government authorities would freely acknowledge the heroism and sacrifices of the Freedom Riders. And even the original architects of the dismissive interpretation of the Freedom Rides, including Burke Marshall and Robert Kennedy, eventually admitted that the crisis provided the federal government with an "education" and a much-needed push toward constitutional enforcement. But as long as the Kennedys were in power, there would be no White House receptions, or even public statements, honoring the risk-takers who had forced a reluctant administration to act.

This policy was grounded in practical politics, and administration leaders thought they had a strong electoral rationale for distancing themselves from the Freedom Riders, even though liberal contemporaries and later historians and political scientists accused them of excessive timidity. Operating without a strong public mandate or a solid Democratic majority in Congress and facing the prospect of losing congressional seats to the Republicans in the fall 1962 elections, the Kennedys calculated that they could ill afford to alienate powerful conservatives within their own party. As early as July 1961 one aide, after concluding that "the dynamics both here and abroad compelling desegregation are accelerating," advised that providing "leadership for those forces and to moderate Southern difficulties without destroying the Congressional coalition at mid-term is the nub of the problem." This problem loomed even larger in the wake of the Freedom Rides and the ICC order. After disappointing the civil rights community in January 1962 with the announcement that he had no immediate plans to "put forward . . . major civil rights legislation," the president tried to assuage the feelings of blacks and liberals by letting it be known that he intended to appoint a black man, Robert Weaver, as the first secretary of a new Department of Urban Affairs. But this gesture backfired when a conservative bipartisan coalition promptly rejected the bill authorizing the new department.

At the same time, Kennedy endorsed a moderately progressive bill prohibiting the use of literacy tests for federal election registration, but even this fairly innocuous challenge to the political status quo in the white South went down to defeat in May. By summer he and other chastened Northern Democrats were in full retreat on legislative issues related to civil rights, and the elevated priority of avoiding sectional disharmony remained in force until well after the fall elections sustained a Democratic majority in both houses of Congress. Only the federal intervention at the University of Mississippi in September interrupted this strategy, but for many white Southerners this anomaly was an acceptable response to violent extremism.

Justified or not, political considerations alone cannot explain the administration's rude treatment of the Freedom Riders, or its continuing inattention to pressing civil rights matters. Ideological commitments also dictated an official postmortem that reduced the Riders to bit players in a government drama. While the crisis provoked by the Freedom Rides seized the Kennedy brothers' attention, forcing them to address an expanded range of issues related to race and democracy, it did not persuade either of them that ending Jim Crow was a moral imperative requiring immediate and uncompromising action. They did not celebrate the achievements of nonviolent direct action in 1962 and 1963, in large part, for the same reason that prevented them from embracing the Freedom Riders in 1961: They did not believe that radical or disruptive change was in the best interests of the nation or the world.

Robert Kennedy was more receptive to the Freedom Riders' tactics and ideas than was his brother, but neither leader was ready to jettison his commitment to what the political scientist David Niven has labeled "glacial change." In the case of John Kennedy, the attachment to glacialism was as broad as it was deep. But, as Niven has pointed out, the young president's response to the Freedom Rides was also guided by a traditional interpretation of Reconstruction that convinced him "that moderation was always a more successful course than coercion." Encumbered by this simplistic model of regional and national history, he had difficulty absorbing the lessons that the Freedom Riders might have taught him. The concept of "freedom now" struck him, as it struck many Americans of moderate and conservative leanings, as an unreasonable expectation that threatened both civic order and evolutionary progress. "Quixotic crusades," the historian Harvard Sitkoff once wrote of Kennedy, "interfered with his careful plans and cautious timetables." Indeed, John Dittmer probably came closest to the truth when he observed that "in the short run, at least," both Kennedy brothers "preferred order to justice."

In the long run, the Kennedys—especially Robert, who had five more years than his brother to rethink his views on race and radicalism—gained some appreciation for the insistent and compelling nature of the civil rights agenda. And when the president finally went before the nation in June 1963 to make the case for a comprehensive civil rights bill, he insisted that Americans were "confronted primarily with a moral issue," not a mere legislative or political problem. In 1962, though, there was little indication that administration leaders had acquired anything more than a superficial and detached understanding of the nonviolent movement's passions and frustrations. The president's continuing preoccupation with the Cold War—both before and after the Cuban Missile Crisis of October—relegated civil rights issues to secondary status in Washington, and even the attorney general seemed more interested in J. Edgar Hoover's relentless search for subversive elements within the movement than in the movement itself. The mixed signals from the top influenced all levels of the federal government. Thus, despite the legal advances of the previous year, federal agencies were still more adept at nurturing moderates and consoling conservatives than at protecting the constitutional rights—and the lives—of grassroots activists.

In a September 1962 letter to the novelist Lillian Smith, CORE's Marvin Rich acknowledged that John Kennedy had "done ever so much more than Eisenhower" for the cause of civil rights, but he also offered the telling qualifier that "when measured against our expectations and against the awesome rush of events he has done little." Rich's lament captures the bittersweet quality of movement life in the aftermath of the Freedom Rides. Caught in the throes of a classic revolution of rising expectations, civil rights activists chafed at the restrictions imposed by the inertial power of institutions and individuals. As the Freedom Riders and others watched and waited for signs of fundamental change, it became clear that neither the American public nor the Kennedy administration could keep pace with the new expectations. But equally clear was the realization that the civil rights movement had undergone a thoroughgoing transformation during the past year. While the barriers of racism remained formidable, the struggle against those barriers had acquired new sources of strength and energy.

Most obviously, the various organizations that made up the movement had established a precedent of working together, building a coalition that crossed regional, racial, and ideological lines. Though loose and uneasy at times, and subject to the full range of problems related to organizational competition and diversity, the coalition that emerged during the Freedom Rides initiated the nationalization of a movement that would later oversee massive mobilizations such as the March on Washington, Freedom Summer, and the Selma to Mont-gomery voting rights campaign later in the decade. The collective efforts of 1961 also exposed deep ideological and personal conflicts within the movement and revealed the difficulty of coordinating local and national initiatives, as in Albany and Monroe. But even the worst of these problems contributed to the matura-tion of a movement that eventually found ways to offset the negative influence of rivalries and disagreements. By 1962, all civil rights organizations, whether their leadership was fully aware of it or not, were being drawn into the vortex of a new insurgent style of protest that would become the trademark of the decade ahead.

The Freedom Rides offered important lessons to anyone willing to acknowl-edge the gap between democratic ideals and the many imperfections of Ameri-can life. Indeed, the Freedom Rides exerted an impact that transcended tangible, quantifiable changes in institutional behavior or public policy. Within six months of the first Ride, travelers of all races were sitting side by side on buses and trains all across the nation without fear of arrest, the "white" and "colored" signs that had blighted the walls of Southern bus and train stations for decades were gone, the nation's major civil rights organizations had undergone significant transfor-mations, and the Justice Department had been pushed into a deepening engage-ment in civil rights matters. But even this impressive list of accomplishments does not capture the full effect of the Freedom Rides. The most important and lasting consequence—the one that confirmed the Rides' status as a pivotal moment in American history—was a revolutionary change in the character of citizen politics. In the course of six months, the nation's first mobile nonviolent army expanded the realm of the possible in American political and social insur-gency, redefining the limits of dissent and setting the stage for the escalating demands and rising expectations of the mid- and late-1960s.

While the Freedom Riders ultimately failed in their effort to bring the nation, or even most of the civil rights movement, into the confines of the "beloved community," they, more than any other activists of their day, foreshadowed the grassroots "rights revolution" that would transform American citizenship over the next four decades. The rising movements for women's rights, military with-drawal from Southeast Asia, environmental reform, gay and lesbian rights, and the rights of the disabled all built upon the foundation of legitimacy and success established by Freedom Riders and other nonviolent activists in the early 1960s. By demonstrating the power of personal commitment and sacrifice in a new and dramatic way, the Freedom Riders countered traditional assumptions of institu-tional authority and top-down politics, pushing American democracy to what the journalist Malcolm Gladwell has called a "tipping point," and beyond. Reflecting on his experiences as a Freedom Rider, Stokely Carmichael used a different metaphor, characterizing the Rides as a "great leap forward" that super-seded the orthodoxy of slow and steady gradualism. But whatever the words used to describe the change, the conclusion that the Freedom Rides created a new context for social activism seems inescapable.

The Rides also nationalized the movement by dramatizing "to any who remained doubters, that segregation was a national concern, rather than a series of local problems," as the journalist Milton Viorst once wrote. Forcing the Kennedy administration to take a belated but ultimately forthright stand on one aspect of racial discrimination, the Rides hastened the day when the federal government would embrace a broader agenda of promoting integrated schools and neighborhoods, equal access to public accommodations, affirmative action in hiring policies, and black voting rights. Although one unintended consequence of the Freedom Rider crisis was the government's turn to voting rights advocacy as a means of diverting movement energies away from additional direct action campaigns, that too was a tribute to the power and influence of the Rides. Indeed, without the pressure exerted by the crises of 1961, the Voter Education Project that led to Freedom Summer, Selma, and the 1965 Voting Rights Act might not have been part of the historical equation.

Looking back after five decades of uneven progress, it is evident that the Freedom Riders' hard-won alliance with federal authorities imposed certain limits on the movement, virtually guaranteeing an emphasis on civil reform, not moral revolution. For some Americans, the Freedom Rides and the nonviolent direct action campaigns that followed brought about a direct transformation of heart and mind. But for most, the lesson of the Rides was the ability of ordinary citizens to affect public policy. Both inside and outside the movement, the primary legacy was the efficacy of direct action, not the moral rectitude of nonviolence. This was not what many Freedom Riders had intended, but such are the ironies of history forged by real people in real time.

Though ultimately problematic, these limitations were barely visible in the immediate aftermath of the Freedom Rides. When the sociologist James Laue talked with several of the Freedom Riders in 1962, he discovered that they were proud of what they had accomplished. They felt they had proven that even a small vanguard of activists could initiate fundamental change through righteous action and moral discipline. All that was needed, they believed, was the physical and moral courage to express their passion for social justice through the medium of nonviolent struggle. And that was what they had done, experiencing unmerited suffering and demonstrating their willingness to "give a little bit of blood to redeem the soul of America," as John Lewis recalled in a 2001 speech. "We allowed the spirit of history to use us," Lewis explained, invoking the sense of destiny that propelled him and so many others down the road to freedom.

Destiny, however, meant something less than determinism. Even with history on their side, the Freedom Riders had faced difficult choices at every turn in the road. At several points during the spring, summer, and fall of 1961, seemingly insurmountable challenges had threatened to push the movement backward, forcing even the most resilient Riders to contemplate retreat or compromise. In every instance movement activists and organizers had found a way to push on, but they had done so with a growing appreciation for the difficulty and magnitude of the task before them. The original CORE Freedom Riders came to the South to teach and preach and spread the gospel of nonviolence, which they did in full measure. But in the process of delivering the movement's message, they, and the other Freedom Riders who followed them, became experiential learners, acquiring essential truths about themselves, the human condition, and the nature of historical agency. Wherever they found themselves—on buses, in terminal waiting rooms, in mass meetings, in the jails and prisons of the benighted South—Freedom Riders absorbed the concrete lessons of struggle. Some were hard and sobering lessons about the intractability of racial hatred and entrenched privilege. But others were hopeful and inspiring, demonstrating the expansive possibilities of individual and collective action and the transformative power of movement culture.

Disseminating these lessons to the American public proved difficult, and the nonviolent movement never realized its full potential. But for a time the Freedom Riders' victory over fear and violence became an object lesson in itself. During the remainder of the Kennedy era and into the mid-1960s, the term "Freedom Rider" took on a special mystique, providing black Southerners and many others with an empowering example of engaged citizenship. Indeed, by 1964, when nearly a thousand college students traveled to Mississippi to participate in the Freedom Summer equal rights campaign, the term had morphed into a generic and iconic symbol only loosely connected to the events of 1961. For a time, the simple phrase "the Freedom Riders are coming" invoked hope among those seeking change and dread among those defending the racial status quo. Later in the decade, as the freedom struggle moved through the stages of Black Power, urban rioting, and ideological fragmentation, memories of both the Freedom Rides and Freedom Summer faded, and the term lost some of its force. But it did not disappear entirely.

The Freedom Riders themselves have done their best to keep the record straight. For the past fifty years, participation in the Rides has been a continuing source of identity, pride, and fellowship. Bound by ties of friendship, memory, and shared sacrifice, many former Freedom Riders have protected and sustained a common legacy. Among the ex-Riders there are distinct subgroups—the original CORE Riders, those who survived the burning bus in Anniston, those who spent time in Parchman, the Interfaith Riders, and so forth—each with its own set of experiences and lore. But there is also a commonality of perspective that binds them all together, setting them apart from everyone else, including the rest of the movement.

Forged in the fires of nonviolent struggle, this sense of common purpose and experience has persisted through the decades, despite the inevitable physical dispersion of the Riders. During the tumultuous years of the 1960s and 1970s, the Riders went their separate ways, passing into a wide variety of careers and private lives. A few either became disillusioned or moved too far to the right or left to remember the Freedom Rides without a measure of embarrassment or regret. And, against the increasingly violent backdrop of the Vietnam War and the Johnson and Nixon eras, many abandoned the nonviolent philosophy that had propelled the Freedom Rides during the relatively innocent years of the early 1960s. Some went to Vietnam as soldiers or sailors, some became antiwar activists, and others filled both functions, turning against a war that ultimately seemed ill-conceived and morally unjustifiable.

Most embraced the liberating themes of 1960s counterculture, but as the politics of reform and revolution became darker and more complicated, there was an inevitable divergence of opinion and belief. And yet, even with this divergence, a large majority continued to identify with a broad-based struggle for human rights and social justice that inevitably drew them to a variety of new causes from environmentalism to gay and lesbian liberation. An inordinate number went on to distinguished careers as social workers, community organizers, health care providers, labor leaders, lawyers, jurists, politicians, writers, journalists, theologians, teachers, college professors and administrators, entrepreneurs, or corporate executives. But whatever their professional experiences or private enthusiasms, they were still Freedom Riders, still part of the small but brave band of activists that had the courage and wisdom to demand "freedom now." Today, five decades later, they are no longer young, and many are no longer with us. But the memory and meaning of what the Freedom Riders accomplished in 1961 is worth pondering in a nation still searching for simple justice and true democracy.

Note on Sources

For a comprehensive list of the primary and secondary sources used in this book, see the bibliography in the original 2006 edition of *Freedom Riders: 1961 and the Struggle for Racial Justice*. This brief Note on Sources directs readers to the most important autobiographical and secondary sources related to the Freedom Rides. The best place to begin in any historical examination of the Freedom Rides is the handful of memoirs written by individual Freedom Riders: James Peck, *Freedom Ride* (New York: Simon and Schuster, 1962); Robert McAfee Brown and Frank Randall, *The Freedom Riders: A Clergyman's View, an Historian's View* (New York: CORE, 1961); Mary Hamilton, *Freedom Riders Speak for Themselves* (Detroit: News and Letters, 1961); James Farmer, *Lay Bare the Heart: An Autobiography of the Civil Rights Movement* (New York: New American Library, 1985); John Lewis, with Michael D'Orso, *Walking with the Wind: A Memoir of the Movement* (New York: Simon and Schuster, 1998); William Sloane Coffin Jr., *Once to Every Man: A Memoir* (New York: Atheneum, 1977); Stokely Carmichael, with Ekwueme Michael Thelwell, *Ready for Revolution: The Life and Struggles of Stokely Carmichael (Kwame Ture)* (New York: Scribner, 2003); and Bob Zellner, with Constance Curry, *The Wrong Side of Murder Creek: A White Southerner in the Freedom Movement* (Montgomery, AL: New South Books, 2008).

See also Dorothy B. Kaufman, *The First Freedom Ride: The Walter Bergman Story* (Detroit: ACLU Fund Press, 1989); Diane Nash, "Inside the Sit-ins and Freedom Rides: Testimony of a Southern Student," in *The New Negro*, ed. Mathew H. Ahman (New York: Biblo and Tannen, 1969), 42–60; Tananarive Due and Patricia Stephens Due, *Freedom in the Family: A Mother-Daughter Memoir of the Fight for Civil Rights* (New York: Ballantine, 2003); Phil Noble, *Beyond the Burning Bus: The Civil Rights Revolution in a Southern Town* (Montgomery, AL: New South Books, 2003); Solomon S. Seay Jr., with Delores R. Boyd, *Jim Crow and Me: Stories from My Life as a Civil Rights Lawyer* (Montgomery, AL: New South Books, 2008); Howard K. Smith, *Events Leading Up to My Death: The Life of a Twentieth-Century Reporter* (New York: St. Martin's, 1996); Hollinger Barnard, ed., *Outside the Magic Circle: The Autobiography of Virginia Foster Durr* (New York: Simon and Schuster, 1985); Patricia Sullivan, ed., *Freedom Writer: Virginia Foster Durr, Letters from the Civil Rights Years* (New York: Routledge, 2003); Bayard Rustin, *Down the Line: The Collected Writings of Bayard Rustin* (Chicago: Quadrangle Books, 1971); Bayard Rustin and George Houser, *You Don't Have to Ride Jim Crow* (Washington, DC: Interracial Workshop, 1947); James Forman, *The Making of Black Revolutionaries: A Personal Account* (New York: Macmillan, 1972); and Roy Wilkins, with Tom Mathews, *Standing Fast: The Autobiography of Roy Wilkins* (New York: Viking Penguin, 1962).

Relatively few books focus specifically on the Freedom Rides, but they are all useful and illuminating. See Derek Catsam, *Down Freedom's Main Line: The Journey of Reconciliation and the Freedom Rides* (Lexington: University of Kentucky Press, 2009), a revised 2003 Ohio University Ph.D. dissertation; David Niven, *The Politics of Injustice: The Kennedys, the Freedom Rides, and the Electoral*

Consequences of a Moral Compromise (Knoxville: University of Tennessee Press, 2003), a solid study written by a political scientist; and Eric Etheridge, *Breach of Peace: Portraits of the 1961 Mississippi Freedom Riders* (New York: Atlas, 2008), a fascinating collection of brief photographic essays. There are also two good books on the Freedom Rides designed for young readers: Ann Bausum, *Freedom Riders: John Lewis and Jim Zwerg on the Front Lines of the Civil Rights Movement* (Washington, DC: National Geographic, 2006); and James Haskins, *The Freedom Rides: Journey for Justice* (New York: Hyperion Books for Children, 1995).

The civil rights historiography of the Freedom Rides is not well developed. Indeed, most of the scholarly commentary on the Rides appears in the various reviews of the original edition of *Freedom Riders*. See especially Thomas Sugrue, "AmeriKKKa," *London Review of Books* 28 (October 5, 2006): 17–19; Peter J. Ling, "Tracing the Movement's Path," *Reviews in American History* 35 (2007): 289–96; David J. Garrow, "Down the Highway to Freedom," *Wilson Quarterly* 30 (Spring 2006): 103–4; Roger Wilkins, "Mission to Dixie," *Washington Post Book World*, January 15, 2006; Michael Kenney, "Catching a Bus Bound for Freedom," *Boston Globe*, January 16, 2006; William Grimes, "When Mile by Fearful Mile America Rode to Freedom," *New York Times*, January 25, 2006; Eric Foner, "Bound for Glory," *New York Times Book Review* (March 19, 2006): 24; Timothy Tyson, "Long Road to Freedom," *Anniston Star*, June 4, 2006; Kenneth T. Andrews, review in *Journal of American History* 94 (June 2007): 356–57; and Todd Moye, review in *Journal of Southern History* 73 (August 2007): 749–52.

Most general treatments of the modern civil rights struggle pay little attention to the Freedom Rides. But there are a few notable exceptions: Taylor Branch, *Parting the Waters: America in the King Years, 1954–63* (New York: Simon and Schuster, 1988), a magisterial work that includes a long chapter on the Freedom Rides; Catherine A. Barnes, *Journey from Jim Crow: The Desegregation of Southern Transit* (New York: Columbia University Press, 1983), a groundbreaking work of legal history; David Halberstam, *The Children* (New York: Random House, 1998), a journalist's riveting but sometimes unreliable account of the Nashville Movement; August Meier and Elliott Rudwick, *CORE: A Study in the Civil Rights Movement* (Urbana: University of Illinois Press, 1975), a comprehensive and insightful study of the organization that launched the Freedom Rides; and Harvard Sitkoff, *The Struggle for Black Equality, 1954–1992* (New York: Hill and Wang, 1993), which offers the best brief account of the Freedom Rides.

Other more specialized works that include significant treatments of the Freedom Rides and the broader context of the civil rights struggle in 1961 include: Timothy B. Tyson, *Radio Free Dixie: Robert F. Williams and the Roots of Black Power* (Chapel Hill: University of North Carolina Press, 1999), which presents a fascinating account of the Monroe Freedom Ride; John D'Emilio, *Lost Prophet: The Life and Times of Bayard Rustin* (New York: Free Press, 2003), a moving biography of the man who started it all; J. Mills Thornton III, *Dividing Lines: Municipal Politics and the Struggle for Civil Rights in Montgomery, Birmingham, and Selma* (Tuscaloosa: University of Alabama Press, 2002), an important study written by Alabama's most perceptive and knowledgeable civil rights scholar; Glenn T. Eskew, *But for Birmingham: The Local and National Movements in the Civil Rights Struggle* (Chapel Hill: University of North Carolina Press, 1997), an incisive study of the city that bedeviled the Freedom Riders; Diane McWhorter, *Carry Me Home: Birmingham, Alabama: The Climactic Battle of the Civil Rights Revolution* (New York: Simon and Schuster, 2001), an imaginative and highly personalized account by a Birmingham native and *New York Times* journalist; Andrew Manis, *A Fire You Can't Put Out: The Civil Rights Life of Birmingham's Reverend Fred Shuttlesworth* (Tuscaloosa: University of Alabama Press, 1999), an authoritative biography of the Freedom Riders' indefatigable and courageous collaborator; Frye Gaillard, *Cradle of Freedom: Alabama and the Movement That Changed America* (Tuscaloosa: University of Alabama Press, 2004), a highly readable survey of the civil rights struggle in Alabama; John Dittmer, *Local People: The Struggle for Civil Rights in Mississippi* (Urbana: University of Illinois Press, 1994), an award-winning study of the Mississippi movement; Charles M. Payne, *I've Got the Light of Freedom: The Organizing Tradition and the Mississippi Freedom Struggle* (Berkeley: University of California Press, 1995), a veritable companion volume to the Dittmer study; and the recently published, definitive account of the "Battle of Oxford" by Charles W. Eagles, *The Price of*

Defiance: James Meredith and the Integration of Ole Miss (Chapel Hill: University of North Carolina Press, 2009).

On the controversial and evolving role of the Kennedys in the Freedom Riders crisis, see Victor Navasky, *Kennedy Justice* (New York: Atheneum, 1971); Arthur M. Schlesinger Jr., *Robert Kennedy and His Times* (Boston: Houghton Mifflin, 1978); Evan Thomas, *Robert Kennedy, His Life* (New York: Simon and Schuster, 2000); Carl M. Brauer, *John F. Kennedy and the Second Reconstruction* (New York: Columbia University Press, 1977); Harris Wofford, *Of Kennedys and Kings: Making Sense of the Sixties* (Pittsburgh: University of Pittsburgh Press, 1992); and Nick Bryant, *The Bystander: John F. Kennedy and the Struggle for Black Equality* (New York: Basic Books, 2006). On the FBI and Gary Thomas Rowe, see Gary May, *The Informant: The FBI, the Ku Klux Klan, and the Murder of Viola Liuzzo* (New Haven, CT: Yale University Press, 2005); and Gary Thomas Rowe Jr., *My Undercover Years with the Ku Klux Klan* (New York: Bantam, 1976).

On SNCC's participation in the Freedom Rides, see Howard Zinn, *SNCC: The New Abolitionists* (Boston: Beacon Press, 1965); Clayborne Carson, *In Struggle: SNCC and the Black Awakening of the 1960s* (Cambridge, MA: Harvard University Press, 1981); Eric Burner, *And Gently He Shall Lead Them: Robert Parris Moses and Civil Rights in Mississippi* (New York: New York University Press, 1994); and Wesley C. Hogan, *Many Minds, One Heart: SNCC's Dream for a New America* (Chapel Hill: University of North Carolina Press, 2007). On Martin Luther King Jr., SCLC, and the Freedom Rides, see David L. Lewis, *King: A Critical Biography* (New York: Praeger, 1970); David J. Garrow, *Bearing the Cross: Martin Luther King, Jr., and the Southern Christian Leadership Conference* (New York: William Morrow, 1986); Adam Fairclough, *To Redeem the Soul of America: The Southern Christian Leadership Conference and Martin Luther King, Jr.* (Athens: University of Georgia Press, 1987); and Harvard Sitkoff, *King: Pilgrimage to the Mountaintop* (New York: Hill and Wang, 2008).

On the legal aspects of the Freedom Rides in Alabama and Mississippi, see Jack Bass, *Taming the Storm: The Life and Times of Frank M. Johnson and the South's Fight over Civil Rights* (New York: Doubleday, 1992); Frank Sikora, *The Judge: The Life and Opinions of Alabama's Frank M. Johnson, Jr.* (Montgomery, AL: New South Books, 2007); William M. Kunstler, with Sheila Isenberg, *My Life as a Radical Lawyer* (New York: Birch Lane Press, 1994); and Constance Baker Motley, *Equal Justice Under the Law: An Autobiography* (New York: Farrar, Straus, and Giroux, 1998). On the press coverage of the Rides, see Gene Roberts and Hank Klibanoff, *The Race Beat: The Press, the Civil Rights Struggle, and the Awakening of a Nation* (New York: Alfred A. Knopf, 2006). On the Cold War context of the Rides, see Thomas Borstelmann, *The Cold War and the Color Line: American Race Relations in the Global Arena* (Cambridge, MA: Harvard University Press, 2001); Mary L. Dudziak, *Cold War Civil Rights: Race and the Image of American Democracy* (Princeton, NJ: Princeton University Press, 2000); Catherine Fosl, *Subversive Southerner: Anne Braden and the Struggle for Racial Justice in the Cold War South* (New York: Palgrave, 2002); George Lewis, *The White South and the Red Menace: Segregationists, Anticommunism, and Massive Resistance, 1945–1965* (Gainesville: University Press of Florida, 2004); and Jeff Woods, *Black Struggle, Red Scare: Segregation and Anti-Communism in the South, 1948–1968* (Baton Rouge: Louisiana State University Press, 2004).

The Journey of Reconciliation and the Freedom Rides have also been reconstructed and interpreted by documentary film makers. The three most notable documentaries that provide visual and sound representations of the Freedom Rider story are a filmed reunion of several of the activists involved in the 1947 Journey of Reconciliation, *You Don't Have to Ride Jim Crow!* (Durham: New Hampshire Public Television, 1995); "Ain't Scared of Your Jails," Episode 3 of the celebrated documentary film series *Eyes on the Prize: America's Civil Rights Years* (Boston: Blackside, 1986); and *Freedom Riders* (Boston: WGBH Public Television, *American Experience*, 2010). The latter film, directed by the award-winning documentary film maker Stanley Nelson, will be shown nationally on PBS in May 2011, as part of the 50th-anniversary commemoration of the Freedom Rides, with the abridged version of *Freedom Riders: 1961 and the Struggle for Racial Justice* serving as the companion volume for the broadcast. The linked websites for the film are www.freedomridersfilm.com and www.pbs.org.

Readers of *Freedom Riders* may also want to visit the Freedom Rider museum exhibits at the Birmingham Civil Rights Institute in Birmingham, Alabama, at the National Civil Rights Museum in Memphis, Tennessee, and at the new Freedom Rider Museum currently under construction at the old Greyhound bus station in Montgomery, Alabama. A mobile exhibit on the Freedom Rides, curated by the Gilder Lehrman Institute for American History, will be available for viewing at selected American public libraries, universities, and museums beginning in January 2011. For the current location of the exhibit, inquire online at www.gilderlehrman.org.